CCJ.

DEVELOPMENT AND ECONOMIC POLICY
IN THE UAR (EGYPT)

Development and Economic Policy in the UAR (Egypt)

BENT HANSEN

Professor of Economics, University of Stockholm
Institute of National Planning, Cairo

and

GIRGIS A. MARZOUK

M. Sc., Ph. D. Econ. (London)
Central Bank of Egypt, Cairo

1965

NORTH-HOLLAND PUBLISHING COMPANY – AMSTERDAM

1965

NORTH-HOLLAND PUBLISHING COMPANY

Printed in the Netherlands

Contents

LIST OF CURRENCY, WEIGHTS AND
MEASURES USED

Currency

1 Egyptian Pound (£E)
= 100 piasters (PT)
= 1000 millièmes (m/m)
1 Tallaris = 20 PT

Exchange rates

– Sept. 1949   1 £E =   US $ 4.133 (parity)
Sept. 1949 – June 1962 1 £E =   US $ 2.872 (parity)
June 1962 –   1 £E = $\begin{cases} \text{US \$ 2.872 (parity – largely nominal)} \\ \text{US \$ 2.286 (effective selling rate)} \end{cases}$

Weights and measures

1 feddan = 0.42 hectar = 1.04 acres
1 kantar (old) = 44.9 kg
1 kantar (metric) = 50.0 kg
(where nothing else is said the kantar used is the "old" kantar)

Preface

In this volume we have tried to draw a picture of the economic development and the economic policies pursued in Egypt – The United Arab Republic since 1959 – during the post-war period. Deep-going economic and social changes have taken place in the country since the beginning of the 'fifties, and the development efforts here have been more serious and persistent than in so many other poor countries. For various reasons – maybe not unrelated to international conflicts – this rich study field has not attracted the attention of Western scholars to any considerable extent as have, for instance, the countries of Latin America and the Far East, not to speak about India. General surveys in foreign languages of the Egyptian economy do exist, but they have mostly the character of economic-historical records of events, general descriptions of the structure of the Egyptian economy, or superficial journalism, in any case containing little of economic analysis proper. This has left us with a gap in the literature on developing countries and their problems. Our aim is to fill this gap.

In our attempt to do that, we have as far as possible tried to build our analysis directly on available statistics on basic matters. Here we met a well known obstacle: that of obtaining unbroken, reliable statistical series covering the whole of the period concerned. Compared with other poor countries Egypt is relatively well equipped with statistics. Population censuses date back to the nineteenth century and agricultural statistics to the years before World War I, while industrial statistics are only slightly younger than industry itself. Yet the Egyptian statistics are far from satisfactory. The gaps in the statistics, the inconsistencies and lack of precision of definitions, and the inaccuracies in collecting and tabulating, and even in publishing the data are often frustrating, and we had to spend quite a long time in company with the primary data and make quite a number of daring assumptions in order to come out with the series needed. In this work we received great help from the Minister of Treasury Dr. Nazih Deif, the former General

Director of the Department of Statistics and Census Abdel-Fattah Farah, and the Undersecretary of Treasury Badr El Din Hamdy. The reliability of the various series used in the analysis is for natural reasons of varying degree, but we have as far as possible – through cross checks and appraisal of the biases inherent in the statistics due to inadequate sampling, incomplete coverage, changes in definitions, etc. – tried to form an opinion about the margins of error involved and in our conclusions done our best to respect such margins of error.

A problem of its own was the national income and related statistics. Here the situation is that several, partly overlapping official estimates exist. These official estimates, made by the Department of Statistics and Census and the National Planning Commission, resp., suffer from various shortcomings with respect to definitions, comparability, completeness, and methods of deflating, and could not be used directly in their original shape. A critical revision and completion of the estimates of the Planning Commission was therefore undertaken by one of the authors (partly in collaboration with Mr. Donald Mead of Yale University and with valuable help from Dr. Rasheed Osman Khalid of the UN, both of them at the Institute of National Planning, Cairo during 1962 and 1963), and although the existing primary data actually do permit some further improvements of these revised estimates of national income and outlay, we judged them to be sufficiently accurate for our purpose. They furnished us with the first consistent national income and outlay estimates extending from 1946 (1938–39) to 1962/63. In an appendix we have presented all the main national income and outlay tables but for the methods of calculation the reader has to return to the original publications; after all this is technical matters of a rather trivial nature. The revision and completion of the national income and outlay estimates owe much to information and help received from Dr. Deif.

We were surprised ourselves to see how complete a statistical picture it was – after all – possible to draw of the Egyptian economy and its development since World War II, at least in relation to the aspects in which we were interested, but we are also fully aware that on the one hand we may not always be justified in our judgements of the margins of error and the general reliability of the statistics used, while on the other hand we may have over- looked useful sources of information. If so we hope that others will step in and improve on our work which in any case, it is our hope, may serve as a starting point for more deep-going, specialized economic studies. Quite apart from all problems related to the statistics available and their interpre- tation, it is obvious that in a general survey like ours many interesting and important special questions will only be superficially dealt with, and maybe not even mentioned. Our book does not pretend to be an encyclopedia on the Egyptian economy, but only a survey and analysis of the main economic trends, problems and policies.

This book is an economic analysis written by economists for economists. This circumstance, together with the authors' special interest in economic stabilization problems, has been decisive for the selection of problems to be dealt with and is also responsible for the weight – in terms of pages – which has been attached to the individual problems. Throughout the analysis we have stayed within the limits conventionally set for economics as a branch of social science, and treated general policies, international as well as domestic, and fundamental institutional changes as exogenous events which have only been discussed to the extent that they have had a specific impact on the economy or have emerged from specific economic problems. And concerning economic policies proper we have followed the principle of considering the policy targets as given and confined the discussion to the question whether the measures taken have been rational from that point of view. This is just a traditional method of procedure although we are aware that in this particular case it may seem unhappy to the general reader and the political economist who might like to find discussions of the process of target-setting itself and the political and ideological developments accompanying – leading or lagging – the transformation of a backward capitalist-feudal society into that mixed state and private enterprise society now called Arab-Socialism. This transformation has not taken place in a politicial and ideological vacuum, and all along the road alternative courses might have been taken. Fascinating and important though such problems may be, we have by and large left them aside, the simple reasons being that they fall outside our field of competence or would have led us into abstract speculations of rather a barren nature. Fortunately, however, competent social scientists are at present working on problems of economic ideology and philosophy in the UAR and their results may soon be available.

The reader will also have to search in vain for general development philosophies and theories in the Hegel–Marx–Rostow manner; the theoretical set-up relied upon here is just ordinary modern economic theory. The reason is, once more, our preoccupation with concrete economic problems where we found no help in sweeping development theories and no need for new revolutionary economic theories for developing countries. In a qualitative sense the fundamental economic problems are the same everywhere. Orders of magnitude as well as the size and even the signs of elasticities and coefficients of reactions may differ, but the general theory needed to handle the problems is in principle the same. By this we do not mean to say that during our work we did not encounter shortcomings in modern economic theory, but our experience is that in spite of all shortcomings modern economic theory does bring us a long way towards a full understanding of the economic problems of developing countries. The situation is in this respect not different from that of highly developed countries, although there the empirical information is much better and the application of theory correspondingly easier. It is not in particular in its relation to the problems of the poor, developing countries that economic theory needs improvements and adjustments. What is needed for a deeper understanding of the economic problems of these countries is above all detailed, reliable empirical information – statistical data and descriptions of institutions. Once such information is available in abundance, they will look much less exotic – and cease to be a playground for theoreticians.

Our manuscript was finished in the fall of 1963 and by and large it follows the situation up to the budget year 1962/63. Still statistics are not available for the budget year 1963/64, and even for 1962/63 some data are missing. We don't think, however, that recent developments to any large extent have upset our analysis and conclusions in a qualitative sense, although they have changed the relative quantitative importance of various of the factors at work. A clear accentuation of the imbalances of the economy has, namely, taken place during 1963/64 and this calls for a few supplementary remarks. In our discussions in chapter 8, 10, and 11 of the development of saving and investment, the problems of inflation and overvaluation of the Egyptian Pound, the price policies and the regulations of foreign trade, we pointed out that already in 1962/63 the economy was characterized by certain commodity shortages, by a large and growing deficit in the balance of current payments, and by a rapid increase in public consumption. We ascribed there the imbalances mainly to inadequate price policies and to an incompetent and bureaucratic regulation of the foreign trade, and although we also pointed to the likely existence of a general domestic excess of purchasing power we judged this to be a problem of secondary importance only. We still think that this was a correct diagnosis for the situation until 1962/63, but there is little doubt that while today – at the fall of 1964 – the problems related to the price and foreign trade controls are as urgent as ever, the major problem has now become that of a general domestic excess of purchasing power created through a continued vigorous expansion of public current expenditures, mainly defence expenditures. The result has been a marked increase of the commodity shortages and bottlenecks at the same time as the price stability which until 1963 characterized the Egyptian economy has been broken by considerable commodity price increases. To what extent these price increases signalize the first round of an inflationary spiral is still questionable. Apart from some sectors where the overheating is most acute, in particular construction and building activities, money wages do not seem to have followed the price increases to any large extent, and since the price increases seem mainly to be confined to import goods and manufactured goods (other than the most essential foodstuffs), the trade with and production of which are to a large extent in the hands of the nationalized enterprises and public authorities, private income may have increased much less than the prices, and if so the price increases may be conceived of as an equilibrating rather than an inflationary process, the price increases being equivalent to increased indirect taxation. Everything will, however, depend on the extent to which the Government has succeeded, and will succeed in preventing wages and private profits from increasing. To judge about this is difficult at present. The process is in progress, new Government policies under formation, and statistics not yet available.

During the years in which we have been working on this book we have enjoyed the advice and criticism of many colleagues and friends, some of whom we have already mentioned above; we cannot here acknowledge our debts and gratitude to each single one of them. In addition to those mentioned above we want, however, to mention also the positive interest shown to our work by the Deputy Prime Minister Dr. Abdel Moneim El Kaissouny, Professor Edward Mason, Mr. Patrick O'Brien, the Minister of Economy and Foreign Trade Dr. Labib Shokeir, and Professor Jan Tinbergen, and their helpfulness in various ways. From the National Council of Social Research (Statens råd for samhällsforskning) in Sweden we received a grant for publication. Finally, we have to thank Mrs. A. Habib for skilful secretarial work in typing manuscripts and assisting with proof-reading.

Cairo, November 1964

B. HANSEN
G. A. MARZOUK

CHAPTER 1

A general survey

1.1 The background

Egypt is a poor country. The annual income of her people per capita is US $125, which on the world income scale places her in the lower brackets. The factors behind this poverty are much the same as in many other under-developed countries. A large and rapidly growing population is squeezed together in the Nile Valley and the Delta. In 1960 the density of population per square kilometer of inhabited and cultivated areas reached 729 persons. Being almost completely dependent on the water from the Nile the cultivated area cannot be extended much further; and since mineral deposits and other natural resources are limited, the only roads out of poverty lie through capital accumulation and the increased skill of her population. Capital accumulation, however, is a relatively recent phenomenon in Egypt, at least outside the irrigation system and transport, where much capital was invested during the nineteenth century and the first quarter of the twentieth. As for the population, centuries of unscrupulous foreign regimes, and scandalous domestic ones, had left it unskilled and ignorant, illiterate, apathetic and in bad health, trained in primitive methods of agricultural production only, and kept down by a corrupt, feudal governmental system, efficient only in oppression. Any appraisal of present developments has to take into account this sad historical background.

Egypt became a part of the world economy as early as the second half of the nineteenth century, when the shift in her agriculture towards cotton cultivation gave her an essentially money-economy, with even the smallest peasant producing for the world market. Disregarding the numerically negligible Bedouin desert population, the "subsistence sector" in Egypt disappeared a long time ago. Cotton also gradually made Egypt a one-crop exporter, heavily dependent on foreign trade. Thus, in contrast with many other underdeveloped countries, where a modern large-scale export sector

1

has been living its own life alongside a big, small-scale subsistence sector, Egypt early on was dominated down to the grass-roots by her export crop and the conditions for its sale abroad. If to this we add that even before World War I, her transport and communication system was adequate, it will be understood that Egypt was already at that time in a sense a developed raw-material producer.[1])

The world depression of the 'thirties, with its sharp fall in cotton prices compared with most other commodities, shook the Egyptian economy and called for new developments. It was then that the present process of industrialization began. With the change in relative prices and rates of return on capital in favour of manufactured industrial products, domestic capital turned its interest from agriculture to industry. At the same time, in 1930, the country gained control of its tariffs, which made it possible to protect domestic industry. These two circumstances together started the modern process of industrialization. Although supported by Government policies, this early development was predominantly the outcome of domestic private enterprise. The process was speeded up by the isolation of the country during World War II and the demands of the campaigning Allied Armies. When later the post-war investment boom petered out as did the Korean boom, and the Revolution of 1952 introduced a new era in the economic history of Egypt, the first, modest foundations for an industry in the country had already been laid. It is futile to speculate about what developments might have taken place without the Revolution. After it a deliberate, systematic Government policy of industrialization was pursued and this, together with radical land reforms and the eventual nationalization of big business, changed the character of the economy completely during the following ten years.

1.2 Income and production over the past fifty years

Let us follow these developments in terms of national income and production. Fairly reliable figures are available for the post-war period, and with an increasing margin of error they extend back to 1937–39. To go back further is a rather risky business, but it is not altogether impossible because the relatively good Egyptian agricultural statistics give us some impression of what the national product may have been as far back as the beginning of

---

[1]) Concerning developments until World War II the reader should consult A. E. Crouchly *The Economic Developments of Modern Egypt*, London 1938.

CHART 1.1

National income and domestic product 1913–1962 (at fixed 1954 market prices)

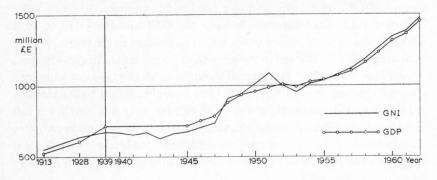

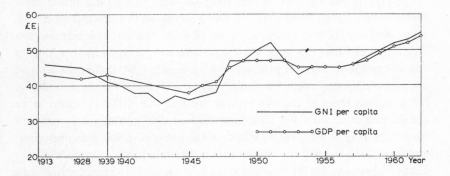

NOTE   The figures for 1939 to 1962 are based on B. Hansen and D. Mead, "The National Income of the UAR (Egypt) 1939–62", *Memo. no. 355,* Institute of National Planning, Cairo, 21 July 1963, and population figures from *Annuaire Statistique,* 1960–61, tableau I, p. 11. The GNI – total and per capita – for the years 1913 and 1928 are based on Ahmed F. Sherif, "General Trends of the Egyptian Economic Growth in the Last Twenty-Five Years", *Memo no. 121,* NPC, Cairo 1959 (in Arabic), corrected for an obvious error in the population figure for 1913, and adjusted to the level of 1939 according to Hansen and Mead. The methods of estimation used by Sherif have never been disclosed, but his results are supported by what is known about the per capita production of agricultural field crops, see Dr. El Imam, "The Production Function for Egyptian Agriculture 1913–55", INP, *Memo. no. 259,* 31 Dec. 1962, p. 25, and about the development of the terms of trade, see Dr. A. M. El Tanamly, "Agricultural Development in Egypt During the Last 50 Years" in *Research on the Fiftieth Anniversary,* Société Egyptienne d'Economie etc. 1909–59, Cairo 1959, p. 123–124 (in Arabic). The GDP figures for 1913 and 1928 were "guestimated" on the basis of the fact that the terms of trade were about the same in 1913 and 1928 as in 1950. The difference between GNI and GDP were therefore assumed to be the same percentage in 1913 and 1928 as in 1950. For figures, see Statiscal Appendix.

the present century. In chart 1.1 we have depicted, year by year, the development of both real gross national income (GNI) and real gross domestic product (GDP) since 1945, and also shown their probable levels in 1939, 1928 and 1913. The difference between the GNI and the GDP at 1954 market prices consists mainly of the effects of changes in the terms of trade compared with 1954 (the net income from abroad being of minor importance, at least after World War II). Like all countries producing and exporting raw materials, income level in Egypt has been strongly affected by fluctuations in her terms of trade, both in the short and the long run, and for a full understanding of her economic life, we have to take this into account. It is characteristic of underdeveloped raw-material producers that national income fluctuates more stronlgy than domestic production, and this is clearly brought out by chart 1.1.

The general trend of GNI is manifestly upwards, though it is broken by a slight decline during World War II, and a sharp fall in connection with the collapse of the Korean boom. In terms of GDP the long-run increase is a little larger and the periods of fall less pronounced; both during the 'thirties and through World War II production fell somewhat, while after the Korean boom it merely stagnated. The figures for GDP before 1939 are very shaky, but accepting them at their face value, we find that GDP increased at an annual rate of about 1 per cent from 1913 to 1928 and about $1\frac{1}{2}$ per cent from 1929 to 1939. By 1950 the effects of the war period had been overcome, and from 1939 to 1950 the annual rate of increase in total production was about $2\frac{1}{2}$ per cent. So far it would seem as if the early industrialization had succeeded in speeding up the rate of growth. During the first half of the 'fifties the gross domestic product again stagnated, but since the middle of the 'fifties, when the Government's industrialization programme was launched and deficit financing became the rule, an annual rate of increase of about 6 per cent has been achieved.

Alongside this acceleration of growth in terms of total income and production there was, however, an acceleration in the growth of the population. To get a full picture of the performance of the economy, we have therefore to turn to the per capita figures, which are also shown in chart 1.1. The diagram reveals immediately that from the beginning of the century (1913 was not a good year and the first decade may have shown better results) until the middle of the 'fifties no significant change in per capita income took place. The stagnation was partly due to the long-term fall in the country's terms of trade; but even if this is allowed for the increase in per capita income over the forty-two years from 1913 to 1955, would only have been some 5 per cent, i.e. an annual increase of about 0.1 per cent. From the time of the Suez War, on the other hand, we find an annual increase in per capita income of about 4 per cent. It would thus seem that 1956/57, by this yardstick, represents the demarcation line between stagnation and development.

Behind the stagnation in the first half of the century there were some interesting short-term developments worthy of comment. If we look at domestic production per capita, we find from 1913 to 1928 a slight fall, and from 1928 to 1939 an increase of about $\frac{1}{4}$ per cent p.a.[2]). The statistical margin of error for the pre-war period is big, as we have already pointed out, but it may be that we have here the first fruits of the nascent industrialization and the improved methods of cultivation in agriculture. However, this slight increase in production was wiped out completely by a heavy fall in terms of trade, and per capita income fell by as much as 10 per cent between 1928 and 1939. World War II brought a further fall of 10 per cent in per capita income, and at the end of the war it may have been about 20 per cent lower than at the beginning of the century; of this fall about half may have been due to the terms-of-trade fall, while half may be ascribed to a fall in domestic product per capita. When after the war imports again became normal, domestic product per capita soon surpassed the pre-war level by about 10 per cent, while owing to the international raw material shortage immediately after the war and the effects of the Korean boom terms of trade rapidly improved to the 1928 level. With the Korean boom the "good old cotton times" returned to Egypt for a year or two, and per capita income rose in 1951 to a level more than 25 per cent above that of 1939 – but only 15 per cent above 1913 and 1928. Just two years later, however, the terms-of-trade gain was lost once more, and per capita income was back at the 1913–1928 level. Compared with 1928, the long-term loss in terms of trade thus outbalanced the small gains in domestic per capita production.

The early attempts at industrialization were thus unable to bring about any radical change in Egypt's economy. From 1928 to 1948 domestic production per capita rose by about $\frac{1}{4}$ per cent per year only, and from 1948 to 1956 it stagnated completely. The slack after the Korean boom contributed to this result, but the main factor was the population explosion, which in Egypt may be dated back to World War II, when the annual rate of increase

---

[2]) The comparison between 1913 and 1928, and 1928 and 1939, conceals a slight fall during World War I and as ubsequent rise, and a strong fall at the beginning of the thirties followed by a stronger increase until 1939.

TABLE 1.1

Production by main sectors (percentage distribution and annual compound rates of increase)

Estimate	Years	Agriculture	Industry and electr.	Transport and communic.	Housing	Construction	Commerce and finance	Other serv. incl. govt.	Total
A	1937–39	49	8	4	7		32		100
	1945	44	10	3	3		40		100
B	1945	42	13	5	7	3	17	13	100
	1954	30	14	9	8	3	18	17	100
C	1954	30	15	6	6	3	16	24	100
	1962/63	26	18	8	5	4	18	20	100
Annual compound rate of increase									
	1937–39–1945—2.4		5.5	n.a.	n.a.	n.a.	n.a.	n.a.	0.0
	1945–1954　0.3		5.4	9.8	4.9	6.3	4.9	7.2	3.8
	1954–1962/63　2.8		7.9	9.4	3.4	10.5	6.7	2.8	5.2

NOTE　For estimate A, see M. A. Anis, "A Study of the National Income of Egypt", *L'Egypt Contemporaine,* 1950 nos. 261–2, Cairo 1950. This estimate is at current factor costs and gives the distribution of GDP. For estimate B, see B. Hansen and D. Mead, op. cit. table 4. This estimate is at fixed 1954 market prices and gives the distribution of GDP. For estimate C, see B. Hansen and D. Mead, op. cit. table 8, alt. I. This estimate is at fixed 1953/54 market prices and gives the distribution of GNP. Finally, it should be noted that the sector definitions vary as between all three estimates, which are, for all these reasons, not mutually comparable. The comparability is best for Agriculture. In judging the size of the individual sectors, it should be observed that the main part of the indirect taxes are included in Commerce and Finance.

rose from less than 1½ per cent to more than 2½ per cent. The conclusion seems to be that while the early phase of industrialization, dominated by private enterprise, did lead to a slow growth in per capita production before World War II, after the population explosion had gained momentum at the end of the 'forties it was only sufficient to maintain per capita production without increasing it; while the small gains in production which were accomplished earlier were only sufficient to pay for the long-term losses in the terms of trade.

CHART 1.2

7

Shares of outlay in gross national product

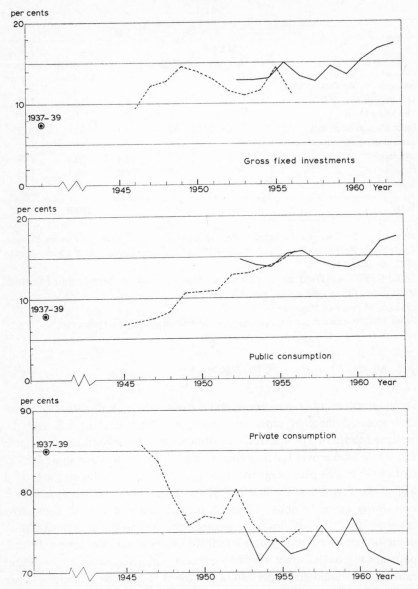

NOTE   The series for 1945–56 shown as -------- are based on a fixed-price estimate.
The series for 1952/53–1962/63 shown as ———— are based on a current-price estimate.
For methods of estimation see Bent Hansen, "The National Outlay of the UAR (Egypt)
1937–39 and 1945–1962/63", INP, *Memo. no. 377*, Cairo, 8 Dec. 1963. In these estimates
private consumption was obtained as a residual and contains some unrecorded stock
changes and capital imports, which may be responsible for some of the violent short-term
fluctuations. For figures, see Statistical Appendix. The level of public consumption
1945–62/63 may be 1–2 percentage units too low, and that of private consumption correspondingly too high.

TABLE 1.2

Investments distributed by sectors (percentages)

	1948/49 Average	1952/53	1955/56	1959/60	1962/63
Agriculture, land reclamation and irrigation	n.a.	11.6	10.5	14.8	16.6
The High Dam	—	—	0.3	2.5	8.0
Industry and electricity	n.a.	29.8	34.1	32.4	30.8
Transport, communication and stocks	n.a.	16.1	14.2	20.9	17.8
Houses	37.3	31.8	30.2	18.1	12.5
Services	n.a.	10.8	10.7	11.4	14.7
Total	100.0	100.0	100.0	100.0	100.0

SOURCES   1948–49, see El Sayed Hafez Abdel Rahman, *A Survey of Foreign Trade in Egypt in the Post-War Period,* unpublished doctoral thesis, University of Cairo, Faculty of Commerce, 1959.

1952/53–59/60, see *Ten Years of Revolution (Statistical Atlas),* Department of Statistics and Census, Cairo 1962, table 11.

1962/63, Ministry of Planning.

From 1952/53 onward some stock changes are included in total investments.

1.3 National outlay 1939–1962/63

Development requires investment, and the statistical records naturally reflect the increased share of gross investment in GNI, see chart 1.2, and the increased share of "productive" investments in total investments, see table 1.2. While total gross fixed investments in the 'thirties stayed at some 7–8 per cent of GNP, this percentage rose to some 13–14 per cent during the second half of the 'forties and the first half of the 'fifties, and after the Suez War it was slowly raised to about 17 per cent. The figure of 7–8 per cent gross investments of the 'thirties corresponds quite well to the slight increase in domestic per capita production which we observed for that period. With a population growth rate of about $1\frac{1}{2}$ per cent, an incremental capital-output ratio of $3:1$ should give a per capita growth in production of about $\frac{1}{2}$–1 per cent[3]). The 13–14 per cent share during the first post-war decennium (until the time of the Suez War) does not fit so well with the continued slow and subsequently vanishing growth in per capita production. It should give, still

[3]) For the years 1946 to 1962/63 the following regression between GNI-increment,

assuming a capital-output ratio of about 3:1, a $4\frac{1}{2}$ per cent growth in production; and with a population increase amounting to more than $2\frac{1}{2}$ per cent we should expect a $1\frac{1}{2}$–2 per cent annual increase in per capita production. A number of circumstances, however, contributed to keep the actual increase in production lower. Part of the post-war investments were pent-up replacement demands from war-time. Also, houses and irrigation canals with a high capital-output ratio absorbed a relatively large share of gross investments during the 'forties with a relatively low production increase later as a result. The area cultivated – at that time still a more important factor of production than capital – did not keep pace with the population; and finally, it seems likely that some idle capacity in industry was created during the 'fifties; the post-Korean slack lasted a relatively long time in Egypt.

The big jump in the rate of growth of per capita production after 1957 does not fit too badly with the share of fixed gross investments, averaging 15 per cent, during the years 1956/57 to 1962/63, and the continued rapid increase of population. From 1956/57 to 1962/63 the domestic product increased by about 6 per cent, whereas an investment share of 15 per cent should give about 5 per cent growth. The deviation is concentrated in the years up to 1959/60, when the average share of investments was only 13.5 per cent, though the average growth rate was above 6 per cent. But the growth rate of 6 per cent since 1959/60 is also a little high for the average investment share of 16.3 per cent for these years; this latter figure, moreover, may be an overestimate, since from 1959/60 the share of investments is measured in current prices, and investment sector prices have probably risen more than in the rest of the economy (see below). Most of the discrepancy can almost certainly be explained by utilization of idle capacity, which means that some of the rapid growth was made possible by earlier investments. That capacity was utilized to a higher degree was due to the expansion of domestic demand created by the budget deficit policies of the Government. Thus the rapid growth since the time of the Suez War has partly to be conceived of as a traditional Keynesian multiplier process; only in the last years of the period, say from around 1961, has increased capacity through investments been a limiting factor in the expansion process. The development of the Industry

---

ΔGNI, and gross investment, I was found:

$$\Delta \text{GNI} = -0.027 + 0.326 \, \text{I}$$

with a low and insignificant correlation coefficient. This result points to an incremental gross capital-output ratio of 3:1.

sector shows this quite clearly: after an increase of production by 12 per cent from 1959/60 to 1960/61, the increase fell in the following two years to 10 per cent and 7 per cent. However, there was also a shift in investments towards sectors with a lower capital-output ratio. Construction expanded vigorously, and the tendency towards a higher share of industrial investments may also have contributed to keep down the capital-output ratio. But, when everything is taken into account, it seems likely that without a further lift in the share of fixed gross investments the 6 per cent increase in total domestic production realized between 1956/57 and 1962/63 cannot be maintained in the future.

The share of public consumption also shows a big increase compared with the pre-war level, see chart 1.2. A sharp increase took place from 1948 to 1952, when the share of public consumption almost doubled. The main reason was increased defence expenditure in connection with the Palestine crisis. At the time of the Suez War there was a further increase in public consumption, but after that the share stayed almost unchanged, at a 13–14 per cent level, from 1952 to 1959/60. Behind this development we find an increasing share of expenditure for education and defence, while other current public expenditure stayed almost unchanged in absolute amount. From 1960/61 public consumption again increased rapidly, this time mainly as a result of the Government's employment policies. Some of this increase, reflected in the GNP, amounts to a form of concealed unemployment benefit.

The large increase in the shares of these two sectors, gross investments and public consumption, was made possible through a fall in the share of private consumption. From a level of about 85 per cent immediately before and after World War II (during the war it must have been lower), it fell to about 79 per cent in 1947–48, and still further to 72–74 per cent around 1954–55. The factors behind this fall are not quite clear. The post-war decline, is to some extent explained by the simultaneous increase in public net income from about 14 per cent of GNP in 1947/48 to 17 per cent in 1954/55, which lowered the share of private disposable income in GNP from almost 86 per cent to 83 per cent. Shifts in income distribution in favour of profits probably also contributed to the fall in the share of private consumption. Concerning the development after the Suez War, it is more difficult to judge. The share of Government income increased rapidly through sequestrations and nationalizations of both foreign and domestically owned companies; but the effects of this on consumers' disposable income is uncertain. The share of taxes in GNP fell, and at the same time price subsidies and interest payments increased; but outside the budget there was a large accumulation of pension and insurance funds, which had the effect of lowering consumers' disposable incomes somewhat compared with the GNP. The land reforms and other Government policies, on the other hand, tending to equalize income distribution, should have led to an increased consumption. We do know, however, that since 1954/55 the share of consumption in GNP has probably been quite constant. The fluctuations in the figures from 1955 to 1962/63 arise partly from unrecorded stock-changes and capital imports, which are included in private consumption owing to the methods of estimating. Since 1959/60 the measured share of consumption has fallen slightly, but this may be a statistical fiction, due to the above factors, and to the fact that the estimate shown in chart 1.2 is a current-price estimate, and most probably consumer goods prices have risen less than other prices[4]).

TABLE 1.3

Prices 1939–1962/63 (1945 ≈ 100)

Year	Implicit GNP-deflator	Wholesale price-index	Cost-of-living index
1939	—	35	34
1945	100	100	100
1948	96	100	96
1951	114	116	109
1954	113–119	104	98
1957	121–128	124	103
1960	124–131	123	104
1962/63	130–137	124	104

SOURCE   The GNP-deflator is based on Bent Hansen and Donald Mead, op. cit. table 4 and El Sayed Hafez Abdel Rahman, *A Survey of Foreign Trade in Egypt in the Post-War Period,* University of Cairo, Faculty of Commerce Library, unpubl. doct. thesis, 1959. For the years 1945 to 1951 the fixed-price series is that of Hansen and Mead, the current-price series that of Abdel Rahman. For the years 1954 to 1962/63 see Hansen and Mead, op. cit. table 8, alt. I, together with information from the Ministry of Planning. From 1954 two figures are shown for each year, with the chaining based on 1952/53 and 1954, respectively. Neither the wholesale nor the cost-of-living index has been used in constructing the national income series; the three price series are therefore independent. All three indexes are based on official prices.

---

[4]) From 1959/60 to 1962/63 the implicit GNP deflator rose by 5 per cent. If we assume that the whole price increase took place in the investment sector – which is a clear maximum assumption – the share of consumption in 1962/63 at fixed 1959/60 prices becomes 73.9 per cent. In 1959/60 the figure was 76.5 and the average for 1952/53 to 1955/56 was 73.3. Most probably the share of consumption at constant prices has been almost un-

We are led to the conclusion therefore, that the policies tending to diminish the share of private consumption were pursued mainly before 1955. After that time little was done in this respect. The rise in public consumption and investments since 1960 has only been made possible through a large increase in the deficit of the current balance of payments. We shall return to this below.

1.4 The structure of production

Since the 'thirties, which is unfortunately as far back as statistics can take us, great changes in production have taken place, especially in terms of sector distribution. The changes are, of course, closely connected with the process of industrialization, though a glance at table 1.1 makes it tempting to speak about de-agriculturization rather than industrialization; for the most striking feature of the table is the fall in the share of agriculture in total production, from about half before World War II to only one quarter in 1962/63. The fall seems to have been greatest between 1945 and 1954, when there was little increase in agricultural value added; after 1954 agricultural production increased more rapidly. The most expansive sector, measured by percentage share, seems to have been industry and electricity (including mining and quarrying); but owing to different sector definitions and methods of measurements, it is difficult to get a clear picture. To judge from table 1.1, its share may have increased by 6–7 percentage units from 1937–39 to 1962–63, which is the largest increase shown by any of the sectors. It is closely followed, however, by the Government sector, which is included in Other services. Government proper has probably increased its percentage contribution to GDP from about 5–6 per cent in 1937–39 to about 11–12 per cent in 1962/63. A clear expansion is also shown by the transport sector, which may have increased its share by 4–5 percentage units. For the remaining sectors long-term comparisons are difficult.

We do not need to look far for an explanation of these developments. The falling share of agriculture is mainly a reflection of the growth of the other sectors; while the increase in the share of industry is the natural result of the change of emphasis in investment. In the transport sector, the relatively large

---

changed. By this token, however, the share of real investments would be as low as 14 per cent in 1962/63, which does not seem likely. Most probably there has been some price increase for consumption also, but less than for investments.

increase is mainly due to the rapid increase in the Suez Canal traffic, which is included in and dominates this sector. The increase in the Government sector is connected with foreign policy problems and the need to build up a defence system, deliberate development policies, such as the creation of an adequate education system, and Government employment policies. There is hardly anything astonishing in all this, except the very heavy fall in the share of agricultural production. More unexpected, perhaps, is the growth that has taken place in the whole "service sector". Considering Agriculture, Industry and Construction as the "commodity producing" sectors and the rest as the "service sectors", we find an increase in the service sector from about 40 per cent in 1935–39 to about 50 per cent in 1962/63. Though some of this may be due to differences in sector classifications and definitions, the increase is nevertheless a real one. It is, however, fully accounted for by the growth of the transport and Government sectors discussed above. The remaining services have hardly increased their share (the apparent fall in the share of housing between 1939 and 1945 is due to rent control during the inflationary period of the war, and the fact that the distributive shares of table 1.1 for 1939 and 1945 are based on a current-price estimate).

The changes in the distributive shares of the sectors arise, of course, from differentials between the growth rates of the individual sectors. At the bottom of table 1.1 we show the annual growth rates for the three periods; from an analytical point of view, this choice of periods is not very interesting, but it is forced upon us by the available statistics. The highest growth rates since 1954 are found in construction and transport, with industry and electricity in third place. Agriculture shows the lowest rate of growth. The sharp increase in construction is closely associated with the Government's investment and employment policies. while the backbone of transport is the Suez Canal. Figures showing the distribution of investment by sectors, corresponding to that of production in table 1.1, are not available. Table 1.2, however, gives some idea of investment patterns, which may be related to those for growth. The conspicuous feature is the steep fall in the share of investment in houses since the second half of the 'fifties, and the increase in the shares of investment in Agriculture and the High Dam, and also services (education, etc.). The shares of Industry and Electricity, and Transport, Communications and Stocks were in 1962/63 about the same as in 1952/53, but since Industry and Electricity still have the largest, it is quite natural to find here the highest growth rates. From a long-run point of view the High Dam investments should be distributed on irrigation and electricity, but to do this is not possible.

1.5 Price stability and balance of payments instability

It is commonly considered almost an axiom that development policies lead to domestic inflation coupled with a deterioration in the balance of payments and an overvaluation of the country's currency. The underlying mechanisms which in many developing countries have made this "axiom" come true are well-known: increased investments lead to increased purchasing power and imports, prices increase, and the wage demands of the trade unions add fuel to the process. In so far as production and real income are in fact pushed upwards, this will in itself contribute further to the deterioration in the balance of payments. The day will then soon come when the IMF, as a condition for short-term loans to support empty foreign exchange reserves, will ask for a cut in Government expenditure and a dose of deflation in order to restore order to the finances of the country; development will be slowed down or stopped, and if the balance of payments has deteriorated very far, depreciation will be called for – and after a suitable interval the country can prepare itself for the next round of development and inflation.

A glance at Egypt's budget and balance of payments figures, with their permanent and in later years sharply increasing deficits, the growing utilization of her industrial capacity, the complete exhaustion of her exchange reserves, the depreciation of the currency, the repeated IMF consultations and drawings on the Fund, make it tempting to conclude that the country is yet another example to bear out the truth of the above-mentioned "axiom". To some extent this is true, without doubt. The balance of payments deficit has persisted, and increased from an average 1.5 per cent of GNP during the period 1946–51, to 2.3 per cent 1952/53–59/60, and 4.3 per cent from 1960/61–62/63, culminating in a deficit of 6.4 per cent for 1962/63. This makes it look likely that the currency is overvalued. At the same time, the total public-sector deficit, i.e., domestic and foreign borrowing, has increased from almost nothing in the 'forties to about 3 per cent of GNP in the middled of the 'fifties, 9–10 per cent of GNP on average for 1960/63, and around 10 per cent in 1962/63, which could be expected to create inflationary tendencies in the economy. The fall of the net exchange reserves from 65 per cent of GNP to nothing at all at the end of 1962, and the depreciation by 25 per cent in the same year, might point to the end of these policies. Yet the Egyptian development has some distinctive features which make a straightforward application of the "axiom" inadequate; the problem of the balance of the Egyptian economy can be thought of as a straightforward inflation problem to a limited extent only, and it is an open question whether the currency is overvalued. We discuss these problems in great detail in chapters 7 and 8 because they are so important for an understanding of past and future policies in Egypt, and also because they have considerable bearing on the problems of financing development in general. Here we shall merely summarize the argument.

First of all, the price level has been relatively stable since the end of World War II. All available price indexes agree about this, as may be seen from table 1.3. The implicit GNP deflator and the wholesale price index agree about a price increase of about 25 per cent from 1945 to 1957; but while the wholesale price index shows constant prices from 1957, the implicit GNP deflator reveals a further price increase of 7 per cent until 1962/63. To this we have to add certain black-market price increases (see below), which are not taken into account in the implicit GNP deflator, nor in the other indexes; but in any case the annual price increase does not seem to have been much more than 2 per cent. The increase is distributed fairly evenly over the whole post-war period (with a certain fall immediately after the war, and after the Korean boom); and even taking into account black-market prices, the increase in the *general* price level has probably not accelerated since 1957, when the Government entered upon its budget deficit policy and development really began. The implicit deflators for agriculture and industry show that price increases have been much greater in industry than agriculture. Deflators for the GNP by use are not available, but it seems clear that investment prices have increased more than other prices; in particular, construction shows substantial price increases. It is quite natural to find the greatest price increase in these sectors, for they are the most expansive. The cost-of-living index shows almost complete price stability, with an increase of only 4 per cent from 1945 to 1962/63. This steadiness is partly due to inadequate weighting (in this respect it resembles the wholesale price index), but also to the fact that controlled rents and other controlled prices, in particular those heavily subsidized, have much higher weights in the cost-of-living index than they would have in a general consumer-goods price index. Indeed, the official price controls and subsidies have been patterned in a way to keep the index stable. But even if the cost-of-living index is disregarded, it is clear that Egypt has experienced a high degree of price stability compared with most other countries.

Alongside the general price stability there have been heavy fluctuations in export prices and balance of payments. Cotton, which accounts for 25 per cent of agricultural production, some 10 per cent of total production, and about 70 per cent of export value, trebled in price from 1945 to 1951, and fell to half again in 1954, to mention the most violent movement. And the current balance of payments shows such extreme positions as a surplus corresponding to 8 per cent of GNP in 1945 and deficits of 6 per cent of GNP in 1952 and 1962/63. Through various "counter-cyclical" measures such as buffer stock policies, export tax variations, concealed foreign exchange rate changes, food price subsidies, etc., the effect on domestic price levels has been scaled down considerably; but only the abundant exchange reserves which the country could dispose of until the end of the 'fifties made such policies feasible. In this short-term instability Egypt resembles most other underdeveloped raw material exporters, but this makes the over-all price stability even more remarkable.

The modest rise in prices may be partly explained by direct price controls, which have been applied to all important commodities, and price subsidies; and the situation might therefore be interpreted as one of repressed inflation with little price increase, but with a large demand spill-over resulting in a balance of payments deterioration. There is of course an excess of total demand for investment and consumption purposes over supply corresponding to the balance of payments deficit, but it is doubtful to what extent this should be taken as a proof of the existence of inflation. Since foreign trade is now completely controlled and most of it directly in the hands of the Government, it is appropriate to study first the state of demand and supply "within the fence", so to speak, i.e. given the controlled levels of imports and exports, and turn later to the balance of payments deficit itself.

A repressed inflation should ultimately show itself through commodity and factor shortages and tendencies to black-market prices. There are without doubt shortages, particularly of imported manufactures but also of certain home-produced goods, and also an incipient black market. But, given the level of imports and exports, these may be partial imbalances rather than the result of a general excess demand for commodities. It is also unlikely that the administration would be able to keep the situation under control with a strong general excess demand within the fence; the price controls would probably break down completely. A basic condition for the price stability is to be found in the labour market. Although the supply of labour is certainly not infinitely elastic in the sense of Arthur Lewis (absolute surplus labour in agriculture probably did never exist in Egypt), there is no doubt that the supply has increased so rapidly during the post-war years that the increasing demand has never led to a real shortage, at least in the major categories of labour. Construction is probably the only sector wheer labour shortage and wage drift has become a real problem. And Government money wage rates have, if anything, been falling for the post-war period as a whole. Since, furthermore, tax and subsidy policies have added to the net disposable incomes of the lower income brackets, and since the trade unions have always been weak, private money wage rates have quite naturally increased less than productivity; and even including fringe benefits, which have been quite important in recent years, they have exceeded the increase in productivity by a negligible amount only. It is symptomatic of the state of the labour market that the Government has never been able to implement its own minimum wage legislation for rural labourers. Excess demands "within the fence" are therefore mainly confined to the commodity markets, and here they may be partial only, though the possibility of slight general excess demand cannot be excluded.

Turning to the balance of payments deficit, there is no doubt that in simple terms of purchasing power, i.e. in terms of unit prices or unit costs converted at actual exchange rates, the Egyptian pound became seriously overvalued during World War II. Prices almost trebled, while the Sterling rate was kept unchanged. Since 1945 unit costs and prices have become more favourable and this, together with the 25 per cent depreciation which took place gradually from 1949 to 1962 must have greatly diminished the overvaluation in this sense. Other factors are, on the one hand, the improvement in the terms of trade, which may amount to some 20 to 40 per cent compared with 1939 or 1945, and, on the other, the shift of domestic demand towards capital goods with a higher import content, and all the obstacles which Egyptian exports have met abroad in connection with the Suez War, etc. What net effect they have had on the balance of payments deficit is difficult to say. They may together explain the tendency for the deficit to amount to 1–2 per cent of GNP from World War II to the end of the 'fifties. Since about 1960 it has grown rapidly. The deficits in 1961 and 1962 can be ascribed in part to the unique cotton crop failure in 1961; but there is no doubt that in 1962 the deficit climbed to a substantially higher level than earlier, and this can only be explained by the rise in excess of Government spending for consumption and investment over revenue. The remedy for this is not simply to cut public expenditure *in general*, or increase public income *in general*, because this would cause a decline in domestic production at the same time as the balance of payments improves.

Although from the above analysis it would seem that the Egyptian pound is overvalued, it would be rash to draw this conclusion. The question of overvaluation should not be judged on the evidence of the present balance of payments deficit only; it has to be regarded as part of the general problem of how a country achieves its economic policy targets, and whether the exchange rates are or are not one of the instruments used for that purpose. Among the targets will usually be the balance of payments, and if this target comprises a period of foreign borrowing followed by a period of repayment spread over five or ten years, there is little point in discussing the possibility of overvaluation in the light of the current deficit. If the long-run targets can be achieved without recourse to the exchange rates, it is of course up to the Government to do so if it wishes. Now it is quite clear that even without altering the exchange rates, the Egyptian balance of payments deficit could in principle be rectified, both in the short run and the long run, with maximum production and unchanged Government spending. In the short run big shifts in the price relationships coupled with an increase of taxation on both commodities and incomes would be necessary; the hardships falling on the population would be very heavy, however, because the drop in consumption would have to be concentrated on cereals and this would lower caloric intake sharply. In the long run some shifts in price relationships and increased taxation would still be necessary, but the emphasis here would be on a return to the modest money-wage pattern of the 'fifties. So far there is no reason to speak of an overvaluation of the Egyptian pound, though a depreciation could, of course, be used as an act of policy, and will have to be used in the long run if the Government does not succeed in keeping down money wages. Two things complicate the picture, however: first, it is not clear what the Government's long-term programme is, and secondly, the attitude of foreign lenders may force the Government to adopt policies which it had not originally intended. Modern international credit transactions are to a large extent political moves, in which lenders do in fact interfere with the borrowers' programmes.

The UAR is a country greatly affected by the political aspects of the international credit market, but we shall not enter here upon an account of her foreign borrowing, which is closely related to the history of her international relations. It is sufficient to say that for the years before 1960 most of the deficit in the balance of payments was covered by the large exchange reserves accumulated during World War II; the big problem at that time was to get the blocked reserves in London released. After 1960, the deficit has been financed mainly by American deliveries of wheat, etc. under United States Public Law 480, which began on a large scale after the take-over of the Kennedy administration and the abandonment of the Dulles attitude to the UAR. The Soviet loans contracted shortly after the Suez War for the

construction of the High Dam at Assuan are quite large ($£$E 113 million)
but they are spread over a ten-year period. Loans from other sources have
played only a minor role, though short-term trade credits have at present
reached considerable figures.

1.6 The changing institutional framework

The developments which we have described, in very broad terms, took place
against a background of radical change in the institutional framework and
in the policies pursued. In some cases a change was made because the
previous institutional frame was considered a hindrance to the success of
certain policies. In other cases institutional changes were an end in themselves. Some changes, finally, are best understood in connection with the
dramatic happenings in the country's foreign relations. A characteristic of
Government policies since the Revolution of 1952 has been the adoption of
a pragmatic approach to problems. Ideologies have grown out of events
rather than the other way round.

Before 1952 the economy was based on private enterprise, with very few
restrictions, except for some feudal remnants still to be found in agriculture.
Distribution of both income and wealth was extremely unequal, and absentee
land-ownership was a characteristic feature of the economy. Government
policies, both monetary and fiscal, were on the whole passive, and mainly
designed to promote the interests of the big landowners, merchants and
industrialists, or the royal family itself. Development policies were not
unknown. Improvements to the irrigation system have always been considered
a Government assignment; early industrialization, as we have seen, was
conditioned by general protectionist tariff policies; and a more specific
though very modest development programme was actually adopted by the
old regime shortly before its fall. But all this was insufficient to cope with the
growing population and the worsened conditions for the country's foreign
trade, as is clearly shown by the stagnating per capita income; and social
legislation was both inadequate and inefficient.

The Revolution of 1952 had as its immediate purpose the carrying through
of land reforms which both Government and Parliament had repeatedly
refused to support. Inevitably therefore, the land reforms of 1952, which
involved an expropriation and redistribution from big to small owners of
about 10 per cent of the cultivated area (later reforms have increased this
figure to about 15), came to dominate policies during the first years after the

Revolution. On other matters the policies of the new Government, until the nationalization of the Suez Canal in 1956, were on the whole quite traditional, though there was a certain modernization of both monetary and budget arrangements, and some direct regulations were introduced, in particular in the field of foreign trade. But none of this went beyond the regulations applied by many Western European countries at that time. Development was an important part of the Government's programme; public investments were expanded somewhat, and a special development budget was introduced. The main policy, however, was still of a general, indirect investment-promoting type; the tariff system was reorganized in 1954 in order to give increased protection for domestic industries and promote capital goods imports, and company taxation included built-in investment incentives.

With the nationalization of the Suez Canal and the Suez War that followed at the end of 1956, policies changed rapidly. It is well-known that the nation-alization was decided upon as a way to finance the Assuan Dam after negotiations with the IBRD broke down. The Suez War carried with it further sequestrations and nationalizations of British and French property, which meant that the Government suddenly found itself, more by chance than design, with the main part of the banking and insurance system in its hands, together with some other sectors of big business. The following year, 1957, development planning was begun on a large scale, with the emphasis on Government investment. A 5-year plan for industry and another for agriculture were adopted, and in 1960 these partial plans were amalgamated in a further comprehensive 5-year plan for the period 1960-65. At the be-ginning of 1960 the big Misr concern, which had played a leading part in the early industrialization, was nationalized, partly because the investment plans of the concern did not conform with those of the Government. Large-scale nationalizations followed in 1961, and these brought the bulk of big industry and wholesale trade under public ownership. A new round of land reforms were put through at the same time. The main economic motive for the nationalizations was to bring investment and company savings under the direct control of the Government; but as a by-product, current production and trade also came to a large extent under Government control.

Since 1961, then, the country has had a mixed economy with Government and private sectors of about equal size. How this mixed economy works will be considered in detail in the last two chapters of this book. Here it is sufficient to say that with a mixed system, Government administration and policies become crucial. So far they have hardly found their final form in the UAR; much experimenting is still going on, and it is therefore too early to appraise their success. One thing, however, should be stressed. Like most other underdeveloped countries, the UAR depends to some extent upon foreign loans to finance its development. About one third of investments are at present financed from abroad. Difficulties are encountered in raising these funds, and sooner or later they have to be repaid. This requires an increase in domestic savings, presumably in public savings; but in both the short run and the long run all attempts to increase domestic savings must prove futile unless the resources set free lead to a corresponding net income from abroad. This means that the country must develop competitive export industries; and it means also that the developed countries must be prepared to let such industries compete within their own borders. The successful development of the UAR is therefore not only a responsibility of the country itself; it is just as much a responsibility of the developed, industrialized countries in Western Europe, America, and the Eastern Bloc.

CHAPTER 2

The demographic picture

2.1 The growth of population

Demographic statistics in Egypt go back a relatively long way. Estimates of the population were made as early as the French occupation under Napoleon Bonaparte, and in 1800 the total was found to be about 2½ million. The first modern census was taken in 1882, and in 1897 regular ten-yearly censuses were begun. This pattern was then maintained until 1957, when owing to the Suez War a simple population count only was made and the census itself postponed to 1960. According to the censuses the population of Egypt has risen from 6.8 million in 1882 to 12.8 million in 1917, and 26.1 million in 1960, i.e. about four times during the past eighty years.

It is generally agreed that, because of improved methods of data collection and the increasing standard of education of the population, recent censuses are on the whole more accurate than earlier ones. The 1960 census probably achieved quite a high standard, but earlier ones may have suffered from some underenumeration. Some of the fall in the rate of population increase which took place between 1882 and 1917 may well be explained by a decreasing degree of underenumeration. In 1947, on the other hand, it has been argued that the census exaggerated the total population, because people expected it to be used to reassess the rations of essential commodities in short supply at that time[1]. This may account for some of the increase in the population growth rate between 1937 and 1947, which implies that the measured annual growth rate of 2.4 per cent from 1947 to 1960 may be too low.

By comparing population statistics with registrations of births and deaths we can get some idea of their accuracy. Registration did not become compulsory until 1912 and at first was not comprehensive; but in recent decades

---

[1] Dr. Hassan M. Hussein, "Contribution to Demography Through New Census Enquiries", *Proceedings of the World Population Conference*, 1954, vol. VI, p. 11.

TABLE 2.1

Population of Egypt, 1882–1960

Census year	Population in millions	Annual compound rate of increase during inter census years, per cents
1882	6.8	—
1897	9.7	2.3
1907	11.3	1.5
1917	12.8	1.3
1927	14.2	1.1
1937	15.9	1.1
1947	19.0 (17.9)*	1.8 (1.2)**
1960	26.1	2.4 (2.9)**

* Estimate of El Badry on basis of the continuation of the 1907–37 rate of increase (see chapter 2, footnote 2).
** Adjusted accordingly.
SOURCE *Population Trends in the UAR,* Central Statistics Committee, 1960, p. 3.

TABLE 2.2

Population increase during intercensus years
(millions)

	Registration statistics	Census results
1927–36	2.3 ⎫ 4.8	1.7 ⎫ 4.8
1937–46	2.5 ⎭	3.1 ⎭
1947–56	5.1 ⎫ 7.1	4.0 ⎫ 7.1
1957–60	2.0 ⎭	3.1 ⎭

SOURCE *Annuaire Statistique* and *Basic Statistics,* Department of Statistics and Census, several issues.

coverage has improved and registrations are now believed to be fairly complete, especially in urban districts. Table 2.2 shows that for the period 1927 to 1960 as a whole, and also for the two sub-periods 1927–1946 and 1947–1960, registration statistics and the census show almost the same population increase, 11.9 millions for the whole period, 4.8 millions from 1927 to 1946, and 7.1 millions from 1947 to 1960. On the assumption that the 1960 census is unbiased, this should give us some confidence in both the 1927 and 1947 census, and in the accuracy of both censuses and registrations.

It should be remembered that for the censuses we must presume a decreasing underenumeration, and therefore an exaggeration of the growth rate, while growth according to the registrations may be over- or underestimated, depending on variations in the quality of birth and death registrations. Table 2.2 suggests a serious underenumeration in the 1957 population count, which was disturbed by the Suez War, and in the 1937 census.

The history of population growth in Egypt during the present century can be divided into two periods, with World War II as a period of transition. During the period 1917–1946 the average crude birth rate (according to registration statistics) was 42.4 per thousand, while the average crude death rate was about 27 per thousand. On the basis of the evidence provided by the age distributions as disclosed by the censuses, and after making certain necessary corrections, Dr. M. A. El Badry[2]) has estimated that for the years 1917–1946 the deficiency in registration of births was up to 11 per cent, and in reporting deaths between 13 and 31 per cent. The actual average annual rate of increase of population during this period may therefore have been as low as 1.2 per cent, although the census figures themselves show a higher rate of increase from 1937 to 1947.

After 1945 the crude death rate fell considerably, through the introduction of antibiotics and insecticides, improved methods of sanitation, and the work of the newly established public health organizations. In recent years the crude death rate has been 16 per thousand, compared with an implicit average rate of 31.9 per thousand during 1937–1946[3]). At the same time the crude birth rate has remained at the pre-war level of about 43 per thousand, with the result that the rate of population growth has increased to something between 2.4 and 2.9 per cent. Because of the big drop in mortality rates, the expectation of life at birth in 1960 exceeded that of 1937 by 16 years for males and 11.7 years for females. For older age groups the increase in life expectancy was smaller. One reason was the larger drop in the infant mortality rate. Mortality of children under one year accounts on an average for about one fourth of the annual number of deaths, and it fell

---

[2]) "Some Demographic Measurements for Egypt Based on the Stability of Census Age Distributions" by M. A. El Badry, repr. from the *Milbank Memorial Fund Quarterly,* July 1955, vol. 33, No. 3, p. 268–305, published by the Milbank Memorial Fund, New York, p. 36.

[3]) "Life-Table Functions for Egypt based on Model Life-Tables and Quasi-Stable Population Theory", by S. H. Abdel-Aty, reprinted from the *Milbank Memorial Fund Quarterly,* April 1961, vol. 39, no. 2, p. 350–377, published by the Milbank Memorial Fund, p. 19.

TABLE 2.3

Expectation of life in Egypt at successive census dates, 1937–1960

	1937		1947		1960	
	Males	Females	Males	Females	Males	Females
At birth	35.6	42.1	41.4	47.0	51.6	53.8
At age 10	47.4	54.5	49.3	56.8	56.6	62.0
At age 30	33.0	38.2	34.1	40.4	39.0	43.9
At age 50	19.4	23.4	20.1	24.2	22.4	26.3

SOURCE   *Population Trends in the UAR*, 1962, p. 48–49.

from 175 per thousand to 108. A second reason was that previous life tables gave unreasonably high estimates for the survival rates and life expectancies of the older age groups [4]).

2.2 *The age distribution*

According to well-established demographic theory, a population without migration and with relatively constant age schedules of fertility and mortality will after a large number of years attain a constant rate of increase and a stable age distribution. It has been shown also that a decline in mortality has a relatively small effect on the stable age distribution provided that fertility rates remain unchanged. Such a decline will result in a new stable population having a higher percentage under 15 years old, a lower average age, a small increase in the percentage of persons over 60 years.

These demographic theories are in harmony with the development of Egypt during the last fifty years. Persistent high levels of fertility between 1917 and 1947 produced in Egypt a relatively constant age distribution. The general form of the age structure disclosed by the censuses was for the whole period the same broad-based pyramid tapering off rapidly with age. The proportion of persons under 15 remained fairly constant, between 38.0 per cent and 39.1 per cent, but in 1960 it rose to 42.8 per cent, as a result of the sharp fall in the mortailty rates after 1947. The proportion of persons in the 15–49 age group, on the other hand, which varied between 53 and 56 per cent from 1917 to 1947, fell to 51 per cent in the 1960 census. The small

---

[4]) S. H. Abdel-Aty, op. cit. p. 2.

TABLE 2.4

Age distribution in successive censuses, in percentages, 1917–1960

Age Group	1917	1927	1937	1947	1960
0– 4	13.8	14.4	13.2	13.6	15.9
5– 9	14.2	13.1	13.9	12.7	14.7
10–14	} 20.3 {	11.1	12.0	11.7	12.2
15–19		9.1	8.4	10.0	8.3
20–29	15.6	16.4	15.3	15.1	14.3
30–39	13.5	14.1	14.6	13.8	13.1
40–49	9.0	9.4	10.1	10.4	9.3
50–59	5.9	5.7	5.9	6.4	6.3
60–69	3.8	3.6	3.6	3.8	3.8
70–79	2.2	1.8	1.8	1.5	1.5
80 and over	1.7	1.3	1.2	1.0	0.6
Total	100.0	100.0	100.0	100.0	100.0

SOURCE　　*Population Trends in the UAR*, 1962, p. 4.

TABLE 2.5

Number of persons by age distribution 1937–1960 (in millions)

	1937			1947			1960			Increase 1960 over 1947
	M.	F.	Total	M.	F.	Total	M.	F.	Total	
0–14	3.2	3.1	6.3	3.7	3.6	7.3	5.7	5.5	11.2	3.9
15–59	4.3	4.3	8.6	5.2	5.4	10.6	6.6	6.8	13.4	2.8
60 and over	0.5	0.5	1.0	0.5	0.5	1.1	0.7	0.8	1.5	0.4
Total	8.0	7.9	15.9	9.4	9.6	19.0	13.1	13.0	26.1	7.1

SOURCE　　ibid.

fraction of persons over 60, which was between 7 to 8 per cent in the period 1917–1947 fell, however, to less than 6 per cent in 1960.

As a result of the continued high fertility and the sharp decline in mortality rates, the Egyptian population has become younger than before: the average age of the population has fallen from 25.8 years in both 1937 and 1947 to 24.4 years in 1960.

Out of the total increase in population of 7.1 million persons since 1947, 3.9 million (or 55 per cent) were persons under 15 years, and 2.8 millions (or 39 per cent) were persons in the group 15–59 years. Persons 60 years and over increased by 0.4 million, or by less than 6 per cent. This age distribution shows that Egypt suffers from the economic handicap of having a large number of children dependent on the adult population, represented by the

15–59 age group. There are now about 8.5 children under 15 to every 10 persons between 15 and 60 years old, whereas the figure for 1947 was 7 children. This compares with a ratio in the economically most advanced countries of Europe, North America, and Oceania of about 4 or $4\frac{1}{2}$ children [5]). One of the traditional explanations of high fertility in countries like Egypt is the possibility of exploiting children productively, and the actual burden of childhood dependence has always been lightened by their beginning work at an early age. In rural areas this is still common in Egypt; children may be working in the fields, during the seasonal peaks at least, at the age of 6 to 10 years. With the spread of compulsory education, however, and the legal prohibition of employing children under 12 years of age, the ratio of labour force to total population, as will be explained later in the chapter, has fallen considerably in recent years. The burden of childhood dependence has therefore increased more than the figures suggest.

Age structure is important not only because of its immediate economic and social consequences, but also because of its influence on the future trend of mortality, fertility, and the natural rate of increase. The present very heavy burden of raising and educating children is likely to continue in the future. "So long as the birth rates are not changed, any addition to the adult population implies a proportionate increase in the number of births. If death rates fall while birth rates remain constant, the size of each successive generation will be larger, but the average number of dependent children per adult will be practically unchanged" [6]).

---

[5]) *The Determinants and Consequences of Population Trends,* ST/SOA series A. Population series, no. 17, New York, 1953. Brief summary presented to the World Population Conference, E/conf. 13/345 meeting, no. 26, p. 14.

	Egypt	USA	Sweden
Children ($<$ 15)	8.5	5.5	3.9
Old People ($\geq$ 60)	0.6	2.3	2.7
Children plus old people	9.1	7.8	6.6

SOURCE   *Demographic Yearbook,* 1959, United Nations, New York, 1959.

The findings are counterbalanced to some extent by the fact that countries with a low proportion of children usually have a high proportion of old people. Comparison with USA (1959) and Sweden (1957) shows that although in Egypt the burden of supporting children *and* old people remains larger than in USA and Sweden, the difference is much smaller when the two are added together. The figures in the table are the number of children and old people per 10 persons in the productive ages 15–59.

[6]) Ibid., p. 15.

2.3 Population forecasts for 1960-1985

The Central Statistics Committee has made a set of five projections for the
population of Egypt for the period 1960 to 1985, and analysed them according
to age and sex. The results are summarized in table 2.6.

TABLE 2.6

Projected size of total population of UAR (population in millions)

Projection	1960 modified census	Estimates for		Compound annual rate of increase		
		1970	1985	1960–70	1970–85	1960–85
I	26.1	34.5	52.5	2.8	2.8	2.8
II	26.1	34.0	48.3	2.7	2.4	2.5
III	26.1	34.5	48.4	2.8	2.3	2.5
IV	26.1	33.4	43.6	2.5	1.8	2.1
V	26.1	31.7	38.8	2.0	1.4	1.6

SOURCE   *Population Trends in the UAR,* Central Statistics Committee, 1962, p. 53.

NOTE   The projections are based on five different assumptions as to the future trend of
fertility. Projection I (as an upper limit): Fertility rates will remain constant from 1960 to
1985 at the actual 1960 level of 190.0 (101 males and 89 females) per thousand females in
the age group 15–49. Projection II: Fertility rates will decline by 1 per cent of the 1960
rates each year up to 1985, with a total decline of 25 per cent. Projection III: Fertility
rates will remain at the 1960 level for 15 years and decline thereafter by 5 per cent each
year for 10 years. Projection IV: Fertility rates will decline by 2 per cent of the 1960 rates
each year during the period, i.e. with a total decline of 50 per cent of the 1960 rates in
25 years. Projection V (as a lower limit): Fertility rates will decrease by 5 per cent of the
1960 rates for 10 years and remain constant thereafter. In all five projections mortality
rates up to age 45 are assumed to decrease exponentially over the period (according to
Makeham's formula) towards certain ultimate values obtained from a study of the minimum relevant mortality rates in various countries. For age 45 and over, mortality rates
are assumed to remain constant at their 1960 level; any further improvement over the
steep decline since 1947 would not significantly affect estimates of the future size of the
population. Similarly mortality rates for age 65 and over are assumed to remain constant.

The most probable rate of growth for the period 1960–85 lies, in our
opinion, between 2.5 per cent and 2.1 per cent. It is true that in the years
1947–1960 the actual rate of growth may have been as high as 2.9 per cent,
but this very high rate was influenced by a temporary spate of births. It
should be remembered furthermore that the 2.9 per cent is an adjusted

figure assuming a population 1.1 million less than measured 1947. The increase actually recorded by the censuses between 1947 and 1960 was only 2.4 per cent. The very high fertility rate of 1960 (see below) was also influenced by temporary factors. We shall deal with these points at some length, for the future growth rate of the population is bound to have a critical influence on any attempts to increase general standards of living. A growth rate of even 2.1 per cent per year is a serious handicap for such a policy.

The trend of fertility assumed has important implications not only for estimates of the annual rate of increase of the total population, but also for its age distribution. A low fertility assumption implies fewer children under 15 years. According to projection I, children under 15 years will form 45.3 per cent of the total population in 1985, as against 42.8 per cent in 1960; but projection II implies that the ratio will fall to 37.1 per cent. The ratio drops further, to 36.8 per cent and 28.1 per cent, under the last three projections based on still lower fertility rates.

2.4 Fertility

Owing to changes in age and sex composition, the crude birth and death rates do not reflect in any precise way fertility and mortality trends. Similarly the crude fertility rate, calculated in terms of births per 1 000 females in the age group 15–49 in a given period, is defective because it does not represent the actual experience of any real generation of women. The crude fertility rate will rise if, other things being equal, a larger proportion of people marry. Similarly, a sudden shift to marriage at an earlier age may increase the fertility rate and the crude birth rate during the years in which this shift takes place, even though the total number of children born during the lifetime of a woman may, for behavioural or physiological reasons, remain unchanged. In such cases the increase in the fertility rate and the crude birth rate is temporary only, and due to speeded-up births. The crude fertility rate, however, has an advantage over the crude birth rate in that it partly eliminates the effect of temporary shifts in the age structure of the population. The following table compares crude fertility rates in the last four census years with the crude birth rates.

The proportion of persons in the 15–49 group fell significantly from 1947 to 1960, as we have seen, while from 1927 to 1947 the age distribution remained almost unchanged. The number of females in this age group increased from 27.1 per cent in 1937 to 28.1 per cent in 1947, but fell to

TABLE 2.7

Fertilit· and crude birth rates, 1927–1960

Year	Crude fertility rate	Crude birth rate
1927	178.5	n.a.
1937	181.4	43.9
1947	171.9	43.6
1960	190.0	42.9

SOURCE   *Population Trends in the UAR,* Central Statistics Committee, 1962, op. cit.

25.8 per cent in 1960. Thus, the slight fall in the crude birth rate shown in table 2.7, at a time when the crude fertility rate increased, may be ascribed, other things being equal, to changes in the age structure of the population.

However, although the fertility rate eliminates some of the effects of changes in the age structure, it suffers from two serious defects: it does not represent long-run trends, and it does not eliminate the effect of temporary changes in the proportion of married women or the age at which they marry. Both defects have serious repercussions on population projections, especially those extending over periods of 25 years or more. In 1959 there was a large temporary increase in the number of marriages, especially in the last quarter of that year, which partly accounts for the increase in the number of children born during the fourth quarter of 1960. This is one of the reasons why we think projection I in table 2.6, based on unchanged 1960-fertility, exaggerates future developments. A further reason is that owing to temporary circumstances such as the high marriage rate during and after World War II, the ratio of married women to all women between 15 and 50 in 1960 was relatively high. Finally, and probably most important, the proportion of married women with a marriage duration of 10–19 years was exceptionally high in 1960, again because of the high marriage rates of World War II. This group of married women has by far the highest fertility in Egypt (see table 2.20), which therefore raises the average fertility for 1960.

As indicators of long-term trends it is usual to use "cumulative fertility rates". We have computed these for 1947 and 1960, and give them in an appendix to this chapter, tables 2.17–2.20. They show the total number of children born to married women classified according to age or duration of marriage. The average number of children per married woman rose from 3.80 in 1947 to 4.17 in 1960. This average, however, does not necessarily reflect long-term trends, since it is calculated on an aggregate of woman-generations. We have to break it down into age and marriage-duration groups. On doing this, we find that the increase may be explained to some extent as the outcome of speeded-up births during and after World War II; and these in their turn were the result of an increase in the marriage rate and a fall in the average marriage age at that time. But the picture is more complicated than that. While the breakdown shows the expected big increase in the number of children born to women who married early during and immediately after the war, it shows also an increase for women past child-bearing age (the size of completed families), and at the same time a fall in fertility among the youngest women. The increase in the figure for women past child-bearing age has little relevance, because it concerns a group which dominated the picture in the past. It is rather the fall in the fertility of the youngest women which concerns us; for this may be the *future* trend. We believe therefore, that a continuation of the high fertility rate of 1960, and the high growth rate from 1947 to 1960, is unlikely, and that projection I, the most pessimistic of the above population projections, is quite unrealistic.

It will be noticed from tables 2.17–2.20 that there is no difference in fertility between urban and rural areas. The figures also indicate that contrary to expectation cumulative fertility rates in 1960 became higher in both Cairo and Alexandria than for the rest of the country. This is explained partly by the fact that in Cairo and Alexandria the increase in marriage rates during the years 1941–51, and the consequent speeded-up births, were more pronounced than in other parts of the country[7]. In addition over 40 per cent of the population of these two cities had moved in from rural areas in a rapid process of urbanization; for Cairo and Alexandria, rather than the rural areas, witnessed most of the industrial expansion. The standard of living in these two cities rose more than in other parts of the country, and this seems to have brought with it some increased fertility, at least temporarily.

It would seem, therefore, that the classical theory of population growth associated with the name of Malthus is more applicable to Egypt at the present stage of the country's economic development than the theory of demographic transition. According to the Malthusian theory, any rise in per capita income for the poor classes tends to increase fertility rates and to decrease death rates. However, there are also factors which support the theory of demographic transition, which asserts that "the high birth rates

---

[7]) Girgis A. Marzouk, "Fertility of the Urban and Rural Population in Egypt", *L'Egypt Contemporaine*, Jan. 1957, no. 287.

and death rates characteristic for an agrarian low-income society are affected by economic development. The changing structure of production with a declining importance of the family as a production unit, with the growth of impersonal system for the allocation of jobs, and with the development of economic roles for women outside of home, tends to increase the possibility of economic mobility that can better be achieved with small families, and tends to decrease the economic advantages of a large family" [8]). The fall in the fertility of the youngest women in Egypt between 1947 and 1960 may be a pointer in this direction. The transition theory also maintains that "in most countries that have undergone the economic transition from an agrarian to an industrialized, market-oriented economy, the custom of the small family has started in the urban groups at the higher end of the socio-economic scale and has spread to smaller cities, lower-income groups, and eventually to rural areas" [9]). In Egypt, again, there are some indications to that effect. In 1959 a study [10]) of family size was made in which information was collected from Cairo and Alexandria, representing the urban pattern, from the workers' town of the Misr Textile Factory at Mahalla El Kobra, semi-urban, and from three villages; about 6 000 women who had married once and were still with their husbands were interviewed. According to this study, there is in Egypt some inverse relationship between average size of completed families and social class. The fertility differentials were more pronounced when married women were classified by the educational status of their husbands; a trend that was noticed also for incompleted families. In urban areas the top socio-economic or educational class had reduced its fertility significantly, the middle class only slightly, and the lower brackets not at all; they had maintained their high fertility rates. In semi-urban and rural areas, too, there was still no indication of a reduction in fertility, even among the highest educational or occupational class.

It may be therefore that while the immediate effects of the improved standard of living in Egypt has been along Malthusian lines, industrialization, urbanization and improved education will slowly make the tendencies stressed by the transition theory dominate.

---

[8]) A. J. Coale and E. M. Hoover, *Population Growth and Economic Development in Low-Income Countries,* Princeton University Press, 1958, p. 11.

[9]) Coale and Hoover, op. cit. p. 11.

[10]) *Social and Psychological Factors Affecting Fertility in the UAR,* by Prof. Hanna Rizk, in mimeograph, issued by the Egyptian Medical Association and the Scientific and Research Department of Schering AG, Berlin, Germany.

2.5 Major demographic features

The major demographic features of the Egyptian population – apart from the high level of both fertility and mortality already discussed – are its youth, the comparatively small ratio of the labour force to the total population, the concentration of the majority of the people in agricultural employment in rural areas, and, finally, the high rate of illiteracy. In recent years structural changes have decreased the share of agriculture and increased the share of services and industry; at the same time the proportion of urban population has increased, and education has become more widespread.

2.5.1 Distribution of population by economic activity

The employment figures revealed by the last three censuses are not directly comparable. Both in 1937 and in 1947 the figures included persons of 5 years of age and over, as well as a large number of persons whose occupation were not stated, whereas in 1960 the census recorded the employment of persons of 6 years of age and over only. Table 2.8 shows the employment figures of the three censuses, together with the adjusted figures of the Department of Statistics.

According to the adjusted figures the economically active population expanded by 1.1 million between 1937 and 1947 and by 0.8 million from 1947 to 1960, that is a total increase of 1.9 million, or 32.5 per cent over 1937. After having stayed unchanged at 37 per cent in 1937 and 1947, the ratio of economically active persons to total population fell to 29 per cent in 1960. The comparable ratio in Europe and the USA varies between 42 per cent and 52 per cent.

Of the total increase of 1.9 million persons since 1937, agriculture absorbed 386 thousand persons, or slihgtly more than 20 per cent, industry and construction 378 thousand, or slihgtly less than 20 per cent, and the remaining 1,132 thousand persons, or 60 per cent, went into services. Of the increase since 1947, agriculture absorbed 320 thousand persons, or 43 per cent[1]), industry and reconstruction 220 thousand, or 30 per cent, and the remaining

---

[1]) The number of persons active in agriculture is probably exaggerated, both in the census and the adjusted figure. The 1960 census was made in September, which is a seasonal employment peak in agriculture, while earlier censuses were taken in March, which in agriculture is a seasonal slack. The increase in agricultural employment since 1947 may therefore be fictitious.

199 thousand persons, or 27 per cent, went into services. As a result of these movements, agriculture now engages 57 per cent of the total economically active population, as against 58.4 per cent in 1947 and 68.8 per cent in 1937. The share of services, on the other hand, swelled from 21.7 per cent in 1937 to over 31.4 per cent in 1947, and has since remained stagnant. The share of industry and construction, as a result of the industrial expansion, grew gradually from 9.5 per cent in 1937 to 10.2 per cent in 1947 and 12.0 per cent in 1960.

As we have seen in section 2.2 of this chapter, out of the total increase in population of 10.2 million persons since 1937, males in the 15–59 age group increased by only 2.3 million, which leaves, after deducting the 1.9 million total increase in economically active persons, 0.4 million, some of whom have been absorbed in secondary or high school education. The high level of fertility rates coupled with the sharp drop in mortality rates contributed much to the fall in the ratio of the economically active to the total population in 1960, but other important factors have accentuated this trend.

2.5.2 Manpower and labour-force[12])

Since November 1957 the Department of Statistics and Census has carried out sample surveys of the labour force, on a nation-wide basis and including both urban and rural areas. So far thirteen surveys have been published. The sampling unit is the household, and the frame of the rotating, multi-stage, and stratified sample is the population count of 1957[13]). Manpower is defined in the surveys as the proportion of the population whose energy can be used in economic activity. The very young, originally those under 6, but from 1961 those under 12, as well as persons over 65 years, and the disabled, are therefore excluded. Manpower is divided into two groups: a) the labour force, which includes both employed and unemployed persons, and b) those outside the labour force, i.e., persons who are able to work but are neither working nor looking for paid work, such as housewives wholly

---

[12]) This section on the results of the labour force surveys is based on two sources: "The Current Labour Force Sample Survey in Egypt", by Prof. Abdel Moneim El Shafei, in the *International Labour Review,* vol. 33, no. 5, November 1960, p. 432–449, and *The Labour Force Sample Survey of Egypt, 1959–60,* by the Central Statistics Committee, May 1961 (in Arabic).

[13]) A positive appraisal of the surveys was given by Morris H. Hansen in *Report on Study of Household Sample Surveys* to Dr. Hassan Hussein, Central Statistics Committee, UAR, May 6, 1962.

TABLE 2.8

Employment by economic activity, 1937–1960 (in thousands)

	1937		1947		1960	
	Census	Adjusted	Census	Adjusted	Census	Adjusted
Agriculture	4284	4020	4215	4086	4379	4406
% of econ. activ.	58.1	68.8	51.2	58.4	57.2	57.0
Industry	476		707		758	
% of econ. activ.	6.5	552	8.6	710	9.9	930
		9.5		10.2		12.0
Construction	118		112		157	
% of econ. activ.	1.6		1.4		2.0	
Services	1168	1266	1617	2199	2255	2398
% of econ. activ.	15.8	21.7	19.7	31.4	29.4	31.0
Not stated	1329	—	1567	—	117	—
% of econ. activ.	18.0	—	19.1	—	1.5	—
Total	7375	5838	8218	6995	7666	7734

SOURCE   Department of Statistics and Census.

TABLE 2.9

Labour force and manpower

	Labour force		Man-power		Total
	Number in millions	% to total population	Number in millions	% to total population	population in millions
Average of first four					
surveys (1957/58)	7.0	29.7	18.1	76.6	23.6
Round 5 (1959)	6.8	28.6	18.3	76.6	23.8
Round 13 (1960)	6.0	25.0	18.8	77.7	24.2

SOURCE   Prof. El Shafei, op. cit. and *The Labour Force Sample Surveys of Egypt, 1959–1960*, Central Statistics Committee, May 1961 (in Arabic).

engaged in household work, full-time students, or persons not looking for work because they have private means of support or are in receipt of subsidies.

According to the surveys, the labour force amounted in 1961 to 6.0 million persons on average, of which 255 thousand, or 4.2 per cent, were unemployed, as compared with 7.7 million recorded in the population census. The difference of about 1.7 million, which is largely absorbed by children under 12 and women, is due to several factors. The sample surveys estimate the total population at 24 million, or 9 per cent lower than the total recorded in the population census. This was because they used as their frame the households recorded in the 1957 population count which, as we have seen, was an underestimate. There is thus an inherent downward bias in the labour force surveys of some 9 per cent, which may account for about 600 000 persons. Concerning the remaining difference of about one million persons, it will be noticed from table 2.9 that while total manpower has increased by almost one million during the thirteen labour force surveys, and thereby remained stable in relation to total population, the labour force has fallen by about one million between the 1957/58 surveys and the 1960 surveys. Two major factors account for this. The first is the issue in April 1959 of Law no. 91, prohibiting certain types of employment of children under 12 years of age. As a result, the number of children 6 to 11 years old in the labour force fell, from 248 thousand in the first four surveys to 39 thousand only in survey no. 13. The second factor is that although the same definition of the labour force was maintained throughout the period, it seems that in more recent surveys the interviewers have excluded unpaid females giving incidental help only in agricultural field work. As a result, the number of females in the labour force fell from 718 000 in the first four surveys to 253 000 in the last survey. This exclusion seriously distorts the comparison over time, and, moreover, females helping in agricultural field work are in practice part of the labour input in production. We have preferred, therefore, to base the analysis which follows on the results of the first four rounds of sample surveys, raised by 11 per cent, to take into account the downward bias in the frame as well as the rise in employment during the two years after they were made. If this is done they almost agree, both in total and in distribution, with the census of 1960. The following table makes the comparison.

TABLE 2.10

Employment according to labour force surveys and population census (in thousands)

	Labour force surveys		1960 population census (adjusted)
	Average 1957–58	1957–58 adjusted upwards by 11%	
Agriculture	3929	4322	4406
Industry and construction	764	840	930
Services	2199	2418	2398
Unidentifiable, not reported	138	152	—
Total	7029	7732	7734

SOURCE   ibid. and information from Department of Statistics and Census.

For industrial employment the 1957/58 figures, after adjustment, are lower than the 1960 figures by 11 per cent, while for agriculture and services the agreement is good. For industry, therefore, there seems to be a real difference between the population census and the labour force surveys. This is a reservation that must be borne in mind in the following analysis.

2.5.3 Sex and age of the labour force

The labour force in Egypt is made up of 90 per cent males and 10 per cent females. The ratio of women in the labour force to the total female population is only 6 per cent, compared with a ratio of 53 per cent for the male population. Children under 16, on the other hand, form a relatively large part of the labour force in Egypt, 13 per cent, the proportion being larger in rural than in urban areas. Since the prohibition in 1959 of certain kinds of employment of children under 12, this ratio is expected to fall, particularly in urban areas.

TABLE 2.11

Percentage distribution of labour force by age groups in rural and urban areas

Age group	Urban	Rural	Total
6–11	2.1	4.1	3.5
12–15	7.1	10.4	9.3
16–19	7.5	9.3	8.7
20–29	19.5	19.9	19.8
30–39	24.0	20.9	21.9
40–49	19.9	16.2	17.4
50–65	17.3	15.8	16.3
65 and over	2.4	3.4	3.1
Total	100.0	100.0	100.0

SOURCE   Ibid.

The ratio of children under 16 in the labour force to the total number of children in the same age group is much larger in rural areas than in urban areas. This is the natural outcome of, on the one hand, the need for children in farm work, and on the other, the fact that in urban areas a larger proportion of children attend school. The larger ratio in rural areas of both children under 16 and women in the labour force accounts for the higher ratio of the labour force to total manpower in rural areas compared with urban areas. Other important differences between urban and rural districts are to be found in the distribution of the labour force by economic activity and by occupation. While 79 per cent of the labour force in rural areas are engaged in agriculture, only 4 per cent are engaged in industry and 17 per cent in services. In the urban areas about 25 per cent of the labour force are engaged in industry and construction, 70 per cent in services, and only 5 per cent in agriculture. Paid employees predominate in urban areas, while in rural areas self-employed persons, as well as unpaid family workers, predominate.

2.5.4 Illiteracy and education

The 1960 census shows a considerable improvement over previous decades in the decline of illiteracy. Between 1937 and 1947 the ratio of illiterate persons to the total population 6 years of age and over fell only slightly, from 78 per cent to 77 per cent. Thereafter, however, there was a big fall, to 56 per cent in 1960.

The distribution of the population according to educational status shows that in 1960 18.5 per cent could write and/or read, and over 4 per cent had completed a primary, secondary or university education. The ratio of illiteracy is largest among females, and in rural areas.

The number of pupils and students has grown rapidly; but so too has the number of children and young people of school age. As a result, although the number of pupils and students rose by almost 120 per cent from 1947 to 1960/61, their share of the age group 5–19 years stayed almost constant at 35 per cent. At the primary school level, however, there has been an im-

TABLE 2.12

Number of pupils and students (in thousands)

	1953/54	1960/61
Primary schools	1 396	2 610
(girls)	(257)	(997)
Preparatory schools	352	295
(girls)	(27)	(94)
Secondary schools	135	226
(girls)	(28)	(55)
Universities	38	98
(girls)	(2)	(15)
Total	1 921	3 229
of which: girls	314	1 161

SOURCE   United Arab Republic *The Year Book 1963*, Cairo.

provement, and it is estimated that about three-quarters of all children reaching the age of 6 years are now enrolled in primary schools; by 1970 it is planned that all children reaching school age shall attend. Since primary school education is at present compulsory only for boys, while girls can attend school if circumstances permit, the percentage of girls attending school is much lower than that for boys at all stages of education.

2.5.5 Urbanization

Intensive urbanization has been taking place during the last 25 years, and it has speeded up considerably during the last decade. The factors behind this are not difficult to find. The depression of agriculture during the 'thirties started the process, and the special conditions during World War II accelerated it. Since 1947 it has been greatly influenced by indust ialization and the expansion of the Government sector.

TABLE 2.13

Urban population as a percentage of total population

1882	19
1907	19
1927	23
1937	23
1947	31
1960	38

SOURCES   *Annuaire Statistique,* several issues.

2.6 Population policies

Although the rate of population growth is smaller in Egypt than in some other underdeveloped countries, it is still high enough to present a serious problem to a country anxious to develop. A $2\frac{1}{2}$ per cent annual increase in the population makes it difficult to achieve a rapid increase in per capita income. Until 1962, the Government's attitude to the problem was relatively passive, but in his speech at the inauguration of the National Assembly in 1962 the President took up the question and advocated family planning as a necessary device in the struggle for a higher standard of living. The country was told that unless the people themselves contributed to keeping down the size of families, the Government's efforts to increase production per capita would be in vain. Since then the Government has pursued a very active family planning policy, supported by the religious authorities, both Moslem and Coptic. In contrast to certain other Moslem countries contraceptives have always been available in Egypt, and their use has by no means been limited to the highest income and education classes. In addition, and quite apart from contraceptives, people have always had their own ways and means of limiting the number of children if they wanted to [14]). Since 1962 however, the question has become public. An official birth control propaganda was launched and during 1963 and 1964 the Government opened a large number of family planning clinics both in urban and rural districts, where people can get advice on family problems in general and birth control in particular, and where both mechanical and chemical contraceptive devices, as well as contraceptive pills are made available gratis or at low, subsidized prices. On the basis of sales figures it has been estimated that about 200 000 women, corresponding to 4 per cent of the total number of married couples, made regular use of contraceptive pills in 1963.

More important perhaps than propaganda and the availability of contraceptives is to increase the average age of marrying for women, which is still low (though recent figures show that it is rising), and to make children an economic burden instead of being a source of income. In both rural and urban districts even small children of 6 and over were until recently a good source of income. In agriculture cotton-picking, weeding, rice planting, etc., has always been considered work for women and children; and in towns even quite small boys helped in workshops, while girls were rented out as servants from the age of 5. Some of these practices have been checked through improved social legislation, but probably only compulsory school attendance, enforced by the authorities, can bring an end to child-labour and turn children into an economic burden for their parents. This is probably the most important way in which increased education can help to bring down the high fertility; if increased education can also help to delay marriages further, much will already have been done, and the rest may be plain sailing, even if it is slow. Nobody, of course, expects the population growth to be retarded quickly; a generation or two may be necessary. But with the present policies of the Government, and the rising standard of living and education, the Egyptian population problem does not look as hopeless as that of many other underdeveloped countries.

---

[14]) H. Rizk, op. cit., found that in urban and semi-urban districts about 10 per cent of the wives of illiterate men practised some form of birth control, while among wives of men with a higher education than secondary school the percentage was as great as 50–60. In rural districts birth control was practically non-existent.

MARRIAGE RATES AND CUMULATIVE FERTILITY

During World War II the crude marriage rate rose from 22.2 to 31.2 per thousand in 1943, but then fell again during the 'fifties to a level below the 1938 level. The marriage rate calculated on the basis of persons of 16 years and over showed a less pronounced rise, from 19.8 per thousand in 1938 to 23.2 per thousand in 1947, and fell back to the 1938 rate in 1960.

TABLE 2.14

Number of marriage contracts and crude marriage rate in some selected years

	Cairo and Alexandria		Other parts of Egypt		All Egypt	
	Number in thousands	Crude marriage rate	Number in thousands	Crude marriage rate	Number in thousands	Crude marriage rate
1938	27	25.8	165	23.2	192	23.4
1939	29	26.4	155	21.6	184	22.2
1941	36	30.0	200	27.0	236	27.4
1943	49	37.8	228	30.0	277	31.2
1945	47	33.6	229	29.2	279	30.0
1947	42	28.0	219	27.2	261	27.4
1949	47	29.4	233	28.0	280	28.2
1951	43	25.8	210	24.0	253	24.2
1953	37	21.2	179	19.4	216	19.7
1959	46	20.4	183	17.6	230	18.1
1960	52	22.6	230	21.6	282	21.8

SOURCE   *Annuaire Statistique,* several issues.

The high level of the marriage rates during the years 1941–51, compared with previous and later years, should in principle lead to an increase in the percentage of married women among women of 16 years and over. Table 2.15 shows that this percentage did actually rise, from 65.8 in 1947 to 67.6 in 1960. If no other influences had been at work, we should at the same time expect a fall in the percentage of never-married women. But in fact the percentage of never-married women rose, while the percentage of divorced and widowed women fell. The explanation for the increase in the number of never-married women may have to do with the low marriage rates at the end of the 'fifties. The fall in the number of divorced women is a complex phenomenon, but obviously the fall is a real one; the percentage of "not stated", which probably contains a high proportion of divorced women, fell from 1947 to 1960. The fall in the percentage of widowed women may also be a sociological one – more widows marry now than earlier – but most probably it has to do with the fall in mortality. In any case a smaller ratio of widows means a higher ratio of married women. The increase in the percentage of married women may thus be partly a temporary phenomenon, partly a more permanent one.

TABLE 2.15

Distribution of women of 16 years and over by marital status (in percentages)

Marital status	Cairo and Alexandria		Other parts of Egypt		All Egypt	
	1947	1960	1947	1960	1947	1960
Never married	22.5	25.3	18.5	19.0	19.3	20.3
Married	63.2	64.8	66.3	68.2	65.8	67.6
Divorced	2.0	1.8	1.7	1.5	1.7	1.5
Widowed	8.6	7.5	11.9	10.4	11.3	9.8
Not stated	3.7	0.6	1.6	0.9	1.9	0.8
Total	100.0	100.0	100.0	100.0	100.0	100.0
Percentage of married persons in total population	38.4	35.5	39.2	37.9	39.1	37.4

SOURCE   1947 and 1960 Population Censuses

The big rise in the marriage rates during the above-mentioned years was naturally accompanied by a fall in the average age of married women at that time. The fall in the marriage rate after 1951 has in turn led to a rise in the average age of married women in 1960, compared with 1947. The implication of this, on its own, for fertility is not clear. The average duration of marriage for married women in 1960 was also greater than that at the time of the 1947 census: and the trend is more pronounced for Cairo and Alexandria than for rural areas. As shown in table 2.16, the ratio of married women with a marriage duration of less than 10 years fell, compared with 1947, while the ratio of women with a duration of 10–19 years increased substantially; and here again the trend is more pronounced in both Cairo and Alexandria than in other parts of the country. The interpretation of this table is made extremely difficult by the big fall from 1947 to 1960 in the number of "not stated". Most probably the "not stated" women are to a

TABLE 2.16

Percentage of married women by duration of present marriage in 1947 and 1960

Marriage duration	Cairo and Alexandria		Other parts of Egypt		All Egypt	
	1947	1960	1947	1960	1947	1960
Below 5 years	25.3	18.7	21.1	17.4	21.7	17.6
5– 9 years	18.6	19.1	17.2	18.3	17.4	18.4
10–19 years	24.0	34.9	25.9	32.5	25.6	33.0
20–29 years	14.4	15.9	16.0	17.3	15.8	17.0
30 and over	7.0	10.7	9.8	12.5	9.4	12.2
Not Stated	10.7	0.7	10.0	2.0	10.1	1.8
Total	100.0	100.0	100.0	100.0	100.0	100.0
Average marriage duration in years	12.27	15.23	14.86	16.12	14.53	15.68

SOURCE   Ibid.

large extent women with a relatively long marriage duration. This cannot, however, change the main features of the table except that the apparent increase in the number of women in the categories 20–29 and 20-and-over may actually be a fall.

In considering trends, we must notice first that women with a marriage duration of 10–19 years constitute by far the most fertile group of all married women (see table 2.20), and the high proportion of these women in 1960 must therefore temporarily increase the average for all married women in 1960. Furthermore, women who marry early have a longer period of exposure to the possibility of pregnancy than women who marry late, and will therefore, on average, bear a larger number of children. And a woman who has married early will, after a given number of years of marriage, have a larger number of children than a late-marrying woman will have after the same number of years of marriage. It is most probably these circumstances that account for the very steep rise in the cumulative fertility rates, shown by table 2.17, for women having a marriage duration of 10–19 years, see tables 2.18–20. This group of women married between 1942 and 1950 and were relatively young when they entered marriage. The higher cumulative fertility rates for women over 45, and those having over 20 years of marriage duration, would normally be taken as a sign of higher fertility; for they have not been influenced by early marriage in the same way as the age groups 30–44 years and the group with a marriage duration of 10–19 years. However, when we look at the average number of children born during specific age limits and marriage-duration periods, we find among the highest groups, which are not influenced by anything except that the women have actually been married a long time and completed their families, that the figures for 1960 are the same or lower than for 1947. Since these women had a larger total number of children in 1960 than in 1947, they must during an earlier period of their marriages have had a higher fertility, and it seems likely that

TABLE 2.17

Cumulative fertility rates (average number of children born to married women*) by age group)

Age group	Cairo and Alexandria		Other parts of Egypt		All Egypt	
	1947	1960	1947	1960	1947	1960
Below 20	0.75	0.48	0.51	0.39	0.57	0.41
20–24	1.62	1.72	1.31	1.41	1.37	1.47
25–29	2.80	3.37	2.43	2.87	2.48	2.97
30–34	3.94	4.68	3.50	4.16	3.56	4.26
35–39	4.99	5.72	4.67	5.23	4.71	5.32
40–44	5.32	5.89	5.19	5.67	5.21	5.71
45–49	5.73	6.38	5.89	6.15	5.87	6.18
50 and over	5.80	6.08	5.94	6.06	5.89	6.16
Not stated	2.84	3.11	2.99	5.31	2.97	5.27
All age group	3.69	4.35	3.82	4.14	3.80	4.17

*) Excluding married women who did not state number of children born.

TABLE 2.18

Cumulative fertility rates (average number of children born to married women*) by marriage duration)

Marriage duration	Cairo and Alexandria		Other parts of Egypt		All Egypt	
	1947	1960	1947	1960	1947	1960
Below 5 years	0.93	0.85	0.75	0.73	0.78	0.75
5– 9	2.38	2.80	2.21	2.50	2.24	2.56
10–19	4.54	5.12	4.25	4.73	4.30	4.80
20–29	6.10	6.76	5.93	6.39	5.95	6.45
30 and over	6.40	7.14	6.67	6.85	6.64	6.89
Not stated	5.43	4.81	5.09	2.41	5.16	2.57
All duration	3.69	4.35	3.82	4.14	3.80	4.17

*) Excluding married women who did not state number of children born.

this was during and after World War II. There is no reason therefore to believe that the rise in the cumulative fertility rates for older women represents a permanent long-term tendency. Finally, when we turn to the youngest age group and those with the shortest marriage duration, we find a fall in fertility; and if anything in present and past events indicates future trends, it must be the behaviour of the youngest generation.

TABLE 2.19

Cumulative fertility rates (averages number of children born to married women*) during specific age limits)

Age group	Cairo and Alexandria		Other parts of Egypt		All Egypt	
	1947	1960	1947	1960	1947	1960
Below 20	0.75	0.48	0.51	0.39	0.57	0.41
20–24	0.87	1.24	0.80	1.02	0.80	1.06
25–29	1.18	1.65	1.12	1.46	1.11	1.50
30–34	1.14	1.31	1.07	1.29	1.08	1.29
35–39	1.05	1.04	1.17	1.07	1.15	1.06
40–44	0.33	0.17	0.52	0.44	0.50	0.39
45–49	0.41	0.49	0.70	0.48	0.66	0.47
50 and over	0.07	0.30	0.05	0.09	0.02	0.02

*) Excluding married women who did not state number of children born.

TABLE 2.20

Cumulative fertility rates (average number of children born to married women*) during specific marriage duration periods)

Marriage duration	Cairo and Alexandria		Other parts of Egypt		All Egypt	
	1947	1960	1947	1960	1947	1960
Below 5 years	0.93	0.85	0.75	0.73	0.78	0.75
5– 9	1.45	1.95	1.46	1.77	1.46	1.81
10–19	2.16	2.32	2.04	2.23	2.06	2.24
20–29	1.59	1.64	1.68	1.66	1.65	1.65
30 and over	0.30	0.38	0.74	0.46	0.69	0.44

*) Excluding married women who did not state number of children born.

CHAPTER 3

Agriculture-production and prices

3.1 The trends of development

Our concern in this chapter will be mainly with the post-war developments in agriculture, leaving aside historical long-term trends. However, to appraise achievements since the war a brief review of the earlier course of agricultural production is useful. In chart 3.1 therefore, we have picked out two important indicators of production in agriculture, and the rôle of agriculture for the economy, and showed their development from 1914 to 1960.

The first, *Production per worker in agriculture*, is an important indicator of productivity and standard of living. Here, instead of growth and progress, we find a sharp fall by one-third from 1914 to the beginning of the 'thirties, when a small recovery took place. This was soon followed by a further heavy fall during World War II. Taking into account certain weaknesses in the statistics on which chart 3.1 is based, it seems safe to say that at the end of World War II, production per man in Egyptian agriculture was only about two-thirds of its 1914 level. After 1945 the trend changed radically, and production per man started rising even more rapidly than it had fallen. By about 1960 the pre-World War I level had again been achieved[1]).

On closer consideration, however, it seems better to consider not 1945 but the low point in 1933, as the turn of the tide. The reasons for this will be clear as we seek the causes of the changes. Behind the fall in production per man up till 1933 lay the pressure of increasing population, which led to a

---

[1]) From 1913 to 1950 the production index used for the calculation of the curves of chart 3.1 does not include animal production and vegetables and fruits. From 1950 to 1960 it does not include animal production. We know that from 1935–39 to 1960 this means an underestimation of the increase of agricultural production of about 2 per cent. If the underestimation is of the same order of magnitude for the years 1913–1935–39, it seems as if production per man should be about 5 per cent higher in 1960 than shown in chart 3.1. This brings 1960 up to 90 almost. Value added, however, may have increased less.

CHART 3.1

Agricultural Plant Production

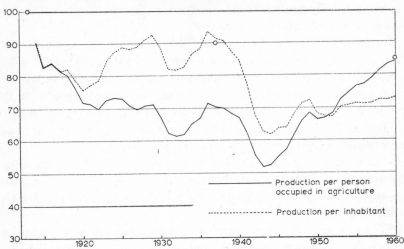

NOTE   Agricultural production from 1913 to 1950 is represented by an index for major
field crops calculated by Dr. M. M. El Imam, "A Production Function for Egyptian
Agriculture 1913–1955", *Memo. no. 259*, Institute of National Planning, Cairo 1962. El
Imam's index is a chained ideal Fisher index. From 1950 to 1960 the index for plant production of the Department of Census and Statistics was used, see table 3.12. Yearly figures
for persons occupied in agriculture were calculated by Dr. El Imam, op. cit. Figures for
total population are from *Annuaire Statistique*. Both curves are based on three-year moving
averages, o indicates food production per inhabitant, 1913 = 100.

rapid rise in the number of workers per acre of agricultural land. According
to the law of decreasing returns, a fall in production per working person is
then exactly what we should expect. Up to this point, development may be
characterized as typically Malthusian. But at the end of the 'twenties and
during the 'thirties, two important things happened: there was an improvement in methods of cultivation through a rapid expansion of irrigation and
draining and a great increase in the use of artificial fertilizers; and the number
of those employed in agriculture stagnated, in spite of a rise in the growth
rate of the population as a whole. These events were connected to some
extent with the world depression from 1929 onwards, which hit Egyptian
agriculture hard. To the low level of production per person at the beginning
of the 'thirties, we must add the effects of a fall in agricultural selling
prices of about 50 per cent. These were years of deep misery for the fellahin,
and the flight to the towns and the big public works to extend the network

of canals and drains were natural consequences. The outcome was an increase in production per worker of about 15 percent over a few years; and at this higher, but still very low level, production per worker then remained during the second half of the 'thirties.

The fall which followed during World War II was due to a temporary shortage of fertilizers, combined with certain unfavourable shifts in the composition of agricultural production during the war years. In any discussion of long-term trends, therefore, these years should probably be left out of the picture. When the supply of fertilizers once more became normal, production slowly recovered; and by the end of the 'forties, with the consumption of fertilizers approaching the level of the second half of the 'thirties, production had recovered completely. The sharp increase during the 'fifties can again be explained by a further rapid increase in the use of fertilizers, together with other factors which we shall study in greater detail in the rest of the chapter.

The present upward trend in agricultural production per man may thus be dated back to certain fundamental events in the 'thirties, and to make a fair appraisal of the achievements in agriculture during the last ten years, they should be seen against this background: a continuous fall in production per worker from 1913, perhaps even from the end of the last century, to the beginning of the 'thirties, followed by a period at a low level lasting till about 1950.

The second indicator, *Agricultural production per inhabitant*, does not have the same direct significance as production per man in agriculture. Agricultural production, it must be remembered, is not identical with food supply, which may be modified upwards or downwards through foreign trade. The fall to be seen in agricultural production per inhabitant indicates that a serious and permanent foreign trade problem has developed. At the same time food production per inhabitant has also fallen, though by not so much, namely by 7 per cent from 1935–39 to 1960. At a given standard of living, and even more so at a rising standard, Egypt is thus no longer self-sufficient in food. In itself there is nothing wrong in this; many other countries have experienced a similar development and profited from it. Its significance as an economic problem is that in the long run exports, obviously of industrial products, must be increased to pay for the increased imports of food.

In this way our two curves indicate two main problems connected with Egyptian agriculture, but of importance for the Egyptian economy as a whole: that of raising the general standard of living through increasing production per man in agriculture, and that of feeding a growing population with a rising standard of living, i.e. balancing foreign trade in spite of an increased food import.

3.2 Agricultural techniques and inputs

3.2.1 The water supply

Egyptian agriculture depends almost entirely on Nile water, for even on the coast the rainfall is inadequate for cultivation, and in the rest of the country there is hardly any rain at all. This circumstance is decisive for the methods and possibilities of cultivation. Irregularities in the Nile water supply, seasonal fluctuations within the year, as well as large variations in the total annual supply, confront the irrigation system with a variety of difficulties. To master these problems, and direct the water supply in an optimal manner, is one of the primary concerns of Egyptian long-term agricultural policy[2]).

The average annual discharge of Nile water, measured at the sluices of the Assuan Dam, amounted to about 82 000 million m³ during the years 1912–42. The variations around this average were large, however. In some years the volume was as low as 42 000 million m³, while in others it was as high as 155 000 million m³ [3]). The seasonal fluctuations are even larger. About 80 per cent of the total annual volume of water passes through the sluices of the Assuan Dam between mid-July and the end of December[4]). During this period there is a surplus of water, and normally a large volume passes "unused" into the Mediterranean Sea. The other 6½ months, from January to mid-July, are a period of shortage with only 20 per cent of the annual total available, and this is not sufficient for optimal irrigation.

With the increase in foreign demand for Egyptian cotton after the American Civil War, the problem of controlling the Nile to increase production came to the forefront. Efforts were concentrated on evening out the natural seasonal fluctuations in the water supply, which were larger than indicated by the above figures, since they refer to regulated fluctuations, by storing untimely water during periods of surplus, and releasing it during periods of shortage. However, the possibilities for storing water in this way

---

[2]) For a general survey of the problems of irrigation and draining, see e.g. Sayed Marei, *UAR Agriculture Enters a New Age, An Interpretative Study,* Cairo 1960, ch. 4 and 5.

[3]) *Sudan Almanac 1955,* An official handbook, Sudan Govt. Khartoum 1955, p. 49.

[4]) Ibid., p. 48.

are limited by the fact that during the early part of the flood, the Blue Nile and the Atbara River carry considerable quantities of silt. If this water is stored, there is some danger of filling up the reservoirs with silt. Generally speaking, a "standard" year, with about 70 000 million m³, is considered to supply one fifth of water as timely water, one fifth as untimely, non-storable water, and three fifths as untimely, but storable water[5]). The first big dam was constructed in 1902 at Assuan. This was capable of storing 1 000 m³, but its capacity has since been enlarged twice: in 1912, to 2 500 million m³; and in 1933, to 5 000 million m³. In 1937, another dam was built at Jebel Aulia in Northern Sudan, which increased total storage capacity to 7 500 million m³. But even with this increase, storage capacity remains far below optimum, and is confined to "seasonal" storage rather than "annual" storage, which is the major objective of the High Dam at Assuan.

Together with the efforts made to increase water supplies during the period of shortage, the river banks were strengthened to protect the fields against inundation by flood water. Deep canals were excavated to draw water from the Nile when at its lowest level. Every year considerable efforts are expended on clearing the silt deposited by the flood water, and on lifting irrigation water from the deep canals to the fields. To control the geographical distribution of the water supply, and to feed the canals with the quantities of water required, a set of barrages were constructed at different places on the Nile. The Delta Barrage, the first to be constructed, was completed during the 'eighties, though its construction was started as early as 1843. It was followed by the Assiut Barrage in 1903, the Esna Barrage in 1930, and the Edfina Barrage, a minor work only, in 1952. A new barrage was built in 1937 to replace the old Delta Barrage, which had become inadequate.

Since the construction of the new Delta Barrage, no major single contribution to the improvement of the irrigation system has been made so far. The completion of the High Dam at Assuan in 1968–69 will become the next big achievement. This does not mean, however, that no improvement of the irrigation system has taken place during the last 25 years. On the contrary, through extending and deepening the irrigation canals and drains for the local distribution of water, improvement has been continuous. The growth in the total length of drains and canals, some of which are navigable and carry a certain amount of traffic, is shown in table 3.1. The period 1925–1940 was one of rapid expansion; from 1940 to 1960 the tempo has been more modest.

---

[5]) Ibid., p. 49–50.

Since all major irrigation canals and drains are public, the administration of water distribution is, and always has been, public. This, of course, gives the State a certain influence on crops and methods of cultivation.

Improvements through the increased use of machinery, i.e. pumps, for irrigation and drainage have taken place since World War II. After a fall in both number of machines and total horsepower at the beginning of the 'thirties, irrigation machinery slowly recovered, and reached at the end of World War II the level attained at the end of the 'twenties. Since then a rapid

TABLE 3.1

Length of irrigation canals and drains

End of year	Kilometres in thousands	Increase last five year period, per cent
1915	24.3	—
1920	24.8	2
1925	25.0	1
1930	26.6	7
1935	28.7	8
1940	32.0	12
1945	33.3	4
1950	35.2	6
1955	36.2	3
1960	38.1	5

SOURCE   *Annuaire Statistique*, 1960–61 and earlier issues.

TABLE 3.2

Irrigation and drainage machinery

| End of year | Number of machines | Horsepower (in thousands) | | | Index of total horsepower |
		Private (licensed)	Public	Total	
1930	12.992	371	37	408	100
1935	10.546	292	46	338	83
1940	11.819	326	61	387	95
1945	12.420	338	65	403	99
1950	n.a.	370	70	440	108
1955	n.a.	428	119	547	134
1960	16.782	460	122	587	143

SOURCE   *Annuaire Statistique*, 1960–61 and earlier, together with information from the Ministry of Public Works.

development has taken place, mainly through the establishment of big
public pumping stations, many of them connected with particular large-
scale reclamation schemes, such as the Tahrir project.

As an expression of the "density" of machinery we can use the amount of
horse-power per kilometre of canals and drains. Defined in this way, the
density was unchanged at 15.3 hp per km from 1930 to 1960. During the
'thirties it actually fell to about 12 hp per km, and not until the 'fifties did it
reach its old pre-depression level.

3.2.2 Area cultivated and cropped

Before the construction of deep "summer' canals, only one crop, a winter
crop, could be grown. At that time the land was divided into basins to which
the flood water was directed, and one basin after the other was inundated and
left, until the excess water receded to the Nile through the drains. Wheat,
barley, beans, clover and other winter crops were then planted in the basins
without need for further irrigation. After the harvesting of this single crop,
the land was usually left fallow till the next flood. With the improvement in
water supply during the season of shortage, i.e. during spring and summer,
it has become possible gradually to extend perennial irrigation to replace the
old basin system[6]. Two or more crops could then be cultivated per year on
the same land. Summer crops, in particular cotton and rice, upon which the
Egyptian economy became very dependent, were now grown. The improve-

TABLE 3.3

Area, cultivated and cropped

Year	Area cultivated		Area cropped	
	million feddans	index 1897 = 100	million feddans	index 1897 = 100
1897	5.0	100	6.7	100
1917	5.3	106	7.7	115
1937	5.3	106	8.4	125
1947	5.7	114	9.2	137
1957	5.8	116	10.3	154
1960	5.9	118	10.4	155

SOURCE   *Annuaire Statistique,* 1960–61, and earlier issues.

[6]) In 1959 about 0.9 million feddans, i.e. about 15 per cent of the cultivated area,
mainly in Upper Egypt, were still irrigated by means of the basin system.

ment in the seasonal and geographical distribution of the water supply made possible also the reclamation of new land. In order to give a full account of the effects of the improvement in irrigation upon the area of land available for agricultural activities, it is necessary to make a distinction between *area cultivated* and *area cropped*. A particular feddan of arable, i.e. irrigated, land is counted as 1 feddan cultivated area and as 1, 2, or 3 feddans cropped area, according to whether it yields 1, 2, or 3 crops per year.

The main effect of the improved irrigation was upon the crop area, which from 1897 to 1960 expanded by 3.7 million feddans or 55 per cent, whereas the cultivated area only rose by less than one million feddans, or 18 per cent. It will be seen also that while in 1897, thanks to the deep canals and the Delta Barrage, about one third of the cultivated area may have yielded two or more crops per year, in 1960 this is true of about three-quarters of the area cultivated.

To understand the trend of development in production briefly discussed in section 3.1, it is important to note that before 1940 the increase in both cultivated and crop area was much slower than after 1940. This is due once again to the depression in the 'thirties, which pushed large marginal areas out of cultivation. From 1913 to 1940 the cultivated area increased by only 0.2 million feddans, and the crop area increased by 0.9 million feddans. For the period 1940–60 the corresponding figures are 0.7 million feddans and 1.9 million feddans, respectively. The increase in cultivated area during the 'fifties is partly due to certain large-scale governmental reclamation projects in the Tahrir province in the Western desert, among other places. A substantial increase in the area will follow from the completion of the High Dam, which at the end of the 'sixties is expected to add about one million feddans to the cultivated area, and to enable the basin system in Upper Egypt to be abolished.

3.2.3 Crop-rotation. Price-elasticities of supply

For a good many problems, the question whether production can be shifted from one commodity to another, and if so, how rapidly and to what extent, is of decisive importance. Rigidities due to technical considerations may be so important that the possible ways of influencing the composition of the output are limited; or the price-incentives necessary to call forth warranted shifts in production may be so large that they are out of the question, owing to side-effects, for instance on the distribution of income, which cannot be corrected in other ways. Such rigidities exist in Egyptian agriculture. The

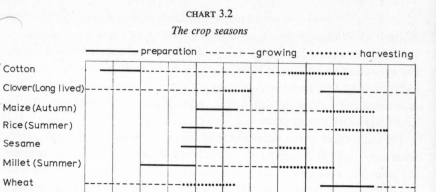

CHART 3.2

The crop seasons

─────── preparation ───────growing ·········· harvesting

Cotton
Clover(Long lived)
Maize (Autumn)
Rice (Summer)
Sesame
Millet (Summer)
Wheat
Beans
Barley
Lentils
Helba
Sugar cane

Jan. Febr. Mar. Apr. May June July Aug. Sept. Oct. Nov. Dec.

fact that the present system of irrigation allows more than one crop per year on most lands leads to rather rigid crop-rotation systems, which are made even more necessary by the detrimental effect cotton-growing has on the fertility of the soil. Cotton has to alternate with other crops, to allow the land to recover. The timing of the cotton crop is of importance, too. For these reasons we find, for instance, that cotton and short-lived berseem (a variety of clover) are complementary in production; and since cattle go with berseem, a certain complementarity between cotton and cattle follows. For a fuller understanding of these things, it is necessary to describe the crop-seasons and the crop-rotation systems at present in use. The above diagram indicates the usual seasons for the most important crops.

The seasons shown in the diagram are to be understood as averages for the country as a whole in a normal year. Some of the crops, e.g. maize and rice, can be grown in other seasons than those shown above. Furthermore, clover can be grown during a shorter time (the above includes four harvests during the season November–May), while sugar-cane usually stays on the land three years, giving three harvests. Vegetables, not shown in the chart, can be grown all the year round, and fruit-growing, of course, stretches over many years.

Given these seasons for the various crops, we find at present two pre-

dominant crop-rotation systems in operation, a *triennial system* with one
cotton crop each third year, and a *biennial system* with one cotton crop each
second year; there is a great difference of opinion about the advantages
and disadvantages of each system [7]. The crops alternating with cotton within
these two main systems may differ, but as typical examples we may have:

Example of triennial crop-rotation with cotton

Grown during	Crops
Year 1	Clover (from year 0) – cotton – wheat or barley
Year 2	Wheat or barley (from year 1) – maize – clover
Year 3	Clover (from year 2) – horse beans or rice – clover
etc.	etc.

Example of biennial crop-rotation with cotton

Grown during	Crops
Year 1	Clover (from year 0) – cotton – wheat or barley
Year 2	Wheat or barley (from year 1) – maize or rice – clover
etc.	etc.

Cotton competes with millet and maize, and, if the water supply is sufficient, with rice. In the event of the rotation system being changed, cotton
also competes with wheat, barley, beans and clover. Four cereal crops (or
three plus clover or vegetables) can be grown per two-year period, and a
cotton-free rotation may, for example, become:

Example of crop-rotation without cotton

Oct./Nov.–Apr./May	Wheat or barley
June/July–Oct./Nov.	Maize, rice, vegetables or clover
etc.	etc.

The choice between cotton and other products is governed not only by the
rotation systems necessary when cotton is grown, but also by several other
factors, the seasons, the availability of water (important for rice), proximity
to urban area or factory (important for vegetables and sugar-cane), the
number of animals to be fed (making clover necessary), etc.

Owing to the necessity for crop-rotation, the proportion of cotton in the

---

[7]) See C. H. Brown, *Egyptian Cotton*, London 1955, p. 7–8.

total area cropped must have a rather rigid *upper limit*. On the other hand, it is also obvious that from a technical point of view, it is possible to shift away from cotton to other crops, and that the possibilities of shifting between other crops must be substantial. The rigid upper limit for cotton seems to be about one third of the cultivated area, i.e. about 2 million feddans, which was the figure reached during the years from 1950 to 1952, when there were no restrictions on the area planted with cotton, and cotton prices were extremely high. With the exception of one year in the 'thirties, this cotton

TABLE 3.4

Average net return on various crops, 1955–59 (per feddan in £E)

	Net value added (1)	Net profit (2)	Rent of land (3)	Surplus to lessee hiring labour (4) = (2) — (3)	Surplus to lessee doing all work himself (5) = (1) — (3)
Cotton	63	46	21	25	42
Wheat	19	11	13	—2	6
Millet	24	14	8	6	16
Barley	20	14	10	4	10
Rice	53	39	8	31	45

NOTE   (1) and (2) are estimated as average yields times average prices minus relevant costs.

SOURCES   *Economic Review*, CBE 1961, pp. 217 and 330–1, and *Agricultural Economics* (in Arabic), several issues, issued by Ministry of Agriculture, for costs and rents.

area has never been surpassed, in spite of an increase of the total area. It is generally believed that the upper limit for the cotton area tends to be a lower limit, too; at least within a wide range of relative cotton prices, and disregarding Government restrictions on area. This is because of the superiority of cotton from a cash-surplus point of view. In table 3.4 we have tried to estimate for some important crops the *average* net profits to tillers who own their land, and the surplus to lessees, i.e. net profit or net value added, depending upon whether he hires labour or not, minus rent of land. Needless to say such calculations are quite arbitrary owing to the prevalence of joint production in agriculture. For the particular use we make of the figures here, however, this is not so important. What we want to estimate is the net profit for a complete rotation, and for this it is immaterial just how the costs have been distributed between the individual crops in the rotation.

Cotton and rice, though the latter is only possible where water is abundant, are on average by far the most profitable field crops, both before and after payment of rent, bearing in mind that rents are always paid per crop and adjusted to the profitability of each particular crop. For growers living near towns or factories, the profitability, per feddan, of vegetables, fruits, and sugar-cane is even higher than that of cotton and rice; the location, however, is very important for these crops and so competition from them becomes limited in general.

In a two-year rotation, the shift from two crops of cereals plus one cotton crop plus one cut of clover (net profit about £E 5 per feddan) to four cereal crops and no cotton would reduce the net profit per two years per feddan from £E 75–59 to £E 50–56; and given the prices of cereals ruling during this period, it would take a fall in the cotton price to less than half the average price ruling in 1955–59, to make the rotation without cotton more profitable on average than the rotation with cotton. This might then be taken as an indication that in a large range around present prices, the price-elasticity of cotton supply is very low. To what extent such conclusions are really justified is a great problem. What we know is that *on average* cotton is much more profitable than most other crops. But the elasticity of supply is governed by the conditions of growing cotton and growing other crops *on the margin*, and about this the average profitability really tells us nothing. However, various studies point to a rather low supply elasticity of cotton. Response elasticities of cotton area to deflated cotton prices of the order of magnitude 0.1–0.4 have been found. The cotton *supply* elasticity is substantially lower than this [8]; but on the other hand all the area elasticities found are short-term elasticities which do not take into account the adjustment period necessary to change the rotation.

Apart from cotton, and complementarities connected with cotton, e.g. clover and cattle, and rice, where water supply will usually be the decisive factor, there seems, on the other hand, to be good reason to believe that at existing prices the price-elasticities of supply are substantial for all field crops. The farmers' own consumption, however, and their probably very rigid consumption patterns, may put a certain brake on the response of food crops to price changes. For vegetables, and at least in the long run for sugar-cane and fruits, there may be a certain elasticity, though factors like proximity to towns and factories may here be decisive.

---

[8] See Bent Hansen, "Cotton vs. Grain. On the Optimum Allocation of Agricultural Land", *Agricultural Research Papers*, Seminar on Economics and Industrialization of Cotton, Ministry of Scientific Research, Cairo 1964, and the literature mentioned there.

3.2.4 The size of the agricultural production unit

Another circumstance that has a decisive influence on the techniques applied in Egyptian agriculture is the small size of the majority of the production units, which together cultivate a substantial part of the available land. The small scale of production is a hindrance to the use of machinery, unless there is some kind of cooperation between tillers; and until recently such co-operation has been limited to areas affected by the land reforms (see below, chapter 4, section 4.2). Information about the number and size of production units is available from the agricultural censuses.

TABLE 3.5

Distribution of holdings according to size, 1950 and 1956

	1950 (census)				1956 (off. estim.)				Average size of holdings feddans	
	Area		Holders		Area		Holders			
	feddans thousands	%	thousands	%	feddans thousands	%	thousands	%	1950	1956
Less than 1 feddan	112	1.8	214.3	21.4	142	2.3	405.3	32.3	0.5	0.3
1– 5 feddans	1311	21.4	572.5	57.1	1427	22.9	619.8	49.4	2.3	2.3
5–20 feddans	1524	24.8	174.9	17.4	1681	27.1	187.7	15.0	8.6	9.0
20–50 feddans	792	12.9	26.5	2.6	797	12.8	28.7	2.3	29.9	27.8
50–200 fed.	1142	18.6	12.4	1.2	1040	16.7	11.0	0.9	92.1	94.5
More than 200 feddans	1263	20.5	2.4	0.3	1125	18.2	1.9	0.1	526.3	592.1
Total	6144	100.0	1003.0	100.0	6212	100.0	1254.4	100.0	6.1	4.9

SOURCE   *Economic Bulletin*, NBE, 1957, vol. 10, no. 1, "Land Tenure in Egypt" p. 46.

It is not clear to what extent a holding in this statistical sense coincides with a production unit. Intermediary holding was earlier a widespread phenomenon, and for this and other reasons, e.g. share-cropping, the production units may have been smaller than indicated by table 3.5. By and large, however, the figures are believed to give a good indication of the size. While the absolute number of very small holdings (below 1 feddan) almost doubled and increased its proportion of the total number of holdings by about fifty per cent from 1950 to 1956, the proportion of all other sizes fell. This is obviously a result of the land reforms, which will be discussed in detail below; but it should be borne in mind that in 1956 the redistribution of land according to the Land Reform of 1952 was not yet completed, and this partly explains the relatively small decline in the area of holdings above 200 feddans. Also, the Land Reform of 1952 did not forbid lessees to rent areas exceeding 200 feddans from different owners. During the years since 1956, a further shift from big to small holdings must have taken place.

The average size of the smallest holdings (of less than 1 feddan) diminished substantially. The total number of holdings increased by about 25 per cent while the cultivated area remained almost unchanged, with the result that the average holding fell from 6.1 feddans in 1950 to 4.9 feddans in 1956. It will also be seen that in 1956 about $\frac{1}{4}$ of the area was held by holders having less than 5 feddan, $\frac{1}{4}$ of the area was held by holders having 5–20 feddan, and the remaining half by holders with more than 20 feddan. All this means that on about half the cultivated area the size of holdings is an obstacle to mechanization unless cooperation takes place; and it seems clear that because of the land reforms this obstacle has increased during the 'fifties. Against this, however, one must set governmental efforts to increase co-operation between tillers and encourage "collective" farming (see chapter 4, section 4.2.3).

Production methods and productivity are probably also considerably influenced by the fact that ownership and enterprise are to a large extent separated. The distribution of land according to ownership will be discussed in the next chapter; here it is sufficient to mention that in 1950 the number of registered owners was about 2.8 million, while the number of holders was only 1.0 million. For various reasons this may imply inadequate methods of production. The following table shows the distribution of holdings according to type of tenure.

TABLE 3.6

Distribution of holdings according to type of tenure

	1950 (census)				1956 (off. estim.)			
	Area		Holders		Area		Holders	
	feddans thousands	%	thousands	%	feddans thousands	%	thousands	%
Ownership	3720	61	657	66	3690	59	730	58
Tenancy	1223	20	207	20	1351	22	346	28
Mixed { Own.	494	8			546	9		
{			139	14			178	14
{ Ten.	706	11			626	10		
Total	6143	100	1003	100	6213	100	1254	100

SOURCE   Ibid. p. 47.

Both in 1950 and 1956 about ⅓ of the area was held by tenants. It is interesting to note that by area pure tenancy increased considerably between 1950 and 1956, while pure ownership declined. This is probably due to the land reforms, though it should be borne in mind that the redistribution according to the first reforms had not been completed by 1956. The increase in tenancy shown by the 1956 estimate was a temporary phenomenon, arising from the fact that the land taken from big owners was at first rented by its future owners, who got formal possession later on. It seems likely that by 1960[9]) the distribution between ownership and tenancy will prove to have returned to about the same as in 1950, with a large increase and shift of owners, from big to small, within the "ownership" group.

3.2.5 Labour in agriculture

It is difficult for many reasons to obtain good figures for the input of labour in agriculture. With small production units, where the wife and children of the tillers more or less regularly take part in production, it often becomes virtually impossible, even for the tillers themselves, to know the input of labour with a reasonable degree of exactitude. What we should like to have is the number of hours worked during a year, hours of work of men, women and children being converted to some standard unit. What we have now is mainly information provided by the population censuses of the numbers engaged in agricultural production. Such censuses were carried out in 1897, 1907, 1917, 1927, 1937, 1947 and 1960[10]). The agricultural censuses also give a certain amount of information about the labour force; and since 1957 the labour-force surveys have provided further valuable figures, and confirmed the total number of persons occupied in agriculture in 1960 (see table 2.10).

The earlier censuses are probably not very reliable; definitions have changed from census to census; and, finally, it is rather problematical how the census questions have been understood and answered by the population. The figures from the population censuses, leaving out those for 1897, which are very unreliable, are given in table 3.7.

After a rapid increase up to 1937, the population occupied in agriculture has been almost stationary, with only a small measured increase of about

---

[9]) A census of holdings was carried out in 1960, but the results are not yet available.

[10]) Attempts have been made to utilize the relationship between rural and town population for estimating the development of agricultural labour year by year, see note to chart 3.1.

3 per cent during the last 23 years. We have already seen, in section 3.1, the far-reaching influence of this change in population development. To what extent the 3 per cent figure can be taken as an indication of the change in labour input in agriculture is not easy to say. The 1960 census was taken in September, which is one of the seasonal peak months for labour in agriculture, whereas earlier censuses were taken in March, which is a seasonal slack. For this reason the adjusted 1960 figures may somewhat exaggerate

TABLE 3.7

Population occupied in agriculture (in millions)

Year	Number
1907	2.40
1917	2.82
1927	3.50
1937	4.28
1947	4.22
1960	4.40

SOURCE   *Annuaire Statistique.* The 1960 figure is the census number adjusted to include all persons over 5 years occupied in agriculture. This figure, however, is still not fully comparable with the earlier figures. See *General Monthly Statistical Bulletin* (in Arabic), vol. 1, no. 7, May 1962, Dep. of Statistic and Census, p. 2, table I, and the text above.

the number occupied in agriculture, and there may even have been a slight fall since 1947. When the agricultural census of 1960 is published more light will be thrown on this question.

Quite apart from changes of definition and other statistical deficiencies, there may be so-called disguised unemployment, which is usually assumed to exist in agriculture in underdeveloped countries according to contemporary development theory, and in Egypt is believed to be large. Disguised unemployment makes the effective labour input smaller than the figures disclosed by censuses, and makes the effective amount of work done grow more slowly than the census figures may lead us to believe. Official figures corresponding to 25 per cent of the total labour force occupied in agriculture have been published[11]. If disguised unemployment is taken to mean that the marginal productivity of labour is near zero, so that labour can be removed permanently without detrimental effects on production, there is good evidence for the opposite view, viz. that there is not disguised unemployment

---

[11] See *General Frame of the 5-Year Plan*, National Planning Committee, Cairo 1960, p. 118.

CHART 3.3

Labour requirements in agricultural field work, 1960 (days per month per person permanently employed in farms)

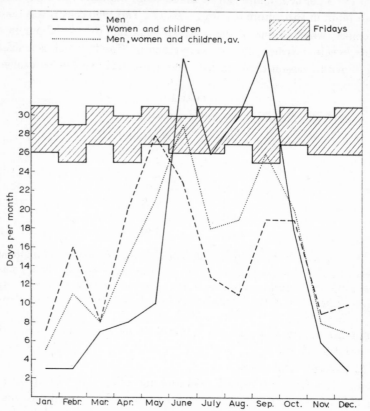

SOURCE   Bent Hansen and Mona El Tomy "The Seasonal Employment Profile in Egyptian Agriculture", *Memo. no. 501*, INP, Cairo 1964. On the basis of figures on labour requirements per feddan for the various kinds of work (sowing, irrigation, harvesting, etc.) for each individual crop the total labour requirement in terms of days of work per month per person permanently employed on farms was calculated. The individual crop figures for labour requirements per feddan were estimated by the Ministry of Agriculture on the basis of unsystematic surveys carried out by the Ministry's district inspectors. They should in principle give the amount of work actually performed, but they may be coloured by the inspectors' personal opinions about labour requirements under conditions of optimal cultivation. Concerning the distribution of work by month, it has sometimes been necessary to use rather subjective assumptions. For this reason, it may be better to consider averages of April-May, June-July, and August-September. The number of persons permanently employed on farms was obtained from the agricultural census of 1950, and was assumed to have stayed unchanged until 1960. This assumption is supported by the population censuses of 1947 and 1960, which show no significant change in the total number of persons engaged in agriculture. The agricultural census for 1960 has not yet been published. Men includes all males 15 years and over. The upper broken line shows the number of days per month, the shaded area the number of Fridays (the Moslem weekly day of rest) per month in 1960; Fridays are not taken off in agriculture to any large extent. Only field work proper is included in the calculations.

in Egyptian agriculture, but that there is some open unemployment, and a large seasonal underemployment. However, seasonality in agriculture is not a special problem for underdeveloped countries, though it may be more serious for poor countries than for rich. The labour force surveys sho an open unemployment in rural districts of as much as 3 per cent, even during the agricultural peak seasons[12]). Calculations of labour requirements, on the other hand, given in chart 3.3, indicate that the more permanent farm labour force is at certain times of the year fully employed, and that there is a seasonal demand for outside labour. Chart 3.3 distinguishes between men, i.e. males 15 years and over, and women and children, on the hypothesis that certain kinds of labour are performed by men only and other kinds of work by women and children only. To some extent this may be true, but there is without doubt considerable overlapping, and for this reason we have also shown a calculation for men, women and children together, on the opposite hypothesis that all work can be performed equally well by men, women and children. In the calculations, which are open to various kinds of criticism, no regard has been paid to work on animals, about the house, or on the cleaning of canals. Bearing this in mind it seems that the men are fully occupied around May (the wheat crop), while there is either full employment, or even an absolute shortage, of women and children from June to September (rice and cotton). The shortage of women and children is met partly by seasonal employment of outside labour, but, on small farms at least, the men step in too. If there were a full substitution of men for women and children, and vice versa, it would seem that there would be about full employment for all permanent farm workers in June and September. The seasonal slack from November to March, on the other hand, is clearly very serious. For the year as a whole field work seems to give full occupation for only about 180 days for men as well as women and children, and even if we add work with the animals, about the house, and on the canals and drains, and consider 300 days a working year, the underemployment of the men is

---

[12]) Prof. El Shafei, op. cit. Owing to the methods adopted the labour force surveys do not disclose the full seasonality of labour demand.

serious. For the women and girls underemployment in this sense probably means just work in the house instead of in the fields, while for the boys, and to a minor extent the girls also, it means, increasingly, school attendance[13]). However, the seasonal underemployment may very well correspond to about 25 per cent of the total permanent labour force, calculated on an annual basis. Since, finally, production function studies for field crops (see below, section 3.4.2) indicate that the value of the marginal productivity of labour, measured on a yearly basis, is of the same order of magnitude as current money wages for agricultural labourers, it seems quite clear that we should not speak of disguised unemployment in Egyptian agriculture, but rather of seasonal underemployment[14]). In other words we cannot, *ceteris paribus*, remove one man *permanently* without detrimental effects on total production. Finally, we would point out that the increase in the area culti-vated, and even more the cropped area, relative to the number of persons occupied in agriculture since 1937 makes it likely that seasonal under-employment has diminished during the last 25 years. The increasing school attendance of children in rural districts points in the same direction.

3.2.6 Equipment, implements and machinery

Methods of production in Egyptian agriculture are on the whole, apart from the highly developed irrigation system and certain recently reclaimed areas, such as the Tahrir province, crude and simple, and on the small holdings the implements seem to a large extent to be the same as in ancient times. The hand-plough that is used hardly scratches the soil, while harvesting and threshing is mainly done by hand. It is estimated that "about 10 per cent of the crop is lost through hand and animal harvesting and threshing"[15]). Statistics on this type of equipment do not exist. Before the war almost no

---

[13]) Saad M. Gadalla, *Land Reforms in Relation to Social Development in Egypt*, University of Missouri Studies, vol. 50, Columbia 1962: "Between the crop seasons, when there is not much work on the farms, about 95 per cent of those enrolled, encouraged by the free meal offered at noon, usually attend the school. When this meal is cancelled, the attendance drops to 65 per cent. During the crop seasons when every possible hand is needed to work on the farm, only 30 per cent of the pupils usually attend school" (p. 70).

[14]) In cooperation with the ILO the Institute of National Planning in Cairo is at present preparing a special survey of labour in Egyptian villages. When finished, this study may give us more detailed and reliable information on unemployment and underemployment.

[15]) *Report of the Sub-Committee on Agriculture*, National Planning Commission, Cairo 1960 (in Arabic).

machines were used in agriculture, apart from machinery used in connection
with irrigation and draining, but since the war development has been rapid.
The number and horse-power of "licensed" machinery, mainly tractors, has
grown since 1935 as follows:

TABLE 3.8

Licensed farm machinery

End of year	Number	Horsepower in thousands
1935	1026	28.6
1939	1178	34.0
1944	2926	78.2
1949	6449	193.3
1952	7582	226.7
1957	10065	316.4
1960	10348	328.0

SOURCE   *Annuaire Statistique* 1959, table 13, p. 288, and earlier issues.

This table does not give a complete picture of the growth in mechanisa-
tion; there is also some unlicensed machinery in use. In spite of the sharp
rise during the post-war period, machinery is still the exception rather than
the rule in Egyptian agriculture, the number of hp of licensed machinery per
working person being 0.1, while the number of hp per cultivated feddan is as
low as 0.05. Yet it has been estimated[16]) that by the end of the 'fifties about
22 per cent of the land was being tilled by tractors, and 13.4 harvested and
threshed by mechanical means, figures which are astonishingly high. It
should be noted, however, that the expansion in machinery is to a large
extent concentrated on the big estates, the cooperatives, and Tahrir province,
where newly reclaimed desert-land is cultivated by capital-intensive methods.
Agriculture in general, the great majority of small holdings outside the
land-reform areas, is therefore still unaffected by the increased use of
machinery for field operations.

3.2.7 Livestock

Table 3.9 shows the number of livestock in the country as a whole, and its
changes since 1937. The table also contains an index of total number of

---

[16]) *Report of the Sub-Committee on Agriculture,* op. cit,

TABLE 3.9
Number of livestock (in thousands)

	1937	1947	1952	1957	1960	£E*
Buffaloes	956	1240	1212	1371	1524	54
Cows	983	1321	1356	1381	1588	53
Horses	31	28	39	44	46	70
Mules	23	12	10	10	10	72
Donkeys	1142	1126	816	938	980	15
Camels	155	197	165	159	173	44
Sheep	1919	1875	1254	1252	1418	8
Goats	1311	1476	703	730	778	5
Weighted index of number of livestock	100	122	113	121	136	—
Area under berseem (clover) index	100	121	134	145	(145)	—

* Approximate prices September 1960 per animal, used as weights in livestock index.
SOURCE   Ibid. p. 219, and *Agricultural Economics,* issued by Ministry of Agriculture (in Arabic), Oct. 1960, p. 19; *Statistical Pocket-Book,* Cairo 1961, NBE *Economic Bulletin,* several issues.

animals and the weights used for calculating this index. An index of the area under berseem (clover), which is the most important fodder for animals, has been added.

The main feature revealed by the table is the considerable increase up till 1947 in the number of big animals, buffaloes and cows, followed by a static period at the beginning of the 'fifties, and then a further increase at the end of the 'fifties. This contrasts with the sharp fall between 1947 and 1952 in the number of small animals. Because of these different developments, we found it useful to compute a weighted index for the total number of animals; as weights we used the approximate price per animal in September 1960. The index of livestock increased by as much as 22 per cent from 1937 to 1947, but remained unchanged from 1947 to 1957, after having declined somewhat at the beginning of the 'fifties. From 1958 to 1960 there was again a substantial rise.

Livestock are used both as a source of power and for the production of milk and meat, and there is no doubt that the shift from small animals to big animals represents a rationalization of agricultural methods of production, the big animals being the main source of power, made possible by, and making necessary, an increase in the production of fodder. An index of the number of livestock does not give a full description of the development, however; for the animals may be more or less well fed. It is interesting here to note that animal production, taking into account changes in the number of livestock, increased by about 15 per cent between 1947 and 1957, although the stock of animals remained stationary. This may be explained by the increased supply of fodder. The area under berseem (clover) increased by about 19 per cent during the same period, though production of clover may not have increased so much; the increase in the clover area from 1947 to 1957 was largely due to the increase in the cotton area, which carried with it an increase in the area under short-lived clover. From 1957 to 1960 the index of animals increased by as much as 12 per cent, while at the same time animal production only increased by 4 per cent. But the area under clover increased by only 3 per cent. For the whole period 1937–1960 we notice a 36 per cent increase in number of animals and a 45 per cent increase in area under clover. Total animal production rose at the same time 48 per cent.

3.2.8 Artificial fertilizers and other chemicals

The use of chemical fertilizers is shown by table 3.10, both totally and per feddan, cultivated and cropped, respectively.

During the inter-war years a big increase can be seen in the supply of fertilizers, beginning in the second half of the 'twenties. This increase, inter alia, put a brake on the falling average return for labour in agriculture, as was pointed out in connection with chart 3.1. The consumption of chemical fertilizers declined to almost nothing during World War II and did not reach the pre-war average until the end of the 'forties. During the 'fifties it increased sharply to more than twice the pre-war level; this was made possible not only by increased imports, but also by a large expansion in the domestic production of fertilizers. Because the big animals, in particular buffaloes and cows, are used as a source of power in the fields, manures are not utilized in any rational way. Insecticides, pesticides and weedicides are of great importance for the yield of crops in Egypt, and available statistics show a sharp increase in their use. While the total value of such chemicals was only about £E 0.1 million at the beginning of the 'fifties, it rose to £E 1.8 million in 1957. However, they are still used in rather limited quantities.

Having now surveyed developments in the major inputs in agriculture, and the efforts made to increase them, we shall turn to agricultural output. Before doing so we would just point out that efforts are being made from the side of the government to improve methods and conditions of cultivation by means of soil surveys, improvements of plant and animal varieties, education of farmers, and agricultural scientific research. The extension of

TABLE 3.10

Use of chemical fertilizers

Year	Total annual supply †) in thousands of tons	Annual consumption		
		Total in thousands of tons	Per feddan cultivated kg	Per feddan cropped kg
1921/24	110.7	...	21 **	14 **
1925/29	266.0	...	48 **	31 **
1930/35	306.4	...	57 **	37 **
1935/39	567.4	...	106 **	68 **
1940/44	202.5	...	38 **	22 **
1945/49	431.5	...	75 **	47 **
1950/54	779.5	762.3	135	79
1955/59	875.7	871.5*	150	85
1955	779.5	757.5	132	76
1956	709.9	787.8	137	76
1957	1005.6	879.0	152	85
1958	1115.3	938.4	162	93
1959	768.3	1158.4*	196	112
1960	1125.8*	1395.1*	237	134

† Production plus import.   *) Prel. figures.   ** Supply per feddan.
SOURCE   Ibid. p. 214, and *Annuaire Statistique*, several issues. The consumption figures
are not calculated as supply minus stock changes but are estimated by the Ministry of
Agriculture as area cultivated with various crops multiplied by certain figures for consumption per feddan obtained through unsystematic surveys.

the agricultural credit system has also in many cases been used as a way to
introduce improved methods of production[17]).

3.3 *Agricultural production and value added*

3.3.1 *The composition of production*

The produce of Egyptian agriculture is largely non-animal, i.e. fibres, cereals,
pulses, vegetables and fruits. This is a feature that Egypt has in common with
most other underdeveloped countries, and which arises from a combination
of shortage of capital and a low standard of living; though it is also due to
special conditions, in particular the almost complete lack of pastures.

---

[17]) A. El Tanamly, "Agricultural Credit and Cooperative Organization", *L'Egypt Contemporaine,* Oct. 1962.

TABLE 3.11

Agricultural production 1959/1960

	Gross value of production		Value added	
	million £E	%	million £E	%
Fibres	135.5	24	114.7	29
Cereals and other field crops	160.3	28	102.6	26
Vegetables, fruit and wood	58.4	10	49.7	12
Fodder	65.9	12	56.0	14
Animal products	134.1	23	58.6	15
Others, incl. fishing and hunting	19.6	3	18.3	4
Total	573.8	100	399.9	100

SOURCE   *General Frame of the 5-Year Plan*, p. 44.

Of the gross value of production less than a quarter, and of value added less than a sixth even (a quarter if fodder is included), is due to animal commodities. The non-animal sector is dominated by fibres, i.e. cotton and cereals, though vegetables and fruits, and fodder to support animal production, play a rapidly increasing rôle. Both by gross value and still more by value added, cotton is by far the largest item of agricultural produce[18]).

3.3.2 Post-war development of gross production

For the inter-war period statistics of production in agriculture are limited to the major field crops, but for recent years comprehensive statistics are available. A detailed picture of the development of the total volume of agricultural *gross production* is given by the volume index calculated by the Department of Statistics and Census for the years 1948–1961 with an average of 1935–1939 as basis[19]). This index and some of its sub-groups are shown in table 3.12, together with the quantity index of non-animal production

---

[18]) The fact that costs are "joint" makes the value added figures for the individual commodities quite arbitrary; this is particularly true for fodder.

[19]) The index of the Department of Statistics and Census is a Laspeyres' volume index with the average unit values of the base period 1935/39 as weights, the weights being kept constant for the whole period considered. The index includes changes in livestock, and also certain outputs used as inputs by agriculture itself, i.e. berseem (clover) and seeds. The index is, in other words, a very gross production index.

computed by the National Bank of Egypt for the years 1935–39 and 1946–59[20]), and the production index of the FAO[21]).

It can be seen that the general development of plant, i.e. non-animal, production is very much the same according to the index of the Department of Statistics and that of the National Bank. For total production the FAO index shows a somewhat larger increase than the Department of Statistics index. In what follows, we keep to the Department of Statistics index. The causal factors behind the main trend of the total production development will be discussed more closely in section 3.4, it being understood that the short-term irregularities are due to irregularities of water supply, plant diseases and climatic factors, and, of course, to inevitable imperfections in the indices.

From 1952 non-animal production increased sharply, but was not able to catch up with the continuous increase in animal production. While the total volume of production increased by 42 per cent from 1935–39 to 1960, animal production increased by 48 per cent and plant production by 40 per cent. It is to be noticed in this connection that "other field crops", which include fodder necessary to support animal production, increased by no less than 97 per cent during the same period. Within the group "plant output", a difference can be seen in the development of the two sub-groups, fibres and cereals. Fibres, which is almost identical with cotton, fell during the war and stayed, apart from 1952, below the pre-war level until 1957, when the pre-war level was reached again. During 1958–60 there was an increase, which disappeared completely, however, during the very bad crop year 1961; from 1960 to 1961 the cotton crop fell by almost 40 per cent because of leaf worm. The crop of 1962 was almost the same as that of 1960. Cereals declined until 1952, but then, after a stationary period, increased sharply during 1953 and 1954. Dry

---

[20]) The index of the National Bank of Egypt is a weighted geometrical average of the relative size of crops, base year 1946/50, the weights being the average total values of each crop, 1946/50, over the average total value of all crops 1946/50. Berseem (clover) enters the index with the area sown instead of the quantity cropped; it is not clear which weight has been attached to berseem. See *Economic Bulletin,* National Bank of Egypt, vol. 7, 1954, p. 252 ff.

[21]) See *FAO Production Yearbook,* vol. 14, 1961. This index is a net production index in the sense that it does not include such outputs, particularly fodder and seeds, which are used as inputs in agriculture itself. But it is a *gross* index in the sense that there are no deductions for current inputs (artificial fertilizers, etc.) other than those produced by agriculture itself. The base period is the years 1952/53–1957/59. Earlier yearbooks had another index based on pre-war years. We have spliced the two together to form one continuous index.

TABLE 3.12

Volume of agricultural output; index of Department of Statistics and Census, and indices of NBE and FAO

	Total volume (plant + animal) output	Total animal output	Total plant output	Plant output sub-groups								NBE quantity index of nonanimal production	FAO index of total production
				Fibres (mainly cotton)	Cereals	Dry legumes	Oil seeds	Other field crops	Vege-tables	Fruits	Total food pro-duction		
1935–39	100	100	100	100	100	100	100	100	100	100	100	100	100
1945	..	..	..	..	..	..	..	..	..	..	..	86	..
1946	..	..	..	..	..	..	..	..	..	..	..	89	98
1947	..	..	..	..	..	..	..	..	..	..	..	93	100
1948	111	124	107	97	109	96	102	104	151	144	115	108	113
1949	109	124	105	98	104	102	96	109	140	148	113	106	114
1950	108	139	99	94	99	72	96	105	121	148	113	102	114
1951	105	132	97	90	94	79	94	120	129	172	110	97	110
1952	110	122	107	112	90	80	116	127	162	207	110	106	119
1953	109	119	107	79	115	73	91	143	170	215	120	98	114
1954	121	131	119	86	130	84	96	168	193	211	133	110	126
1955	119	128	117	83	126	89	96	171	200	226	132	108	128
1956	123	140	118	81	133	75	96	168	212	191	138	109	133
1957	130	140	127	101	130	89	111	180	224	229	140	121	144
1958	131	142	127	113	118	86	121	180	245	242	137	123	143
1959	136	145	133	115	127	76	122	196	292	222	143	128	149
1960	142	148	140	122	131	99	128	197	303	244	148		153
1961	123	148	116	78	119	56	96	197	321	223	127		

NOTE   The "years" of the three indices do not coincide completely. This gives rise to large differences for individual years.

legumes have been falling continuously. Behind all of these developments, we find Government price policies and physical regulations, which will be explained in detail in the next chapter, together with shifts in demand due to urbanization and a rising standard of living. The most conspicuous feature of table 3.12, however, is the very sharp increase in vegetables and fruits, in response to a rising demand, domestic and foreign; and this, taken with the increase in animal production, is closely connected with the change in the long-term trends in chart 3.1.

3.3.3 Value added in agriculture

Estimates of value added, both in current prices and in constant prices, have been made by the Department of Statistics and Census for the years 1950 to 1960, and they show the picture given in table 3.13.

We have already shown the composition of gross output and value added, in section 3.3.1. Here we shall concentrate on the composition of inputs and the net value added. Amongst the inputs seeds and fodder dominate and constitute more than half the total of the inputs that are deductible in a value-added calculation. The calculation of these two items, fodder in particular, is quite arbitrary, both in volume and in value. The high level of the value of fodder from 1954 to 1958 must be a statistical error; this does not matter for the net value added, since both seeds and fodder appear in the value of gross output, and thus cancel out in value-added figures; but it does matter for the output, which is obviously too high for the years 1954 to 1958. It will be observed that the input of fertilizers has increased less according to table 3.13 than according to table 3.10. Net value added at fixed 1954 prices shows little increase from 1950 to 1954; but from then on there is a continuous rise. Over the whole period from 1950 to 1960 it increased by 32 per cent, and up to 1962/63 there was a further increase of 5–6 per cent. Calculations before 1950 are more uncertain. The output indices suggest that the level in 1950 was 10 per cent higher than 1935–39, but available information about physical inputs point to an increase of value added by at most a few percentage units. The year 1949, however, was considerably higher than 1950, when the crop was bad.

Measured at current prices net value added fell by about 25 per cent from 1950 to 1952, and then climbed back to the 1950 level in 1957. This development was largely governed by the price fluctuations, especially the big drop in cotton prices from 1950 to 1952, the revival which followed up to 1956, and the increase in the price of cereals in 1954 and 1956. In table 3.18 we show the implicit value added deflator.

TABLE 3.13

Value added in agriculture, 1950–60

Year	Gross output at fixed 1954-prices, million £E	Inputs at fixed 1954-prices, £E million							Net value added at fixed 1954-prices		Net value added at current prices	
		Seeds	Fertilizers	Fodder	Fuel	Maintenance and depreciation	Other inputs	Total inputs	million £E	Index	million £E	Index
1950	376	14	19	30	5	3	3	73	303	100	369	100
1951	379	14	20	31	5	3	2	75	304	100	352	95
1952	409	14	19	30	6	3	2	74	334	110	272	74
1953	391	15	18	32	6	3	2	76	315	104	278	75
1954	416	16	20	57	6	3	2	104	312	103	312	85
1955	426	16	19	54	8	4	3	105	321	106	318	86
1956	434	16	19	52	9	4	3	101	333	110	361	98
1957	454	16	21	60	9	4	4	112	342	113	369	100
1958	472	16	21	52	9	4	3	106	367	121	371	101
1959	482	24	24	33	9	4	5	99	383	126	392	106
1960	498	23	24	34	9	4	5	99	399	132	422	114
1961											372	101

SOURCE   *National Income from the Agricultural Sector,* 1950–60, (in Arabic) Department of Statistics and Census, Cairo (no year). Due to roundings, the figures do not always add up to the totals. An estimate made by the Ministry of Agriculture shows an increase of "Cash Agricultural Revenue" from £E 306 million in 1951 to £E 412 in 1960. This is a current price estimate, but the definition of "Cash Agricultural Revenue" is not quite clear. See *Agricultural Economy,* issued by Agricultural Economics and Statistics Department, Cairo, Jan. 1962, p, 12. 1961-figures provisional, see *Economic Bulletin,* NBE, 1964, 3.

3.4 Productivity in agriculture

The most usual way of measuring productivity and its development is to calculate value added in constant prices per employed unit of labour, capital or land; developments in these measures are then supposed to give information about development in productivity. Productivity, however, is a many-dimensional phenomenon and such measures do not in themselves give a full understanding of how it is changing. We shall therefore first consider productivity in its relation to gross output, and as far as possible discuss the productivity of *all* the factors of production involved in agriculture.

3.4.1 Output productivity

We have already described the statistics of physical output and physical inputs and factors of production. This information is summarized in table 3.14, for the years 1937, 1947, 1957 and 1960. The table enables us to discuss *productivity in terms of output*, which is related to, but should not be confused with *productivity in terms of value added*. We shall therefore in what follows use the terms "output productivity" and "value-added productivity".

It should also be made clear that since we have only four time-points of ob-servation and no less than 8, or even 9, if we include area cropped, explana-tory variables, statistical inference concerning the form of the production-function and its coefficients is, of course, impossible. A multiple regression analysis, which was actually in the minds of the authors, would probably require series of reliable and comparable statistics going back 40–50 years, and to make such an analysis, would, if possible at all, take an amount of work beyond our present limits. Studies of this kind have been made, but only for field crops [22]. In spite of this limitation certain interesting conclusions can be drawn from the available information.

We are dealing here with agriculture, and it is a well-known and empirically well-established fact that in agriculture production obeys the law of de-creasing returns, if not to scale then at least to each factor of production. Decreasing returns to scale means that if we increase all factors of produc-tion, including land, in the same proportion, total output will increase less than in proportion to the increase in the factors. Diminishing returns to a factor means that if this factor is increased, all other factors being kept constant, both the average and the marginal output-productivity of this

---

[22] Dr. M. El Imam, op. cit., fitted a Cobb-Douglas function for field-crops to time series for the years 1913–55 and obtained the coefficients (elasticities) for area 0.3, for labour 0.3, and for fertilizers 0.03. All coefficients are significant. Curiously enough El Imam did not find any significant influence from water supply. Hanaa Kheir El Dine, "The Cotton Production Function in the UAR and its Relation to Technical Progress and to Disguised Unemployment", *Memo. no. 370*, Institute of National Planning, Cairo 1963, estimated a Cobb-Douglas function for cotton (and cotton seeds) and found the coefficients 0.7 for area (weighted), 0.4 for labour, and 0.04 for fertilizers (nitrates); the last coefficient was not significant. Both of these estimates conform with constant returns to scale and decreasing returns for all factors. In both estimates time was found to have no significant influence. This result is interesting because it might be interpreted as if there had been no technical progress. A more reasonable interpretation, however, is that techni-cal progress is "embodied" (in Solow's sense) in the factor fertilizers. We cannot dis-tinguish between improved technique and increased use of fertilizers.

factor will fall, while the average output-productivities of all the other factors will rise. From table 3.14 the development of the *average* output-productivities can be obtained and they are shown in table 3.15[23]). It should be noticed that for the three post-war years shown in that table, the water-supply, measured by the annual discharge at the sluices at Assuan, was slightly above average, whereas for 1935–39 it was somewhat lower. Some of

TABLE 3.14

Physical output and inputs in agriculture, 1937–1960 (1937 = 100)

| Year | Agricultural output | Area (feddans) | | Labour force in agr. (number) | Artificial fertilizers consumed (tons) | Livestock | Canals and drains (length) | Irrigation and drainage pumps (hp) | Agricultural machinery (hp) | Water supply (discharge at Assuan) |
		Cultivated	Cropped							
1937	100*)	100	100	100	100**)	100	100	100	100	100*)
1947	100	108	110	98	75	122	117	114	479	116
1957	130	109	123	101 †)	155	121	127	161	1011	124
1960	142	111	124	102	246	136	130	164	1048	121

SOURCES   See all earlier tables of this chapter, except for water supply (discharge at Assuan): *Annuaire Statistique*, 1960–61.

*) Average of 1935–39
**) 1935–39 average supply
†) Estimated

TABLE 3.15

Average yield in terms of output in agriculture 1937–60 (1937 = 100)

| Year | Per feddan | | Per unit of labour force | Per ton of fertilizers | Per unit of livestock | Per km of canals and drains | Per hp of irrigation and drainage pumps | Per hp of agri-cultural machinery |
	Culti-vated	Cropped						
1937	100	100	100	100	100	100	100	100
1947	93	91	102	133	82	86	88	21
1957	119	106	129	84	108	102	81	13
1960	128	115	139	58	105	109	87	14

[23]) Special indices of yield per feddan of major field crops are published by the Central Statistical Committee and in *Annuaire Statistique*. Apart from a more detailed picture they show the same developments as the material used here.

the increase in production must be ascribed to the higher water supply during the post-war years, which has favoured rice production in particular.

Studying table 3.15, we observe that from 1937 to 1960 certain average output-productivities have increased, namely those of land, labour, animals and canals and drains, while the average output-productivities of fertilizers and machinery show a big fall. This is a simple consequence of the fact that fertilizers and machinery, as can be seen in table 3.14, have increased much more than output, which in its turn has increased more than area, labour force, animals and canals and drains. While the first group of factors has increased on average by at least 64 per cent, the average increase in the second group is at most 36 per cent. This fits well with the idea of decreasing returns, which makes it impossible for *all* average productivities to rise simultaneously, on the assumption of given technical knowledge. Loosely expressed, it seems permissible to say therefore that the relative increase in fertilizers and machinery has "paid" for the increase in the average output-productivities of land, labour, animals, and canals and drains, considered as a whole. It should be added that the increase in fertilizers and pumps is undoubtedly far more decisive than the increase in agricultural machinery; for fertilizers and pumps are big factors of production, while agricultural machinery is still only a secondary factor.

A remarkable feature of the development concerns the labour force active in agriculture. Since *all* other factors increased more or less from 1937 to 1960, while the labour input remained constant, the law of decreasing returns would lead us to expect an increase in both the marginal and average output-productivity of labour. We can check this concerning the average output-productivity of labour, which actually has increased by as much as 39 per cent between 1937 and 1960; and with a Cobb-Douglas production function marginal productivity increases in the same proportion. The same reasoning holds for the development from 1947 to 1960. Just how the increase in the other factors have helped the average output-productivity of labour to increase so much, we do not know; to answer such questions we need longer series[24]. However, prior knowledge combined with the figures of the tables allow us to suggest that the increase in canals and drains and irrigation pumps, i.e., the improved irrigation, has helped the cultivated area to increase by 11 per cent and the cropped area by 24 per cent, and this alone can have increased the average output-productivity of labour by at most 24 per cent. This means that at least 15 percentage units of the 39 per-

---

[24]) See, however, footnote 22.

cent increase in the average labour output-productivity must have been called forth by the increased use of fertilizers[25] (and other chemicals not included in table 3.14) and agricultural machinery, together with the increased stock of animals and the larger water-supply (discharge at Assuan).

From 1937 to 1960 a dramatic development took place in the use of fertilizers and other chemicals. From 1937 to 1947 fertilizers fell by 25 per cent (during the war the fall was much greater), while from 1947 to 1960 they trebled. With the input of labour more or less unchanged, total production in 1947 was at the same level as in 1937. This shows that the 25 per cent fall in fertilizers, plus delayed effects from the much lower supply of fertilizers and the unhappy crop-rotation during the war, was sufficient to wipe out the effects on total production of a simultaneous increase in land by 8 per cent, animals by 22 per cent, canals and drains by 17 per cent and pumps by 14 per cent. In fact, the only factor of production which could show a significant increase in average output-productivity 1937–47 was fertilizers. This demonstrates once more their importance.

The picture of post-war Egyptian agriculture given here is quite remarkable. With a stagnating labour input, an increase in land, and increasing average output-productivity of both land and labour, we are far away indeed from the Malthusian nightmares usually associated with the agricultural situation in underdeveloped countries; but they did in fact overshadow the Egyptian economy until the middle of the 'thirties.

3.4.2 Value-added productivity and average income

Measured per man and per feddan, we find the following development in nominal and real value added for 1950 and 1960.

Both per feddan and per unit of labour force value-added productivity has increased by 25–30 per cent from 1950 to 1960. At current prices the increase in value added per feddan or per man was only about 10 per cent. However, neither the nominal value added (income) nor the value added at constant prices indicates the development of *real income* in agriculture. To arrive at this the value added at constant prices should be increased, or decreased, by

---

[25] If we apply the elasticity of 0.03 found by El Imam, op. cit., for fertilizers to the 146 per cent increase in fertilizers, we find that the increased use of fertilizers explains only 5 per cent of the increase in production.
Table 3.13 seems to indicate that the value of even a 5 per cent increase in output is somewhat higher than the costs of the input increase for fertilizers, etc. The increase of these inputs seems therefore to have been "good business".

TABLE 3.16

Net value added per feddan and per unit of labour

	Per feddan (cultivated)		Per unit of labour-force	
	In current prices, £E	In fixed 1954-prices, £E	In current prices, £E	In fixed 1954-prices, £E
1950	64.7	53.2	87.9	72.1
1960	71.5	67.6	95.9	90.7
percentage increase 1950–1960	10.5	27.1	9.1	25.8

the gains or losses in "terms of trade", in a wide sense, between Egyptian agriculture and "the rest of the world". Alternatively, to arrive at real income in agriculture in terms of consumer goods, we can deflate net value added at current prices by a cost of living index for the agricultural population. No such index exists, but the official cost of living index increased by 3 per cent from 1949 to 1960, while value added in current prices per unit of labour force increased by 10 per cent according to table 3.16. From this it would follow that real income in agriculture per until of labour force increased only by about 7 per cent from 1950 to 1960. 1950 was namely a year with extremely good terms of trade for agriculture. Measured in the same way, but from 1952, we find an increase of about 11 per cent. For a fair judgement about the standard of living of the working population in agriculture, regard should also be had for the substantial shift in the distribution of value added between absent land-owners on the one hand and active owners and tenants on the other, in connection with the land reforms. To judge from the calculations in chapter 4, almost 10 per cent of value added has been transferred from absent owners, who are not included in the agricultural labour force, to active owners and tenants in particular. It seems, therefore, that the real income of the labour force units has increased by 15–20 per cent from 1950 to 1960.

Wages for agricultural labourers rose from about 3 piasters per day in 1937 to about 9 piasters in 1945, and to about 12 piasters in 1951, which is somewhat more than the cost-of-living index. During the 'fifties the wage rate remained unchanged[26]. For a labourer employed full-time, i.e. 300 days, this

---

[26]) Ministry of Agriculture, *Agricultural Economics* (In Arabic), several issues. The introduction of minimum wages for agricultural labourers of 5 piasters per day from 1942, 10 piasters per day from 1945 and 18 piasters from 1952 does not seem to have had any great influence on actual wage developments.

corresponds to about £E 35 per year. It is interesting to notice that according to the estimate of Dr. El Imam, the labour coefficient in the Cobb-Douglas production function for agriculture should be about 0.3, which means that the marginal productivity of labour should be about one third of the average output productivity at current prices. Since the latter fluctuated between £E 90 and 110 during the 'fifties, the value of the marginal productivity of labour seems to have been of the order of magnitude £E 30–37, i.e., about the same as actual money wages[27]. The equality of wages and marginal value productivity holds true back to 1937, at least.

3.4.3 Agricultural growth rates

We have collected and summarized our findings concerning the development of production and productivity in the following table of growth rates.

TABLE 3.17

Growth rates in agriculture; annual percentage changes (compound)

Period	Gross real output per unit of			Net value added at fixed prices per unit of			Total real income
	Total	Land	Labour	Total	Land	Labour	
1935/39–1960	1.5	1.0	1.4	...	...	...	...
1935/39–1950	0.6	0.0	0.6	...	...	...	...
1950–1960	2.8	2.3	2.5	2.8	2.3	2.5	1.4–1.8

The growth rate for total production during the 'fifties seems then to have been between $2\frac{1}{2}$ and 3 per cent annually, and measured per unit of labour or land 2–$2\frac{1}{2}$ per cent. The growth in total real income is slightly lower than the total gross real output or net value added at fixed prices. The explanation for this is that the assumptions behind the calculation of total real income include a certain loss through terms of trade; whether such a loss has really taken place is quite uncertain and depends largely on the time points of comparison; from a price point of view 1950 was perverse. In any case, we find a rate of growth which is not in itself very high, but compared with the continuous fall by about $1\frac{1}{2}$ per cent annually in production per man from 1913 to 1933, and the almost stationary level from 1935 to 1950, it is nevertheless an improvement.

---

[27]) See Hanaa Kheir El Dine, op. cit.

3.5 The general price development for agricultural products

As a background to the discussion of Government policies a survey of price developments since the end of World War II is necessary. In table 3.18 we have gathered together some important price indicators, an implicit value-added deflator for the agricultural sector and wholesale prices for the major commodity groups. The implicit deflator and the commodity group indices fit fairly well together, taking into account the weights of the various groups.

The general price level showed a big increase up to 1950/51, in connection with the Korean boom. During 1952 and 1953 it fell back to the earlier level. This development was mainly governed by cotton prices. After 1952/53

TABLE 3.18

Prices of agricultural products, 1947–1962 (indices, 1950 and 1950/51 = 100)

Year	Implicit value-added deflator	Sept.–August	Cotton		Wholesale prices		
			MEB spot quotations Ashmouni Good	Total crop average price	Cereals	Dairy-products	Meat and fish
		47–48	55	49	91	85	87
1948	67	48–49	43	44	91	85	90
1949	76	49–50	78	59	91	91	95
1950	100	50–51	100	100	100	100	100
1951	95	51–52	70	73	99	98	102
1952	67	52–53	47	49	103	85	86
1953	72	53–54	51	48	114	85	85
1954	83	54–55	62	50	112	89	87
1955	81	55–56	61	57	127	91	89
1956	89	56–57	68	68	127	97	95
1957	88	57–58	59	59	120	104	92
1958	84	58–59	57	54	121	98	90
1959	84	59–60	61	60	121	98	90
1960	86	60–61	56		124	101	91
1961		61–62	(58)		131	106	94

NOTE   From 1950–60 the implicit value-added deflator is calculated from table 3.13. For 1948–50 it was obtained from the total output value as estimated by the Ministry of Agriculture, see *Agricultural Economics,* Jan. 1961, p. 17 (in Arabic) and the output index from table 3.12 above. For total crop average price of cotton, see *Annuaire Statistique,* 1960–61, p. 252, table 40. For the rest of the figures, see *Economic Bulletin,* NBE, and *Economic Review,* CBE, several issues.

cotton prices recovered at the same time as the price of cereals increased. Since 1956 agricultural prices have on the whole been fairly steady. Cotton prices have been governed mainly by the course of the world market prices, while prices of cereals and other agricultural produce have been governed more by Government policies. These relations will be discussed in detail in the next chapters.

CHAPTER 4

Agricultural policies

4.1 Introductory survey

The fact that the Government control the Nile and manage the irrigation system makes their intervention and participation in both the daily routine and the long-term development of agriculture almost a necessity. It is hard to imagine how the water supply could be organized in any other way, and it has in fact always been an undisputed axiom in Egyptian politics that these two vital matters should be in the hands of public authorities. Granted this, however, the important implication follows that long-term structural development is shaped to a large extent by deliberate Government decisions on public investment in improvements of the water supply. There is little room here for ideological controversy about Government interference in the economy. Now, with the High Dam south of Assuan the last big step has been reached. When it is completed at the end of the 'sixties, with its related irrigation canals, drains and so on, Nile control will have been brought to an optimum, and the cultivated area and perennial irrigation extended to their maximum. In the previous chapter we touched briefly upon the effects this great project is likely to have; at present, however, and for five to six years to come, its main impact on the economy will be through the investment expenditure necessary for the work in progress. In this respect the High Dam resembles any other investment project.

In addition to this inevitable intervention, the present Government has for social and political reasons brought about radical changes in the ownership-structure in agriculture and in the marketing of agricultural products. Intimately connected with the Revolution, the Land Reforms of 1952, with their later extensions, have annihilated the previous mixed capitalist-feudal rural structure and laid the foundations of a cooperative small-owner agricultural system, which, if successful, will combine the advantages of small-scale private ownership with large-scale cultivation and trading. In a sense the structural effects of the land reforms are much more revolutionary than those of the High Dam. The High Dam after all is merely the last of a series of big water-regulation projects that have slowly changed the conditions for agricultural production over the last century. It is the end of a development, most of which has already taken place. The Land Reforms on the other hand meant a sudden break with a way of life inherited from the past; they are the beginning of a new development. The effects of the High Dam are a relatively simple matter of mechanical and agronomical calculation; and they are limited. The effects of the Land Reforms are incalculable; the immediate economic effects may be trifling compared to the rich variety of long-term effects that may spring from this social awakening and upgrading of the working rural population.

The policies affecting structure have been accompanied by current regulations of a more trivial kind, concerned with both prices and production. Since World War II, when the present regulations were initiated, a large variety of methods of Government intervention in the markets for agricultural products have been applied. The *ad hoc* regulations used during the war years have been subject to many changes, also *ad hoc*, during the postwar years, mainly because of changes in the conditions of foreign trade. The present methods of regulation are, of course, strongly influenced by the nationalization policies adopted since 1961, and they may prove more permanent and better integrated with economic policy in general; but the problems to be solved remain very much what they were in the 'fifties.

Without Government intervention in the markets Egyptian agricultural prices would to a large extent be determined by the state of demand and supply in the world market. This is particularly true for cotton, the big ex-

TABLE 4.1

Rents and prices

			Wholesale prices		
	Average rents per feddan £E 1938/39 = 100		Foodstuff June– Aug. 39 = 100	Cotton average price	Maize 1938 = 100
1938/39	7	100	100	100	100
1942/43	12	171	n.a.	236	226
1944/45	17	243	n.a.	344	255
1950/51	27	386	334	1089	238
1951/52	30	429	350	790	238

SOURCE *Bulletin of Agricultural Economics,* (in Arabic), Ministry of Agriculture, several issues. *Annuaire Statistique,* 1959, p. 250 and 390. *Economic Bulletin,* NBE, several issues.

port commodity, and for cereals, some of which are imported, such as wheat, and others exported, such as rice. While world-market cotton prices have fluctuated heavily, cereals prices, dominated by the international wheat agreement, have developed more quietly. Since the Korean boom most international agricultural prices have had a tendency to fall. The main aim of the market regulations in Egypt has been to stabilize agricultural income at a suitable level in spite of these international developments, and to influence the general income distribution in a way found appropriate. In addition, however, the regulations have tried to adjust the terms of trade favourably in order to increase the national income and improve the balance of payments.

4.2 The land reforms[1])

4.2.1 Tenure and rents

The pressures behind the far-reaching land reforms, both of ownership and methods of cultivation, were much the same as in other countries with a small industrial sector, a rapidly increasing population and an antiquated social organization[2]). It was shown in the introductory pages of chapter 3 how the rapid increase in the agricultural labour force made the average output-productivity of labour fall continuously from 1913 to 1933; at the same time the average yield per cropped feddan, and even more per cultivated feddan, rose. Although reliable statistics are not available, it seems natural to believe that a serious fall in agricultural labour income per man, in terms of output, and an increase in rents per feddan, also in terms of output, must have taken place during the first three decades of this century. Production per worker may have fallen by about 35 per cent from 1913 to 1939, while production per cultivated feddan rose by about 10 per cent during the same period. (In terms of money, rents fell heavily of course during the 'thirties.)

---

[1]) A broad description of the agrarian reforms and their effects is to be found in Doreen Warriner, *Land Reform and Development in the Middle East,* London 1955, and *Agrarian Reform and Community Development in UAR,* Dar El Taawan Publishing and Printing House, Cairo 1961. Our remarks here are based mainly on Warriner's books, to which this note is a general reference. See also Sayed Marei, *UAR Agriculture Enters a New Age, An Interpretative Survey,* Cairo 1960, and two United Nations Reports on *Progress in Land Reforms.*

[2]) A background description of the development of land-ownership has been given in Gabriel Baer, *A History of Land-ownership in Modern Egypt, 1800–1950,* Oxford 1962.

Even before World War II this trend was broken with respect to labour productivity, as we have described. To judge the development of "real" rents and wages for the period 1933–51 is difficult, because here the increased use of fertilizers comes into the picture. With an almost unchanged yield per feddan and a slightly increased production per man compared with 1933, it seems quite unlikely, however, that in 1951 rents, in terms of agricultural output, should have risen further and agricultural labour income fallen further. Rents certainly rose sharply during and after the war in terms of money, but this increase must be ascribed altogether to the rise in agricultural prices up to the Korean boom year.

After the Korean boom cotton prices fell sharply and so, after a certain time lag, agricultural rents could in any case have been expected to fall even without government action. However, the Agrarian Reform Decree (Law no. 178, 1952), as one of its measures, fixed the rents of land and regulated the conditions for tenure and share-cropping. Rents were fixed, in the summer of 1952, at 7 times the basic land tax, which was levied at the rate of 14 per cent. As the tax assessments, made in 1949, were low, £E 2–4 per feddan, with an average of £E 3, the average rent fixed by the Government was about £E 21 per feddan, i.e. roughly 2/3 of the average prevailing in 1951/52; and these maximum rents have been kept unchanged since 1952. There seems to have been no difficulty in restricting rents at the time they were fixed, with cotton prices falling substantially after the Korean boom. But later, when agricultural prices picked up again and land-productivity rose, there was a natural tendency for rents also to rise; and this has undoubtedly exerted a pressure on the maximum rents, and caused a certain amount of illegal increasing of rents. But against this there has been the changed legal position of the fellahin vis-a-vis the landowner. While earlier a tenant would usually only rent the land for a year or a crop, the compulsory period of tenure, which was extended several times, is now 3 years; and while earlier the landowner had all the support and sympathies of the authorities in his attempts to make the fellahin pay, the attitude of the authorities now is exactly the opposite. Although it is admitted that "rentals fixed by the law have not always been fully observed by some landowners" [3]), it seems clear that the rent restrictions have put a serious brake on rents, which in other circumstances would inevitably have risen since the slump years 1952/53. In addition to the rent restrictions and changes in the conditions of tenure, the rules for regulating share-cropping also favoured the fellahin.

---

[3]) Sayed Marei, *UAR Agriculture Enters a New Age*, Cairo, 1960.

As we have seen in chapter 3, section 3.2.4, the area under tenure may amount to about one third of the total area cultivated, to which should be added areas under share-cropping. The probable income redistribution effects will be estimated in section 4.3.

4.2.2 The redistribution of land

The most conspicuous feature of the reforms, however, is the redistribution of land. Owing mainly to the rules of inheritance, the number of registered owners of land increased rapidly from the end of the last century, with a consequent fall in the average size of land property.

TABLE 4.2

Number of owners, area and average size of properties

Year	Number of owners registered in thousands	Area owned million feddans	Average size of properties, feddans
1897	767	5.1	6.5
1913	1557	5.3	3.4
1929	2176	5.8	2.7
1939	2482	5.8	2.4
1945	2506	5.9	2.3
1952	2802	6.0	2.1
1957	2885	5.9	2.1

SOURCE   *Annuaire Statistique,* several issues. This table does not include state and public domains, with a total area of 2.5 million feddans (mainly uncultivated) in 1957. Area owned and area cultivated do not coincide.

By 1952, the average size of registered properties had fallen to one third of what it had been at the end of the last century. This fall was brought about, in particular, by a rapid increase in the number of very small owners, though there was also a fall in the number of big owners, and their area. The total number of owners increased by about 1.25 million from 1916 to 1957, while owners with less than one feddan increased by about 1.05 million[4]. Distribution according to size of property just before the land reforms in 1952 was as follows:

---

[4] For a detailed study of these developments, see Gabriel Baer, op cit. chapter 3.

TABLE 4.3

Distribution of owners and land by size of property, 1952

	Number of owners		Area		Average area of property, feddans
	Thousands	%	Thousand feddans	%	
1 and less	2018.1	72.0	778	13.0	0.4
over 1 to 5	623.8	22.2	1344	22.5	2.1
over 5 to 10	79.3	2.8	526	8.8	6.6
over 10 to 20	46.8	1.8	638	10.7	13.6
over 20 to 30	13.1	0.5	309	5.0	23.6
over 30 to 50	9.2	0.3	344	5.7	37.4
over 50 to 100	6.4	0.2	429	7.2	67.3
over 100 to 200	3.2	0.1	437	7.3	137.2
over 200	2.1	0.1	1177	19.8	550.9
Total	2802.0	100.0	5982	100.0	2.1

SOURCE   *Annuaire Statistique*, 1952–53.

In any discussion of the size of properties owned by individuals, it is important to note that the statistics exaggerate the number of owners. A person who owns land in several provinces is registered as an owner in each province. Furthermore, land property should not be confused with "holdings" in the sense discussed earlier, in chapter 3, section 3.2.4. It is a common misapprehension that the tenure system leads to actual holdings being even smaller on average than the average property owned. It is usually taken for granted that the land is split up by tenancy even more than the ownership statistics suggest. This is not so. From the statistics on holdings (tables 3.5 and 6) it is clear that the average actual holding before the reforms was about three times the size of the average property owned. The tenure system has actually tended to concentrate the land into larger production units than the freeholds. The many very small properties are to a large extent rented by farmers who already have some land themselves, or collect a number of small properties into a larger tenancy-holding. Observe that while in 1952 the number of owners with one feddan and less was above 2 million with 778 000 feddan, the number of holdings less than 1 feddan was only 214 300 with 112 000 feddan in 1950, see table 3.5.

The Agrarian Reform Decree of 1952 originally declared that "no person may possess more than 200 feddans of agricultural land". From this general rule exemptions were granted to 1) companies reclaiming land for sale later, 2) private persons reclaiming desert land (exempted for 25 years), 3) existing industrial companies and agricultural and scientific societies, and 4) certain Wakf land[5]). In an amendment of 1958, total family ownership was limited to 300 feddans, in order to prevent evasion through sales to children. Land in excess of the limits set by the decree was to be expropriated and redistributed to small farmers in holdings of between 2 and 5 feddans. At first landowners were given the chance of selling the land privately in small lots, and the opportunity was immediately taken on a large scale. To prevent all the excess land being disposed of in this way, private sales of excess land were forbidden from October 1952. It has been estimated that out of a total of 600 000 feddans to be expropriated about 145 000 feddans were sold privately. In 1957, therefore, new laws were enacted which extended the expropriations to include the Wakfs and the land-reclaiming companies; certain areas belonging to the state were also included in the reforms.

The land earmarked for expropriation and redistribution was subsequently requisitioned by the Government. By the end of 1960 the figures amounted to:

Requisitioned end of 1960

Under the Agrarian Reform Decree	467 257 feddans
Under the Wakf law	104 785 feddans
From foreigners	9 670 feddans
Total requisitioned	581 712 feddans

Redistributed end of 1960

Under the Agrarian Reform Decree	299 282 feddans
Under the Wakf law	81 594 feddans
From foreigners	3 200 feddans
Total redistributed	384 076 feddans

If we add to the 384 076 feddans redistributed the 145 000 feddans sold by the owners prior to October 1952, it will be realized that more than 10 per cent of the cultivated area was affected by the reforms, and carried over to

---

[5]) Wakf land is land voluntarily put under permanent public administration by its owner to secure all future income from it for religious purposes or for the descendants of the benefactor; the latter type of Wakf was abolished by the land reforms. See Gabriel Baer, op. cit. p. 147 ff. In 1957 Wakf land amounted to about 5 per cent of the total area registered as privately owned.

TABLE 4.4

Distribution of owners and land by size of property, 1957

	Number of owners		Area		Average area of property, feddans
	Thousands	%	Thousand feddans	%	
1 and less	2 058	71.3	827	13.9	0.4
over 1 to 5	660	22.9	1447	24.3	2.1
over 5 to 10	81	2.8	539	9.1	6.6
over 10 to 20	50	1.7	670	11.3	13.5
over 20 to 30	14	0.5	337	5.7	23.5
over 30 to 50	10	0.4	369	6.2	37.2
over 50 to 100	8	0.3	501	8.4	67.1
over 100 to 200	3	0.1	464	7.8	136.5
over 200	1	0.0	791	13.3	543.3
Total	2 885	100.0	5945	100.0	2.1

SOURCE *Annuaire Statistique,* 1959.

new small owners. The requisitioned but undistributed areas consist mainly of uncultivated land previously under private ownership. The effect on land distribution can be estimated from table 4.4.

By comparing this with table 4.3 it can be seen that the total area of the properties between 5 and 200 feddans had increased since 1952 by as much as 197 000 feddans, which was probably caused by private sales from areas to be expropriated. A substantial increase can be seen in the 1 to 5 group, but to get a full picture of the redistribution, the 384 000 feddans redistributed up to 1960 from properties over 200 feddans must be deducted from that group and added to the 1 to 5 group. Because of the conditional ownership of redistributed land the state is held to own all the land in the over 200 group. If we do this, we find that the area in the 1 to 5 group increases from 22.5 to 30.8 per cent of the total area, while the area in the over 200 group falls from 19.8 to 6.8 per cent. The proportion of very small properties remained almost unchanged, while the medium-sized ones, between 5 and 200 feddans, increased their share of the total acreage from 44.7 to 48.5 per cent. That a substantial equalization in the distribution of land property was accomplished is clear.

The land was given in conditional ownership in the first place to tenants who had previously held it and cultivated it, to be acquired through instalment payments extending over 40 years, the price being equal to the compensation to be paid to the old owner. This compensation was fixed at ten times the rental value, which was estimated at seven times the basic land tax. Compensation was thus fixed at rates a good deal below the current market prices of land. Interest at three per cent, later lowered to $1\frac{1}{2}$ per cent, was to be paid together with an over-all addition of ten per cent of the price, to cover the expense of requisitioning and redistribution. Eventually, in 1961, half the instalment payments (including interest payments) were written off by the government. Obviously, all this meant a substantial improvement for tenants, who had earlier had to pay rents to a landowner, and for earlier sharecroppers. There have been various estimates of the income increase enjoyed by tenants becoming owners under the land reforms. Such estimates are made difficult by the fact that the land reforms took place during a period in which value added and farm income changed rapidly because of changes in agricultural prices. The following estimate of income per feddan on redistributed land, assuming an average income and rent, can be made:

TABLE 4.5

Income on redistributed areas

£E per feddan	Before land reform	After rent restriction	After redistribution
Gross income	60	60	60
Land rent	30	21	
Instalment payments			9–12
Net income	30	39	48–51

NOTE   Gross income is calculated on the basis of the value added in 1951. Gross income fell at the time of the reform almost in proportion to the regulated rents, but recovered later to the 1951-level. For rents see table 4.1. Land tax is assumed to have been paid by the owner as a deduction from his rent. On land reform areas no land tax is paid. The installment payment includes both interest and amortization.

This estimate suggests an increase in income of 60–70 per cent, but the actual increase may be lower, for certain compulsory payments from the new owners to the cooperatives have to be taken into account. Survey studies made on a sample group of land reform estates and a control group of other estates point to a similar improvement for the tenants: "In 1956, the average net return per feddan in the land-reform estates was £E 26.60 as compared to £E 17.70 in 1952 – an increase of £E 8.90 per feddan, or 50.3 per cent. The large part of this increase was due to the average annual instalments on the purchase price being substantially lower than the average paid in 1952. By comparison, the average net return per feddan in the control estates was £E 21.50 in 1956 and £E 17.00 in 1952 – an increase of £E 4.50 per feddan or 26.5 per cent. Practically all this increase is due to rents being fixed at seven times the basic land tax, considerably lower than rents paid in 1952[6])".

Compensation to the previous owners was to be paid in non-negotiable government bonds, redeemable in 30 (later 40) years, bearing interest at 3 per cent (later reduced to $1\frac{1}{2}$ per cent). However, all the compensation payments do not even now seem to have been made. The total amount of Agrarian Reform Bonds issued by the end of 1961 was £E 42 million, while the total value of the requisitioned land must have amounted to about double. Even if all the payments had been made, the land reform expropriations would still have reduced the income of the old owners to about one sixth of that obtained (at maximum rents) from the expropriated lands.

4.2.3 Production and cooperation

One alleged drawback of land redistribution is that it tends to make the average production unit smaller, and this is generally believed to make production less efficient. It was shown in table 3.5 that the average size of holding fell somewhat from 1950 to 1956, but in spite of this, it seems possible that the Egyptian land reforms have succeeded in raising production on the redistributed areas. The explanation for this lies in compulsory cooperation in production and sales, which has made it possible to combine large-scale production and small-scale ownership on the redistributed areas. This is probably one of the most interesting features of the Egyptian land reforms.

The new owners are compulsory members of cooperatives which plan overall production and take care of sales. Each expropriated and redistributed big estate is formed into a cooperative, which then divides the total area into two or three parts, on each of which a certain crop is grown according to a planned crop-rotation system. The individual farmer is thus compelled to follow the general rotation, and has the advantage of having his plot of land ploughed at the same time as all the other plots in the same part by the tractor belonging to the cooperative. The cooperative, under the leadership of an agronomist (with veto-rights) and under the supervision of the Ministry of Land Reform, decides on crop-rotation, irrigation, use of

---

[6]) Saad M. Gadalla, op. cit. p. 61.

fertilizers, insecticides, etc., which are delivered from the cooperative. Sowing, harvesting and work in between, however, are done by the individual farmers themselves, who are responsible for their own plot of land. Production in excess of the farmer's personal needs is sold through the cooperative, and the proceeds credited to the farmer, while the cost of the various services provided by the cooperative are debited to his account. This ingenious combination of collective farming and individual ownership seems, according to survey studies, to have brought about an increase in production[7]). The system also seems to be appreciated by the farmers. Attempts have been made to introduce *voluntary* systems of cooperative farming, coupled with individual ownership, in villages outside the land reform areas. These have proved a success and it is possible that the system may spread to all agriculture in Egypt.

To prevent further fragmentation, the land reforms stipulated that in cases where agricultural land is to be divided as a result of inheritance, sales, exchange, gifts, etc., the parties concerned must agree to a single person assuming ownership of the land. In the event of disagreement, the case is to be settled by the authorities. This part of the land reforms, however, does not seem to have been put into effect.

4.2.4 The land reforms of 1961

In 1961 the maximum permissible area owned by one person was reduced to 100 feddans, and at the same time a maximum limit of 50 feddans was fixed for land rented by any one person. These new restrictions were put into effect immediately; the compensation terms were somewhat improved. The reforms of 1961 meant that, according to the statistics of land distribution, about 250 000 feddans were to be redistributed; a good deal of this area, however, seems to have been already sold before the law of 1961 was put in force, since new reforms had been expected for some time. From general policy statements by the Government, it would seem that the plan is to lower the limit for ownership to 25 feddans. This is not expected to take place until the end

---

[7]) "The average yield of cotton per feddan in the three surveyed land-reform estates during 1952–1956 was 12 per cent higher than the same average during 1948–1952. The corresponding increase in the control estates was only 2.6 per cent. The average yield of wheat per feddan increased by 21.4 per cent in the land-reform estates and by only 5 per cent in the control estates. The average yield of corn increased by 10.5 per cent in the land-reform estates and by 2.3 per cent in the control estates". Saad M. Gadalla, op. cit. p. 60.

of the 'sixties, but already it has led to sales from owners with more than 25 feddans.

4.3 Distribution and redistribution of income in agriculture

Concerning the distribution of the value added created in agriculture, the information available is very scanty. The National Planning Committee[8]) estimated that for 1959/60, when the net value added amounted to a little less than £E 400 million, about two thirds was income from ownership, while one third was wages and salaries. Here, however, income from ownership includes returns imputed to owners working on their own land, while wages and salaries include wages imputed to such owners. This makes the estimate quite arbitrary, and at best it gives us information only about the *functional* distribution of income between factors of production. But it is interesting because it points to a very low share of labour in agricultural value added; when we come to industry we shall find the same phenomenon there.

For the year 1950 it is possible to obtain an estimate of the distribution of value added between absent owners, tillers owning the land which they till, and tillers renting land. Value added was at that time £E 60 per feddan[9]), while the rent per feddan may have been about £E 30[10]). These figures can be applied to the distribution of holdings according to types of tenure in table 3.6, assuming the value added per feddan to be the same for all types of holdings. A similar calculation can be made for 1956, with value added per feddan again about £E 60 and the average rent per feddan now as low as £E 21[11]). We shall try, moreover, to estimate the distribution of income on the assumption that the redistribution of land according to the land reforms had been completed, which was in fact not the case in 1956. The land reforms implied a transfer of land from big owners to small owners. To some unknown extent, this means a transfer from absent owners to owners tilling their own land; but some land must also have been transferred from big owners tilling their own land to small owners tilling their own land. With the distribution of holdings according to type of tenure (table 3.6) in

---

8) See *General Frame of the 5-Year Plan*, p. 12.

9) Value added per cultivated feddan was about £E 65, but the total recorded area of holdings was 10 per cent larger than the area cultivated.

10) See table 4.1.

11) See section 4.6.1.

1952 and 1956 as a starting point, we can get an idea of the distribution between absent owners and tillers (owners and lessees) after the redistributions were completed. It has been estimated that in 1956 new holders still held about 200 000 feddans as lessees waiting for the ownership to be transferred to them from the Land Reform Committee, which temporarily took over all lands to be redistributed. If, therefore, in table 3.6 we move 200 000 feddans from the tenancy group to the ownership group, we should have the approximate distribution according to tenure after the completion of the land reforms, and to this distribution we can apply the above-mentioned figures for rent and value added in 1956. On these assumptions, we find the following distribution of value added "before" and "after" the land reforms of 1952.

TABLE 4.6

Distribution of agricultural value added
(percentages of total value added)

Derived from	"Before" land reforms of 1952	"After" land reforms of 1952
Absent ownership	18	10
Active ownership	68	71
Tenancy	14	19
Total value added	100	100

Needless to say, this calculation is crude and the margin of error large, but the figures do, we think, give an impression of the order of magnitude of one aspect of the distribution of income from agriculture, and the change in distribution resulting from the Land Reforms of 1952. Taking into account that the value added accruing to active owners includes payments to the Government (interest plus amortization), by the new owners, the net share of active owners has actually increased less than from 68 to 71 per cent of the total value added. The interest payments to the Government, however, are very modest, and the amortizations can be left out of the picture in this connection, since they are a kind of compulsory savings. The outstanding feature of the development is then the big drop, to almost one half, of the absent owners' share in agricultural value added, and the rise by about one third in the tenants' share. The main cause was undoubtedly the lowering of rents, which applied to *all* rented land. Two things have not been taken into account, illegal rent increases and the effects of the new conditions for share-cropping. They pull in different directions, but we have not found it possible to estimate their impact on the distribution of income. Finally, it should be remembered that both active owners and tenants have to pay wages to workers, interest on loans, taxes, etc., out of their shares of the value added [12]).

Although the main work on the farm is done by the tiller himself and his family, hired labour still plays a substantial rôle, especially on the bigger farms and in the seasonal peaks. Of the working population in agriculture more than one quarter may be employees. In connection with the land reforms a maximum wage (of 18 piasters per day for men) was introduced, but it has never become effective. In each agricultural district wages were to be settled by special committees, but as a matter of fact it was decided to leave them to the normal economic laws of demand and supply [13]), which fixed actual wages a good deal below the minimum, namely at about 12 piasters per day for men. Only in districts near places where public works are going on do agricultural wages seem to have increased during recent years, e.g. in the area round Assuan [14]). It is commonly held that the land reforms have actually worsened the situation for the remaining landless rural population through diminishing the demand for hired labour; but on the other hand public demand has increased.

4.4 The cotton policy

4.4.1 The background

Although cotton regulations were applied during World War I and up to the

---

[12]) The above calculations produce a somewhat lower rise in the tenants' share than other estimates. The Ministry of Agriculture has estimated that the reduction of rents has "added £E 40 million annually to the income of the tenant class", see *Progress in Land Reform,* Second Report U.N., Dept. of Economic and Social Affairs, New York 1956, p. 136. The increase by five percentage units in the share of tenants which we found above corresponds to about £E 20 million annually. The difference between the estimates has to do with the area supposed to be under tenancy. According to our table 3.6, about one third of the land was under tenancy in 1950, while the Ministry of Agriculture seems to have assumed that "two thirds of the cultivated area" (ibid.) is affected by the reductions in rent; this again may have to do with share-cropping. The calculations in the text take no account of share-cropping, but this can hardly account for the whole difference.

[13]) Sayed Marei, op. cit. p. 59.

[14]) Average daily wage rates paid by the Ministry of Public Works for the cleaning of irrigation canals increased from 15 pts in 1960/61 to 18 pts in 61/62 and 20 pts in 62/63. The corresponding figures for improvement works were 25, 27 and 29 pts (information from the Ministry).

great depression, it seems natural to consider the post-war system of regulations as originating from World War II. When the war extended to the Mediterranean area, Egypt suddenly found herself cut off from her major traditional export markets and confronted with the need to supply not only her rapidly growing urban population, but also the Allied armies, operating in and from Egypt, with food from domestic production. In this situation, the authorities restricted the area under cotton in order to avoid a large cotton surplus and to ensure a sufficient supply of cereals, vegetables, etc. To leave the solution of this problem to the price mechanism, by letting cotton prices fall sufficiently and the prices of cereals, etc., rise, seems to have been out of question. The policy was not very successful. Large quantities of cotton had eventually to be bought by the Egyptian Cotton Commission (ECC) at fixed support prices and stocked till the end of the war[15]). The production of cereals did not increase owing to the simultaneous distortion of the normal rotation and the decrease in the supply of fertilizers (see chapter 3, section 3.4.1.). After the war production of cereals remained at a low level, while demand for them from the towns increased continuously. As the authorities also had to face the problem of selling the huge accumulated stocks of cotton, the war policy of restricting the cotton area continued, but since cotton prices at the same time improved, the support-prices of the ECC and the area restrictions gradually lost their importance. In the field of cereals, price policies were still effective. With the Korean boom and its aftermath, however, a new situation arose, which led to new regulations. The change of Government in 1952 introduced new policy targets and methods, which gradually led up to the nationalization measures of 1961, and the general introduction of the cooperative marketing system in 1963.

Interventions concerning the production and price of agricultural products have been most extensive with respect to cotton. This is quite natural, not only because cotton is the largest single crop in Egyptian agriculture, but also because it is by far the most important source of foreign exchange, accounting for 60–70 per cent of export value, and because trade in this commodity has been hit by serious disturbances. The possibility of increasing foreign exchange earnings through intervention in the cotton trade has always been at the back of the Government's mind. Because of World War II, and later the Suez War and the trade dislocation that followed, the traditional Egyptian cotton export markets have at times been closed

---

[15]) That these stocks happened to be relatively easy to sell at good prices after the war is another matter, which ex post facto may justify the war-time policy.

completely or partly. Furthermore, during the whole post-war period the international cotton market has been disturbed by foreign regulations and export policies, especially those of the United States. At the same time, the long-staple varieties, the Egyptian speciality, have suffered from increasing competition from the short-staple varieties and from synthetic fibres, and from new long-staple producers, the Sudan and the Soviet Union. Owing to technical improvements goods made from short-staple cotton have now many of the qualities of those produced from long-staple cotton. Cotton policies have also had to take into account a rapidly growing domestic demand for raw cotton from the Egyptian cotton spinners. The spinning industry has expanded vigorously not only to meet domestic demand for cotton textiles, but also for increased exports of cotton yarn and textiles. While domestic consumption of raw cotton amounted to about 20 per cent of the total crop immediately after World War II, this had increased to 30 per cent in 1956 and is now close to 40 per cent. Finally, the market mechanism itself, the cotton bourse in Alexandria in particular, was believed to work in an unsatisfactory way making for instability.

The cotton markets and the prices made in them are complicated phenomena. For almost a century, interrupted only by wars, the international trade in cotton has been carried on through highly developed and very refined cotton bourses with futures markets in addition to the spot market, and with a well organized system of forward dealing. The market at Alexandria was the first futures market in the world. For such markets to work in a satisfactory manner there should be a large number of sellers and buyers and speculative activity should be of a stabilizing kind. In these circumstances, the bourses fulfil an important function in supplying producers, exporters, and consumers of raw cotton with facilities for hedging against unexpected price fluctuations. Futures markets, however, have always been suspect as the playground of speculative forces. Against the activities in the Alexandria futures market in particular, it has been objected that since it is in the hands of a limited number of powerful dealers, with expectations shifting continually between bullishness and bearishness, and since an increasing number of very big buyers, foreign governments, in particular from Eastern bloc countries, organizations, and so on, have entered on the demand side, it has become unable to offer the hedging facilities so much needed by producers and others, which were its original raison d'être. Against this background, the futures market in Alexandria has been closed several times, and reopened only with increased controls from the side of the Government. The market was closed from 1940 to September 1949, and again from November 1952 to

September 1955. From then on it was open, with a short interruption during the Suez War, until 1961, when it was finally closed for good in connection with the nationalization of the cotton trade. It should be observed, however, that the spot market was open most of the time and forward dealings were going on as usual.

4.4.2 Four kinds of intervention

Apart from direct interventions in the futures market, which from a national point of view may be a minor thing, although it has always been considered big news, Government intervention has worked along four main lines: 1) area restrictions, 2) cotton export taxes, 3) purchases for and sales from buffer stocks, and 4) encouragement of cotton exports through straight-forward subsidies or disguised, partial depreciations of the Egyptian pound.

4.4.3 Area restrictions

The war-time area restrictions were abolished in 1950, when the big stocks of cotton accumulated during the war were finally sold and the Korean boom gave the cotton export trade unprecedented opportunities. In 1953, after the market had again been slack for some time, area restrictions were reintro-duced, cotton being limited to 30 per cent of all areas. During 1954 and 1955, the cotton area in Northern Lower Egypt, producing mainly the long-staple Karnak variety, was maintained at 30 per cent, while in the rest of the country, producing mostly medium-staple varieties, it was increased to 37 per cent. These percentages were maintained until 1959, when cotton was restricted to 33 per cent for the whole country; and this limit is still in force. However, owing to the relatively high profitability of cotton-growing there has been in most years large scale evasion of the area restrictions[16]). With the distribution of cotton seeds under its control the Government has also been able to influence the proportions of the various varieties grown. Policy here has been to limit the area with longer-staple varieties and expand that with shorter-staple varieties.

The rationale of cotton area restrictions, and all other attempts to restrict

---

[16]) "The *minimum* area fixed by law for wheat throughout 1955–59, for example, was exactly the *maximum* fixed for cotton, but in actual fact the wheat area – supposed to be higher than or at least equal to that of cotton – was 19% lower". *Economic Review*, CBE, vol. I, no. 2, p. 217.

supply, must obviously be *either* the existence of an irrational tendency for farmers to neglect crop-rotation, and keep the cotton area larger than is profitable even from a private economic point of view (to counteract this was the original aim of the area restrictions in the period of the first World War), *or* the possibility of calling forth an increase in export prices in terms of foreign currency, which will improve the country's terms of trade. We shall consider only the latter motive. This is an old controversail issue in Egyptian cotton policy, and important contributions to the discussion were made as early as 1930[17]), when the main arguments for and against area restrictions were developed. Although the opposite has been maintained,

TABLE 4.7

Egypt's share of world cotton production, 1958/59 (in thousands of bales)

	Total cotton production (estimated)	Long staple production	Extra long staple production	Long and extra long staple production
UAR	2 057	877	1 185	2 062
World	44 797	3 115	2 518	5 633
Non-Communist World	29 095	2 610	1 998	4 608
UAR as per cent of:				
World	5	28	47	37
Non-Communist World	5	34	59	45

SOURCE   *Cotton-World Statistics.*

it seems fairly clear that Egypt is able to influence world market prices of long-staple cotton, less in the long run, of course, than in the short run. This follows directly from her large share in the total world production of long and extra long staple cotton.

Provided that foreign demand is not perfectly elastic and that the resources released from cotton production will contribute to the national product in their alternative use, it will usually pay the country as a whole to restrict supply, i.e. exports. To what extent depends, inter alia, on the elasticities of demand and supply of cotton. Existing elasticity estimates indicate that it may pay the country to limit the cotton area to 10–20 per cent below the

---

[17]) C. Bresciani-Turroni, "Relations entre la Recolte et le Prix du Cotton Egyptien", and the discussion that followed with the Cotton Bureau, Mr. Mahmoud El Darwish, Mr. J. O. Craig, Mr. Minost and Bresciani-Turroni, all in *L'Egypte Contemporaine*, 1930. The discussion has continued since then.

area which the farmers themselves would choose without intervention, but the gains to be obtained seem to be so small (the order of magnitude may be about $\frac{1}{2}$ per cent of the total value added in agriculture) that they may easily be wiped out by the negative effects of retaliatory measures by the buying countries[18]). There is perhaps also an ethical question involved, whether a country should apply this kind of "monopolistic" policy in its foreign trade. But for a poor country which is itself in any case exposed to plenty of monopolistic practices from foreign governments and private companies in its imports, this question is certainly not difficult to answer; the policy may simply be considered as self-defence. It should be mentioned also that the policy is perfectly in line with recent proposals for adjusting the terms of trade in favour of the underdeveloped countries in general[19]).

It will be understood, however, that if area restrictions really pay the Egyptian economy as a whole, the optimum limit for the cotton area will tend to fluctuate up and down with foreign demand, and if foreign demand is sufficiently high it may pay to drop the area restrictions completely; this may occur if the limit is reached at which, owing to the necessity for crop-rotation, the marginal costs of cotton growing become very high.

4.4.4 Export taxes

Export taxes are a natural supplement to area restrictions in exporting countries. Export taxes on cotton were introduced in 1948, when export prices rose to a level which made it impossible for domestic spinners to continue production at the regulated domestic sales prices. Domestic spinners were forced to use Egyptian raw cotton even if imported raw cotton would have been cheaper and more suitable. The export taxes were officially intended to finance, at least in part, a subsidy to domestic spinners. With given area restrictions, however, the taxes would also help domestic spinners directly by depressing domestic raw cotton prices, and this would presumably be their most important effect.

The decrease in production and increase in export price brought about by area restrictions can be achieved by the alternative device of an export tax of suitable size; and the conditions for an export tax to benefit the country

---

[18]) See Bent Hansen, "Cotton vs. Grain. On the Optimum Allocation of Agricultural Land", op. cit.

[19]) See Raul Prebisch, "Commercial Policy in the Underdeveloped Countries", *American Economic Review,* 49, May 1959; and Robert F. Gemmil, "Prebisch on Commercial Policy for Less-developed Countries", *Review of Economics and Statistics,* vol. 44, May 1962.

are very much the same as they are for area restrictions. From an allocation point of view, the export tax is superior to area restrictions, which, depending upon their nature and administration, may happen to push intra-marginal cotton lands out of cotton cultivation, and keep extra-marginal cotton lands in. But leaving aside the problem of allocation, a moderate export tax added to area restrictions will only have effects of an income distributive nature. Instead of the cotton farmers alone benefiting from the area restrictions, while domestic consumers of cotton are losing, some of the benefit accrues to the Government as export tax revenue, while at the same time cotton prices for domestic consumption are prevented from increasing, and may even fall; from an income distribution point of view, it may be considered unjust to let the whole benefit be enjoyed by the cotton farmers, while consumers suffer a loss. By combining area restrictions with a moderate tax, the revenue of which is used by the Government to subsidize domestic cotton textiles production, we may secure a rise in export prices and farmers' selling prices, though less than in export prices, and a fall in the consumers' buying prices. It will be understood also that it may be rational to let the export tax move up and down according to foreign demand, i.e. according to export prices, and in the oppostie direction to area restrictions. In the event of increased foreign demand, rising prices and increased cotton area, the export tax should be increased to stabilize both producers' prices and consumers' price.

In chart 4.1 we have shown the course of the export tax on two typical varieties: Karnak (Good), which is a long-staple variety, and Ashmouni (Good), a medium-staple variety. In the same chart the reader will find the Alexandria spot prices for the two varieties; these are equal to export prices *less* export tax, see chapter 7, section 7.5). The chart does not suggest that as far as the export tax is concerned the authorities have been particularly preoccupied with optimizing export revenue from year to year. The tendency for the export tax to vary with short-term changes in the level of demand abroad is weak. From a supply point of view, of course, this is immaterial, since in most years area restriction may be supposed to have been the effective limitation to production. An interesting feature is that during the years 1950 and 1951, when no area restrictions were in force, the export tax rose and reached its maximum. To this extent the export tax has in fact, whether intended to or not, served as an alternative method of restricting production. During the following years, until 1954/55, the tax remained at a high level in spite of lower export prices. The explanation probably lies in fiscal considerations of an unsophisticated nature. From 1955/56 export taxes are progressively reduced, and domestic textile prices rise. In 1959/60 the export tax on Karnak is completely abandoned, but a low export tax on Ashmouni (and other medium staples) is still in force. This has to be seen as a measure to keep up the farmers' income in spite of the tendency for cotton prices to fall. The other side of the medal, of course, is that buying prices for the domestic textiles industry have risen in relation to export prices (including export tax), and for most varieties the difference, hitherto in favour of domestic industry, disappears completely from 1959. Thus from a longer term point of view it may be said that the cotton export tax, though with rather bad timing, has followed demand conditions abroad, and has to some extent served to stabilize producers' prices.

4.4.5 Buffer stock policies

The buffer stock policies which the authorities, i.e. the Egyptian Cotton Commission, have carried over from the war years aim primarily at counteracting short-term fluctuations in cotton prices and income to cotton producers. They influence the world market as well as domestic prices. The ECC has worked in part by fixing each year certain support prices at wich it has committed itself to buy from producers. Throughout the 'fifties these have been *on average* lower than the Alexandria market quotations, usually quite a good deal lower, though vis à vis the *producers*, the support prices have probably for long periods been effective; for owing to margins for merchants and ginning mills, transport costs, etc., the producers' selling prices are always lower than the Alexandria quotations. The support prices have not only served as an extra hedge for the producers; while most ECC selling has actually taken place at prices higher than the support prices, buying has been mainly at support prices and thus an active determinant of the prices received by the farmers. The course of the support prices and the stocks held by the ECC is shown in chart 4.1. At times the ECC has worked in the futures market, buying futures contracts at fixed prices[20]), and it has also announced selling prices to influence the market. Its purchases and sales, i.e., its "open market operations", have naturally had a general influence on market prices. Sales to exporters and domestic industries at prices below the current market prices have also taken place. The ECC has tended to increase its stock in years of slack demand and decrease its stock in years of strong

---

[20]) Particularly in 1951/52, when the Government made a herostratic attempt to prevent cotton prices from falling after the Korean boom.

CHART 4.1

Cotton spot prices, support prices, export taxes and ECG-stocks

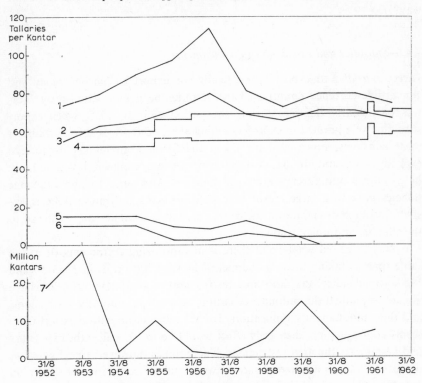

1. Karnak, G/FG, spot MEB (51/52–55/56 FG est.)
2. Karnak, G/FG, EEC buying prices
3. Ashmouni, G, spot MEB
4. Ashmouni, G, ECC buying prices
5. Average export tax Karnak G.
6. Average export tax Ashmouni G.
7. ECC stock (total) at beginning of season

demand from abroad. In addition it has evened out fluctuations in supply caused by erratic crops. In this way the buffer stocks have absorbed fluctuations from both the demand and the supply side. At times the stocks have amounted to more than one third of the total crop; at others they have been negligible (the crop has fluctuated between 6 and 10 million kantars during the last decennium). There has been no long-run stock-piling. The result must have been a certain short-run stabilization of domestic prices, but the effect on international cotton prices in the long-staple markets is more uncertain. On average foreign exchange earnings may be increased in this way[21]).

4.4.6 Subsidies and exchange rate adjustments

Direct *subsidies* to exporters, especially for export to hard-currency and convertible-currency countries, have at times been used extensively. This was particularly the case during the period 1952 to 1955, when export subsidies were granted to exporters selling at reduced prices abroad. Most of these subsidies, however, have taken the form of premiums on foreign exchange, etc., and are therefore better reviewed in connection with balance of payments and foreign exchange policies. And since foreign exchange policies have to a large extent been cotton-price stabilization policies, we shall postpone discussion of the degree of stabilization actually achieved to the chapter on foreign trade.

It may be asked what point there is in subsidizing cotton exports at the same time as taxing them, as happened in 1952–55; or, as in 1953–55 and 1957, to subsidize, tax, and area-restrict cotton simultaneously. We have already explained the rationale of cotton export taxes and area restrictions, and their simultaneous application. To add subsidies to cotton export taxes seems contradictory; their only effect would be to neutralize the export tax and counteract the area restrictions. The point is, however, that Egypt has not been living in a free-trade world with uniform conditions of sale to all countries. The subsidies have been varied according to the nature of the particular export deal, while the taxes have been more uniform. The combination of taxes and subsidies may therefore be considered as some kind of price-differentiation in which Egypt has tried to adjust the price to the conditions in each particular market. That such policies may be profitable from the seller country's point of view is obvious; whether they have actually been so is difficult to judge. The ever-present danger of a price differentiation policy is that reselling may take place; and such reselling at dumping prices did in fact take place to a considerable extent. In this respect especially the policies of the Soviet Union and Czechoslovakia were very disturbing from an Egyptian point of view. Even the possibility of retaliation has to be taken into account.

---

[21]) The GATT report *Trends in International Trade,* A Report by a Panel of Experts, Geneva 1958, has for this reason strongly recommended national buffer-stocks of raw materials.

4.4.7 The nationalization of the cotton trade

After the *nationalization of the cotton trade* in 1961, the fixing of prices has been almost completely in the hands of the authorities. The Alexandria futures bourse was closed in 1961, and the open spot market (Minet El Bassal) was closed in 1962. All sales of raw cotton for export or local consumption are now effected through the ECC, which buys cotton at fixed prices, and fixes selling prices both for export and for local consumption.

At the beginning of the seasons 1962/63 and 1963/64, the cotton authorities announced fixed buying prices for the whole season, September 1 to August 31, for deliveries from the ginning mills; in principle the ECC thus takes over the whole crop. It would, of course, be more rational to announce buying prices before sowing, and this has actually been done for the season 1964/65. The price received by the farmers is lower than the fixed price by the margins of the mills and the intermediaries handling the cotton. To make these margins as small as possible the cooperative societies and the Cooperative and Agricultural Credit Bank were ordered to compete with the private merchants at this stage of the cotton trade. From 1964, however, all trade is to be through the cooperative societies. A glance at chart 4.1 reveals immediately that the margin between Alexandria spot prices and ECC buying prices has narrowed considerably during the last 7–8 years, and this must in all probability imply squeezed margins for the intermediaries[22].

Concerning export prices it has already been mentioned that ECC export quotations are changed from time to time according to the state of foreign demand[23]. From the beginning of the 1962/63 season uniform prices were applied to all foreign buyers, so that the price discrimination pursued during the 'fifties was brought to an end. This probably means that price discrimination proved to be more trouble than it was worth. Domestic selling prices are also fixed at the beginning of the cotton season, for the whole season. To give an impression of the price relationships fixed by the ECC, we show in table 4.8 quotations for the quality Good/Fully Good of some important varieties during the seasons 1962/63 and 1963/64.

---

[22] El Gritly, *The Structure of Modern Industry in Egypt,* Cairo 1948, mentions that before World War II the margin between the Alexandria quotations and the producers' prices may have amounted to almost fifty per cent.

[23] During 1962/63 and 1963/64 export prices were fixed to avoid any carry-over of exportable qualities at the end of the season. But whether this really indicates a new policy with respect to stocks is doubtful. During these two seasons demand has been relatively good, in particular in 1963/64.

TABLE 4.8

ECC price quotations (tallaries per metric kantar)

Variety	Buying prices, seasons 1962/63 and 63/64	Selling prices for local consumption, seasons 1962/63 and 63/64	Export prices for commitments effected from the following dates				
			27.5 1962	12.8 1962	9.12 1962	7.4 1963	10.11 1963
Giza45,G/FG	85.00	105.00	91.20	86.50	87.50	86.50	90.50
Karnak,G/FG	78.00	95.75	85.20	80.00	81.00	80.00	84.50
Giza47,G/FG	71.60	87.25	77.90	72.50	72.50	72.50	78.50

SOURCE   *Economic Review*, CBE, 1963, p. 3.

The buying prices are the prices paid for deliveries from ginning mills. The selling prices for local consumption are the prices paid by domestic spinners no matter whether they are producing for the domestic market or for export. However, when the textile industry exports yarn or cloth a subsidy is paid to them from the Government corresponding to the difference between the ECC selling price of raw cotton for export and that for local consumption. Thus when the domestic textile industry produces for foreign markets, it gets the raw cotton at the low export prices quoted by the ECC. When it produces for the domestic market, raw cotton prices are somewhat higher, 10–15 per cent in August 1962. Domestic final consumers in this way now pay a higher price for the raw cotton in the products they buy than foreign final consumers[24]. In relation to foreign textile industries using Egyptian cotton, the domestic textile industry still has a small advantage when it comes to exports, for the export tax that is still levied on some medium-staple varieties of raw cotton does not affect domestically produced goods for export. Obviously this situation is radically different from that at the beginning of the 'fifties. Then, raw cotton exports were taxed in favour of domestic textile production, whether for local or export sale. Today[25], domestic final consumers are taxed in favour of all exports of cotton, whether

---

[24]) It should be remembered, however, that domestic consumption is concentrated on the cheapest, largely non-exportable qualities, and for these qualities the price difference is smaller.

[25]) I.e. the beginning of 1964. During 1964 export prices actually rose above prices for domestic consumption due to the good demand abroad.

raw or manufactured; and at the same time there is a slight taxation of raw cotton exports in favour of manufactured cotton exports. And this "subsidization" of exports takes place while area restrictions in principle limit the total supply of Egyptian raw cotton. We shall return to these problems in chapter 6, on industrial policies.

4.4.8 Summary and conclusions

Here we end for the moment our attempt to describe the methods applied by Egypt in connection with her cotton trade during the post-war period. What has been the combined impact of all these policies? To answer such a question is certainly not easy; it may even be impossible – at least with the information available. The following conclusions, which should be appraised in connection with the relevant discussions in the chapters on industrial and foreign trade policies, are therefore highly tentative.

First of all, we notice that the various methods of intervention may well fit together into a logical system of measures intended to influence the terms of trade favourably to Egypt, and at the same time stabilize domestic raw cotton prices and domestic textile prices at levels judged satisfactory from the point of view of income in and outside agriculture. The area restrictions and the export taxes, together with the stocking policies of the ECC, may in principle be able to influence international prices, production, and foreign sales in a manner optimal to the country, influence income distribution, and exert some stabilizing influence on domestic prices; and the foreign exchange rate policies should in principle be able to stabilize domestic prices in spite of fluctuations in the optimum export prices. The objections sometimes raised against domestic stabilization policies in connection with the export of raw materials[26]), namely that they may be in conflict with general optimization targets and lead to a bad allocation of resources, obviously lose all relevance when a Government simultaneously uses all the above-mentioned instruments of policy. Most of the discussion in this field is suffering from a lack of understanding of a fundamental proposition in the theory of economic policy: that the number of instruments has to be at least equal to the number of targets. If this provision is fulfilled, and the instruments are chosen and used in an appropriate manner, no conflicts need arise between such targets as domestic stabilization, optimum use of resources, and an

---

[26]) See Ragnar Nurkse. "Trade Fluctuations and Buffer Policies of Low Income Countries", *Kyklos,* 1958.

acceptable distribution of income. The large number of policy instruments actually used in the Egyptian cotton trade should not be taken as an indication of confused policies, but rather as an indication of the degree of complication of the policy problem to be solved.

So much for principles. How well these policies have been designed from a practical point of view is, of course, quite another matter. That the timing of policy has not always been successful with respect to changing international conditions is one thing; this has inevitably to do with difficulties in forecasting international economic developments, but it may also perhaps have something to do with conservatism in policy. Disregarding the short-term timing of the policies there seems to have been a continuous adaptation to changing international demand conditions in the directions one would have expected. An exception perhaps is the export tax during the period 1952–55, when the level of the tax was kept amazingly high. It seems that unsophisticated fiscal considerations gained the upper hand here. Also the policy towards domestic consumers followed a course which is difficult to understand from the point of view of pure optimization. Other considerations seem to have supervened. Finally, it should be stressed that since cotton is an important article in Egypt's foreign trade, cotton policies, e.g. area restrictions, may have been influenced by the general foreign policies of the country, not only to avoid retaliation, but also as an element among many others in a larger, partly political frame. In such a wide context seemingly irrational economic measures may after all have their rationale, or at least their explanation. Aid without strings is still the exception rather than the rule. It is known that American sales of surplus commodities were not without strings with respect to Egyptian cotton policies.

4.5 The grain policy

As we have already indicated, price and production policies concerning cereals have been influenced by the rapidly growing demand for food and, at the same time, the wish to stabilize farmers' incomes. Already during the war a minimum area for wheat production was fixed, together with a maximum for cotton; and the minimum area regulations have been maintained during the whole post-war period, though there have been large scale evasions because of the higher profitability of cotton. Egypt came out of the war period with relatively low grain prices, owing to war-time price regulations. Such regulations are still in force for all cereals in the sense that the Government fixes support prices to the producers or maximum prices in trade. During the 'fifties these support prices have – with the exception of rice – gradually been increased, and at the time of the exchange reform, when the currency was depreciated in July 1962, they were – once more with the exceptions of rice – relatively high compared with world market prices. At the exchange rates effective after July 1962, the prices of cereals other than rice have been more or less in line with world market prices; rice has been relatively low. But for various reasons comparisons of this kind are hard to make. The regulations affecting agricultural production and prices in force in most countries, together with American export policies, make it difficult to say what exactly are "world market prices".

The above comparisons of Egyptian cereal prices with world market prices are made in terms of US cents, with domestic prices expressed in US cents via the official exchange rate. This may distort the picture. In bilateral trade agreements special exchange rates may be applied. Partial depreciations of the Egyptian pound took place during most of the 'fifties through the import entitlement systems, the pound discount given to cotton exporters (see chapter 7), etc. Also the import duties have been raised, though in general imports of cereals have been exempt from duty. Imports of food grains are now mainly effected through special arrangements with the US authorities, see later. There has been some export of cereals at special rates, but exports have on the whole been small compared with imports.

In fixing prices the Egyptian authorities seem to have been mainly concerned with the average earnings of the farmers; the possibility of affecting supply does not seem to have played any great rôle. An important exception, however, is the increase in prices of 1954, which was partly intended to give farmers more incentive to grow cereals. Against the background of this price fixing, it is remarkable that the average net returns on wheat and maize, with prices in line with "world market" prices, are much lower than the average net return on rice, with a price which is probably below the "world market" price.

The commodity balance for grain, i.e. wheat, maize, rice, millet, and barley, is given in table 4.9. "Net production" is production less the cost of seeds. "Domestic supply" includes changes in stocks, and the figures for "domestic supply per caput" are therefore not identical with consumption per caput. The yearly fluctuations are partly due to stock changes. The conspicuous feature of table 4.9, is the change in Egypt's international position, from being a net exporter of grain to the extent of about 100 000 tons annually before the war, to being in 1961 a net importer, to the extent of almost 1¼ million tons. This is the problem we have already described in

TABLE 4.9

Commodity balance for grain* (thousands of tons)

| Average of year | Net production | Imports | | Exports | Domestic supply | Domestic supply per caput, kg |
		Total	of which, from USA under public law 480(Title I)			
1936–38	3 708	26		142	3 591	229
1948	3 856	767		355	4 266	218
1950	3 482	530		234	3 780	185
1952	3 323	960		12	4 271	199
1954	4 597	48		175	4 471	199
1956	4 754	834		282	5 304	223
1957	4 593	1 089		391	5 293	216
1958	4 345	1 112	(800)	360	5 097	206
1959	4 554	1 261	(900)	23	5 792	228
1960	4 768	1 155	(1 000)	280	5 643	218
1961	4 404	1 133	(1 200)	203	5 334	201
1962	5 548	1 741	n.a.	144	7 145	262

* Includes wheat, maize, rice, millet and barley; imported flour is converted into grain.

SOURCE   *Annuaire Statistique*, several issues, and *Economic Review* 1963. From 1958 our estimates; the net production figures calculated according to the rules laid down in *Annuaire Statistique*, 1959. Table 7, p. 212, notes; the import figures comprise only wheat and maize, the export figures only rice. The figures for imports from the US were estimated on the basis of information concerning agreements signed between the US and the UAR Government on Egyptian purchases to be paid in £E of wheat and food grains during the years 1958 to 1961. The total agreed upon amounted to 4 149 thousand tons, of which 977 in 1960 and 1 483 in 1961. The shipments by calendar year are not known, but we estimated them to be as shown in the table. See *Fifteenth Semi-Annual Report on Activities Carried on Under Public Law 480, 83rd Congress*, etc., 87th Congress, 2nd Session, House Document No. 385, US Government Printing Office, Washington, 1962, Appendix.

section 3.1 of chapter 3. Imports are almost exclusively of wheat, while exports consist mainly of rice. Since 1961 imports have increased strongly.

In spite of the substantial increase, by about 30 per cent, in net production since 1936–38, and the huge increase in imports, offset by only a modest increase in exports, which together have permitted the domestic supply to rise by almost 60 per cent, the supply per inhabitant has only in 1962 surpassed the pre-war level. During the years 1945–55, it was even lower by about 10 per cent, than during the years before the war. The later increase up to the pre-war level was made possible by the American sales from surplus stocks, together with a large Russian delivery in 1957. During the years 1958 to 1962 these American sales provided between 15 and 25 per cent of the total supply of grain in Egypt. They are regulated through US Public Law 480, according to which agricultural surplus products may be sold to foreign governments against payments in foreign currency, in this case Egyptian pounds, at an exchange rate favourable to the US. These Egyptian pounds are paid into so-called counterpart-funds, i.e. accounts in banks in Egypt. In practice it is as if Egypt had obtained an interest-free loan in the US to purchase agricultural products[27]. The commodities are bought by the Egyptian authorities in the open market in the US at the ruling (subsidized) American export prices, which are more or less in line with "world market prices".

The retail prices of bread, flour, etc., are in general fixed at a level which is low compared with both import and producer prices of food grains. There is thus a substantial subsidizing of the consumer. Finally, it should be mentioned that most prices of fruit, vegetables, beans and lentils, etc., are subject to price control, and that marketing is being taken over more and more by government agencies and cooperatives.

4.6 *Agricultural marketing*

Government agencies have been increasingly active in the markets for agricultural products since the price and quantity interventions started during World War II. Cotton purchases and sales were handled by the Cotton Commission, while grain policies have been pursued through the Agricultural Bank; the private commercial banks have also always been active in agricultural products. Since the nationalizations of 1961 foreign trade in all major products have been carried out by Government-owned companies, and the same has applied to a good deal of the domestic wholesale trade in agricultural products. During the last year or two, however, the cooperative societies have come to play a bigger part in agricultural marketing. The Egyptian cooperative societies have traditionally been credit societies, serving earlier mainly as intermediaries for credits to big land owners, but from the time of the land reforms cooperative organizations immediately took on a

---

[27]) See Prof. Said El Naggar, *Foreign Aid to United Arab Republic,* Institute of National Planning, Cairo 1963, for a detailed discussion of the mechanism and effects of this kind of foreign aid.

new importance. The cooperatives in the land reform areas take an active part in both production, selling farmers fertilizers, and so on, and the buying of their products. The policy at present (1963/64) is to extend the scope of the local cooperative societies, buying produce and selling production necessities, beyond the Land Reform areas. Intermediaries will in this way disappear, and all the individual farmer's cash transactions connected with production will be recorded by the cooperative society. The Government may thus get price formation completely under its control, quality controls may become better, and, finally, an administrative basis may be created for a reform of the system for taxing farm incomes. So far this marketing scheme has only just started to function, and it is too early to judge its effects.

CHAPTER 5

Industry

5.1 Introductory remarks

In spite of the improvements which have taken place in agriculture, and the upward surge it will enjoy when the High Dam is finished and put to work, industrialization is necessary to obtain a satisfactory rate of growth in Egypt. We shall show in this chapter that between the 'thirties and the middle of the 'fifties a considerable expansion of industry had already taken place[1]). Since 1957 the 5-year plans have aimed at accelerating this expansion, and some acceleration does in fact seem to have been accomplished.

It is no more than one would expect that Egypt concentrated first on the production of those goods for which she had natural comparative advantages, owing to resources, climate, domestic demand, and the capacity of her people. The availability of raw materials and a domestic demand for consumer goods made it natural that industrialization should begin in the food and cotton industries. As early as the beginning of the twentieth century we find, therefore, a number of industrial enterprises in cotton ginning, pressing, spinning, and weaving, sugar, flour-milling, beverages, tobacco, etc. Besides these industries, we find others typical of industries based on raw materials, such as salt, soda, cement and pottery. The numbers employed in industry and the extent of production were extremely modest until World War I, which caused a certain expansion. With peace and the return to the traditional free trade policy, the war-time industries could not survive to any large extent. It was not until the 'thirties, when the foreign trade policy of the country was changed, that industry started developing at a more rapid tempo. High duties were imposed on competing import goods, such as cotton fabrics,

---

[1]) For the earlier development a general reference can be given to Ali El Gritly, *The Structure of Modern Industry in Egypt,* publ. as Nos. 241–242, *L'Egypte Contemporaine,* 1947, Cairo 1948. See also F. Harbison and J. A. Ibrahim, *Human Resources for Egyptian Enterprise*, New York 1958.

TABLE 5.1

Output of selected commodities (thousands of metric tons unless otherwise indicated)

		1928	1938	1946	1950	1955	1959	1960	1961	1962
Cotton										
Yarns		3	20	41	49	73	91	104	111	121
Woven fabrics	mill.m.	...	93	195	255	380	499			
	thous.t.						62	64	73	78
Seed oil		...	53	80	85	83	97	110	106	94
Oil products		...	281	1 025	2 107	2 456	3 127	3 997	4 209	4 815
Cement		90	375	588	957	1 371	1 778	1 848	2 141	2 313
Super-phosphate		...	20	15	69	137	167	188	178	164
Nitrates		...	...	...	83	191	246	257	274	270
Iron bars		...	...	...	25	89	130	160	176	189
Refined sugar		109	209	168	231	289	287	338	330	333
Steel products		...	...	...	...	...	50	113	132	132

SOURCE   1928–1959 (in some cases 1960), *Annuaire Statistique,* 1960–1961. The other figures are taken from NBE *Economic Bulletin.* 1963. The latter figures may not in some cases be fully comparable with those for the earlier years.

matches, refined sugar, alcohol and cigarettes. At the outbreak of World War II domestic industries satisfied the following percentages of the country's consumption: sugar 100, alcohol 100, cigarettes 100, salt 100, flour-milling 99, cotton yarn 96, shoes 90, cement 90, soap 90, furniture 80, matches 80, beer 65, vegetable oils 60, caustic soda 50 and cotton textiles 40 per cent [2]).

The very recent origin of Egyptian industry can also be appreciated from table 5.1, which shows how production of the early "big" commodities developed. In all of them a rapid growth has taken place, and successively more and more commodities come into the picture. Although these "big" commodities still occupy a substantial part of total industrial production (perhaps half the industrial value added), the table does not do justice to the range of diversification achieved in later years. It does at least show, however, how oil and fertilizers have become significant since the war, and that even a certain iron and steel industry has grown up.

5.2 Production, prices and value added, 1939–1962/63

5.2.1 Industrial production

An official industrial production index, similar to the agricultural output

---

[2]) *Economic Bulletin,* NBE, 1948, p. 113.

index (table 3.12), showing development from before World War II does not exist. We have ventured, however, to splice together existing indices and other information to make an unbroken production series from 1939 to 1962/63. The result is given in table 5.2. The problems connected with establishing this index series were great and the quality of the result is probably inferior to the corresponding index series for agricultural output, in particular for the period before 1951. Various kinds of biases affect the figures, arising partly from well-known index problems, and partly from special circumstances. The index may have an upward bias for the years before 1950, but not for the rest of the period, in which a downward bias

TABLE 5.2

Industrial production (1952 = 100)

Year	Total industry and electr.	Manufacturing industry		United Nations Index	Annual increase per cent	
		Total	Textiles		Total ind. and electr.	Textiles
1939	(48)	(49)	(34)			
1945	67	66	57		5	7
1946	68	69	59		1	4
1947	74	74	65		9	10
1948	83	83	75		12	15
1949	93	90	88		12	17
1950	98	92	88		5	0
1951	97	97	93		— 1	6
1952	100	100	100	100	3	8
1953	101	102	103	103	1	3
1954	106	109	112	108	5	9
1955	115	119	119	118	8	6
1956	122	128	129	125	6	8
1957	130	135	138	133	7	7
1958	144	146	151	147	11	9
1959	148	150	156		3	3
1960	161				9	
1961	179				11	
1962	193				8	
1959/60	152				—	
1960/61	170				12	
1961/62	187				10	
1962/63	199				7	

SOURCE   See below "Note on the industrial production index", p. 116. The 1939 figures have been put in brackets to indicate their inferior quality.

is not to be excluded, at least before 1960. But in any case, we do not think the various biases, which we discuss in detail in the "Note on the industrial production index" attached to this section, disturb the main picture. For the sake of comparison, we have added a UN index of production for the UAR for the years 1952 to 1958[3]). This index does not include electricity, mining and quarries, rubber and metal ore manufacturing, and should thus be roughly comparable with the index for manufacturing industries; the two series fit well together.

Throughout the period there has been an almost continuous increase in total production. In only one year is a decline recorded. Until 1956 textiles grew the fastest, but since 1957 other industries have taken over the lead. The average compound rate of growth from 1939 to 1962/63 has been quite high, namely 5 per cent; but the growth rate has fluctuated widely. To some extent this merely reflects the business cycles of the highly industrialized countries of Europe and America, but from the time of the Suez War, when foreign trade was shifted towards the Eastern Bloc countries, the growth rate has probably been determined more by domestic factors. During the years 1947–49 expansion was vigorous, at an average level of 11 per cent per year, a rate of growth which was never surpassed later. The following slack from 1950–54, with an average increase of $2\frac{1}{2}$ per cent only, was clearly due to the general post-Korean recession. From 1955 onwards we find relatively high but very uneven increases year by year. Here the average annual growth is 8 per cent. During the first three years of the 5-year plan, 1960/61 to 1962/63, the average rate is as high as 10 per cent, but it is noteworthy that the rate of growth has been falling during these three years, from 12 per cent in 1960/61 to 7 per cent only in 1962/63. The reason seems to be that during 1960/61, and to a lesser extent 1961/62, idle capacity was utilized. 1962/63 may also have been affected by shortages of imported raw materials, but there is the further possibility that the rate of growth may have been influenced by the nationalizations of 1961.

Note on the industrial production index

The indices were made as follows:

Total industry and electricity　　From 1939 to 1945 the estimate is that of M. A. Anis[4]). Anis' estimate is a value added estimate, and is based largely on employment figures. From 1945 to 1951 the index is based on the National Planning Commission's estimate of gross

---

[3]) *Statistical Yearbook,* UN, New York 1961.

[4]) M. A. Anis, "A Study of National Income of Egypt", *L'Egypte Contemporaine,* no. 261–262, 1950, p. 685.

value added at fixed 1954-prices[5]). This estimate is also to some extent based on employment figures. The 1951–59 figures are the National Bank of Egypt Index of Industrial Production. This index is a weighted geometric average with weights based on net value added 1950[6]). It is also to some extent based on employment and other input data. Production in Allied military establishments during and after World War II are not included in any of these indices. The same holds true for Government industrial production, which became particularly important after 1952. The figures for 1960 to 1962 are based on gross value added at constant 1959/60-prices for 1959/60 to 1962/63, as estimated by the National Planning Commission[7]). The necessary chaining and interpolation was made by us. For these years production in Government establishments is included.

Manufacturing industry   From 1939 to 1945 the estimate is our own, based on statistics of production of selected commodities, weighted (arithmetic average) on the basis of net value added as disclosed in the 1945 census of production. Our estimate of a 36 per cent increase in manufacturing output from 1939 to 1945 tallies well with J. W. Tailor's[8]) estimate of a 34 per cent increase from 1938 to 1945. The figures for 1945–51 are the estimates of the NPC[9]), with 1945 weights. The 1951–59 figures are sub-indices of the National Bank of Egypt index for total industrial production, see above. The remarks concerning Allied military production and Government industrial production apply here, too.

Owing to the natural difficulties in collecting the information required, production indices in Egypt, like those in all other countries, tend to exclude production in the smallest establishments and outside establishments proper. Since the very small establishments are known to have been and still are very important in Egypt, and to have developed less rapidly in terms of employment than the larger establishments (see below section 3 and table 5.7), this may imply a tendency for the production index to show too great an increase. We have tried to estimate a maximum limit for this bias. On the assumptions (1) that the production index actually applies only to establishments employing 10 persons and more, while (2) in other establishments and outside establishments proper there has been no increase in productivity, so that production here would only have increased in proportion to employment, and that finally, (3) from 1952 to 1960 employment in these small establishments and outside establishments proper increased by 11 per cent (according to table 5.8 the increase from 1947 to 1960 was 17.5 per cent), we find a production increase in 1952–60 of 45 per cent, against the 61 per cent in table 5.2. The *maximum limit* for this bias should then amount to 16 percentage units, i.e. 10 per cent for the eight years 1952–1960.

Other biases, however, point in the opposite direction. For certain industries the production indices from 1945–59 on which our index is based are actually input indices, owing to the difficulty of measuring output directly. This is to a large extent true of the important food industry. It means that for certain industries increased labour productivity is not shown by the production index, but it means also that production in very small enterprises is in fact to some extent included.

---

[5]) See Hansen and Mead, op. cit. table 4.

[6]) *Economic Bulletin,* NBE, several issues. For a description of the index and its calculations, see *Economic Bulletin,* vol. X, no. 1, 1957.

[7]) See Hansen and Mead, op. cit., table 8.

[8]) See, *Overseas Economic Surveys: Egypt,* Nov. 1947, p. 37.

[9]) Information in the NPC.

A special problem concerns the rôle played by Government industrial establishments. From 1959/60 these establishments are included in the production estimates, but from 1939 to 1959/60 they are not. From 1939 until the withdrawal of the British forces in 1956 foreign military establishments employed a large number of Egyptians. The incomes of these employees are rightly recorded as invisible exports, and should not be included in domestic industrial production. But from the beginning of the 'fifties national military and other Government industrial establishments developed rapidly, producing both military equipment for the army and civil products for sale. It has been estimated that in 1959/60 (see *General Frame of the 5-Year Plan,* p. 162) the gross output of these establishments was about £E 86 million, against £E 1094 for the whole of industry. Output in Government establishments thus amounted to 8.5 per cent of total industrial output, excluding output from Government establishments. On the assumption that output from Government establishments was negligible in 1952, and that no part of this output is included in the calculations underlying our index, we should thus have to add 14 percentage units to the index for 1959/60. The downward bias of our index arising from the exclusion of output from military establishments may therefore be of the same order of magnitude as the possible maximum upward bias arising from the non-inclusion of small enterprises for the period 1952–60.

For the period 1951 to 1954 two indices are available, namely the NPC index, which we used for the years 1945 to 1951, and the NBE index, which we have used for 1951 to 1959. For these years the NPC index shows about the same increase as the NBE index.

Index-making is always difficult during a period of rapid industrialization because *new* commodities, i.e. commodities previously imported and not produced in the country, keep appearing. Ordinary quantum indices will obviously tend not to catch them immediately and will for this reason have a downward bias. This is in all probability true of the period 1939–59. For the period 1959/60 to 1962/63 the index calculations are based on information from the establishments concerning their total output value at 1959/60 prices. Quite apart from the possibility that the establishments have actually reported in current prices, owing to misunderstandings, it is obvious that *new* commodities, and perhaps all production in new factories, will be reported at current prices, for the simple reason that no 1959/60 prices will have been available for the reporting establishment; and this may imply an upwards bias for the years 1959/60–1962/63.

Finally, we would point out that while the index link 1939–45 and 1945–51 (for Total Industry) is of the Paasche type, which tends to show a low rate of increase, the links 1945–51 (for Manufacturing Industry), 1951–59, and 1959–1961/62 are of the Laspeyres type, which tends to show a high rate of increase. We want to stress, however, than this is not a question of biases from a "true" index, but a question of a fundamentally arbitrary choice of method of weighting. The Paasche index is no more right or wrong than the Laspeyres index. But while the Laspeyres index evaluates with standards taken from the past, the Paasche index evaluates in more recent terms, and since we actually live in the present and the Paasche index employs contemporary, or at least more recent, standards, the Paasche index is usually preferred in measurements of long-term developments[10].

---

[10] Simon Kuznets, "Some Conceptual Problems in Measurements", in *Studies in Economic Development,* ed. B. Okun and R. W. Richardson, New York 1961.

5.2.2 *Industrial price development*

During World War II prices rose steeply as a result of the general inflation. The official Wholesale Price index contains, from 1947, a sub-index for industrial products and materials, in which obviously raw materials predominate. As a more general expression for industrial prices we have calculated the implicit value added deflator for the sector Industry and Electricity for the period 1952/53 to 1959/60. We did not find it possible to extend this calculation backwards or forwards. The developments shown by the two indices are quite different, and obviously the wholesale price industrial sub-index is not a good indicator of prices for industrial output, although the implicit deflator is not perfect either, and will show too high a price increase to the same extent as the downward bias of the production index on which it is based (see the note above)[11]). The wholesale price index may overestimate the rise from 1947 to 1951 and the following fall. Industrial output prices have probably been more stable than this. It seems to underestimate the next increase, up to 1960; and the fall after 1960 is certainly not true for industrial output prices, which have on average probably risen somewhat during recent years. The 40 per cent price increase for industry 1952/53 to 1959/60, although probably exaggerated, contrasts with an increase of only 20 per cent for agricultural products during the same period. The terms of trade are shifting in favour of industry, mainly because of deliberate protectionist Government policies (see chapter 6).

5.2.3 *Value added in industry*

The National Planning Committee has made the estimate of industrial output and gross value added in 1959/60 presented in table 5.4.

The importance of the various industries is entirely dependent on whether we look at gross output or gross value added. Measured by value added cotton ginning and pressing are quite unimportant, but the whole crop passes through the industry and its gross output is enormous. Similarly with the food industries, though measured by value added they still form the largest

---

11) It is worth mentioning that if we apply the production index of the NBE to the nominal value added recorded by the production censuses 1952 and 1960, we find an implicit deflator of only 117, which suggests only half the price increase shown by the implicit deflator of table 5.3. Between the calendar years 1952 and 1960 the wholesale price sub-index rose by 7 per cent.

TABLE 5.3

Industrial prices

Year	Wholesale prices, sub-index for Industrial Products and Materials		Implicit value added deflator for Industry and electr.
	June-Aug. 1939 = 100	1952/53 = 100	
1947/48	327	84	n.a.
1948/49	355	91	n.a.
1949/50	361	93	n.a.
1950/51	429	111	n.a.
1951/52	431	111	n.a.
1952/53	388	100	100
1953/54	377	97	108
1954/55	374	96	112
1955/56	376	97	115
1956/57	462	119	122
1957/58	461	119	126
1958/59	435	112	131
1959/60	457	118	139
1960/61	451	116	n.a.
1961/62	435	112	n.a.
1962/63	438	113	n.a.

SOURCES   Wholesale prices, sub-index for Industrial Products and Materials, end of December figures, see *Economic Bulletin,* NBE, several issues, Statistical Appendix. The official wholesale price index is based on weights from 1939 chosen by the Director of the Department of Statistics at that time according to his personal judgement. The prices are collected in Cairo and Alexandria. The implicit value added deflator for Industry and Electricity is based on the current price estimate of value added published in *Ten Years of Revolution (Statistical Atlas),* Department of Statistics and Census, Cairo 1962, table 9 (the figures in that table from 1960/61 onwards are estimates based on fixed 1959 prices), and the fixed prices estimate in Hansen and Mead, op. cit. table 8. The latter is based on the NBE index for industrial production.

single industry. It is closely followed by spinning and weaving, which have a much more industrial character than most sections of the food industry, including as it does butchers and bakers. Oil extraction and processing, the chemical industries (fertilizers), clothes and shoes, and beverages and tobacco are also important industries.

Value added in industry shows the same development as our production index in table 5.2; indeed, for most years they are identical and based on the same volume indices. There is no point, therefore, in distinguishing between output and net production in industry as we did in agriculture.

TABLE 5.4

Industrial output and gross value added 1959/60 (at 1959/60 current market prices and in millions £E)

Industry	Gross value of domestic production	Value of production requirements	Gross value added
Cotton ginning and pressing	149.7	145.8	3.9
Crude Oil extraction	14.5	1.5	13.0
Other mines and quarries	7.5	2.0	5.5
Total oil, mines and quarries	22.0	3.5	18.5
Food	419.0	351.5	67.5
Beverages and tobacco	67.1	57.3	9.8
Spinning and weaving	160.3	113.1	47.2
Clothes and shoes	28.9	18.6	10.3
Wood and wood manufactures	17.1	9.5	7.6
Paper, etc.	2.9	1.8	1.1
Printing and publishing	20.3	10.8	9.5
Leather and rubber	14.8	11.2	3.6
Chemical industries	31.2	18.3	12.9
Petroleum	43.3	22.1	21.2
Non-metallic products	21.3	12.2	9.1
Basic metal industries	18.8	11.5	7.3
Metal products	18.4	12.1	6.3
Machinery	8.3	2.9	5.4
Means of transportation	14.5	6.3	8.2
Miscellaneous	18.0	5.9	12.1
Total manufacturing	904.2	665.1	239.1
Electricity	18.3	6.4	11.9
Total industry and electricity	1094.2	820.8	273.4

SOURCE   *General Frame of the 5-Year Plan*, p. 45, table 20.

5.3 Industrial employment

Information about employment in Egyptian industry and its development is available from various sources, population censuses and labour force surveys, censuses of production and censuses of establishments. The last two sources are defective in so far as they do not include persons employed outside recorded establishments, which in Egypt are of great importance from an employment point of view. Furthermore, the information about employment in small establishments is useless. We have therefore chosen to base our estimates of total employment in industry on the information contained in the population censuses, although these suffer from other well-known deficiencies.

5.3.1 Development of industrial employment

We saw in chapter 2 how the economically active population rose much less from 1937 to 1960 than the total population. The percentage increases were 33 and 64 respectively. The number of persons in industrial occupation,

TABLE 5.5

Population in industrial occupation

	1937	1947	1960
Total population in thousands	15 924	19 021	26 089
Economically active population (adjusted) in thousands	5 838	6 995	7 734
In industrial occupation (adjusted) in thousands	440	610	770
As percentage of total population	2.8	3.2	3.0
As percentage of economically active population	7.5	8.7	10.0

SOURCE   See table 1.15. The figures are based on the census figures as adjusted by the Department of Statistics and Census. In the case of industry, it is obviously necessary to use the adjusted figures. Adjusted figures for industry separately were not available, so the adjusted figures for industry plus construction have been used, by splitting them between industry and construction in the same proportions as the original census figures, rounded off to the nearest ten thousands.

however, has risen more rapidly than the economically active population, and slightly more than the total population, namely by about 70 per cent. The share of the economically active population occupied in industry rose therefore from 7.5 per cent in 1937 to 10 per cent in 1960.

It is noteworthy that about half the increase in industrial employment from 1937 to 1960 took place between 1937 and 1947. From 1937 to 1947 the increase was 150 000 persons or 34 per cent, while for 1947–1960 the corresponding figures were 160 000 and 26. For several reasons the figures for 1947 are not very reliable. Quite apart from adjustments to the census figures, which are particularly large for 1947, the figures for 1947 (and to a lesser extent 1937) include people employed by the British Forces. The total

number of civilians so employed amounted to 165 000 at the end of 1945[12]),
and many of them were in industrial occupations. By 1947 there may have
been fewer, but a significant number of people were still engaged in this kind
of employment, which should not be counted as Egyptian industry but rather
as "invisible" exports. If, for the sake of argument, we deduct 20 000 persons
in 1937 and 60 000 in 1947 on this account, the percentage increase in the
number of persons in industrial employment changes to about 30 per cent
for 1937–47 and about 40 per cent for 1947–60. We shall make no attempt
to adjust the employment figures for this factor, but it should be kept in
mind.

For the most recent developments, up to 1962/63, the NPC gives the
following figures[13]).

TABLE 5.6

Industrial employment 1959/60–1961/62

Year	Number of employed persons	Increase over previous year, per cent
1959/60	612 700	—
1960/61	638 700	4.2
1961/62	694 100	8.7
1962/63	740 300	6.7

SOURCE   Hosein Omar, *Economic Development in the UAR*, (in Arabic), Cairo 1964, p.131.

The big increase between 1960/61 and 1962/63 should be viewed in connection with the reduction in working hours per week from 48 to 42, which
was carried through in 1961. The 16 per cent increase in employment during
these two years should not therefore be interpreted as a corresponding increase in labour input; for the total number of hours increased much less.
For the period 1937 to 1960 this problem is not so important, because the
number of hours worked per week was fairly constant. It is true that the
Labour Code of 1959 reduced the legal maximum number of working hours
from 9 per day (introduced in 1937) to 48 per week, but this legislative
change had little effect upon actual hours worked. The change to 42 hours

---

[12]) M. A. Anis, *A Study of National Income of Egypt*, p. 786.

[13]) The explanation of the lower level of industrial employment in table 5.6 as compared
with table 5.5 is mainly that the former table includes persons employed outside recorded
establishments.

in 1961, however, became effective in the whole Government sector, which by that time included all the nationalized industries. We shall return to this question in sections 5 and 6 below.

5.3.2 Employment in establishments

Alongside each of the population censuses of 1937 and 1947, censuses of industrial and commercial establishments were undertaken. Besides manufacturing, the census covered mining and quarrying, electricity, gas and water distribution, and certain small services, including hairdressing, laundry, etc. Certain Government establishments, on the other hand, were not included; neither were any Allied military establishments and their industrial activity. Employment figures in the 1937 and 1947 censuses refer only to hired labour and do not include owners and their relatives. In addition to these censuses, censuses of industrial production were made in 1944, 1947, in each second year from 1950 to 1956, and annually from 1956 onwards. Since 1960 quarterly censuses of industrial production have been carried out. All these production censuses cover the same industries as the censuses of establishments, with the exception of services such as hairdressing, laundry, and repair shops. Furthermore, after 1952 the production censuses cover only establishments employing 10 persons or more; in the production censuses "persons employed" are defined as wage earners and salaried employees plus working owners and unpaid members of the family.

Owing to changes in definitions and so on, all figures for the very small establishments (1–9 persons) are highly uncertain. In table 5.7 we have given figures for the number of these establishments, but when it came to employment figures for them we gave up. Instead, we have calculated employment in establishments with 1–9 persons *plus* persons employed outside establishments proper; this figure was obtained by subtracting the probably quite reliable figures for establishments employing 10 persons and more from the less reliable adjusted population census figures for persons in industrial occupations. The significance of this residual is certainly questionable, but we have used it – with all its shortcomings – as an expression for the size and development of employment in very small-scale industry, i.e. handicrafts. It will then be seen that while employment in very small-scale industry increased by only 42 per cent from 1937 to 1960, employment in the rest of industry increased by 136 per cent. Between 1947 and 1960, the difference is less pronounced. Very small-scale industry increased its employment by 13 per cent against 45 for the rest of industry. For very small-

TABLE 5.7

Establishments and employment in industry, 1937–60

Year	Number of recorded establishments in thousands			Number of persons employed in thousands		
	Employing 1–9 persons	Employing 10 persons and more	Total	In recorded establishments employing 10 persons and more	In recorded establishments employing 1–9 persons and outside recorded establishments	Total
1937	89.3	2.7	92.0	153	287*	440*
1947	130.2	3.4	133.6	249	361*	610*
1960	84.0	3.4	87.3	361**	409	770

* Including persons employed in industrial occupations by Allied forces.
** Including 34 000 workers estimated to be employed in Government establishments; the number of these establishments is small and no correction has been made for this in the number of establishments. No adjustment was made for owners and unpaid relatives; for establishments employing 10 persons and more this would amount to less than one per cent of the total number employed.

SOURCE   Total number of persons employed: population censuses, see table 5.5. Total number of establishments: 1937, census of establishments; 1947, census of production; 1960, census of establishments. Data on establishments employing 10 persons and more; 1937, census of establishments; 1947, cencus of production; 1960, census of production. The figures in the penultimate column are obtained as residuals.

scale industry the results are, however, seriously distorted, because they include people employed by the British Forces in 1937 and 1947. Deducting, again for the sake of argument, 20 000 in 1937 and 60 000 in 1947 the rate of increase of employment in very small-scale industry becomes 13 per cent for 1937–47 and 36 per cent for 1947–60. The picture of stagnation in small-scale industry is clearly wrong, although it has increased less than the rest of industry. The expansion in small-scale industry seems to have taken place outside establishments proper, as a natural consequence of the population pressure.

5.3.3 Employment and value added by size of establishment

A comparison of table 5.8 with table 5.7 shows that the increase in industrial employment has been most marked in the biggest and in the smallest establishments, and outside establishments proper.

Information concerning the distribution of establishments and employment in establishments employing 10 persons and more does not exist for years before 1952. It is difficult to judge whether the tendency for big enterprises to dominate the development of employment is of recent origin or whether it goes back to the pre-war period. For 1937–47 the increase in employment in small-scale industry was modest, but at the same time the increase in the number of establishments for 1937–47 must have taken place through an

TABLE 5.8

Industrial employment by size of establishments, 1952–60

| | Establishments employing | | | | | | | |
| | 10–49 persons | | 50–499 persons | | 500 pers. and over | | Total | |
	Number of establ.	persons employed*	Number of establ.	persons employed*	Number of establ.	persons employed*	Number of establ.	Persons employed*
1952	2 734	53	633	90	78	130	3 445	273
1960	2 583	58	682	98	103	171	3 368	337
1961	—	—	676	101	121	196	—	—

* Figures given in thousands.

SOURCE   Censuses of production. Government establishments are not included; the 1961 figures date from before the big nationalizations of that year.

increase in the number of establishments with 10–499 persons; whereas this group shows a decline in numbers for 1952–60. Also the average number of persons per establishment in establishments with more than 10 persons increased much more rapidly from 1937 to 1947, when the average rose from 58 to 87, than from 1947 to 1960, when it rose only from 87 to 97 (or about 106 if Government establishments are included). For 1961 and after only quarterly censuses of production are available covering establishments with 50 employees and more. It seems that in 1960–61 the increase in employment is concentrated in big establishments with 500 employees and more.

From an employment point of view, small-scale industry is in any case still predominant. More than half the population occupied in industry is to be found in establishments with 1–9 persons and outside establishments proper. On the other hand, the concentration in big establishments is noteworthy, too; almost one fourth of the population occupied in industry is employed in establishments with 500 employees and more. And it is in these two extreme groups that the employment increase takes place. For obvious reasons the big establishments are of even greater importance when the contribution to production, measured in terms of value added, is considered. In big establishments value added per person will normally be larger than in small establishments.

If it is assumed that Government establishments are mainly big ones employing more than 500 persons, it will be seen that the big establishments,

TABLE 5.9

Gross value added by size of establishments, 1960

Establishments employing	Number of establish- ments	Persons employed (in thousands)	Av. number of persons employed per establ.	Gross value added £E millions	Gross value added per pers. empl. £E
Under 10 persons	83 969	409	—	97	238
10–49 persons	2 583	58	22	16	281
50–499 persons	682	98	144	43	441
500 persons and over	103	171	1.660	111	650
Government est.	...	34	—	18	526
Total	87 337	770	—	286	360

SOURCE   Total number of establishments, see table 5.7 and 5.8. Details of establishments with 10 employees and more, 1960 census of production, provisional figures.
Persons employed, see table 5.7 and 5.8. The class "under 10 persons" includes people employed outside establishments proper. No average number of employees has therefore been given for the class under 10 persons or for the total. Government establishments: number of establishments is unknown to us. Value added acrued in Government establishments, see *General Frame of the 5-Year Plan*, p. 162. In the financial year 1959/60 wages and salaries paid by Government establishments amounted to £E 5.9 mill. Average annual wage per employee in large establishments was £E 171 according to the 1960 census of production. On this basis the number of employees in Government establishments was estimated by us to be about 34 000. Note that all figures for the class "under 10 persons" are residuals.

which together employ 27 per cent of all persons occupied in industry, produce about 47 per cent of total value added. Very small-scale industry, employing 53 per cent of those engaged in industry, produces only 34 per cent of value added. This suggests an average productivity of labour two to three times larger in big establishments than in small; which does not, however, prevent small-scale industry from being important as far as production is concerned.

5.4 The stock of capital and the capital-output ratio in industry

The problem of capital in agriculture did not offer many difficulties, for although a good deal is invested there, real capital takes on a few specific, quite homogeneous forms which are relatively easy to measure physically, such as fertilizers, canals and drains, pumps, etc. The various items of capital can therefore be dealt with individually, and there is no need to work with an aggregate comprising all real capital. It is otherwise in industry, where productive equipment is infinitely more differentiated, even in a relatively new industry such as the Egyptian. In defining and measuring aggregate capital one comes up against well-known difficulties, which are certainly no fewer in Egypt than elsewhere. Also the role played by real aggregate capital in the process of growth is quite uncertain and not very well understood. In spite of all this, we found it necessary to try to measure the size and development of industrial capital. In doing so we have used three different methods, and although the results do not coincide very well, and are open to many kinds of criticism, many of which we are ourselves only too well aware of, they may give a true idea of the trend. The results, together with a brief description of the methods of calculation, are given in table 5.10.

The various estimates give an increase of physical capital in industry of from 169 per cent to 306 per cent between 1939 and 1960; three of the estimates agree upon an increase of about 200 per cent. All the estimates have this in common, that by far the largest part of the increase has taken place between 1950 and 1960; part of the quite substantial industrial investments during the second half of the 'forties was used to make up for the fall in the stock of capital during the war period.

Concerning the capital-output ratio, a 200 per cent increase in the real stock of capital together with a 235 per cent increase in industrial production (see table 5.2) points to a fall in the capital-output ratio of about 10 per cent. A comparison of the value of the stock of capital (estimate A) and the value of industrial value added suggests a fall in the capital-output ratio from about $3\frac{1}{4}$ in 1939 to about 2.5 in 1960; since the capital value figures found are book-values the latter figure may have to be raised to about 3. In the study of the incremental capital-output ratio mentioned in chapter 1 a figure of almost 3 was found as an average for the period 1945 to 1962/63 for the economy as a whole. All these circumstances taken together show that our capital estimates are not completely out of touch with realities.

TABLE 5.10

Capital estimates for industry

	Estimate A			Estimate B				Estimate C
	£E millions		Index at	Alt. 1.	Alt. 2.	Alt. 3.	Alt. 4.	Index
	current prices	1939– prices	1939–pr. 1939 = 100	1939 = 100	1939 = 100	1939 = 100	1939 = 100	of h.p. 1939 = 100
1939	50	50	100	100	100	100	100	100
1950	200	53	106	180	164	149	132	130
1952	...	...	...	219	198	177	156	152
1960	700	152	304	406	354	301	269	295

NOTE   *Estimate A* is based on figures for financial capital invested in establishments with more than 10 employees, see production censuses; on information about long-term capital invested in joint stock companies, and estimates of the market values of shares in such companies, see *Economic Bulletin,* NBE 1959, and earlier issues, and *Annuaire Statistique,* 1959, tableau XI, p. 356 ff., and corresponding tables in earlier issues; and finally on information about capital invested in certain Government establishments, see *Annuaire Statistique,* several issues. Deflation by the Wholesale Price sub-index for Industrial Products and Materials.

Estimate B was made by the flow of capital goods method. Two different base values for 1939 were chosen and real gross investments, less depreciations, were cumulated yearly to obtain the capital values at fixed prices for subsequent years. Investment figures are from tables in National Planning Commission; deflation by the Wholesale Price sub-index for Industrial Products and Materials. Rates of depreciation alternatively 5 per cent and 7 per cent of stock of capital. The values for base capital and rate of depreciation respectively are in Alt. 1 £E 30 million and 5 per cent, Alt. 2 £E 30 million and 7 per cent, Alt. 3 £E 40 million and 5 per cent, and Alt. 4 £E 40 million and 7 per cent. The base capital values were set lower than the value found in estimate A because estimate B does not include inventories.

Estimate C is an estimate of the total number of installed horsepower, from information in *Annuaire Statistique,* several issues, *Basic Statistics,* Dept. of Statistics and Census, 1960, and *Development of Manufacturing in Egypt, Israel and Turkey,* UN, New York 1958. The estimate consists of the installed h.p. of all licensed non-electrical machines in industrial establishments plus the h.p. of electrical power stations. The three estimates are independent, apart from the common deflator used in A and B.

5.5 The development of productivity in industry

5.5.1 Productivity of labour and capital, 1937–60

In the preceding sections we have dealt with the development of industrial production together with the development of the two factors of production, labour and capital. Table 5.11 gives a summary of these findings for the years 1939, 1947 and 1960. Some interpolation has been necessary to make this table, but it is not on the whole considered to give rise to much uncertainty. The years 1937 and 1947 were chosen for very much the same reason as in the corresponding summary tables for agriculture (see tables 3.14 and 3.15): these are the years of the censuses. In the case of capital, several divergent calculations were made in section 5.4. Here we have chosen to use the horsepower measure, partly because it happened to coincide with two other calculations of the increase and partly because statistically it is probably the most sound of our capital estimates. In table 5.12 we have then

TABLE 5.11

Production and factors of production in industry 1937–1960

Year	Index of total production	Labour input			Capital (number of h.p. installed)	
		Number of persons		Number of hours worked, Index	in thousands	Index
		in thousands	Index			
1937	100*	440	100	100	762**	100
1947	154	610	139	139	799	105
1960	335	770	175	166	2 246	295

* According to M. A. Anis, op. cit. p. 684, output of manufactures remained about constant in 1937, 1938 and 1939.
** 1939.
SOURCES   For total production, number of persons and number of h.p., see above. For number of hours worked per week, see below.

TABLE 5.12

Average productivity of labour and capital, 1937–60

Year	Per employed person	Per hour worked	Per unit of capital (h.p.)
1937	100	100	100
1947	111	111	147
1960	191	202	114

NOTE   The inclusion in 1937 and 1947 of those employed by the British military forces among the number of persons employed overestimates the 1960 figures per employed person and per hour worked slightly by about 5 per cent, and makes the 1947 figures somewhat too low. But this qualification does not disturb the main picture.

calculated – on the basis of the figures given in table 5.11 – the development of the average productivities of labour and capital in terms of real gross output[14]).

The development differs in many respects from that of agriculture. Industrial production increased over the whole period 1937–60, although the largest part of the increase took place in the second half of the period. Employment, too, increased over the whole period, but with the largest increase in the first half. Capital, finally, was about the same size in 1947 as in 1937, but after 1947 grew rapidly, and by 1960 had reached a size which makes the total percentage increase in the stock of capital from 1937 to 1960 almost the same as the increase in production. Remarkable shifts in capital intensity seem therefore to have taken place during the period. Dividing the index of horsepower installed by the index of persons in industrial occupation, we get the following figures for capital intensity in industry.

TABLE 5.13

Capital intensity in total
industry

Year	Index
1937	100
1947	76
1960	169

The note to table 5.12 applies here, too, mutatis mutandis.

After a drop in capital intensity, i.e. capital per person employed, from 1937 to 1947 – a drop caused perhaps by increased utilization of capacity and the erection of a lot of small labour-intensive shops supplying the Allied Forces, and profiting from the general shortage of goods during the war – capital intensity more than doubled from 1947 to 1960, to reach a level almost 70 per cent above that of 1937. Post-war investment has been to a large extent in relatively capital-intensive establishments. However, capital intensity is still low in Egyptian industry. In 1960 it may have approached £E 7–800 per person employed for the whole of manufacturing industry, and £E 1500 per person employed for establishments employing 10 persons and more. In an industrialized country like Sweden, the corresponding figure

---

[14]) Note that what is here called "average productivity of capital" is the inverted value of the so-called "capital-output ratio".

for the whole of manufacturing industry might be about £E 3000 per person employed. There is also no doubt that at the end of the 'fifties there was a good deal of excess capacity in certain industries.

As an arithmetical consequence of these shifts in capital intensity, the figures for average productivity are relatively higher for capital than for labour in 1947, and relatively higher for labour than for capital in 1960. It is interesting, however, that both in 1947 and 1960 the average productivities are higher for both labour and capital than in 1937. From 1937 to 1947 the increase in production was accomplished almost exclusively by an increase in employment; capital seems to have been almost unchanged. As a natural result, in accordance with general production theory, the average productivity of capital rose by 47 per cent. The average productivity of labour rose also, but only by 11 per cent. In addition to margins of error in the productivity estimates, this may be explained by increasing returns to scale, falling short-term marginal costs, or technical progress. From 1947 to 1960 the average productivity of labour (measured by hours of work) almost doubled, while at the same time the average productivity of capital seems to have fallen heavily. This is in full conformity with the idea of decreasing returns to factors of production, but has no implications with respect to the question of returns to scale or technical progress.

Finally, we observe that from 1937 to 1960 the average productivity of both labour and capital increased; but while average labour productivity doubled, we find an increase of only 14 per cent for capital. That labour productivity increased much more than the productivity of capital is again a simple arithmetical consequence of the increase in capital intensity, but the fact that even average capital productivity could increase can only be explained once more by increasing returns to scale or technical progress. Both of these factors may have been at work.

5.5.2 Growth rates of productivity, 1937–1960

On the basis of the figures in table 5.12 we have calculated the growth rates of productivity in table 5.14. As a check on the calculations we have also calculated the growth of labour productivity 1952–60 for establishments with 10 employees and over, by relating employment in such establishments according to the production census to the production index in table 5.2. These two sets of figures are not quite comparable, because the production index includes some production in enterprises with less than 10 employees. The employment figures from the population censuses, on the other hand, include some employees whose production is not included in the production index. We have therefore good reasons for believing that the "true" figures for productivity growth for the 'fifties lie between the figures for 1947–60 and those for 1952–60. These two sets agree very well[15]).

We have already discussed the main causes behind the development of the productivities. That for the period as a whole the increase in average productivity of capital is less than the increase in average productivity of labour, and is even negative in the sub-period 1947–60, is nothing exceptional or surprising. It is partly an expression of the simple fact that an increased input of capital is the price to be paid for an increased productivity of labour. We found the same in agriculture (table 3.15) and the phenomenon is well known from other countries, although in industry a short-term decline in the average productivity of capital will often be the result of a down-swing in the business cycle, or the appearance of excess capacity for other reasons[16]). Sharply decreasing returns to factors in industry may produce the same

TABLE 5.14

Annual rate of increase in productivity in industry, 1937–60
(per cent, compound)

Year	Per employed person	Per hour worked	Per unit of capital (h.p.)
1937–47	1.0	1.0	4.0
1947–60	4.2	4.7	— 2.0
1937–60	2.8	3.1	0.6
1952–60*	3.5	4.0	—

* Establishments with 10 employees and over.

15) We would draw the reader's attention once more to the problem of employees in British military industrial establishments in 1937 and 1947. Because of this the measured productivity increase for 1937–47 is biased downward and that for 1947–60 upward. The latter bias may amount to 1/2 per cent.

16) The following figures for the US may be of interest, see J. W. Kendrick, *Productivity Trends in the United States,* Princeton 1961, p. 70 and 72, tables 3 and 4.

Annual average per cent rate of change in	Output per unit of Labour input	Capital input
1889–1919	0.8	0.1
1948–1957	3.1	— 0.2

result in spite of an increase in technical knowledge. A falling average productivity of capital alongside an increasing average productivity of labour is therefore not necessarily an indication of bad economic management; on the contrary it may, though not necessarily, of course, be the outcome of an optimum use of capital. The final goal of all economic activity is after all to increase income per *man*. Whether, to attain this goal, the input of capital should be increased more or less rapidly than the total product is increasing is partly a matter of technology, about which a government can do little except pick out the most efficient methods, and partly a matter of the resources available. In any case, even the most efficient technique may necessitate a fall in the productivity of capital. It must be remembered also that a fall in the average productivity of capital is nothing but an increase in the capital-output ratio, which is a phenomenon frequently observed during a process of growth. In the present case it seems fairly clear, however, that excess capacity is partly responsible for the fall in the average productivity of capital.

5.5.3 Productivity under the 5-year plan

The development of productivity during the years 1959/60 to 1962/63 is of special interest, because the period is characterized by heavy industrial investment (compared with the years 1956/57–1959/60 it almost trebled), by the nationalizations of 1961, and by a large employment drive, including a shortening of the working week from 48 to 42 hours in larger establishments from 1961/62. Some problems arise in calculating productivity per hour worked. The number of hours fell by about 2 per cent from 1959/60 to 1960/61, to judge from the wage censuses. For later years statistics are not yet available, but it has been estimated that the "theoretical increase" in number of persons employed owing to the reduction in working hours in

TABLE 5.15

Increase in productivity of labour in industry
1959/60–1962/63 (per cent)

Year	Per person employed	Per hour worked
1959/60–1960/61	7.3	9.5
1960/61–1961/62	0.9	3.0
1961/62–1962/63	0.0	2.1
Average	2.7	4.9

SOURCES   Table 5.6 and Hansen and Mead, op. cit.

the affected industries would be 28 000, corresponding to about 4 per cent of total employment in industry. Applying these figures to the actual figures for employment and production during these years, assuming that the average 4 per cent fall in number of hours since 1961 is evenly distributed over 1961/62 and 1962/63 (the reduction occurred during the year 1961/62 and must therefore also imply a fall in the average for 1962/63 compared with 1961/62), we obtain table 5.15.

For the period as a whole the increase in productivity measured per hour worked is about the same as that in table 5.14 for the years 1947–60, and for 1952–60. So far it would seem that labour productivity is continuing to grow at about the same rate as during the earlier post-war years. Per person the increase in productivity is, of course, lower. The puzzling thing is the very high increase in labour productivity from 1959/60 to 1960/61 and the rather low increases during the following two years. Furthermore, if the whole fall in the number of hours worked actually took place in 1961/62 (we assumed it to be evenly distributed over 1961/62 and 1962/63), the increase in productivity per hour would be 5 per cent from 1960/61 to 1961/62 and nil for the last year. It would seem therefore that growth in labour productivity has fallen off and perhaps even ceased completely during the last two years. Apart from the possibility of errors in the basic statistics, two explanations offer themselves: the employment drive, which began in 1961/62 and which may have led to "under-employment" within the enterprises concerned, and secondly, the nationalizations, which may have influenced productivity. It is certainly too early to judge which factors have been at work here; a much larger volume of statistics will be necessary to appraise the effects of the nationalizations. But it is nevertheless disappointing that the big increase in industrial investment has not led to an increase in the rate of growth of labour productivity[17]).

5.6 *Wages and profits*

Existing statistics do not permit a complete historical survey of how the distribution of income in industry has developed from pre-war years up to to-day. Sufficient is known, however, to make the main picture clear.

---

[17]) If the Government had invested in more labour-intensive techniques than hitherto, the result might have been a fall in average labour productivity – and this fall would have been perfectly rational. But the Government's investment policy has certainly not been to favour labour-intensive projects (see below, chapter 11).

5.6.1 Distribution of value added

The NPC has estimated the distribution of total gross value added in the whole of industry for the year 1959/60. Total gross value added is divided into Wages and Salaries, including salaries attributable to owners and payments to social insurance funds, etc., and Returns to Ownership, which is the residual between gross value added and wages and salaries.

TABLE 5.16

Distribution of income in total industry, 1959/60

£E millions	Wages and salaries*	Returns to ownership	Gross value added	Wages and salaries as per cent of gross value added
Cotton ginning and pressing	1.2	2.7	3.9	30.8
Mines and quarries	3.6	14.9	18.5	19.5
Manufacturing industries	83.5	155.6	239.1	34.9
Electricity and gas	2.9	9.0	11.9	24.4
All industry	91.2	182.2	273.4	33.4

* Including salaries attributable to owners and social insurance payments.
SOURCE   NPC, *General Frame of the 5-Year Plan,* p. 107.

Labour's share is remarkably low; only one third of gross value added is wages and salaries, while two thirds are gross profits[18]). We found the same tendency in agriculture; but it is in sharp contrast to what is usually found in developed countries, where the "normal" is rather two thirds to wages and one third to profits. And it should be stressed that the inclusion of salaries attributable to owners in wages and salaries tends to exaggerate the share of labour. It should also be emphasized that the share of labour has been falling during the last ten years.

For 1952 and 1960 information about gross value added, and its distribution between wages and salaries (not including salaries attributable to owners and social security payments) and profits, was collected in the production censuses for establishments employing ten persons and more.

---

[18]) If we accept the figure for total depreciation given in section 2 below, total net value added becomes £E 238 million, and the share of labour – including salaries attributable to owners – becomes 38 per cent. This figure too is very low, particularly since it includes salaries attributable to owners and social security payments, the latter amounting to 5–10 per cent of all wages and salaries.

Although the figures in tables 5.16 and 5.17 are not directly comparable, they point in the same direction. Labour's share of industrial gross income in 1960 was below one third. In 1952 it was about 40 per cent. Since 1952, therefore, a substantial fall in the share of labour seems to have taken place. This fall is the outcome of the development of money wage rates, industrial prices, and average labour productivity. Wages and salaries per employee in

TABLE 5.17

Development of industrial income distribution 1952–1960;
(establishments employing 10 persons and more, £E millions)

Establishments employing	Wages and salaries*		Profits		Gross value added		Wages and salaries as per cent of value added		Wages and salaries per employee in £E	
	1952	1960**	1952	1960**	1952	1960**	1952	1960**	1952	1960
10– 49 persons	4.7	5.4	4.9	10.0	9.6	15.4	49.0	35.1	88.7	93.1
50–499 persons	9.8	12.2	14.7	29.8	24.5	42.0	40.0	29.0	108.8	130.0
500 persons and over	17.4	29.9	27.3	61.5	44.7	91.4	38.9	32.7	133.8	170.8
Total	31.9	47.5	46.9	101.3	78.8	148.8	40.5	31.9	116.8	145.3

* Not including salaries attributable to owners and social security payments.
** Provisional figures.

SOURCE   1952 and 1960 censuses of production, Department of Statistics and Census.

establishments with more than 10 persons rose by 24.4 per cent from 1952 to 1960, corresponding to an annual increase of 2.7 per cent. At the same time, there was a rise in industrial prices. For this we have two measures (see table 5.3). Industrial wholesale prices rose by 7 per cent, the implicit price index by about 35 per cent, or, annually, 0.9 and 3.9 per cent respectively. Calculating the average productivity per person by applying these two deflators to the nominal value added figures of table 17, we get a productivity increase of 5.0 and 2.0 per cent per year respectively. Productivity increase and price increase together amount in both cases to about 6 per cent per year, compared to a wage increase of 2.7 per cent per year. These developments account for the fall in the share of labour in value added.

For establishments employing 50 persons and more the fall in the share of labour continued in 1961. For such establishments the share of labour in value added was 26.7 per cent in 1960, and 24.4 per cent in 1961.

5.6.2 The rate of profits

To get an idea of the level of profits and their development it is appropriate to calculate net returns (before payment of direct taxes) to capital invested in industry. According to our very uncertain estimates in section 5.4 above, the book value of total industrial capital in 1960 may have amounted to about £E 700 million. Estimated at replacement costs, total capital in 1960 can hardly have exceeded £E 850 million. Total industrial (nominal) gross profits for 1960 may have been about £E 200 million (see table 4.16); in this figure salaries attributable to owners are not taken into account. At a 5 per cent rate of depreciation, total depreciation may be taken to be about £E 45 million and net profits accordingly about 145 million. This leaves us with an annual net rate of return (before payment of taxes) on total industrial capital of 17–18 per cent. There is a wide margin of error in these calculations, but it seems that the rate of profit in Egyptian industry in 1960 was rather high. It seems also that the net rate of return on industrial capital was even higher in 1952; according to available information it was about 20 per cent. The stock of industrial capital has grown more rapidly than profits, which is quite natural.

5.6.3 Money wages, real wages, and wage costs

The modest increase in money wage rates between 1952 and 1960, compared with developments in productivity and prices, has to be judged against earlier figures. Wages seem in fact to have lagged seriously behind profits since the end of the 'thirties. Table 5.18 sets out information about money wages and real wages from before the war to 1962. Money wages are the average weekly earnings of workers in all establishments, including commercial, as found by the semi-annual wages sample surveys that have been held since July 1942. The exclusion of commercial wages does not seem to affect the average significantly, and the pay of salaried employees seems to have followed wages closely. Changes in coverage have taken place during the period, but such changes were not found important [19]). We shall therefore use the overall average weekly earnings for workers as an expression for industrial wages.

Considering first *real wages income,* in the sense of average weekly wages

---

[19]) For a discussion and appraisal of the wage statistics, see "Statistics of Wages and Working Hours in Egypt", *Economic Bulletin,* NBE, 1957, p. 101 ff.

TABLE 5.18

Money and real wages, 1938–1962

Year	Average weekly wages per worker, all establishments		Prices		Real wages income	Real wage costs
	Piasters	Index 1952 = 100	Cost of living 1952 = 100	Industr. prices 1952 = 100		
1938	54–45	29–24	32	23	91–75	126–104
1942	89*	48	59		81	
1943	90	48	77		62	
1944	112	60	88		68	
1945	119	64	93		69	
1946	127	68	91		75	
1947	135	72	89		81	
1948	146	78	89	82	88	95
1949	146	78	88	79	89	99
1950	170	91	93	88	98	103
1951	189	101	101	103	100	98
1952	187	100	100	100	100	100
1953	205	110	93	89	118	124
1954	220	118	91	86	130	137
1955	227	121	90	86	134	141
1956	238*	127	91	97	140	131
1957	232*	124	96	108	129	115
1958	235*	126	96	103	131	122
1959	233*	125	96	104	130	120
1960	236	126	96	107	131	118
1959/60	235*	126	96	106	131	119
1960/61	236	126	97	105	130	120
1961/62	237*	127	96	102	132	125
1962/63						

SOURCES   Average weekly wages: 1942–1955, "Statistics of Wages and Working Hours in Egypt", *Economic Bulletin*, 1957; 1955–59, *Annuaire Statistique*, 1960–61, p. 274; 1960–62, information in the *Department of Statistics and Census*. The average is a simple unweighted average of responding establishments. The two 1938 figures are taken from Ali El Gritly, op. cit. p. 530, and M. A. Anis, op. cit. p. 803. Both authors refer to unpublished official surveys which we have not been able to locate. All yearly figures are averages of beginning, middle and end of year figures except where marked by*, in which information about one or two of these figures has been missing. For cost of living index, see *Economic Bulletin*, NBE, several issues. The cost of living index is a Laspeyres index based on weights from 1939 as chosen by the Director of the Department of Statistics at that time, according to his personal judgement of the expenditure of a middle-class income household in Cairo. The weights do not tally very well with information from the household surveys carried out in subsequent years. The index is based on controlled prices and uses official prices only. Industrial prices: the Wholesale Price sub-index for Industrial Products and Materials; based on controlled prices and uses official prices only.

over cost of living index, i.e. the standard of living of employees, we find a rapid drop at the beginning of the war, with a low point in 1943 at 15–30 per cent below the pre-war level. Real wages income then recovered slowly, and before 1950 regained their pre-war level. A rapid increase then took place in the first half of the 'fifties, and in 1956 real wages income reached a peak 53–87 per cent higher than the pre-war level. Between 1956 and 1957 an increase in the cost of living (arising from the agricultural price policies described in chapter 4) caused a fall in real wages income by about 7 per cent, and at this lower level it remained until 1962, when a slight rise followed the increase in the statutory minimum wage[20]). From 1954 to 1961 real money wages were practically unchanged. No regard is paid here to the profit-sharing scheme introduced when the big industries were nationalized in 1961; from a standard of living point of view his share in the profit should of course be added to the employee's wage. Measured against the total of wages and salaries in industry, the employee's share in the profits may amount to something like 5 per cent[21]). Altogether it seems therefore that in 1962 real wages income in this sense reached a level about 50–80 per cent above the pre-war level, and 80 per cent above the immediate post-war level. It will be recalled that the real wages of agricultural labourers show a smaller improvement compared with pre-war conditions.

From a *wage cost* point of view deflation of money wages by a cost of living index has no meaning. Instead deflation here should be made by means of a selling price index for industry. No such index exists, and we have therefore used (once more!) the Wholesale Prices sub-index for industrial products and materials as a deflator, in spite of its weaknesses, which we have already pointed out (see section 5.2.2). Real costs in this sense seem to have fallen during World War II and were in 1948 10–25 per cent below their pre-war level. Since then they have risen somewhat, but still seem to be on much the same level as before the war, or at most 25 per cent higher. Since the implicit value added deflator showed a much larger increase, there is little doubt that so far real wage costs have not risen significantly above their pre-war level.

------

[20]) The statutory minimum wage was fixed at 10 piasters per day in 1944. From 1950 it was 12½ piaster per day for persons over 18 years. It was raised to 25 piasters per day in June 1962 for industrial workers over 18 years. How many workers were affected by this, and to what extent, is impossible to say. 25 piasters per day corresponds to 150 piasters per week, which is less than two thirds of the average weekly wage. The number of workers affected must therefore be quite limited.

[21]) By the end of May 1962 £E 3.75 million had been distributed.

In any discussion of wages from a cost point of view, the employee's share of profits in the nationalized industries should not be included. Profits are not costs, at least not from a short-run point of view. From a long-run point of view the question is very intricate; here profit-sharing should probably be treated as a tax on distributed profits. The cost of all the new *fringe benefits,* on the other hand, i.e. paid holidays, employers' social security payments, etc., must be included, at least from the point of view of the individual enterprise[22]). Before 1952 fringe benefits were negligible. In that year a Goverment decree introduced paid holidays of 14 days per year after 1 year's work, and 21 days after 10 years continuous work, plus, in establishments with more than 100 workers, 5 public holidays. In the event of sickness, the worker was to receive three quarters of his pay for the first 10 days, half for the next 10 days, and finally 10 days with one quarter of his pay. In 1955 an act decreed that certain publicly administrated insurance and provident funds should be created. The employers' contribution to these funds was fixed at 7 per cent of wage payments, while that of the employees was 5 per cent. A further act of 1958 introduced accident insurance. This system of fringe benefits was revised in 1959, when a Social Security Act raised the social insurance contribution from employers to a total of 10.1 per cent of wage payments. Of this, 5 per cent is paid into an old age pension fund and will for a long time ahead represent compulsory savings[23]). The Labour Code at the same time fixed, unchanged, the number of days of paid holiday but extended the number of public holidays to 7 and the number of days of sickness with pay, at 70–80 per cent of wages, to 180 per year. In 1961, finally, the pension scheme was extended; contributions were raised to 7 per cent from the employee and 17 from the employer.

It is hard to say what these benefits amount to as a percentage of wages in the whole of industry, partly because the laws do not apply to all industrial activity as defined here, and partly because there has in all probability been a good deal of evasion. The 21 days paid holiday since 1959 should in

---

[22]) In principle whatever is gained by the employees from the fringe benefits should be included in real wages income, while the 7 per cent paid by them should be deducted. It is difficult, however, to express in terms of money the exact value of the benefits, one reason being the accumulation of social security funds, which will return to the employees as money payments only after many years. And the security obtained is hard to measure in terms of money.

[23]) From a social point of view such accumulations can hardly be said to represent a cost.

principle amount to something like 7 per cent of wages actually paid. Adding social insurance payments at 10.1 per cent, we have a total of about 17 per cent. But this 17 per cent applies to only part of industry and has only gradually become effective. It seems clear that since the nationalizations in 1961 the provisions of the Labour Code and the Social Security Act have been rigorously applied in all the big industries. If, therefore, we assume that in 1961 the 17 per cent applies to about half the wages paid in all industry, and that it has gradually become effective since 1952, we should find an increase in the cost of fringe benefits for *the whole of industry* from almost nothing in 1952 to about 10 per cent in 1960 (including an estimated 2 per cent for paid sickness), or about 1 per cent increase per year. For the larger establishments the increase has probably been the full 17 per cent, or about 1.6 per cent per year. After 1961 the figure for all industry becomes 13½ per cent and for larger establishments, 24 per cent.

Finally, we must mention the reduction in the number of working hours, which from a cost point of view is of great importance. The Labour Code of 1959 limited the number of hours per week to 48, against the 9 per day worked since 1937, and in 1961 there was a further reduction to 42 per week in certain industries. For the period 1939–47, for which no statistics are available, we shall assume that hours of work were unchanged. From 1947 to 1960 they fell, according to wage statistics, by about 5 per cent, and from 1952 to 1960 by about 4 per cent. Between 1959/60 and 1960/61 the number of hours per week is known to have fallen by about 2 per cent, and between 1960/61 and 1962/63 we have already estimated the fall to be in the region of 4 per cent (see section 5.5.3).

On these assumptions we have constructed table 5.19. Column (1) shows the annual rate of increase in weekly earnings for paid workers. In column (2) we have tried to show the rate of increase in *money wages income* per employed worker by adding for the year 1961/62 the share in the profits of workers in the nationalized industries; and column (4) shows the corresponding changes in *real wages income*. In column (3) we have in the same way tried to estimate the rate of increase in the *money costs per unit of labour input* by calculating money wages per hour worked plus the cost to the establishments of fringe benefits; and column (5) shows the corresponding increase in *real labour costs*. Finally, in column (6) we give the rates of change in productivity per hour worked.

Disregarding the first period, i.e. the years of inflation 1939–47, when money wages rose much more than productivity, while real wages fell (and accordingly rose less than productivity), and the year 1961/62, the general impression given by table 5.19 is that the increase in money wages, money labour income, real labour income and real labour costs have tended to stay within the limit provided by the increase in average labour productivity, while the increase in money labour costs have slightly exceeded the increase in labour productivity. In the period 1959/60–1961/62, i.e. the first two years of the 5-year plan, things changed. In the last year, 1960/61–

TABLE 5.19

Annual rates of change in wages and productivity; all industry, 1939-1961/62
(per cent compound)

	(1)	(2)	(3)	(4)	(5)	(6)
	Money wages, weekly earnings of workers	Money wages, weekly earnings, *plus* share of profit in nat. ind.	Money wages, earnings per hour, *plus* fringe benefit costs	(2) deflated by cost of living index	(3) deflated by wholesale price sub-index for ind. prod.	Productivity per hour
1938-1947	7.9-12.8	7.9-12.8	7.9-12.8	—1.5-+0.9	—3.1-—1.0*	1.0
1947-1960	4.4	4.4	5.5	3.8	3.4	4.7
1952-1960**	2.9	2.9	4.7	3.5	3.9	4.0
1959/60-61/62	0.5	2½-3	4.7	2½-3	6.8	6.2
1959/60-60/61	0.4	0.4	2½	—½	4	9.5
1960/61-61/62	0.4	4½-5½	6½	5½-6½	9.6	3.0

* 1938-1948.
** Establishments with 10 employees and more.

1961/62, both labour income and labour costs, in money and real terms, rose much more than labour productivity, although it must be borne in mind that the labour productivity figures may have been depressed that particular year by disguised unemployment within the establishments. Money wages proper rose very little, by less than half a per cent, but the profit-sharing and the reduction in the number of working hours in certain industries, together with a fall in the price indices applied and the increase in social insurance payments, pushed both real labour income and real labour costs upwards to a level above even a "normal" increase in productivity. In the case of real labour costs the deflator (the Wholesale Prices sub-index) is probably misleading; but it is nevertheless clear that in 1960/61–1961/62 real labour costs rose much more than productivity. This represents a break with earlier years, but it should be realized, on the other hand, that the three events responsible for it – profit-sharing, increased social insurance payments, and the shorter working week – are all of a non-recurring nature. To judge developments in 1962/63 is difficult. As we noted earlier the increase in productivity seems to have been very low that year. But at the same time there was little if any rise in wages, and it is probable that in 1962/63 things returned to their old course, with increases in wage costs staying within the limits of the increase in productivity. However, the figures in table 5.19 tend to hide the effects of profit-sharing, the shorter working week and fringe benefits, in the sense that these measures have been applied mainly in the big industries, while we have measured their effect on all industry. Concerning profit-sharing, we shall return to this later (see chapter 6, section 6.7.2); here we would only mention that the employee's share of the profits has to be considered against the reduction in payments made by the nationalized companies to the previous owners, and since the latter exceeds the former, profit-sharing from any point of view can hardly be considered a burden on the nationalized companies. Concerning the burden of fringe benefits and the shorter working week in 1961/62, we have applied the percentages $13\frac{1}{2}$ and 2[24]) (of total wages) respectively to *all* industry, while these percentages must have been about 25 and 4 for big enterprises and almost nothing for small ones. Taking this into account, it would seem as if the big enterprises had an increase in money labour costs per hour of about 6 per cent annually from 1952 to 1961/62, while small enterprises had an increase of only about 3 per cent during the same period. If we assume, as seems reasonable and is supported by statistics, that the big enterprises had a higher increase in productivity than the small enterprises, the differential in labour-cost increase might have been counterbalanced by a similar differential in productivity increase, and it seems likely that even for the big enterprises the increase in money labour costs remained within the limits of the increase in productivity as an average for the whole period 1952–1961/62. However, since a good part, some 15–20 per cent, of the increase in labour costs in big enterprises took place during 1961/62, it is obvious that for that year, taken by itself, the increase in labour costs was much higher than the increase in productivity, perhaps three or four times higher. But even here 1962/63 will probably show a return to the old development.

---

[24]) Some of the reduction in the working week may have taken place between 1961/62 and 1962/63, as mentioned earlier.

5.7 Company finance and profits disposal

5.7.1 Assets and liabilities

A full survey of industrial finance, business savings, and distributed profits is not possible, since no information is available for the non-incorporated part of industry and for Government industrial establishments. For the greater part of incorporated industry relatively detailed information exists for the period before the nationalizations of 1961, but this information is based on the private book-keeping of the big companies, with all its many pitfalls. Since the nationalizations complete accounts for the companies have not been published. For 88 private industrial companies, assets and liabilities in 1958 and changes since the previous year are given in the following table.

TABLE 5.20

Assets and liabilities of 88 industrial joint-stock companies, 1958 (£E millions)

Assets	1958	Change 1957–58	Liabilities	1958	Change 1957–58
Fixed assets	78.0	+ 4.1	Paid-up capital	81.2	+ 8.4
Stocks	58.7	+ 10.9	Reserves	44.6	+ 3.2
Clients and debtors	37.2	+ 2.9	Provisions	19.0	+ 1.9
Cash	21.0	+ 2.0	Long-term debts	8.3	+ 2.3
Other	12.1	+ 0.3	Bank loans	13.5	+ 2.7
Losses of assets	5.9	+ 1.2	Suppliers and creditors	29.8	+ 0.9
			Other current liabilities	6.4	+ 1.2
			Dividends (to be distributed)	10.1	+ 1.0
Total assets	212.9	+ 21.4	Total liabilities	212.9	+ 21.4

SOURCE   *Economic Bulletin*, NBE, 1959, "Company Finances in the UAR in 1956/57 and 1957/58", pp. 85–104.

Paid-up capital, reserves and provisions amounted to almost the same as the book-keeping value of the fixed assets plus stocks, which partly justifies the method we used in capital estimate A in section 5.4.2. Measured at book-values, we find that of the total assets about two thirds (68 per cent) were financed by share capital plus reserves and provisions, which from the point of view of general solidity indicates a good degree of self-finance. The figures for reserves, however, may have been dilated, owing to inadequate depreciation charges [25]), and this would exaggerate the proportion of self-finance.

---

[25]) See thesis presented to the Faculty of Commerce, University of Cairo, 1962: "The Valuation of Industrial Enterprises in the Case of Inflation", by Hosny Hussein El Sayed.

5.7.2 Self-finance and dividends

From a national point of view it is more interesting to see to what extent real investments, in fixed assets and stocks, have been financed by ploughed-back profits. Since there are both real and financial assets, this is strictly speaking a nonsensical question; one cannot say how much of ploughed-back profits has been invested in real assets and in financial assets respectively. Nevertheless, we shall follow the traditional procedure and confront real investments with ploughed-back profits and net change in debts. The result depends very much upon whether we measure investment and profits gross or net. In table 5.21 we have done both.

TABLE 5.21

Real investment and self-finance in 88 joint-stock companies 1957-58 (£E millions)

		Net self-finance	
Net investment in fixed assets and inventories	15.0	(reserves + provisions)	5.1
Re-investment	7.8	Depreciation charges	7.8
		Capital issues and net borrowing . .	9.9
Gross investment in fixed assets and inventories	22.8	Total means of finance	22.8

SOURCE   *ibid.*

Net real investment here consists of the increases in the book-values of fixed assets and stocks; this may have little to do with net investment in a national accounting sense. Net self-finance, measured by the increases in reserves and provisions, amounted to one third of net real investment. Considering in the same way gross real investment and gross self-finance, by adding book depreciation charges to each side, we find a degree of gross self-finance amounting to 57 per cent. That re-investments must be self-financed is obvious; indeed, it is a necessity to avoid distributing paid-up capital and in the long run bankruptcy. A similar analysis for a smaller number of companies for the years 1954–1955 indicates a very high degree of self-financing at that time, net 98 per cent, gross 99 per cent. The fall in the degree of self-financing, apart from purely book-keeping matters, is connected with a simultaneous increase in investments and in dividend payments. An appraisal of the degree of self-finance has, of course, to take into account the size of dividends and the, so to speak, potential capacity for self-financing.

For this purpose we show in table 5.22 the aggregated profit disposal accounts of the companies hitherto discussed.

Against the capital issues and net borrowing of £E 9.9 million (table 5.21) stand dividend payments of £E 10.5 million. In other words, actual gross self-finance *plus* actual dividends could have brought self-finance up to 100 per cent. On the other hand, with private ownership high dividends may be necessary to make people buy new shares in industrial companies. It is worth

TABLE 5.22

Profit account of 88 joint-stock companies, 1958
(£E millions)

Credit		Debit	
Gross profits	22.2	Depreciation	7.8
Other revenues, net	3.7	Provisions	2.9
		Reserves	3.3
		Dividends	10.5
		Carried forward, net loss.	1.4
Total	25.9	Total	25.9

SOURCE   See table 5.21. Taxes included in Provisions.

observing, nevertheless, that industrial net fixed investment in 1958 may have amounted to about £E 25–30 million at current prices, so that the dividends of the companies surveyed here amounted to 30–40 per cent of total industrial net investment.

On the basis of published statistics, it is possible to get an idea of how distributed industrial profits developed from 1952 to 1960. In a selected number of industrial joint-stock companies that operated throughout the period 1952–60 dividend payments increased by 91 per cent[26]. The paid-up capital of these companies increased during the same period by 47 per cent, while total paid-up capital in all registered industrial joint-stock companies increased by 68 per cent[27]. Assuming the same amount of dividend per unit of capital in all companies, total dividend payments would have increased by 118 per cent. According to the production censuses, total value added in industrial establishments increased during the period by 89 per cent only, while total profits increased by 116 per cent (see table 5.17). Company

---

[26] *Economic Review,* CBE 1961, no. 2, p. 221 ff.
[27] *Economic Bulletin,* NBE 1963, p. 154, and *Annuaire Statistique,* 1960–61.

dividends thus seem to have followed the profit development closely, and, like the profits, their share of value added seems to have increased somewhat from 1952 to 1960. Still assuming uniform dividend payments, not only for the companies mentioned above but for all registered industrial companies, we find that total company dividend payments in 1960 may have amounted to £E 16.6 million, that is, about 16 per cent of total profits in industrial enterprises with 10 employees and more. Total net profits in all industrial companies may have amounted to £E 25–30 million in 1960, and company taxes were negligible; gross profits may have been some 10 million higher

CHAPTER 6

Industrialization and industrial policies

6.1 The genesis of Egyptian industry

As in all countries dominated by agriculture, there has in Egypt always been some small-scale handicraft activity in textiles, leather, wood-work, etc., but it is characteristic of modern Egyptian industry that it did not grow organically from this basis. One can imagine a process of growth in which small-scale hand industry slowly grows bigger, and in which demand and supply develop together. The same thing may happen more abruptly if big investments are made simultaneously in a large number of lines of production, so that both demand and supply are created for a broad range of commodities in one big jump, to take advantage of economies of scale, external economies of various kinds, and complementaries. This is the kind of process envisaged by those who favour the doctrine of balanced growth.

Egyptian industrial growth has little in common with such processes. In Egypt when a domestic industry has been built up, a demand for the commodity in question has existed in advance, a demand which up till then had been satisfied by imports from abroad, and which was big enough to offer a market for modern establishments. This is true for all the pioneering modern industries, sugar, cement, cotton-ginning and pressing, spinning and weaving, and chemical fertilizers, which were started and developed before the Revolution of 1952, most of them even before World War II. And it is true also for most of the industries begun after 1952.

What then is the origin of the domestic demand for the products of the pioneering industries? The demand for sugar needs no special explanation, desire for sugar being a fundamental defect in human nature. More interesting is the demand for all the other commodities, for here we have to search for the explanation in the development of agriculture. The large-scale extensions to the irrigation system during the last and the present century, together with the introduction and rapidly expanded cultivation of cotton, an export and cash crop, are the natural explanations of the demand for cotton-ginning and pressing, and for cheap textiles and other simple consumer goods. The expansion in cotton cultivation and the crop-rotation system involved, created, moreover, a rapidly growing demand for chemical fertilizers. While behind the demand for cement lay not only the large works for regulating the Nile and for irrigation, but also the rapid urbanization dating from the 'thirties, which was connected with the agricultural crisis.

We thus find, behind the rise of a monetary demand for industrial products, a special technological and sociological development in agriculture, which gave the farmers cash from abroad and created a need for certain products. We see here how the development of a single export crop, a raw material, provided the impetus for a far-reaching structural change in the whole economy of a backward, primitive agricultural society. Given this demand, which in the 'twenties and 'thirties led to a rapid increase in imports, and given the existence of domestic raw materials for the production of textiles, cement and fertilizers, two other things were needed for domestic industries to arise: protection against foreign competition, and capital. Protection against foreign competition was provided by the Government through the tariff reforms in the 'thirties, and later amendments. Prior to that Egypt had been committed to a free trade policy under which a general *ad valorem* duty of 8 per cent was levied on all imports. Needless to say this policy conformed to British interests. For Britain a cheap, abundant supply of cotton and a market for British manufactured goods were essential. But most probably it was also in the interests of Egypt herself, until the Great Depression, to invest mainly in agriculture. The capital for industrialization came to some extent from abroad, partly tempted by concessions and monopolies granted by the Government, but also from domestic sources, domestic capital being switched to industry in connection with the agricultural disaster in the 'thirties.

The depression of the early 'thirties naturally affected Egyptian industry, but its main impact on the country was a heavy deterioration in the terms of trade, by about 50 per cent. Egypt here shared the fate of all other raw-material producing countries. The shift in terms of trade, with its much larger fall in the prices of cotton and other agricultural products compared to those of imported manufactured goods, itself gave a strong impetus towards increased industrialization; and with the gloomy prospects in agriculture compared to industry, it was natural not only that domestic capital should switch from the land to industry, but also that the efforts of the Government to meet the depression should take in part the form of in-

creased support to industry, in particular through loans to industrial enterprises. At that time the All-Egyptian Bank Misr embarked on the creation
of a large number of big industrial establishments, financed exclusively by
domestic capital, ranging from the ginning, spinning and weaving of cotton,
silk and linen, to leather manufactures and motion pictures. The bank, which
played a vital role in the early industrialization of Egypt, also acted as intermediary in extending government loans to industrial enterprises.

The early industrialization of Egypt thus proves quite clearly that price-
mechanisms do work in underdeveloped countries, at least when they are
monetized to the extent that Egypt was before the Great Depression.
Whether they work sufficiently rapidly is another matter, of course.

6.2 The protection of industry in Egypt

We have already noted that after 1930 Egypt's foreign trade policy became
protectionist. During the 'thirties higher, in some cases very high, duties
were imposed on competitive goods such as cotton piece goods, cement,
matches, refined sugar, alcohol and cigarettes; and both before and during
World War II the tariffs were raised several times, both for protectionist and
fiscal reasons. Although the tariffs were differentiated, so that raw materials
and capital goods were taxed less than finished consumer goods, the tariff
system was influenced by fiscal considerations. From the beginning of the
'fifties, however, it becomes wholly protectionist. Duties on machinery and
raw materials not competing with Egyptian raw materials were lowered or
abolished completely, while tariff rates for competing manufactures, and
so-called non-essential goods were subsequently raised. At the same time
essential foodstuffs, etc., were exempted from duty in order to keep down the
cost of living and money wages, and hence the cost of production.

When tariffs are not uniform, but vary from commodity to commodity,
it is impossible to give a single unambiguous quantitative expression for the
"degree" of protection. The usual approach is to measure the average
level of tariffs, i.e. total customs duties collected over total import value,
and use this average as a measure. This method has many shortcomings, and
in the case of Egypt it does not work at all. Applying it, we find no increase
in the average level of tariffs from 1952 to 1961. While total imports rose
from £E 222.9 million to £E 243.7 million, total import duties fell from
£E 31.1 million to £E 29.1 million. This result arises, on the one hand, from
the shift in tariff policy towards the abolition of tariffs on capital goods,

raw materials and essential foodstuffs, and increased tariffs for manufactured "non-essential" goods and luxuries; and, on the other, from the fact that the Government, through its import-licensing policy, has expanded imports of the first "essential" group of commodities and limited the second. From total imports we have therefore deducted capital goods, raw materials, and "essential" consumer goods and in this way arrived at a residual group labelled "other imports", which may be compared with total import duties.

TABLE 6.1

Total import duties and "other imports" (£E millions)

Year	Total import duties	"Other imports"	Total import duties as percentage of "other imports"
1952	31.1	44.5	69.9
1959	28.8	22.0	130.9
1961	29.1	25.6	113.6

NOTE   Total import duties are here defined as the sum of import duties, *ad valorem* duties, quay duties, sundry duties, and additional duties, as recorded by the Customs Department; see *The Federation of Egyptian Industry*, July 1962, p. 92. Tobacco duties are not included.

Although the level of tariffs for "other imports" is in fact very high at present, the figures in the table exaggerate the level. Some of the duties in 1961 were still being paid on the "essential" group of imports. On the other hand, the figures understate the increase in the level of tariffs for "other imports"; a larger proportion of the duties were collected from the "essential" group in 1952 than in 1961. The increase by about two thirds in the average level of tariffs shown by the table may therefore underestimate the increase in the degree of protection afforded to industry by the tariff system. Since the so-called essential goods are to a large extent agricultural (wheat) and compete with Egyptian agriculture, the changes in the tariff system mean that the protection of agriculture through tariffs has ceased almost completely.

Another and probably much more powerful method of protecting domestic industries has been exerted during the last ten years through the licensing of imports. After a period with almost free imports from 1947 to 1952, varous systems of import control have been applied, and the tendency has been to make it more and more comprehensive. The policy has been to prevent the import of commodities which could technically be produced within the country, and shift imports to "essential" foodstuffs, raw materials and capital goods, in that order of priority.

6.3 Cotton policies and the textile industry

The Egyptian cotton textile industry is obliged to use domestic high-quality, long and medium staple cotton as its raw material[1]). The import of cheap, short-staple cotton from abroad has always been forbidden[2]), and as the capacity of the spinning factories has increased the import of foreign, short-staple yarns has been cut down to nothing. This means relatively high costs and high prices in the domestic market, where the low standard of living of the majority of the population would make cheaper qualities more appropriate. During the 'fifties the increasing capacity of the cotton textile industry exceeded what was necessary to satisfy domestic demand for both yarns and fabrics, and the industry began to increase its exports rapidly. In the export markets, however, Egyptian goods have had difficulty in competing with the cheap products, based on short-staple cotton, of the Asiatic textile industries of Hong-Kong, Japan, Malaya, India and Pakistan. At the same time, the markets for fine quality cotton textiles in Europe and USA have to a large extent been closed, owing to protectionist measures there, codified in the World Textiles Agreement sponsored by GATT.

These problems have been partially solved by Government support to the textile industry. Direct subsidies and sales of raw cotton from the ECC below the ruling market prices have been made on several occasions, but the main device during the post-war period has been the export tax on raw cotton. We have already discussed this tax and its possible rationale in chapter 4, section 4.4. From the point of view of the domestic textile industry its importance is to push world market prices for long staples upwards, which means higher raw material prices for foreign spinners of fine quality

---

[1]) Actually the industry uses mainly lower qualities of Egyptian cotton for domestic purposes. But low quality Egyptian cotton is high quality compared with many foreign short staple cotton varieties and qualities.

[2]) In 1963 an agreement was made with the USA-Government about sales to Egypt of cotton within the frame of P.L. 480. The cotton concerned was, however, old Egyptian cotton which had been bought by the USA in connection with the Korean crisis and stored in the USA for strategical reasons.

yarns, and keep the raw material prices of the domestic industry down; both *vis à vis* the domestic market and *vis à vis* foreign competitors, the export tax served in this way as a measure of support for the domestic industry. In spite of this, the raw material costs of the Egyptian textile industry were higher than those of the foreign industries consuming short staples, while *vis à vis* the European and American protection of their own fine textile production the relatively low raw material costs in Egypt have had little importance; low costs do not help to break down foreign import quota barriers – the effect may even be the opposite.

Since the end of the 'fifties cotton policies have changed substantially. Export taxes on raw cotton have become lower and have even disappeared for most varieties; and since the nationalization of the cotton trade (see chapter 4, section 4.7), the situation is that in producing for home consumption the domestic industry pays a higher price for raw cotton than the export price, while in producing for export the only advantage the domestic industry has *vis à vis* foreign spinners is a low raw cotton export tax on a few varieties. For these reasons the textile industry, which considering its low wages and relatively high technical efficiency should in principle be competitive, needs protection in the domestic market against cheap quality competition from abroad, and experiences difficulty in the fine quality export market. In the export market the difficulty now seems to be mostly due to foreign protection. The export of yarn has in fact increased rapidly during the last five years, and some improvement in export possibilities may be achieved by Egypt's joining GATT and the World Textiles Agreement; but there is no doubt that protectionism in Western Europe and the USA is the main hindrance to Egyptian textile exports at present.

Policies concerning the buying price of raw cotton for the domestic industry must, of course, be appraised as part of general cotton policy. If cotton textile goods were not exported at all, general welfare considerations would suggest that raw cotton should be sold for domestic consumption at a price equal to the marginal revenue obtained from sales abroad, and to an extent determined by the consumers' free choice between cotton at that price and other goods. This would result automatically if the total raw cotton supply had been limited only by the application of an export tax of appropriate size. Since this has not usually been the case, what we can say in general is that the marginal revenue from cotton sales abroad must have been lower than the export price less export tax. It is obviously not possible, then, to find support in general welfare ideas about optimum allocation of resources for a policy which keeps domestic prices *higher* than export prices. The higher consumer prices may even be taken as an indication of inoptimal resource allocation.

In this connection mention should also be made of the possibility, often advocated by critics of past and present policies, of exporting a larger amount of Egyptian cotton and importing short-staple cotton for domestic use. Disregarding the deterioration in the quality of domestic goods which this might imply, such a policy would pay from a national point of view only if the import price of short-staple cotton were lower than the marginal revenue from selling more Egyptian cotton abroad. Since the marginal revenue is certainly lower than, and at most equal to, the export price less the export tax, and may be considerably lower, depending upon the elasticity of foreign demand at the ruling export price, the rationality of the present policy of not importing short-staple cotton for domestic purposes cannot be ruled out *a priori*. But then, disregarding costs other than raw material costs, cotton textiles should be sold to domestic consumers at prices lower than competing foreign cotton textiles produced from short-staple cotton.

We would not wish to press this argument too hard, however. The policy may have been designed to counteract an overvaluation of the domestic currency. And instead of considering the difference in the price of raw cotton for export and for domestic use simply as an encouragement to exports, it may be looked upon as part of the general system of direct and indirect taxation motivated by a host of policy targets, amongst which income re-distribution may have played an important role. This again may make the resource allocation problem much more complicated than our previous reasoning might suggest. But we would stress that there *is* a serious resource allocation problem involved in the price policies of the ECC *vis à vis* the domestic textile industry, and it is not apparent that sufficient attention has been paid to it.

6.4 *Other government supports; the industrialization plans*

Besides supporting domestic industry in a general way through customs duties and licensing, and in addition to its handling of the special problems of the textile industry that we have been discussing, the Government has promoted industries by a variety of other methods, such as direct subsidies, tax exemptions, which are discussed in chapter 9, cheap loans, bulk purchases, etc. As an example we can take the rubber and tyre factory built in 1956. Besides providing the necessary protection against foreign competition, the

Government secured cheap loans for the investment, guaranteed the sale of the whole production, provided certain quality requirements were fulfilled, and exempted the company from profits tax. Many similar examples could be taken from the years before the nationalizations in 1961. After that most investments have been in a certain sense Government supported.

Of special interest are the Government's own industries, which were important even before the nationalizations of 1961. Apart from the traditional public utilities, these were mainly military factories. During the British occupation a certain amount of industrial activity was concerned with supplying the British and American armies. Little is publicly known about this activity and here it is considered as belonging to foreign territory. After the evacuation of the British troops, national military factories, usually of relatively large size and very modern and capital-intensive, grew up rapidly. Their production was at first reserved exclusively for the Egyptian Army, but eventually these factories, many of which are metal-manufacturing, took up civil products, in particular durable consumer goods. Begun originally as non-market enterprises, they have been important also in training a large staff of skilled workers and engineers, upon which other industries have been able to draw.

After 1957 the Government co-ordinated its efforts for industrialization in the *First Five Year Industrial Plan,* covering the period 1957–1961. A special Ministry of Industry was established, and various public organizations formed to implement the plan, under which about £E 330 million were to be invested in industrial projects. This would have amounted to something like doubling the level of gross industrial investment, and maybe trebling net industrial investment, at that time. The investments actually made, however, were only about two thirds of the planned amount. After 1960/61 the Industrial Plan was incorporated into the general 5-Year Plan, to which we shall devote a special chapter; we postpone discussion of the Industrial Plan till then.

6.5 The infant industries and their competitiveness

The pioneering Egyptian industries were thus typically *infant industries;* at the given exchange rate and variable costs, notably wages, they would propably have run at a loss without protection[3]). And the same holds for most

---

[3]) Exceptions did exist, for instance the famous Egyptian cigarette industry, which until

of the industries built up since World War II. Almost always we find the same picture: a domestic demand, met by imports; then, protection against competition from abroad plus capital investment in the field – and an industry is born.

It is one thing to create infant industries. It is quite another, however, to make the infants mature. Here the development of industry in Egypt offers another interesting illustration of the process of industrial growth. It seems quite clear that to-day the pioneering industries have in fact grown to maturity. As early as 1954 a United Nations report found that "among the industries which could probably dispense with protection are most minerals, fertilizers, cement, vegetable oils, soap, leather products, cigarettes and some food-processing industries[4]). Also the largest single industry, textiles, was already at that time judged competitive from a technical efficiency point of view, considering the wage level[5]); here, however, the special factors connected with cotton policy made protection necessary. Since then the competitiveness of some of these industries has shown itself in increasing exports.

It is not difficult to understand how the pioneering infant industries slowly grew mature and competitive. First, they were started in fields in which Egypt had obvious comparative advantages; all that had to be overcome were certain initial difficulties. This is true for probably all the raw-material based industries. It is not true, unfortunately, for all the industries started in later years, where inadequate investment criteria, a matter that is discussed in chapter 11, have led to the establishment of some highly doubtful undertakings, the Nasr motor works being perhaps the most notorious example.

Another explanatory factor is the favourable development of wage costs in Egyptian industry. We studied this question in the preceeding chapter and found that, with the exception of the year 1961/62, the increase in money labour costs had for a long time remained within the increase in labour productivity. Another important factor is the gradual depreciation of the Egyptian pound, by about 20 per cent from 1952 to 1962. These factors suggest improved competitiveness though they do not definitely prove it. For a more definite proof comparisons with costs and productivity in other, competing countries, taking into account alterations in rates of exchange,

---

the end of the 'twenties had a big market abroad; it was knocked out by the American "blended" types.

[4]) *Economic Development in the Middle East, 1945–54,* Supplement to World Economic Report, 1953–54, United Nations, New York, 1955, p. 40.

[5]) Ibid. p. 41.

have to be made. Table 6.2 brings together some information about the increase in hourly output per worker, hourly wage earnings, and money wage costs per unit of output in manufacturing industry, together with the export prices of manufactured goods in some important, highly industrialized countries in Europe and America. For the sake of comparison, we have

TABLE 6.2

Wage costs and export prices for selected countries, manufacturing industries, 1955–1961
(annual average increase, per cent)

	Output per hour of work	Hourly wage earnings	Wage costs per unit of output (national curr.)	Wage costs per unit of output (US dollars)	Export prices of manufactured goods (US dollars)
USA	2¾	3½	¾	¾	2¾
UK	2¼	6	3½	3½	2
The Six (EEC)	4½	7¾	3	−¼	1
Egypt	4¼	3½	−¾	−2½-3	—

SOURCE   For USA, UK and The Six: *Economic Review*, no. 21, August 1962, p. 30, table 7, National Institute of Economic and Social Research, London 1962.

calculated the corresponding figures for hourly money wage costs (not including fringe benefits) per unit of output for Egyptian manufacturing industry.

Concerning the increase in average productivity, i.e. output per hour of work, Egypt seems to be above both the USA and the UK and only slightly below, perhaps equal to, the six EEC countries. Turning to the hourly wage earnings, we find that the increase in Egypt is at the same level as in the USA and only half that in the UK and the Six. This implies that wage costs per unit of output must have developed favourably in Egypt compared with the USA, the UK and the Six. This is also clear from the third column, which shows wage costs per unit of output measured in the national currencies; whereas Egyptian wage costs per unit of output have fallen slightly, American and European costs have risen from ¾ to 3½ per cent per year. To appraise competitiveness, alterations in the exchange rates have also to be taken into account. This has been done in column four, in which the rise in the dollar rate expressed in £E has been taken to be 15–20 per cent (a certain amount of depreciation had already taken place by 1955). Whereas wage costs per unit of output measured in dollars seem to have fallen $2\frac{1}{2}$–3 per cent per year in Egypt, in the Six there was only a slight fall (mainly owing to depreciations of the French franc), and in the USA an increase of $\frac{3}{4}$ per cent, and in the UK $3\frac{1}{2}$ per cent[6]). Even if we disregard the depreciation of the £E, and add the costs[7]) of fringe benefits (other than paid holidays, which have been included in hours per week) Egyptian labour costs per unit of output would have developed in much the same way, i.e. remained more or less unchanged, as in the Six, and be definitely lower than in the USA and in the UK. Taking into account the fact that fringe benefit costs have also risen in Europe and America, we can safely conclude that Egyptian industry, as far as labour costs are concerned, has improved its competitiveness substantially during the last 5–10 years. And it is worth stressing that due regard has been paid to all the cost-increasing labour-market measures taken in Egypt 1961/62. For the year 1961/62, the competitiveness of Egyptian industry may have declined, particularly since the competing industries are the big ones, which bore most of the total increase in costs; but this seems to have been an isolated phenomenon.

It seems then that labour-cost conditions ensuring the soundness of an "infant industry" policy were in fact present in Egypt up to 1961/62. During 1961/62 this was probably no longer so; but in 1962/63 the situation improved again. Whether it will be so in the future depends very much upon the Government's wage policy. As we shall see below, the fundamental state of the Egyptian labour market is such that there is every reason to believe that the favourable development from the 'thirties up till now will continue also in the future, if the labour market is left to itself. However, with a substantial part of industry nationalized, the Government's wage policy automatically comes into the picture.

6.6 *Labour market policies and the falling share of labour*

It is time now to consider in more detail what lies behind the conditions necessary for an "infant industry" policy to succeed, i.e. for infant industries

---

[6]) The Egyptian figures pertain to total industry 1952–1961/62. Calculations for big industry for the period 1955–1961/62 show almost the same result. The larger fall in hours per week in big industry is counteracted by the circumstance that most of the increase in weekly money wages 1952–1961/62 actually took place 1952–1955.

[7]) It is not quite clear to what extent fringe benefits should be included as an element of costs from a social point of view. Pension funds accumulations can hardly be said to represent a social cost, and the same may be true for other insurance fund accumulations.

to become competitive through a favourable development of unit costs compared with competing foreign countries. We have seen that in Egypt it was very much the modest increase in money wages which led to the fulfilment of the necessary conditions. And if money wages developed modestly compared with foreign countries, they did so even more compared with domestic profits. It may be time therefore to discuss also the important fact that emerged in the preceeding chapter; that the share of labour in industrial value added (at factor costs) seems to have fallen sharply since the end of the 'thirties. Our figures for employment, wages, output and prices point to a share of labour, i.e. wages and salaries of about 70 per cent in 1939[8]). By 1952 this share had fallen to about 40 per cent. And in 1960 it was a little more than 30 per cent. In 1961 it seems to have fallen still further, and although the events of 1961/62 must have raised it somewhat, perhaps even to about 35 per cent, it is clear that the share of labour is extremely low judged by all possible standards. This shift in distribution towards profits is of special importance from a development point of view because it suggests the possibility of increasing ploughed-back profits in industrial companies and higher investments, not only in an absolute sense, but also in relation to value added. We find here a mechanism which could have provided accelerated domestic savings to finance increased investments. Many authorities on growth problems have pointed to ploughed-back profits as a powerful way to accelerated growth. However, owing to the dividend policies of the big private companies this mechanism has only functioned to a limited extent (see chapter 5, section 5.7).

6.6.1 The labour market

It is obvious that the falling share of labour and the modest development of money wages are intimately connected and must have a common cause in the conditions under which wages are formed. According to a well-known theory, in overpopulated, underdeveloped countries with disguised unemployment in agriculture, industrial expansion can take place with little or no increase at all in money wages[9]). The low incomes of the agricultural working population tend to fix the level of money wages in industry at a

---

[8]) For 1937–39 Anis, op. cit. p. 811, calculates the share of wages and salaries to be about 60 per cent. For 1945 his figure is 50 per cent.

[9]) See in particular W. A. Lewis, "Economic development with unlimited supplies of labour", *The Manchester School*, 1954.

low level, too. A very rapid expansion of industrial employment may result in a certain increase in agricultural money wages, but as long as there remain reserves of labour in agriculture and in domestic and public service, industrial wages must stay at a low level, and at most increase only slowly.

It is doubtful whether this theory of surplus labour in agriculture, and an unlimited supply of labour, applies to Egypt, although those who favour it have always referred to Egypt as a typical case. The available evidence points to a large *seasonal* surplus of labour in agriculture, as we saw in chapter 3, section 3.2.5, but industrial expansion can not be based on a seasonal surplus, apart from special cases where counter-seasonal industries can be established. Nevertheless, the supply of labour is big. With an annual increase in population of $2\frac{1}{2}$ to 3 per cent, and an almost stationary working population in agriculture, a vigorous expansion in urban occupations is necessary to absorb the annual increase in the supply of labour. And although the Government sector, traffic and construction have all in fact expanded rapidly during the last 10–15 years, industry has not been able to take in the remaining increase in the labour force. In 1957–58 there was some open unemployment in both rural and urban areas – 7 per cent in large cities, 5 per cent in towns, and 3 per cent in villages, according to the labour force surveys[10]) – and although it has fallen it has not disappeared. To this must be added the great attraction which the Government-owned factories, in particular with their pension schemes and other social security arrangements, exert on household servants and other workers in inferior urban occupations.

Even under such circumstances strong trade unions might have been able to push industrial money wages upwards. It is true that the degree of organization is relatively high in Egypt compared with many other underdeveloped countries. In 1958 about 125 000 industrial workers were registered as members of the syndicates. This means that about half the employees in establishments with more than 10 employees were organized. Trade unions are concentrated in the larger establishments; in small-scale industry, which employs half the industrial workers, very few are organized. The number of unions is big, the individual unions small and weak, and the number of collective agreements very limited; but such agreements are legalized and regulated by law. Most contracts between workers and enterprises are still individual. Legal stipulations for such contracts are laid down in labour legislation to protect the workers against abuse, but in spite of this there is

---

[10]) A. M. El Shafei op. cit.

no doubt that – at least until the nationalizations of 1961 – the workers have always been at the mercy of the employers. Feudalism was not limited to agriculture. With weak trade unions and an ample supply of unskilled, illiterate labour, the bargaining position of the employers has always been terribly strong.

Until the nationalizations of 1961 Government efforts to improve money wages were negligible. During World War II statutory minimum wages were introduced and Government proclamations were issued concerning cost of living allowances. But little was done to make them effective until 1961, when the industrial minimum wage was raised and enforced in all the state-owned companies, and after 1962 in many of the remaining private companies, too. Profit-sharing schemes in both the private and public companies should also be mentioned in this connection (for details, see section 7.2 below).

Instead of attempting to improve real wages by raising money wages, the Government has helped to keep money wages down by keeping the prices of elementary consumer goods low. To achieve this it has used price controls, rent controls, the rationing of sugar and kerosene, tariff reductions for imported, essential foodstuffs, and direct subsidies on bread, flour, sugar, etc.[11]). The effect upon the cost of living is clear, though the official index is far from perfect. The index was slightly lower in 1962 than in 1952; and from 1939 to 1962 the cost-of-living index rose by only about 200 per cent, whereas the sub-index for industrial prices and raw materials rose by about 350 per cent. This development in the cost of living is important if one is to understand how money wages could lag so far behind profits without calling forth social unrest. Another important point here may be that the individual worker does not feel this lag. After all, many of the workers come from villages or urban service where wages are considerably lower, and they may thus enjoy a big rise in income on entering industry. Even if industrial real wages had not risen at all each individual worker might in this way have experienced a substantial rise in real income.

Apart from minimum wages and the cost-of-living policy, legislation has hitherto mainly been concerned with general conditions of work, and been directed towards correcting the worst exploitation of defenceless children and adult workers. Objective observers have compared working conditions during the inter-war period to those prevalent in England in the early days of the industrial revolution, so well-known from Friedrich Engels' descriptions.

[11]) For the year 1962/63 the total expenditures on the budget for reducing the cost of living were about £E 50 million. Total private consumption is estimated at £E 1182 million for the same period.

Much progress has been made in this respect. Legislation regulating conditions for children in factories was begun even before World War I, and it is now forbidden to employ children under 12 years in factories. Conditions of work for adult workers have also been improved in many respects, though lack of supervision has often reduced the effectiveness of legal stipulations.

The nationalization of the big industries in 1961 changed the institutional framework in which money wages are determined. With a high proportion, between a third and a half, of all industrial workers employed in public enterprises, Government decisions concerning wages will in future become a dominant factor in industrial money wage development. This does not mean, however, that supply and demand have ceased to influence industrial wages. In the private sector, which still embraces more than half the total number of people employed in industry, supply and demand will continue to play their cruel game; and indirectly supply-and-demand conditions may influence Government decisions, and the extent to which such decisions become effective in individual public enterprises. Even in a socialist economy the managers will usually be interested in buying labour as cheaply as possible. But all this cannot hide the important fact that with the nationalizations of 1961, the Government took over direct responsibility for the future development of money wages, and hence the competitiveness of Egyptian industry. And the need to improve competitiveness continuously fixes very limited margins for the Government's wage policy.

6.6.2 *Capital intensity and labour's share*

It may be thought that the explanation for the falling share of labour lies simply in the increased capital intensity of Egyptian industry (see chapter 5, table 5.21). But increased capital intensity does not necessarily lead to a shift in income distribution in the direction of a higher share for profits. Along with the increase in capital intensity may go a fall in the rate of profit on capital, and the fall in the rate of profit may more than counteract the increased intensity of capital, so that the share of profits remains constant or even declines. This is in fact what seems to have happened in most developed countries. The increased capital intensity may, of course, have influenced the distribution of income in industry, but *a priori* it is impossible to say in which direction[12]).

---

[12]) W. A. Lewis, op. cit. has argued that under conditions of unlimited labour supply the share of profit in *total* national income, (value added) will increase. Here we are, however, discussing the share of wages in *industrial* value added only.

6.6.3 Industrial selling prices

Given the modest development of money wages the development of industrial prices has been extremely favourable to profits. We have already noticed the remarkable difference between the present level of the cost-of-living index and the index of industrial products and raw materials, not to mention the implicit value added deflators for industry; this is probably partly due to index imperfections, but the difference is without doubt also partly real. To some extent it is the outcome of deliberate policy, though it has also something to do with the present tendency all over the world for agricultural products to fall in relation to prices for industrial products.

It is well known that during an *inflation*, which arises from the "demand" side through increased spending on commodities, money wages will tend to lag behind prices; real wages will fall, or at least increase less than productivity. A development of this kind took place during and immediately after World War II. For the period 1947–1952 imports were on the whole free, and whatever inflationary demand-pressures there may have been found an outlet in increased imports rather than rising prices. Prices did actually rise between 1945 and 1952, but this was intimately connected with the rising prices of imported goods, and a rise in prices would probably have taken place even with a domestic deflationary pressure. The rapid increase in imports for this period shows clearly that demand was at a high level. For the period 1952–1960/61 it is more difficult to gauge the general demand-forces at work, owing to increased Government regulations concerning both imports and prices. Finally, during the next two years of the five-year plan, i.e. 1961/62 to 1962/63, it seems clear that a large excess demand for commodities developed because of increased Government spending; once more, however, the result was mainly increased balance of payments deficit rather than rising prices. We shall return to this question, which we have already touched upon in chapter 1.

Since 1952 *import regulations* and *other protectionist measures* against foreign competition, together with certain partial *depreciations* of the domestic currency (see chapter 8), have given Egyptian industry ample opportunity to increase its profit margins. It may therefore be asked whether rising profit margins would not prove that the protectionist measures have been overdone. The "infant industry" policy in particular should only ensure that the new industries are able to run at a "normal" profit, and not necessarily that profits should rise. It is not easy to judge whether the protectionist measures, together with domestic demand, have been kept at an unnecessarily high level since 1952. They may have been; for the pressure from industrialists for more protection was very strong, and the Government was anxious not to prevent industrial growth. Restrictions on profits and price controls have been in existence during the whole post-war period (see below, chapter 10), but to a large extent they have probably been evaded. Rising profit margins may, on the other hand, have been a necessary condition for industrial expansion, as they would be if the supply price of capital to industry were rapidly rising.

The tendency for industrial prices to develop favourably compared with money wages, and for profit margins to increase, is thus easy to explain. Now, if competitive conditions had prevailed in Egyptian industry in spite of the protection against competition from abroad, the lower real wage costs would certainly have led to the use of less capital-intensive methods, and for a given volume of capital employment would have tended to increase. To say, *a priori*, what would then have been the outcome concerning the distribution of value added would be impossible. However, the possibility that the expansion of industry necessitates higher profits owing to the rising supply price of capital in itself points to a relative increase in the share of profits. And, what is probably decisive, competitive conditions have been the exception rather than the rule. As in all other countries, import regulations and other protectionist measures have created domestic monopolies in the commodity markets in Egypt (indeed, protectionist measures have sometimes been taken in order to give an industrialist a monopoly); and this, given the amount of industrial capital, counteracts the tendency towards more labour-intensive methods, in addition to the direct increase in profit margins arising from the increased monopoly power. To this must then be added the fact that in recent years a growing part of investments have been directed by the Government towards highly capital-intensive production. The Government has pursued this policy not so much because of a special preference for capital-intensive methods, but more because it has favoured such commodities as petroleum and steel, in whose production even the most labour-intensive methods available are necessarily very capital-intensive. If then such production is provided with a domestic market at prices which allow "normal", i.e. very high and increasing, profits, the result must of course be a tendency towards a higher share for profits and a lower share for labour.

6.7 The nationalization of industry

6.7.1 Developments before 1961

By a series of Presidential laws and decrees in July 1961, half the country's industry and the whole of its banking and insurance activities, together with the cotton trade and many construction, transport and trading companies were nationalized. July 1961 may therefore be considered as the point in time when the Egyptian economy was decisively changed in a socialist direction. This is not to say that no nationalization had taken place before 1961. On the contrary, the events of 1961 should not be thought of as a sudden break with earlier conditions and policies, but rather as the end-result, for the time being, of a development which began at the time of the nationalization of the Suez Canal. The Suez War in 1956 was followed by the taking over of British and French companies and other economic interests, called Egyptianization. Since a large part of banking and insurance business was in British and French hands, the Suez War in itself actually led to the nationalization of a substantial sector of the business world. With the later take over of the Misr Bank in 1960, and an earlier law of 1957 providing for the full Egyptianization of the insurance market within a maximum period of five years, little was in fact left to be done in the field of banking and insurance when the laws and decrees of 1961 were published. In the industrial field some foreign-owned companies had already been taken over earlier under sequestrations in connection with the Suez War, and for other reasons, and had subsequently become Egyptianized. In 1957 an Economic Development Organization was created, which was empowered to take over Government interests in various joint-stock companies and also to acquire the capital of public enterprises. It was given the right to participate in and establish all kinds of companies, and it did in fact take over part of the share capital of a series of industrial concerns. The investments of the organization in industrial companies already in 1957 amounted to £E 38 million[13]) and grew to £E 49 million in 1960. Besides nationalizing the Misr Bank the Government obtained control over all the companies belonging to the Misr

---

[13]) Forty per cent represented shares handed over to the organization by the Government, while the value of shares acquired through sequestrations of foreign property was 42 per cent. The rest were shares bought in the market. The total capital of the companies in which the organization held more than 25 per cent of the paid-up capital amounted to £E 94 million (nominal value), which may have been about half the total paid-up capital of all the joint stock companies in the country.

concern; a special Misr organization was established in 1960 to run the bank and the many companies belonging to it.

6.7.2 *The nationalizations of 1961*

According to the July decrees 44 companies and establishments, apart from banks and insurance companies, were to be taken over completely by the state, while state partnership to the extent of not less than 50 per cent of the capital was imposed on 82 companies and establishments. In addition to this there were a large number of companies in which the Government took over less than 50 per cent of the shares; and a good many of these were taken over completely in 1963. The shares were to be taken over by the state. Furthermore, it was forbidden for any person or organization to own shares in certain specified companies exceeding a total market value of £E 10 000, the excess to be taken over by the state. Compensation in all three cases was to be paid to the previous shareholders in the form of negotiable Government bonds, maturing after 15 years and redeemable after 10 years, at a nominal interest of four per cent, to be paid by the companies. An individual could only receive compensation up to a maximum amount of £E 15 000. The amount of compensation was to be determined by the market value of the shares on the stock exchange according to the last closing prices before the passing of the law, or, in cases where no stock market price was available, to be estimated by a special committee. In this way compensation became in effect relatively small, and large shareholders were compensated for only part of their holdings. All the companies and establishments affected were in principle, and until further notice, to maintain their legal form and continue their activities and functions. They were to be supervised by special authorities, who were given the right to discuss the management of the companies and make fresh appointments.

By a further decree the supervising authorities were set up. A Supreme Council for Public Organizations was created, consisting of all the members of the Government (President and Ministers). The individual companies and establishments, including both existing public enterprises and the newly nationalized private concerns, were attached to the various ministries according to the nature of their activity. The duties of the ministers were to "undertake the responsibilities of extending advice and guidance, organization-control and supervision" and "implement the annual production schedules arranged for organizations within his competence and approved by the Supreme Council for Public Organizations according to plans. Plans shall stipulate the size and kind of resources whether financial, material or concerning manpower; they shall also indicate means of ensuring the availability of required potentialities. Plans shall also regulate the use of these potentialities in production, investment, consumption, export and import, means of financing the organizations, means of promoting the production efficiency of the workers"[14]), etc. In this way a series of special organizations were established. Attached to the Ministry of Industry were the General Egyptian Organization for Metallurgy, for the Foodstuffs Industry, for Weaving and Spinning, for Chemical Industries, for Building Materials and Ceramics, for Metallic Industry, for Engineering Industries, for Petroleum, and for Co-operative Organizations and Small Industries. Attached to the Ministry of War was an Organization for Military Factories. And so on for agricultural enterprises, communications, trade, building, land reclamation, social insurance, etc. We shall return to these organizations in connection with our description of the present economic system in chapter 10.

In connection with the nationalizations a series of benefits were extended to employees. We have already mentioned the most important: the higher statutory minimum wage, the reduction of the working week to 42 hours, and the system of profit-sharing. Employees of all the companies, private and public, were given the right to 25 per cent of the distributed profits with an upper limit of £E 50 per employee; of this 25 per cent 10 per cent was to be paid in cash, while the remaining 15 per cent was to be paid into certain public funds for eventual disbursement to employees according to the decisions of the Government. From a report by the Minister of Industry in April 1962, it emerged that 140 industrial firms were at that time under the organizations of the Ministry of Industry. The number of workers in public-sector plants has been given at 249 000 in 1962, i.e. about one third of the employees in the whole of industry, by the definition we have been using.

6.7.3 *The philosophy of nationalization*

It is usual to connect nationalization with socialist ideology, and the public take-overs in Egypt are now undoubtedly considered part and parcel of the "Arab Socialism" that was adopted as a constitutional principle in the Charter, presented by the President at the Inauguration Session of the National Congress of Popular Forces in May 1962. But the beginning of nationalization was in fact more *ad hoc* and perfunctory, and mainly carried

---

[14]) Articles 1 and 2 of decree, defining duties and responsibilities of the Ministers.

out in connection with international conflicts. To some extent it "just happened". If anything, the first nationalizations were nationalistic rather than socialistic. This was obviously so at the time of the Suez War.

Since then, however, an ideology of nationalization has grown out of events, and in Government directives on the nationalization decrees of 1961, as well in the drafting of the Charter of 1962, this ideology is quite articulate[15]). Apart from political considerations, the motivation behind the nationalization measures seems from an economic point of view mainly to be based on two arguments, one of which could have come from traditional socialism, though it is probably directly inspired by factual circumstances in Egypt, while the other is more akin to modern discussions of growth.

According to the *first kind of argument* a large public sector is necessary to prevent *exploitation* of the working population by a limited number of private owners of big industries. Our discussion of the falling share of labour leaves no room for doubt concerning the source of inspiration for this argument. One can hardly think of anything more deserving of the epithet "exploitation" than the earlier conditions of work in Egyptian factories and the rise in profits experienced by Egyptian industry during the last 25 years. And yet the Government's reaction to this development cannot be just a question of social indignation, as the choice of terminology might suggest. After all it is the Government itself which by its protectionist measures has created the hot-house atmosphere that has allowed profits to grow so excessively. Quite apart from any pressure from industry, the Government's motive for protection was to promote industrialization and growth. With a rising supply-price of capital, an increase in private capital investment means a rising rate of profit. If the increased profits are ploughed back, the result is a rising supply of capital, which can eventually bring down the supply-price of capital and provide the source for accelerated growth. If, however, an increased supply of private capital for industrial investment requires not only increased profits, but also increased *distributed* profits, the mechanism ceases to work. A mechanism for growth then turns out to be a mechanism for exploitation. The real income of the working population becomes sacrificed, not so much for the sake of growth, as for the sake of lavish spending by industrial capitalists. The estimates in chapter 5 did in fact show an increasing share of distributed profits in total industrial value added. – This is probably how the accusation of "exploitation" should be understood.

The *second kind of argument* refers to the "mobilization of national

---

[15]) *The Charter*, published by the Information Department, Cairo 1962.

savings". It is not quite clear from the context exactly how this should be understood. One line of interpretation is that nationalization is intended to lead to increased business savings and therefore increased national savings. This would be the case if the nationalizations led to a fall in distributed profits, everything else being equal. Now, the previous owners of shares taken over by the Government receive 4 per cent on the market value of the shares, while the employees' share of the profits amounts to 10 per cent of the total distributed profits, which include dividends paid to the Government in its capacity as shareholder, plus a further 15 per cent to be accumulated in special funds. Before the nationalizations company statistics showed that dividends paid amounted to 9 per cent of paid-up capital and 6 per cent of the market value of shares. If employees receive 25 per cent of total distributed profits and the previous shareholders 4 per cent of the market value of shares, the result is that the previous shareholders and employees together receive 5.2 per cent of the market value, in a company in which all the shares have been taken over and full compensation given. But only about 4.5 per cent would be paid in cash; furthermore, compensation has not been at full market value, and there is also an upper maximum limit to each employee's share of profits. So far the system would seem to ensure an increased share of retained profits in nationalized enterprises.

It may be asked whether an increase in national savings could not have been achieved by simply increasing the tax on company profits. It is questionable, however, whether taxing profits could really have solved the problem. If the supply of new capital to industry is very sensitive to the rate of distributed profits, the private supply of new capital might have declined more than the increase in public savings arising from the increased budgetary income. That the marginal supply-price of capital for industrial investments was high is clear; that the private supply of capital was very sensitive seems likely.

On another possible interpretation, the "mobilization of national savings" is more a question of controlling the way in which a given total of national savings is invested in real capital. If the savings are there and the Government really controls all real investments, it does not need to bother about "mobilizing the savings" unless it is also concerned with what people actually do with their cash. If people hoard bank-notes, the Government can borrow correspondingly from the central bank; if people keep their savings in bank accounts the Government can borrow from the commercial banks, etc. The problem is then only a question of the appropriate way of arranging financially for Government borrowing. If, on the other hand, the Government does not control investments completely, private investment may take place in lines of production considered socially undesirable. National savings, in the form of investments, will then be allocated in a way which may be optimal from the point of view of maximum private profits, but inoptimal from the point of view of Government policy. Instead of speaking about the "mobilization of national savings" it would be better therefore to speak of the "allocation of national savings". It is known that divergencies between the Misr Bank and the Government concerning investment policy was one of the main reasons for the nationalization of the Misr concern in 1960; the concern wanted to invest in the textile industry, while the Government wanted investments in other branches of industry. Nationalization obviously led to a much more detailed control over the investments of the nationalized companies.

It could be asked, once again, whether more traditional methods of directing investment could not have been used instead of nationalization. This is partly a question of the size of the divergency between the preferences of the Government and those of private investors, partly a question of the efficiency of fiscal and monetary policies in channelling private investment, and finally, a question of the efficiency of the Government departments in directing investments by administrative action. We shall return to these questions.

Finally, it will be readily understood that the two interpretations of the catch-phrase the "mobilization of national savings", which we have ventured upon here do not contradict each other, and may both have been in the mind of the Government when the decisions about the nationalizations were taken.

CHAPTER 7

Foreign trade and foreign payments

7.1 Egypt's foreign trade

It has been said that Egypt is on a Cotton Standard. Cotton dominates the export revenues of the country and is the biggest cash crop, on which farmers depend for the payment of rents, taxes, etc. These facts are and always have been of paramount importance for Egypt's foreign trade and balance of payments policies[1]. And although Egypt has never formally been on a Cotton Standard, in the sense that the Government has committed itself to sell and buy cotton in unlimited quantities at fixed prices in terms of Egyptian pounds, it is nevertheless true that since World War II she has concentrated on stabilizing cotton prices in terms of her domestic currency, which is a *sine qua non* for a quiet, stable development of domestic prices and incomes in general. Being a big cotton exporter, Egypt belongs to the group of raw-material-producing countries which have been exposed to heavy fluctuations in their export revenues and terms of trade. The difficulties have been accentuated by foreign political tensions, which at times have created almost chaotic conditions for her foreign trade. That a fair degree of stabilization has actually been accomplished in spite of all these factors is in itself remarkable. The stabilization problem, however, is only one side of Egypt's balance of payments difficulties. What has become of greater and increasing importance is the question of financing development and increasing the import of capital goods; and here the country has large problems still to solve.

7.1.1 Foreign trade and national product

Compared with pre-war years, in value both exports and imports are now

---

[1] Concerning long-term developments see Dr. Abdul Moneim El Kaissouny, "Egypt's

172

at a much higher level. This is partly due to the rise in prices at home and abroad. To form an impression of the level of foreign trade it is therefore appropriate to compare the ratio of exports and imports to the national product at current prices. This has been done in table 7.1. For the pre-war years, exports and imports were about 16 and 18 per cent, respectively, of the national product. During the war years the ratio of foreign trade to national product fell to a very low level,- but recovered its pre-war ratio again around 1947/48. It would be of great interest to know whether there has been any "natural" tendency since the war for foreign trade to rise or fall in relation to national product, but this is not easy to judge. From 1952 onwards trade became increasingly regulated. During the years 1948 to 1951 and most of 1952 imports were on the whole unregulated, but for 1950 and 1951, and part of 1952 also, the value of foreign trade was inflated by the Korean boom. There is nothing, however, in the figures for the ratio of exports to national product which points to a fall in the relative value of exports 1938/39 to 1952. The ratio is about the same in 1952 as in 1938/39, and in both of these years export conditions were relatively bad. For imports there may even have been a tendency to increase, though most of the increase in the ratio of imports to national product in 1950–52 was probably due to inflationary conditions. From around 1952, on the other hand, there is a clear tendency for the ratio of exports to national product to fall; by 1959 it had dropped to about 12 per cent. This level was then maintained through to 1962/63, interrupted by a sharp drop in 1961 and 1962 owing to the failure of the cotton crop in 1961. Imports touched a minimum of 16.5 per cent in 1957, but at once began to rise again and in 1962/63 reached a ratio of 20 per cent, i.e. higher than before World War II.

Development in the volume of exports, see table 7.2, is quite remarkable: it has remained almost stagnant for the last twenty-five years. From 1938 to 1959 Egypt increased her volume of exports by only 12 per cent; while "underdeveloped countries" in general increased theirs during the same period by 51 per cent on average[2]), and "non-industrial countries" by 39 per cent[3]). After a fall during the war, the volume of exports rose in 1948–50 to a level 15–20 per cent above the pre-war level; this was made possible partly by sales from stocks of cotton accumulated during the war

foreign trade during the last fifty years", *Research on the Fiftieth Anniversary*, Societé Egyptienne d'Economie, Cairo 1959 (in Arabic).

[2]) *Statistical Year-book*, United Nations, 1961.

[3]) *Trends in International Trade*, A Report by a Panel of Experts, GATT, Geneva 1958, p. 20.

TABLE 7.1

Merchandise exports and imports 1938–1963

Year	Exports value, f.o.b., £E million	Imports value, c.i.f., £E million	GNP at current market prices £E million	Exports as % of GNP	Imports as % of GNP
1938	29.4	36.8	199	14.8	18.5
1939	33.4	34.0	201	16.6	16.9
1945	45.2	58.9	580	7.8	10.2
1946	69.0	80.0	563	12.3	14.2
1947	88.4	98.1	608	14.5	16.1
1948	143.1	160.3	756	18.9	21.2
1949	137.8	166.6	872	15.8	19.1
1950	175.4	200.4	963	18.2	20.8
1951	207.3	236.5	1069	19.4	22.1
1952	150.2	222.9	968	15.5	23.0
1953	142.5	179.7	934	15.3	19.2
1954	143.9	164.4	989	14.5	16.6
1955	146.0	187.2	1043	14.0	17.9
1956	142.3	200.8	1099	12.9	18.3
1957	171.6	191.5	1160	14.8	16.5
1958	166.6	233.1	1225	13.6	19.0
1959	160.5	225.9	1314	12.2	17.2
1960	197.8	225.9	1415	14.0	16.4
1961	168.9	243.8	1508	11.2	16.2
1962	158.3	302.9	1609	9.8	18.8
1962/63	197.9	342.2	1679	11.8	20.4

NOTE   The export and import figures are customs authority statistics based on records of actual exports and imports. They do not coincide, for obvious reasons, with the figures of table 7.9, which are payments figures based on exchange authority statistics; and apart from definitions the principles of valuation and coverage differ in the two sets of statistics. The import figures do not include Russian deliveries for the High Dam at Assuan, amounting to £E 35 million from 1959 to the end of 1962/63, and certain military equipment.

SOURCE   *Yearbook of International Trade Statistics,* several issues, for the export and import figures from 1938 to 1960. For 1961 and 1962 see *Economic Review,* CBE, 1963, no. 1.

The series for GNP at current prices is a chain made from Hansen and Mead, op. cit. table 8 for the years 1952–62 and table 1 for the years 1949–45; the years 1945–53 were obtained from El Sa yed Hafez Abdel Rahman, *A survey of foreign trade in Egypt in the post-war period,* unpub lished thesis, University of Cairo, 1959. The two latter periods are adjusted to the level of the first period.

(see chapter 4). After 1950 there was a sharp fall, but during the 'fifties and the beginning of the 'sixties the pre-war level was reached again, and perhaps surpassed by about 15 per cent. Real national product rose at the same time by 132 per cent. That the share of exports in national product (at current prices) shows a fall of only 2–3 percentage units is due to the relative rise in export prices. The volume of imports followed a different course. After a sharp fall during the war it rose until 1951, when it was 60 per cent above the pre-war level. During 1952 and 1953 there was again a sharp fall almost to pre-war level, but then it rose again until in 1959/60 it was about 40 per cent above the pre-war level. During the following three years the volume of imports may have risen by a further 30 per cent, to which must be added Russian High Dam deliveries. This latest increase in imports and the share of imports in GNP has been made possible mainly by American deliveries of surplus commodities.

The volume of imports will usually tend to increase with increasing real national product; the income-elasticities of imports found in other countries varies from about one in the USA to about two in certain small countries in NW Europe. To make a statistical estimate of the income-elasticity of imports in Egypt is not possible, the available time series being too short. The figures in table 7.3, however, may give some impression of its size. From 1938–39 to 1952 both import volume and gross national product at fixed prices increased by about a half. This points to an "unregulated" income-elasticity of imports of about one, which *a priori* does not seem unreasonable. From 1952 to 1960, when imports were increasingly regulated by physical controls, the total import volume rose by only about 15 per cent, compared with an increase in real national product of about 35 per cent. But after 1960 imports rose rapidly and in 1962/63 seem to have caught up completely with national income. If the unregulated income-elasticity for imports had really been about one, this would mean that the demand for imports would have been fully satisfied in 1962/63. This was certainly not the case. To get a true picture of the situation, we must study the volume of imports other than capital goods proper and compare it with the development of real disposable private income. By this procedure we take some account of the shifts in the structure of demand which took place during the 'fifties, when investment became more and more a matter of deliberate government decision, and as a consequence the conception of a "propensity to import" capital goods lost some of its meaning. Figures for the volume of imported goods other than capital goods do not exist, but we have made an estimate on the basis of the percentage composition of imports shown in table 7.7

TABLE 7.2

Volumes, unit prices and terms of trade, 1938–60

Year	Volume indices 1953 = 100		Unit price indices 1953 = 100		Net barter terms of trade 1938/39 = 100
	Exports	Imports	Exports	Imports	
1938	96	85	22	25	104 ⎫ 100
1939	112	72	22	27	96 ⎭
1945	56	45	56	77	86
1946	82	72	58	66	104
1947	99	81	64	72	105
1948	105	131	99	75	155
1949	114	136	88	75	137
1950	112	160	113	76	176
1951	82	160	179	87	243
1952	77	120	136	103	155
1953	100	100	100	100	118
1954	89	95	113	96	127
1955	91	106	111	99	132
1956	86	106	121	100	143
1957	93	99	134	106	149
1958	104	138	116	99	138
1959	108	140	105	88	141
1960	(120)	(140)	(113)	(92)	145

SOURCE   *Yearbook of International Trade Statistics*, 1959. The figures for 1960 are our "guestimates". The import price index covers only part of total imports. Machinery and equipment are not included and this probably means that the import price fall from 1952 to 1960 is exaggerated, and the increase in the volume index correspondingly. The indices are Fisher's ideal indices with base year 1938, and are probably not very reliable. In particular the import price increase by 20 per cent from 1951 to 1952 is difficult to understand, see *International Financial Statistics*, Supplement to 1962/63 issues, IMF, p. 225. The unit price indices measure prices in terms of £E. After 1953 the multiple exchange rate system gives rise to difficulties. The concealed increases in the exchange rates were on the whole larger on the export than on the import side. This has influenced to some unknown extent the improvement in the terms of trade since 1953. It should be noted that the volume indices are not affected because the values are correspondingly biased.

below. Figures for disposable private income are available[4]). Using the cost of living index as deflator, we find an increase in real disposable income of about 55 per cent from 1952/53 to 1960, and about 80 per cent to 1962/63; using the implicit national income deflator[5]), we find 33 and 50 per cent,

---

[4]) Bent Hansen, "Savings in the UAR (Egypt), 1938/39 and 1945/46–1962/63", *Memo. no. 551*, Institute of National Planning, Cairo 1965.

[5]) Hansen and Mead, op. cit.

TABLE 7.3
Import volume and real national product

Year	Import volume 1938/39 = 100	Gross national product at fixed prices 1938/39 = 100
1938/39	100	100
1952	153	149
1960	178	200
1962/63	230–240	232

SOURCE   Hansen and Mead, op. cit. The 1962/63 figure for import volume is our "guestimate".

respectively. We shall adopt the latter method of deflating, since it appears more suitable in this context. The volume of imported goods other than capital goods seems to have been unchanged from 1952 to 1960, and to have increased by about one third from 1960 to 1962/63. With an import income-elasticity of about one the demand for imports other than capital goods would accordingly have been 35 per cent higher than actual imports in 1960, but only 10–15 in 1962/63. In terms of money this would correspond to some £E 60 million in 1960 and about £E 30 million in 1962/63; these figures should be taken as an illustration of the problem only, rather than as an estimate of the actual demand kept back by the import controls.

However, the real problem is what the propensity to import would have been during the 'fifties in the absence of controls. We have based our calculation of the hypothetical demand for imports in 1962/63 on the assumption that the income-elasticity for imports remained unchanged at one. But this can at most be an upper limit, and the burden borne by direct import control must have been less than the amount suggested by this upper limit. Apart from direct controls, important factors have helped to keep down the demand for import goods other than capital goods in spite of rising incomes. The higher import duties and the depreciation of the Egyptian pound must have reduced the volume of import demand at a given total income; by how much would depend upon the unknown price-elasticity for import goods other than capital goods. Another factor is the growing capacity of domestic industrial production, and the actual increase in production of industrial goods, which now satisfies most of the demands which in other circumstances would have been directed towards imported goods. To what extent this demand would revert to imported goods if the controls were abolished is an open question. Finally, mention must also be made of the change in

income distribution in favour of the lower income brackets, in particular
in agriculture; the propensity to consume imported goods is undoubtedly
much lower for the low-income groups than for the top incomes (the old
landowner class had a great tendency to live abroad, or, if at home, to
adopt a European way of life). This last factor, however, is matched by
effects on the export side. The lower import propensity of low-income groups
is accompanied by a higher propensity to consume exportable goods, such
as rice for instance in agriculture. The shift in income distribution from
landowners to peasants may therefore tend to imply a fall in the level of
foreign trade in general, compared with national income. In itself there is
nothing wrong in such a decline in foreign trade, neither from an efficiency
nor from a development point of view. The problem is only which group,
the old landowners or the fellahin, has the highest net import propensity.
Taking all these factors into account, the amount of imports kept back by
control in 1962/63 may have been less than the 10–15 per cent, or £E 30
million, mentioned above.

7.1.2 Foreign trade prices and terms of trade

Egyptian export prices are dominated by cotton prices. After the war they
moved strongly upwards until in 1949 they reached four times their pre-war
level. The Korean boom doubled them again during 1950 and 1951; but
by 1953 they had already fallen once more to about half the peak-level
recorded in 1951, and with some fluctuations they have remained since
1954 around the level of 1950. Import prices have followed a steadier
course, with a somewhat smaller rise than export prices. In 1957 a peak
was reached after some fluctuations, and since then the import-price trend
seems to have been downward. Compared with the domestic price level,
measured by the Wholesale Prices index export prices show a greater increase, and import prices a smaller one; this is quite natural, since both
export and import prices enter the Wholesale Prices index (see table 7.4).

   The more rapid rise in export prices compared with those of imports
means a corresponding improvement in the net barter terms of trade, see
table 7.2. The improvement amounted to about 40 per cent from pre-war
years to 1960, but some of this improvement (in particular since 1953) is
due to index imperfections (see the note to table 7.2). During 1961 and
1962 the terms of trade must have deteriorated somewhat, but with rising
cotton prices in 1963 they may have recovered to their 1959 level. It is partly
this improvement in the terms of trade that has permitted the volume of

imports to rise in spite of a stagnating export volume. Behind the 40 per cent improvement lie wild fluctuations. During the war years terms of trade deteriorated to almost half their pre-war level. In 1946 the pre-war level was recovered, and by 1949 a 40 per cent improvement had been obtained. From 1949 to 1951 a further improvement of almost 100 per cent was recorded as a result of the Korean boom; but from 1951 to 1953 this im-

TABLE 7.4

Domestic and foreign prices

Year	Wholesale prices	Import prices	Export prices
1939	100	100	100
1950	345	304	514
1951	383	352	814
1952	372	412	618
1960	417	(368)	(514)

SOURCE   *Annuaire Statistique,* several issues, and table 7.2.

provement, and more, was lost again. Since then a slow recovery, perhaps fictitious, has taken place, with terms of trade relatively stable since 1956.

If the Korean boom is regarded as a strange interlude having no connection with long-term trends, this picture of how the Egyptian terms of trade have developed scarcely fits the general complaint of long-term losses in terms of trade for underdeveloped, raw-material-exporting countries. Without entering upon the intricate question of whether these countries in general are really facing such an adverse long-term trend it is nonetheless clear that a fair judgement of how Egypt has fared requires comparison with other underdeveloped countries, and with Egyptian developments before World War II. Dr. El Tanamly has calculated the Egyptian terms of trade back to 1910, and the result is depicted in chart 7.1. Concerning the earlier development, we notice that a severe loss in terms of trade during World War I was regained in the second half of the 'twenties. From 1928 to 1931 there was then a sharp fall, by more than a third, and this has never been regained. The level to-day seems to be about the same as at the beginning of the 'thirties. Rather than a continuously downward long-term trend in the Egyptian terms of trade, a heavy structural shift seems to have occurred during the years around 1930 to the disadvantage of the country.

Reliable figures of this kind for underdeveloped countries in general do not

CHART 7.1

The terms of trade, 1911–1957 (3-year mov. average) and 1938/39–1960

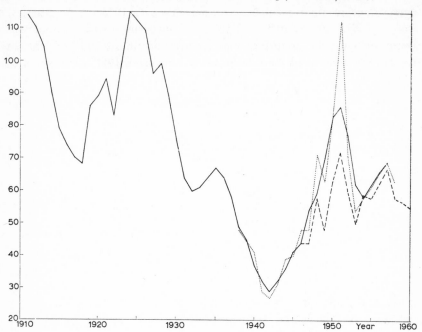

SOURCES   1911–57 depicted as ——————, see A. M. El Tanamly, "The Agricultural Development in Egypt During the Last 50 Years", *Research on the Fiftieth Anniversary*, Société Egyptienne d'Economie, 1900–1959, Cairo 1959, p. 123–4 (in Arabic). El Tanamly's index is an attempt to extend backward in times the index for 1939–1960 depicted as ...., see *Yearbook of International Trade Statistics*, 1959; the full curve in the diagram is a 3-year moving average. The index depicted as – – – – – – was calculated in the State Planning Commission by Pål Bog, see unpublished memoranda in the SPC. Bog's index is a fixed weight index with weights from 1954; this weighting implies a lower weight for cotton during the Korean Boom than in the preceding index which explains the main difference between these two indexes.

seem to exist. In table 7.5 below we have compared the terms of trade of so-called non-industrial countries and Egypt from 1928 to 1957. Compared with immediate pre-war conditions the development in Egypt may have been more favourable than in "non-industrial countries" in general, though the index for Egypt has an upward bias as already pointed out. From 1937/38 to 1957 there was an improvement of 42 per cent for Egypt, against 19 per cent for non-industrial countries. For "underdeveloped countries" the improvement in terms of trade was 31 per cent from 1938 to 1957 (28 per cent to 1960) [6]). The fall in Egypt's terms of trade during the 'thirties, on the other hand, was much heavier than the fall in non-industrial countries, 48 per cent against 14 per cent. The result for Egypt is thus a fall by one quarter from 1928 to 1957, while non-industrial countries have on the whole maintained their position.

TABLE 7.5

Terms of trade for Egypt and non-industrial countries

Year	Non-industrial countries	Egypt
1928	100	100
1937/38	86	52
1957	102	74

SOURCE　　*Trends in International Trade,* A Report by a Panel of Experts, GATT, Geneva, 1958, p. 26, and Dr. A. M. El Tanamly, op. cit.

7.1.3 The composition of trade

Although raw cotton has declined in relative importance it is still the dominant export commodity. In 1938 about 75 per cent of export value was cotton. The present share is hard to judge because of the crop failure in 1961, which lowered the share of cotton in both 1961 and 1962; the "normal" share may now be around 60 per cent. (The shares for other exports goods in 1961 and 1962 are, of course, correspondingly exaggerated.) From year to year there are rather heavy fluctuations, partly because of crop fluctuations, but also because of the well-known price instability of raw-material markets. For rice, which has sometimes been the second export article, and sometimes negligible, the instability is even more pronounced, but here crop fluctuations alone are the cause. The decline in the importance of raw cotton is partly a consequence of the increase in domestic consumption of cotton textiles, and partly of the fact that cotton is to an increasing extent exported in the form of textile manufactures, both yarn and fabrics. From practically nothing in 1938 the export share of cotton manufactures rose to about 2 per cent in 1953 and 12 per cent in 1962. Noteworthy also is the increased export of minerals, fuels, etc., and recently cement. We have already dis-

---

[6]) United Nations, *Statistical Yearbook,* 1961.

cussed, in chapter 6, sections 6.2 and 6.3, the background to this increase in the export of industrial products from the old "infant" industries. Tyres and footwear are other, more recent industries that have just begun to export. Although still modest the tendency is obviously for industrial exports to gain in importance, and for agricultural exports to lose. The share of industrial products in total exports has been calculated at 11 per cent in 1950 and 17 per cent in 1959 [7]).

The composition of imports has undergone more substantial changes. The main trend from 1938 to 1962 has been for the share of food, etc., and capital goods to increase; while the share of manufactured goods has fallen, and that of raw materials has remained fairly constant. This is clear from table 7.7, which permits direct quantitative statements only to a limited extent, because of differences in the commodity classification for various years. These differences are of importance, however, only in the case of raw materials and manufactured goods. It is therefore possible to say that while the share of food has increased from about 12 per cent in 1938 to about 27 per cent in 1962, the import of capital goods has risen from about 13 per cent to almost 25 per cent in 1962. The whole increase in the share of food took place in the 'forties; by 1953 the share was above 30 per cent, the cause being the fall in agricultural production per capita, coupled with the Government's policy of keeping down the price of elementary food-

TABLE 7.6

Exports by main commodities, 1938–1961 (percentage shares)

	1938	1953	1958	1961	1962
Raw cotton	74.4	85.6	67.4	61.9	53.0
Rice	2.4	0.0	8.3	4.8	4.2
Vegetables	3.3	3.2	2.9	3.2	6.7
Minerals, fuels, lubricants, etc.	1.4	0.7	2.8	4.4	9.5
Cotton yarns and fabrics	...	1.9	7.1	9.5	11.8
Cement	...	0.5	0.7	1.7	1.3
Rest	...	8.1	10.8	14.5	13.5
Total	100.0	100.0	100.0	100.0	100.0

SOURCE   *Yearbook of International Trade Statistics*, several issues, and *Economic Review*, CBE, 1963, 1.

---

[7]) *The Economy of the United Arab Republic during the Nineteen-Fifties*, National Bank of Egypt, Cairo 1963, p. 96.

stuffs. The increase in the share of capital goods has taken place almost entirely since 1953, and is a result of deliberate Government policy.

For raw materials (i.e. crude materials, fuels, chemicals, etc.) and manufactured goods direct comparisons cannot be made, the differences in classification being too serious. However, within all of the three periods, 1938–1953, 1953–1959 and 1959–1962, the share of raw materials has been more or less constant, changes in level representing changes in classification. It is also clear that from 1938 to 1959 the share of manufactured goods has been falling continuously; and here it is interesting to see that the main fall seems to have taken place before the physical regulations became important in 1952/53. This fall was almost entirely due to a decline in the import of

TABLE 7.7

Imports by main commodity groups, 1938–1961 (per cent of total)

	Crude Classi-fication I		Standard Intern. Trade Classification		Crude Classification II		
	1938	1953	1953	1959	1959	1961	1962
Food, beverages and tobacco	11.5	25.9	30.4	24.5	25.6	22.4	27.4
Crude materials, fuels, chemicals	26.4	25.8	29.1	31.7	37.5	37.8	...
Manufactured goods	24.3	13.3	20.3	15.7	9.8	10.7	...
Machinery and transport equipment*	13.1	15.1	16.0	25.2	26.3	28.0	23.8
Rest	24.7	19.8	4.3	2.9	0.9	1.1	...
Total	100.0	100.0	100.0	100.0	100.0	100.0	100.0

* Includes passenger motor-cars besides buses. They amounted to 1.8 percentage units in 1938, 0.6 percentage units in 1953, and 0.5 percentage units in 1961. Russian High Dam deliveries not included; if included they might raise the share of machinery and transport equipment by 3–4 percentage units during the years 1959–62. Also some military equipment in excluded.

SOURCE   *Yearbook of International Trade Statistics,* several issues. The figures for 1953–59 using "Standard International Trade Classifications" are taken directly from the Yearbook. The "Crude Classification I" figures for 1938–53 were made by us on the basis of the 1954 yearbook's table on Principal Commodities (p. 173–4). The figures using "Crude Classification II" for 1959–62 were also made by us on the basis of the classification in *Annuaire Statistique* 1959, table III, p. 366, *Monthly Summary of Foreign Trade,* Dec. and Jan. to Dec. 1961, Dept. of Statistics and Census, Cairo, table V, p. 24, and *Economic Review,* CBE, 1963, no. 1. The figures from the three classifications are not directly comparable, though in the case of "Food, beverages and tobacco" and "Machinery and transport equipment" the differences in classification are small.

cotton yarn and fabrics, and this again can be ascribed to the tariff policy and the increasing capacity of the domestic textile industry, see chapter 6.

Summarizing, we can say that the period 1938–1952 was characterized by a sharp increase in the share of food imports, and a fall in the share of manufactured goods, while the shares of raw materials and capital goods were about unchanged. From 1952 onwards, we find a further fall in the share of manufactured goods, more or less unchanged shares for food and raw materials, and a large increase in that of capital goods.

7.1.4 Geographical distribution

The largest structural changes in foreign trade, however, have taken place in its geographical distribution, and here both economic and political forces have been at work. The most conspicuous feature is the almost complete disappearance of trade with the United Kingdom, before World War II Egypt's main trading partner, the big increase in trade with the Eastern Bloc and with underdeveloped countries, and the increased imports from the United States.

By 1954 the share of the UK in both exports and imports had already fallen drastically. In that year only 10 per cent of exports went to the UK against 33 per cent in 1938 and 29 per cent in 1948; most of this drop was compensated by increased exports to "other countries", which includes only underdeveloped countries, such as Ceylon, India, etc. This shift mainly reflects the exit of Egypt from the sterling area, and the increase in cotton textile production in many underdeveloped countries. From 1954 to 1956 exports to Britain fell to almost nothing, and exports to Continential Western Europe also declined somewhat, the fall being compensated during these years by increased exports to Eastern European countries other than the USSR. All of these developments took place before the Suez War. With the Suez War and the ensuing trade blockade by Britain and France, a new decline in exports to Continental Western Europe took place, this time compensated by the USSR, who for political reasons stepped in with bulk purchases of cotton. Since then the distribution of exports has slowly swung back to Western Europe and the USA again, and the present distribution is about 35 per cent to Eastern Bloc countries, 35 per cent to Western Europe and the USA, and 30 per cent to the rest of the world.

The import side shows much the same picture with respect to the UK. Before the Suez War imports from the UK were already down to half their pre-war level. With the Suez War they vanished almost completely,

TABLE 7.8

Geographical pattern of Egypt's foreign trade, percentage distribution

	Middle East	United States	United King-dom	Continental Western Europe	USSR	Other Eastern European countries	Other count-ries
Exports							
1938	4	2	33	36	—	10	15
1948	4	3	29	24	8	5	27
1954	8	5	10	36	1	10	31
1956	12	3	3	27	4	24	26
1958	5	2	5	17	18	22	31
1960	4	5	2	16	16	20	37
1962	7	6	5	22	15	23	22
Imports							
1938	5	7	23	40	1	9	16
1948	7	8	22	30	7	4	23
1954	8	11	13	45	1	4	18
1956	7	13	12	36	4	8	19
1958	2	8	5	36	13	19	17
1960	4	18	6	31	10	12	19
1962	5	25	8	23	8	15	16

SOURCE   1938 and 1948, *Direction of international trade,* UN publ., Sale no. 59 XVII. 12 p. 187–88; 1954 to 1960, several issues of *Economic Developments in the Middle East,* supplements to World Economic Survey, UN. Russian High Dam deliveries and some military equipment not included.

though there has been some revival in recent years. Also dating from the time of the Suez War is the big increase in imports from Eastern Bloc countries, a natural consequence of the bilateral nature of Eastern Bloc trade. For other areas, however, the development of imports differs from that of exports. The share of "other countries" to-day is the same as before the war, and the decline in imports from Continental Western Europe has come later than the decline in exports to that area. Imports from the USA, on the other hand, have increased greatly since 1959, mainly through Egyptian purchases of food grains of American surplus commodities, in accordance with US Public Law 480. Thus in 1962 we find that only about 25 per cent of the imports come from Eastern Bloc countries, 55 per cent from Western Europe and the USA, and only about 20 per cent from the rest of the world.

TABLE 7.9

The balance of payments, 1946–1962 (£E mil

£E millions	1946	1947	1948	1949	1950	19
Exports, f.o.b.	52.8	68.5	132.6	140.3	188.5	2
Imports, f.o.b.	− 88.6	− 106.1	− 162.5	− 158.3	− 221.7	− 2
Balance of trade	− 35.8	− 37.6	− 29.9	− 18.0	− 33.2	−
Suez canal dues	+ 12.0	+ 13.1	+ 18.4	+ 23.0	+ 26.2	+
British military expenditure	+ 20.7	+ 11.5	+ 23.2	+ 11.5	+ 13.0	+
Interest and dividends, net	− 9.3	− 4.9	− 3.1	− 8.2	− 11.2	
Government expenditure	− 1.0	− 2.3	− 6.5	− 6.4	− 5.1	−
Other invisibles, net	0.0	− 1.0	− 9.4	− 5.6	− 0.7	+
Net of invisibles	22.4	16.4	22.6	14.3	22.2	
Balance of current payments	− 13.4	− 21.2	− 7.3	− 3.7	− 11.0	−
Fall in reserves of gold and foreign Exchange*	11.8	33.2	11.8	1.4	9.4	
Net of other capital movements**	− 0.8	− 12.5	− 8.4	− 4.5	− 3.6	
Balance of capital payments	11.0	20.7	3.4	− 4.1	5.8	
Errors and omissions	2.4	− 0.5	3.9	0.4	5.2	

* Including change in IMF position.

** − indicates capital export. Includes Suez Canal compensation payments, net increase in counterpart funds, and change in net liabilities to Sudan.

7.1.5 Invisibles

Both on the receipts and payments side invisibles are important and of a rather special nature. On the receipts side, there are the Suez Canal dues, income from which has risen substantially. Before the nationalization of the Canal in 1956, the income from Canal dues, taking the average for 1946–1955, amounted to about 18 per cent of export value, compared with 27 per cent, taking the average for 1958–1961, after nationalization. Against this increase in income must be set the indemnities paid on capital account to the old owners (see below); but even when this is taken into account, the nationalization of the canal was, in itself, good business for the country. On the other hand, we have the fall in revenue from expenditure by the British Army. During World War II this expenditure must have been very large – no figures are available – but after the war it declined gradually and disappeared after 1954 (see table 7.9).

2	1953	1954	1955	1956	1957	1958	1959	1960	1961	1962
5.6	135.3	139.8	133.1	129.9	166.0	161.0	164.3	200.2	161.3	145.2
0.5	− 165.2	− 150.7	− 190.3	− 192.3	− 217.5	− 214.0	− 235.3	− 255.2	− 237.8	294.2
4.9	− 29.9	− 10.9	− 57.2	− 62.4	− 51.5	− 53.0	− 71.0	− 55.0	− 76.5	− 149.0
6.6	+ 29.1	+ 30.6	+ 31.8	+ 29.3	+ 24.3	+ 43.0	+ 44.4	+ 50.1	+ 51.2	53.7
5.8	+ 9.0	+ 5.6	—	—	—	—	—	—	—	—
2.1	− 11.1	− 13.1	− 9.8	− 5.1	+ 1.9	+ 2.8	+ 4.1	+ 2.1	+ 1.3	− 2.2
5.7	− 6.6	− 9.4	− 11.0	− 12.9	− 16.9	− 21.7	− 27.9	− 25.3	− 30.9	− 28.4
3.1	+ 1.6	− 6.4	+ 12.2	+ 18.4	+ 11.0	+ 8.8	+ 14.4	+ 4.6	+ 1.6	+ 8.3
1.5	22.0	7.3	23.2	29.7	20.3	32.9	35.0	31.4	23.2	31.4
3.4	− 7.9	− 3.6	− 34.0	− 33.0	− 31.2	− 20.1	− 36.0	− 23.6	− 53.3	− 117.6
9.8	8.6	− 3.1	31.4	36.8	51.9	22.3	22.8	19.4	25.3	43.1
2.0	− 0.4	− 0.3	2.2	− 3.3	− 19.6	+ 1.5	11.4	11.1	33.9	78.5
7.8	8.2	− 3.4	33.6	33.5	32.3	23.8	34.2	30.5	59.2	121.6
4.4	− 0.3	− 0.2	0.4	0.5	− 1.1	− 3.7	1.8	− 6.9	− 5.9	− 4.0

SOURCE *Economic Bulletin*, NBE, and *Economic Review*, CBE several issues. Russian High Dam deliveries and corresponding capital transactions not included for 1959–61.

On the payments side we notice in particular the item Interest and dividends, net, which until 1955 amounted to about 15 per cent of the value of imports, but after 1956 almost disappeared, mainly as a result of the sequestrations and nationalizations of foreign companies and properties in connection with the Suez War. Instead we find a very rapid increase in Government expenditure. This item covers payments for a multitude of purposes; no breakdown is available. It probably includes some expenditure on military items which in other countries are usually included in the commodity import figures, a fact which should be taken into account when discussing import trends. About half the amount seems to be ordinary expenditure for diplomatic services and grants for students sent abroad. Government expenditure has risen from a modest level before 1952 to about 10 per cent of import value in 1962. The net result of the invisible items is a surplus which covers part of the large deficit in the balance of trade; and this surplus seems to be slowly growing.

7.2 Capital movements; the balance of payments

7.2.1 The balance of payments deficit

A summary of the balance of payments from 1946 to 1962 is given in table 7.9. Export and import figures represent actual receipts and disbursements as recorded by the Central Exchange Control, which we use here in order to give an unbroken record from 1946. These figures differ from the foreign trade returns, which record the movement of goods as and when they pass the customs authorities. Over and above this difference in timing there are differences in valuation and coverage[8]). This means that the trade figures in this table differ from those in table 8.1; it means also that among the capital items up to 1961 changes in trade credits ("leads and lags") were left out of the picture; for 1962 such capital movements have to a large extent been taken into account. For year-to-year comparisons this may be of importance and give a distorted picture of capital movements; in the longer run it is·a secondary source of error. For the years 1959 to 1961 it means, for instance, that some of the imports and inflow of capital connected with certain development projects are left out of the picture. The deficits shown by table 7.9 are therefore systematically too small for those years. IMF statistics for 1959–61 show an annual deficit larger by £E 4–7 million, but for earlier years they correspond with the Exchange Control figures. Also excluded from the import figures are Russian deliveries for the High Dam [9]), which may amount to some £E 25 million from 1959 to 1961.

Apart from the years 1949 and 1953, which had small surpluses, the whole post-war period has been characterized by deficits in the balance of current payments, and hence by a net capital inflow. From 1946 to 1954 the balance of current payments fluctuated widely, with large deficits in 1946–47 and 1950–52, and only small deficits or surpluses in the years 1948–49 and 1953–54. The cumulative deficit for this period was £E 120.1 million. From 1955 onwards the yearly deficits have been persistent and

---

[8]) In the trade returns imports are recorded c.i.f. and exports f.o.b., while in the Central Exchange Control figures all transport costs are recorded under invisibles. Barter transactions and passengers' baggage, as well as goods not paid for in the year, are not recorded in CEC figures, though they are included in trade returns. Goods on credit are recorded as and when they are paid for.

[9]) This is a consequence of the traditional statistical procedure of not recording parts of a delivery until the whole delivery has taken place. Because of the big amounts involved this is a rather unhappy procedure in this special case.

large, and from 1955 to 1962 the cumulative deficit was £E 348.8 million, and about £E 35 million more if the Russian High Dam deliveries are included. The total cumulative deficit for 1946–62 thus amounts to £E 468.9 million (plus 35 million). The recent tendency has obviously been for the deficit to increase, though the enormous rise in 1962 is partly explained by the failure of the cotton crop in 1961. For 1962/63, however, the deficit was still £E 107 million, and although the first two months of 1962/63 may have been affected by the cotton failure of 1961, it is pretty clear that compared with the deficit of around £E 30 million in the years 1958–60, the level for 1963 must be considerably higher. It is important to notice that the increasing deficit is due to the rapid expansion of imports, while exports seem stagnant.

7.2.2 Exchange reserves and foreign loans

The reduction in net foreign assets corresponding to the net commodity inflow has been accomplished mainly through a fall in the reserves of foreign exchange, the total fall amounting to £E 377 million during the years 1946–62[10]); which brought the net reserves of gold and foreign exchange down from about £E 370 million in 1946 to −7 at the end of 1962 (see table 7.10). The fall in the reserves has also covered net capital exports to a cumulated value of £E 56 million from 1946 to 1958, and certain capital outflows amounting to £E 66 million from 1959 to 62. These large capital outflows relate mainly to sequestrations of foreign property, various payments to Sudan in connection with the withdrawal of Egyptian currency formerly in circulation there and the construction of the High Dam, and compensation payments to the previous owners of the Suez Canal.

Before 1960 foreign loans were small. That direct foreign borrowing began so late was partly because of foreign political tensions, but also because on the whole Egypt was simply not in need of foreign loans earlier, since her foreign exchange reserves were still substantial. In 1959 imports of American surplus commodities began, with corresponding accumulations of US counterpart funds; and at about the same time Russian deliveries for the High Dam started, covered by the Soviet loans agreed upon in 1958. These two sources have provided the main part of the foreign loans since 1959, though other sources, among them the IMF and short-term trade

---

[10]) Disregarding the effects of the depreciation of 1949 on the value in Egyptian pounds of the gold and dollar reserves.

TABLE 7.10

Gold, foreign spot assets, and net foreign reserves of all banks in Egypt
(book-values, £E million)

| Ultimo | Gold | Sterling pounds | | | US dollars | Other currencies | Total exchange reserve gross | Total exchange reserve net **) |
		No. 1 (free)	No. 2 (blocked)	Total				
Dec. 1945								379
Dec. 1948	13	71	264	335	6	10	364	323
Dec. 1949*)	19	63	247	309	21	8	357	321
Dec. 1950	34	52	224	277	26	18	355	312
Dec. 1951	61	24	196	220	37	12	330	292
Dec. 1952	61	6	174	180	20	11	272	232
Dec. 1953	61	19	164	183	12	10	266	224
Dec. 1954	61	35	146	181	13	15	270	227
Dec. 1955	61	21	125	146	21	10	237	195
Dec. 1956	66	7	100	107	21	17	210	159
Dec. 1957	66	27	61	87	16	19	188	109
Dec. 1958	61	45	42	87	4	10	162	85
Dec. 1959	61	63	—	63	7	19	150	62
Dec. 1960	61						157	43
Dec. 1961	61						136	16
Dec. 1962	61							−7
Dec. 1963	61							n.a.

*) The rise in the value of the gold reserve in 1949 is partly related to the devaluation of the Egyptian pound in Sept. 1949. Here Egypt followed the Pound Sterling. This also affects the reserve of US dollars.

**) Figures for the net reserve are obtained by cumulating, backwards from the figure for 1960, the changes shown by table 7.9. No regard is paid therefore to the effect of the devaluation in 1949.

SOURCE   NBE *Economic Bulletin,* vol. VII, no. 3, 1954, p. 162, and later issues of the Bulletin, *Economic Review,* CBE, vol. II, no. 1, 1962, p. 26, and vol. III, 1963, 2.

credits, have contributed. Table 7.11 gives details of the capital account since 1959, excluding Russian High Dam deliveries[11]).

[11]) For details concerning imports of American surplus commodities and the Russian High Dam deliveries and aid, see Said El-Naggar, "Foreign Aid to United Arab Republic", *Memo. no. 382,* Institute of National Planning, Cairo 1963. While the counterpart funds are insterest-free, the Russian loans bear a rate of interest of 2½ per cent p.a. from the time of drawings upon the loan. While no fixed repayment scheme exists for the American

TABLE 7.11

Foreign capital transactions, 1959–1962 (£E million)

(− indicates outflow)	1959	1960	1961	1962
Net capital remittances	0.8	0.1	− 2.5	− 2.6
U.S. counterpart funds and loans in £E	17.1	33.8	27.7	59.6
IBRD loan to Suez Canal Authority	−	10.6	3.2	5.6
Other inflow	−	−	13.5	26.2
Compensation payments (Suez Canal and High Dam)	− 6.5	− 33.4	− 8.0	− 8.1
Change in IMF position	− 0.9	6.2	− 0.9	20.0
Net fall in exchange reserves	23.7	13.2	26.2	20.9
Net capital inflow	34.2	30.5	59.2	121.6

SOURCE   *Economic Review*, CBE, 1962, 1, and 1963, 2. Capital inflow corresponding to Russian High Dam deliveries (£E 25 million) not included before 1962.

7.3   Balance of payments policies

7.3.1   The pre-war system and World War II

> "... count your blessings. I have often reminded you of the many advantages which Egypt possesses – her fertile soil and hardworking peasantry, finances that have been carefully nursed, a public debt which is probably unique in being lower than before the Great War, and a currency which is sound."

These fatherly words by the British Governor of the National Bank of Egypt to the General Assembly of the Bank in 1938 probably give a better impression of the passive conservatism of economic policy in Egypt under the British regime than any detailed study. "Sound", balanced public finances, preferably with a small surplus, not too big, of course, as this would put an unnecessary burden on the shoulders of the tax payer, and a "sound" currency with a fixed exchange relationship to, and full convertibility with the Sterling pound, these were the two great aims to which all policies were subordinated.

Little is known about Egypt's balance of payments as a whole before 1946, except for her balance of trade, which before the outbreak of war

---

loans, the Russian loans are to be repaid over 12 years, beginning one year after completion of deliveries (i.e. in 1964).

usually ran with a certain surplus, on average about £E 3 million, during the years 1932–1937. Egypt was on a Sterling exchange standard with a fixed sterling parity and free movement of funds between Britain and Egypt. Most of the banks in Egypt, moreover, were at that time branches of British and other foreign banks, and so Egypt could not pursue any monetary policies of her own. The banks kept most of their assets with the foreign head-offices and regulated fluctuations in their domestic net lending through corresponding changes in their foreign short-term assets. In this way the domestic money market became part of the British market, and was bound to follow closely British monetary policies.

During World War II this system served to finance Allied military expenditure in Egypt. Sterling pounds were automatically taken up by the National Bank of Egypt at the given parity, and although Egypt had big deficits in her balance of trade during the war years, Allied military expenditure was sufficient not only to cover them but also to increase the sterling assets held in London by the Egyptian banking system to £E 365 million at the end of 1945, plus £ 60 million held by others. The counterpart to this increase in foreign assets was a similar increase in domestic liquidity. The inflation brought on by this heavy Allied spending during World War II was made worse by the fall in domestic production.

7.3.2 The period of liberalization, 1945–1952

The sterling balances accumulated during the war years represented Egypt's only foreign exchange reserves when the war was over. These reserves were very large, more than half the national income at that time, and represented about three years normal import. But although, on the one hand, there was a substantial pent-up demand for import goods, to make good war-time wear and tear on the production apparatus and to replenish the depleted commodity stocks, Britain and Continental Europe, on the other hand, were unable to deliver commodities to any satisfactory extent owing to the damage they had sustained in the war. Import goods could be obtained from America, but this required payment in dollars.

Egypt had long been a member of the Sterling Area, and immediately on the outbreak of World War II the Egyptian Government instituted a system of exchange control over transactions in foreign currencies other than sterling. This exchange control followed the British model. As a member of the Sterling Area, Egypt delivered all her foreign exchange earnings to the London Pool against payment in sterling, and drew dollars and other foreign exchange to an extent determined by London. Egypt's big sterling reserves were thus of limited value and could not be used for the purchase of import goods to any satisfactory extent[12]).

Egypt therefore had little interest in staying within the Sterling Area, and in June 1947 an agreement was reached concerning her departure from it, and the release of some of her blocked sterling assets. This agreement, which has to be seen as part of Britain's unsuccessful attempt in 1947 to introduce full general convertibility for sterling arising from current transactions, rested on an undertaking by the British Government that it would not restrict the use of the released assets, or the sterling proceeds accruing to Egypt from its future current transactions with any other monetary area. Five weeks later, however, the UK had to suspend the general convertibility just introduced, and Egypt was given only a small amount of dollars to cover her needs until the end of the year.

As a result of the British convertibility adventure Egypt thus ended up outside the Sterling Area, but with all its foreign exchange reserves blocked in London. Exchange controls were therefore introduced for all transactions abroad, including those with Sterling Area countries. After a new agreement in 1948, which released further sterling assets, all controls in Egypt were removed except for goods from certain hard-currency countries. Through triangular transactions Egypt succeeded during these years in using some of its sterling assets to buy dollar goods and acquire gold. The stocks of cotton accumulated during the war were a great help as they were easy to sell against hard currency. At this time Egypt began to make bilateral trade agreements, which later became predominant in Egyptian trade.

When the pound sterling was depreciated against the US dollar in September 1949, Egypt followed suit. Since most of her foreign trade was at that time still with the United Kingdom, Continental Europe, and countries belonging to the Sterling Area, almost all of whom followed the pound, the depreciation had but little immediate impact on the Egyptian economy; and in any case what impact it had was soon drowned in the effects of the Korean boom. It is worth noticing that during the war years domestic

---

[12]) The British Government proposed in 1945 that part of these reserves should simply be written off. This would have had serious repercussions upon the future possibilities of financing development in Egypt and was rejected by the Egyptian Government. "The Egyptian Government appreciated the post-war difficulties of Britain, but the talk of scaling-down the balances seemed to Egypt an unworthy attempt to pass these difficulties on to a poorer country with a much lower standard of living." *National Bank of Egypt, 1898–1948*, Cairo 1948, p. 97.

prices and wages rose considerably more in Egypt than in the UK, North America and most European countries. This may suggest an overvaluation of the Egyptian pound *vis à vis* the big currencies, though it is true that during the years from 1946 to 1951 there were only few direct signs of this. The big exchange reserves fell by about £E 90 million, but this was only natural, taking into account depletion of stocks and replacement-needs after the war. What prevented a much larger fall were the sales from accumulated cotton stocks and the big improvement in the terms of trade during the Korean boom, both of them temporary phenomena.

For a full understanding of the depreciation in 1962 one must therefore go back to World War II; and as a matter of fact a policy of partial depreciation against the Pound Sterling, and of course dollar and other hard currencies, was started as early as October 1949. Through varying arrangements the Government continued this policy until an almost general depreciation of the Egyptian pound was finally carried through in 1962. The first device for a partial depreciation was the creation of so-called Export Accounts. Payments for imports could be made in £E to these accounts, and such £E could be bought by foreign buyers in "soft currency" countries for payment of Egyptian export goods. Since the rate of exchange for such £E was free and actually fell below the official parity, this arrangement implied a partial depreciation and the introduction of multiple exchange rates. While the official parity against US$ was kept at $ 2.88 (per £E) the free rates quoted in Tangier for export-£E was $2.48 to $2.63 in 1950, $2.33 to $2.63 in 1951, $2.31 to $2.73 in 1952, and around $2.50 in 1953.

The Korean boom brought with it a big rise in cotton export prices, though the volume of exports did not increase; it actually fell during 1951, partly because war-time stocks of cotton were exhausted, partly because the cotton area was already at its maximum in 1950, while at the same time yields were rather low owing to crop failures in 1950 and 1951, and finally because the Government, when the peak-levels were over and prices had begun to fall, made an attempt to keep prices up by sales restrictions and purchases to ECC stocks at prices above the world-market level. This increased government stocks of cotton financed through Central Bank credits, and added to the already strong inflationary tendencies which the large export incomes had provoked. The result was a very large increase in imports, some of which arrived in the country in 1952 when export revenues had already declined. A fall in the exchange reserves followed and it was felt necessary to take strong counteracting measures. To pursue such policies became one of the first tasks of the Revolutionary Government.

It should be stressed, however, that at the end of 1951, and even at the end of 1952, Egypt's free reserves were still substantial. Gold plus Sterling no. 1 and dollars amounted to £E 122 at the end of 1951, and £E 87 at the end of 1952. This means that at the end of 1951 the free reserves in fact amounted to more than half the total import value for 1951, and at the end of 1952 they were still about a third of the import value for that year. The net reserves were smaller, but including the gold reserves, still substantial. The blocked reserves, too, were very big. The gold reserves, however, according to statements by the National Bank, seem to have been considered untouchable, as a note cover! They have been kept almost unchanged at £E 61 million, since 1950. Behind this luxurious gold policy there may have been political cautiousness, natural in a country that has had its foreign balances blocked several times, but undoubtedly gold-fetishism and Central Bank conservatism have played their roles, too.

7.3.3 Increasing intervention, 1952–1961

The period from 1952 to 1961 was one of increasing Government intervention which finally led up to the nationalization of foreign trade in 1961. Early in 1952 the inflationary conditions that had prevailed since 1950 receded, and deflationary forces made themselves felt in connection with the sharp fall in cotton prices and export income. Measures were taken to bring Egyptian cotton prices down, in line with other cotton prices on the world-market, and although the cotton export tax was temporarily abolished, the drop in agricultural incomes was substantial. A change in agricultural policy was inevitable, see chapter 4. The Government chose to reduce the cotton area considerably and to increease the price of cereals, in order to expand their production and compensate farmers somewhat for their loss of income. Budgetary policy was also revised in a deflationary manner, see chapter 9 below. In the field of foreign trade and payments the most important measures taken in 1952 and the beginning of 1953 were: (1) the introduction of a licensing system for imports from countries accepting sterling, and restrictions on all remittances abroad, (2) a big increase in import duties on so-called non-essential goods, (3) a tax of 10 per cent on payments connected with certain specified invisibles, (4) extended arrangements for payments through the Export Accounts (introduced in 1949, see above), and (5) the introduction of the Import Entitlement system.

The Import Entitlement system resembled the Export Account system in one important respect: it implied a partial depreciation of the £E. Under the Import Entitlement system Egyptian exporters of goods against payment in US or Canadian dollars, or sterling, were entitled to obtain import licences up to a certain, varying percentage of their exports. These licences were transferable and could be sold at a certain premium to Egyptian importers. The premiums increased somewhat between 1953 and August 1955, when the system was abolished. On US dollars the premium was 8 per cent at the end of 1953 and 14 per cent in August 1955; for sterling pounds the figures were 5 and 10, respectively[13]).

At the beginning of 1955 the Export Account system was abolished, having lost much of its value because of the Import Entitlement system. Then, in September 1955, when the situation in the cotton export markets had improved substantially, owing to a general upswing all over the non-communist world, and after the conclusion of a series of bilateral agreements with Eastern Bloc countries and mainland China, and also because its multiple exchange rates had certain disadvantages, the Import Entitlement system too was abolished. To compensate for the partial appreciation this implied, the export tax on cotton was reduced and a general import tax of 7 per cent was introduced on imports from all countries, with exemptions for raw materials and machinery. In April 1956 a further increase in the import duties was imposed.

The nationalization of the Suez Canal later in 1956, with the ensuing fall in income from it, the blocking of Egypt's sterling assets in the UK and dollar assets in the USA, and the general trade blockade on the part of the UK and France, which led to a fall in cotton exports to Continental Europe, necessitated a series of measures. Global and group quotas were fixed for imports and the general 7 per cent import tax was extended to all non-essential commodities and later raised to 9 per cent. Imports in US dollars and certain other currencies in short supply were subjected to a special 10 per cent *ad valorem* fee. At the end of 1958, however, a large number of commodities were exempted from these taxes.

On the export side the most important event was the appearance of the Soviet Union as a large buyer of cotton, and along with a series of bilateral trade agreements special measures were taken to promote exports of cotton. In April 1957 a system of premiums ranging from 10 to 20 per cent on proceeds from cotton exports were introduced. In May the premiums were raised to 15–25 per cent, depending upon the currency involved. At the

---

[13]) *International Financial Statistics,* Dec. 1955, vol. VIII, no. 12, p. 91.

beginning of 1958 these premiums were abolished and replaced by a general premium of about 35 per cent of the official par rate for most exports and imports. As the country's foreign payments position gradually improved this general premium was lowered to about 33 per cent in June and about 21 per cent in September 1958. An attempt was also made to introduce a new Export Account system, but it never acquired any significance and was abolished in September 1959, when a new system of premiums on foreign currency was launched. Proceeds in convertible currencies from exports of raw cotton and a few other items received a variable premium, while most other export proceeds in convertible currencies received a fixed premium of 17.5 per cent. Most receipts in convertible currencies from invisibles received a premium of 27.5 per cent. Payments in convertible currencies for all imports and most invisibles were subject to a premium of 27.5 per cent, but half the premium collected on imports of capital goods, raw materials, and foodstuffs was refunded. During 1960 all these premiums were reduced, owing to an improvement in cotton prices and the foreign payments situation; and in September 1960 the premium for raw cotton exports and certain other commodities was reduced to 6.38 per cent, while the premium for all imports and invisibles was reduced to 10 per cent.

Egypt thus ended up in 1961, after this period of increasing intervention, with a general licensing system for imports, a series of bilateral trade agreements, a system with non-uniform export prices, a complicated and rapidly shifting system of variable, multiple exchange rates, and the Egyptian pound depreciated, though to a fluctuating degree. The aims behind these policies were not only to prevent too large a deficit in the balance of current payments, but also to stabilize domestic cotton prices and direct the composition of imports towards capital goods and food.

7.3.4 Nationalization of foreign trade and the return to uniform exchange rates

In connection with the other nationalizations which took place in July 1961 the import trade was concentrated in a dozen state-owned agencies. At the same time all the leading cotton export companies were made public companies, and under the new cotton policy declared in August 1961, the Egyptian Cotton Commission was made the central agency for marketing Egyptian cotton. The principles of price fixing adopted have already been explained (see chapter 4, section 4·4.7). One of the aims of the new cotton policy was to maintain uniform export prices to all buyers.

In the field of foreign exchange a policy of gradually abolishing the multiple rate system began. In July 1961 the variable premium, fixed for almost a year at 6.38 per cent, on receipts in convertible currencies from exports of raw cotton, textiles and cotton yarn was abolished. The premium of 10 per cent payable on imports in convertible currencies, on the other hand, was extended to apply to all imports. A further step to unify the exchange rates was taken at the end of 1961, when a general premium of 20 per cent on par value was applied to all payments and receipts, with some exceptions. The 20 per cent premium replaced all premiums previously applied, as well as the import license fee of 9 per cent and the tax of 10 per cent on purchases of foreign exchange for certain invisibles.

Finally, in May 1962, the multiple rate system was officially abandoned, and a single rate of US$2.30 per Egyptian pound was announced. The old official rate, which is still in force *vis à vis* the IMF and Suez Canal dues, and in which the gold and exchange reserves are still evaluated, was US$2.8375 per £E; the depreciation of the Egyptian pound thus amounted to about 19 per cent, while the foreign exchange rates rose by about 23 per cent compared with the old par rate. From our description, however, it follows that although the exchange rates had on average been fluctuating, this depreciation of the Egyptian pound took place gradually during the 'fifties and had already begun in 1949. The depreciation had therefore probably had its main effect years before the official announcement in 1962. The background to the unification of the exchange rate in 1962, and the general depreciation, was an acute worsening of the balance of payments position. On top of the chronic deficit came the effects of the failure of the cotton crop in 1961 and certain large payments which the Government had to make to fulfil earlier obligations (Suez Canal indemnities, High Dam compensations, etc.). All this made the Government contact the IMF concerning credits. With the unification of the exchange rate Egyptian exchange policy was brought into close conformity with IMF ideals, and a basis was created for extended credits from the IMF[14]). These credits carried Egypt through her acute difficulties without gold sales, but did not, of course, solve any long-term problems.

7.3.5 *The stabilization of cotton prices*

We have already discussed the most important aspects of the cotton policies

---

[14]) For a detailed description of the Stabilization Programme, see *Economic Review*, CBE, vol. II, no. 2, 1962.

in their relation to agriculture (chapter 4, section 4.4) and industry (chapter 6, section 6.3). What remains here is mainly to study the impact of these policies on domestic cotton prices, and the degree of stabilization accomplished; in this the exchange rate policies have played an important role.

It is widely accepted that the long-staple and the short-staple cotton markets are to be considered as separate markets, with a good deal of interaction but still sufficiently independent to develop in their own special ways. This is immediately confirmed by a glance at the development of international raw cotton prices during the 'fifties. Chart 7.2 shows the average spot prices, c.i.f., quoted in Liverpool, for the years 1951/1952 to 1960/1961 for five varieties of cotton, including two Egyptian, Karnak F. G. and Ashmouni F. G., one Peruvian, Pima no. 1, 1–9/16″, one Mexican, Matamoros S.M.1 – 1/32″, and one from the United States, Memphis Terr. S.M.1 – 1/16″. Karnak and Pima are typical long-staple varieties, Matamoros and Memphis are short-staple varieties, and Ashmouni is a medium variety.

Chart 7.2 demonstrates, first, the well-known fact that the longer the staples are, usually, the higher the price.

Secondly, there is a general downward trend from 1951/1952 to 1960/1961. This is partly due to the fact that 1951/1952 was still under the influence of the Korean boom and its very high prices. But even if 1951/1952 is disregarded, the downward trend is obvious, the slack years 1952/1953 and 1953/1954 showing higher average prices than the prosperous years 1959/1960 and 1960/1961. The downward trend seems to have been stronger for the short-staple than for the long and medium staple varieties. Comparing averages for the years 1952/53–1953/54 and 1959/60–1960/61, we find a price fall for Ashmouni of 8 per cent and for Karnak of 12 per cent, but for Memphis 24 per cent. The extraordinary weakness of the long-staples in 1958/1959 may have been a temporary phenomenon, though the present development seems again to be against the long-staple varieties. Comparing the two important Egyptian varieties, Karnak and Ashmouni, we find that since 1958/1959 the gap between the prices has become quite narrow. This is believed in certain quarters to be a permanent tendency, owing to increased competition from the shorter staple varieties and the synthetic fibres. It is worth noticing, however, that the price-gap between Ashmouni and the American short-staple varieties seems to be larger in 1959/60–1960/61 than before World War II. Compared with prices for American short-staple cotton the price development for Egyptian cotton has not been unfavourable.

CHART 7.2

Liverpool cotton spot prices, c.i.f., US cents per pound

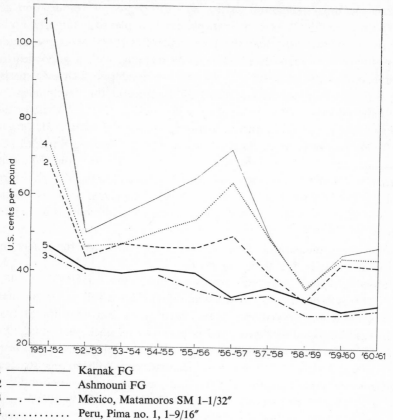

1 ——————— Karnak FG
2 — — — — — Ashmouni FG
3 —.—.—.— Mexico, Matamoros SM 1–1/32″
4 .... Peru, Pima no. 1, 1–9/16″
5 ——————— US Memphis Terr. SM 1–1/16″

A third characteristic feature of chart 7.2 is that the shorter the staples are, the more stable is the short-term development of the prices. This probably has nothing to do with staple length in itself, but is a result of the fact that the short-staple varieties are dominated completely by American cotton policies, which aim at stabilizing both domestic and export prices at levels suitable from the point of view of American domestic agriculture. The price developments of the other varieties will, of course, be affected by the stabilizing influence, the influence being weaker the longer the staples are, i.e. the less keen the competition is. The long-staple varieties are also affected by Government policies in Egypt, the Sudan, the Soviet Union and certain other countries; and it would be highly interesting to know to what extent the Egyptian area restrictions, export taxes, buffer-stock policies, etc., have been successful in influencing the level and fluctuations of the *international* prices of the Egyptian varieties. To trace these influences is not an easy task; a host of known and unknown demand and supply factors go to form prices and among them Egyptian policy is only one, probably even a minor one. The fact that Egyptian long-staple varieties have fluctuated much more than short-staple varieties indicates the huge difference in regulating power on the international markets between American policies and Egyptian.

To make a comparison between the international and domestic prices of Egyptian cotton, we have prepared chart 7.3, taking as our starting point the quotations in Liverpool for Karnak F.G. and Ashmouni F.G., c.i.f., and the spot quotations in Alexandria for the neighbouring quality G/FG. For the sake of comparison, both sets of prices were converted to US cents per pound. Unfortunately, published statistics did not allow us to obtain unbroken series of converted Alexandria quotations for identical qualities for the whole period. For the years 1951/52 to 1954/55 quotations for the quality FGF only were available; since FGF is a lower quality than G/FG the prices too are lower, of course. The conversion to US cents has been done not only at the official par rates, but also at rates taking into account the foreign exchange premiums allowed to the exports (see above). In this way four series have been obtained: (1) showing the Liverpool spot quotations, c.i.f., in US cents, (2) showing the Alexandria spot quotations, f.o.b., converted into US cents *at the official par rate of exchange*, (3) identical with the second series, but including the Egyptian export tax, and finally, (4) identical with the third series, but converted *at the exchange rates actually applied*. This latter series is calculated and published by *Cotton-World Statistics*.

Chart 7.3 shows that for Ashmouni up to 1956–1957 all these series moved more or less parallel to each other[15]). During the years 1955–56 and 1956–57, when the price quotations are very nearly comparable, Alexandria quotations plus export tax coincide almost exactly with the Liverpool quotations, no matter how the conversion to US cents is made, and this is also what we should expect from the policies pursued by the Egyptian authorities. It is true that the measures adopted in 1957, following the Suez War, should have increased the Alexandria quotations somewhat in

---

[15]) A similar diagram for Karnak, not included here, shows the same picture.

CHART 7.3
Ashmouni

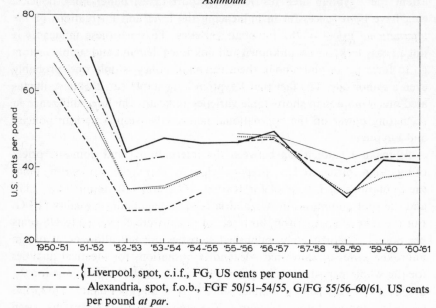

— . — . — . { Liverpool, spot, c.i.f., FG, US cents per pound
— — — — — Alexandria, spot, f.o.b., FGF 50/51–54/55, G/FG 55/56–60/61, US cents
per pound *at par.*
———————— Alexandria, spot + export tax, US cents per pound *at par.*
. . . . *Cotton World Statistics's* series: Alex. spot as above at *actual* exchange
rates + export tax.

relation to those in Liverpool, but at least until August 1957 these played a
minor role only; and the fact that the Liverpool quotations are for a slightly
higher quality than the Alexandria quotations (FG and G/FG respectively)
points in the opposite direction. Finally, we have the influence abroad from
the dumping of Egyptian cotton by Eastern Bloc countries.

For the years before 1954/55, the three series based on the Alexandria
quotations also follow the Liverpool quotations, but at a somewhat lower
level. This is on the whole due to the fact, already mentioned, that for this
period the Alexandria quotations are for a lower quality. However, the
difference may also to a minor extent be explained by the transport costs
between Alexandria and Liverpool[16]); the policy instruments for this period,
on the other hand, Export Accounts and Import Entitlements, ought to
have raised the Alexandria quotations somewhat in relation to those

---

[16]) This holds for the whole period, of course.

in Liverpool, though reselling may have put a brake on this tendency.

For the years after 1956/57 the series develop quite differently. It is here that domestic stabilization becomes significant. From the beginning of 1958, i.e. from the year 1957/58, the exchange premium makes itself strongly felt. During 1956/57 the Liverpool quotations almost coincided with those in Alexandria, including export tax, converted both at par rates and actual rates; by 1958/59 the Alexandria quotations, including export tax, converted at actual rates, had followed the Liverpool quotations closely in their fall, but the fall in the Alexandria quotations, including export tax, converted at *par rates*, was much smaller. The difference between the slim full curve (par rate conversion) and the dotted curve (actual rates conversion) shows then the effect of the foreign exchange premiums, while the difference between the slim full and the dashed curve (par rate conversion with and without export tax) shows the effect of the changes in the export tax, which was raised temporarily in 1957/58 and later reduced. From 1958/59 to 1960/61, Liverpool prices rose again; the Alexandria quotations, including export tax, converted at actual exchange rates, rose too, but not so much, owing to the differences in quality involved (FG rose more than G/FG).

The effect of the measures adopted has obviously been to stabilize domestic prices since 1956/57, domestic prices being shown by the dashed curve, i.e. Alexandria quotations, excluding export tax, converted at par, and the comparable foreign prices by the dotted curve, Alexandria quotations, including export tax, converted at actual rates. The individual effects of the export tax and the foreign exchange premiums are shown in table 7.12, where both the export tax and the premiums applied are measured as percentages of the foreign price, i.e. of the Alexandria quotations, with the addition of export tax, converted to US cents at actual exchange rates.

It should be recalled that during the whole of this period area restrictions were in force, so that one would expect the main impact of changes in the export tax and in the premiums to have been upon the incomes of the cotton producers and not upon the supply, although, of course, evasion of the area restrictions would probably have been less if the export taxes had not been reduced and the premium system introduced.

7.4 Summarizing discussion

7.4.1 The balance of payments deficit

The outstanding feature of Egyptian foreign trade and balance of payments

TABLE 7.12

Export tax and foreign exchange premiums 1956/57–1960/61

Relative numbers	Foreign price	Export tax	Foreign exchange premium	Domestic price
Karnak				
1956–57	100	− 6.7	(+ .4)	93.7
1957–58	100	− 14.5	+ 13.5	99.1
1958–59	100	− 11.5	+ 26.9	115.4
1959–60	100	−	+ 19.2	119.2
1960–61	100	−	+ 19.0	119.0
Ashmouni				
1956–57	100	− 2.6	(+ .5)	97.9
1957–58	100	− 8.1	+ 14.3	106.2
1958–59	100	− 7.2	+ 27.3	120.1
1959–60	100	− 6.4	+ 20.2	113.8
1960–61	100	− 6.2	+ 18.1	111.9

NOTE   The small "premiums" found in 1956–57 indicate the margin of error in the calculations.

is the deficit in both the balance of trade and the balance of current payments during the whole of the post-war period, with the resulting continuous depletion of foreign exchange reserves. This development, which is in contrast to pre-war conditions when small surpluses in the balance of trade were the rule, led finally to foreign exchange difficulties which became critical after 1962, with a formal depreciation of the Egyptian pound, drawings on the IMF, and some adjustments in domestic policies. Behind this development lay an almost stagnant export volume and, simultaneously, an expanding import volume. The improvement in the terms of trade and the increase in the net of invisibles (the Suez Canal) helped to meet part of the increase in imports; but even this favourable development was not sufficient to prevent a growing deficit. Since 1955 the deficits have been large and persistent, and continuously increasing, and in 1963 it may run at a level of 6.4 per cent of GNI.

Until 1958 deficits in the balance of current payments were financed exclusively through a fall in the reserves of gold and foreign exchange, which even had to cover a certain net outflow of capital. Since 1959 a growing part of the deficit has been covered by capital inflows, in particular US counterpart funds, in which the net increase amounted to almost £E 140 millions during the years 1959–1962. This did not, however, prevent the exchange reserves from falling to an unprecedentedly low level. But even during 1962 the gold reserve, which at the new exchange rates amounts to almost a quarter of the present yearly import value, was kept untouched.

Explanations of these deficits are not difficult to find. For the period as a whole an overvaluation in terms of purchasing power owing to the inflationary effect of World War II has made itself felt. The extent of this overvaluation is difficult to appraise. The improved competitiveness of industry must have reduced it during the 'fifties (see chapter 6.5), but even without it, deficits would probably have arisen owing to factors on the demand side. For the first period of heavy deficits, 1946 and 1947, we need only point to the pent-up demand from the war years. The second period, from 1950 to 1952, is dominated by inflationary tendencies, arising partly from the unhappy cotton policies adopted by the Government during and after the Korean boom. The large and persistent deficits in foreign trade since 1955, finally, are closely connected with the expenditure policies of the Government, besides payments of compensation for the Suez Canal, foreign properties and to the Sudan.

One of the important factors on the demand side is the shift towards more investments. An expansion of investments tends in itself to increase imports, even at an unchanged level of national income and outlay. For an underdeveloped country with only a negligible domestic production of machinery and equipment there is, *a priori*, every reason to expect the marginal propensity to import to be larger in investment activities than in consumption activities, in particular when investments are concentrated in the industrial sector. For industrial investments calculations in the NPC point to an average import propensity as high as about 45 per cent, and the marginal content may be even higher; non-industrial investments will probably have a lower propensity. Furthermore, the development 1938–52 suggests an over-all marginal propensity to import, measured upon net national income, of about 25 per cent, for consumption purposes the marginal propensity must have been lower. Increased investment activity should therefore, given the national income and outlay, not only lead to an increased share of capital goods out of a given total import, but also to an increase in total imports.

To find out to what extent the shift in demand towards capital goods is responsible for the present deficits, we may answer the following hypothetical question: what would be the level of imports if investment activities to-day were cut down to a level where only necessary replacements were made, and other activities expanded so that the present national income remained unchanged, though further growth would naturally cease? To fix our ideas let us work on the figures for 1960. Calculations point to a share of replacements of between a third and a fourth of industrial gross investments in 1960. That year total imports of capital goods amounted to almost £E 70 millions (including Russian High Dam deliveries) of which we shall assume, for the sake of argument, that about £E 20 million were for replacement purposes. We then imagine that net investments fall to nothing in order to save £E 50 million imports. If we assume, again for the sake of argument, the marginal import propensity for investments to be about 50 per cent, and in other activities to be about 25 per cent, an expansion of other activities to compensate, with respect to current national income, for the fall in investment activity will lead to an increase of imports by £E 25 million, and the net of imports saved will be the same amount. Even this heavy fall in investment activity would not be sufficient to cover the deficit on the balance of current payments; for 1960 the deficit (including Russian High Dam deliveries) may have been £E 35–40 million. And compared with the deficits in 1962 and 1963 the 25 million would help but little. To this must be added the demand kept back by import controls (see above). It is clear then that a complete stop in net investments at given national income would probably only cut imports sufficiently to wipe out less than one quarter of the present deficits, and it would contribute nothing to the relaxation of import controls. Since, furthermore, some net investments were made already before the war, and even more so during the 'forties, the increase in the share of investments can only explain a minor part of the present deficits.

Since the change in the composition of demand towards more capital goods explains only a minor part of the present deficits, and competitiveness seems to have increased during post-war years together with the terms of trade, it is clear that we must turn to the development of *total demand* in order to explain the deficits. The investment policy has in itself created the possibility of a higher level of income by expanding the production capacity of the country; but, as we shall see in chapter 8, the main expansive factor has been the budget policy, including investments, of the Government. We shall therefore postpone further discussion of the balance of payments problem to the general discussion of savings and investments in chapter 8.

7.4.2 The exchange rate policies

The partial depreciation of the exchange rate which began in 1949, and had already probably reached its peak in the 'fifties, was made with the intention of encouraging exports, as well as to stabilize cotton prices in Egyptian pounds. For a depreciation to improve the balance of current payments certain well-known conditions have to be fulfilled. First of all domestic prices and costs must not be allowed to increase in proportion to export and import prices. This condition has in all probability been satisfied, in particular with respect to industrial costs, see chapters 5, section 5.3 and 6, section 6.5. Secondly, low elasticities of foreign demand for Egyptian export goods and domestic demand for import goods might together even bring about a deterioration in the balance of current payments as a result of depreciation. The theoretical condition for an improvement is that the sum of the two demand-elasticities exceeds one. This condition also has in all probability been fulfilled. There seems to be no doubt (see chapter 4, section 4.3) that the foreign demand for raw cotton is elastic, and even the short-term elasticity may be a good deal greater than one. This settles the issue directly. A further point is that the improvement may be small, at least in the short run, owing to a relatively low supply-elasticity of export goods and demand-elasticity for import goods, though here much will depend on simultaneous Government policies with respect to domestic prices. The short-term supply-elasticity of cotton seems to be quite low, perhaps of the order of magnitude 0.2, and if cereal prices are allowed to rise, owing to higher import prices, there will probably be no increase at all in cotton cultivation. Idle capacity in the cotton textile industry guarantees, of course, a high export supply-elasticity for yarn and fabrics, but increased exports of these products will imply lower exports of raw cotton. On the import side capital goods can be left out of the picture, since investments are almost completely in the hands of the Government, and it is up to them to decide whether to cut the demand for these imports or not. The price-elasticities of demand for both food and raw materials are also probably low. We are left therefore with only about 10–15 per cent of imports in which any short-term elasticity of importance can be expected. In the longer run things may, of course, be radically different.

It is a point of interest that the depreciation of the Egyptian pound has not been a simple one-way street. The average actual exchange rates fluctuated considerably from 1949 to 1962. To some extent the official premiums were governed by the actual state of the current balance of payments, which seems to show that the Government expected fairly quick results from the partial exchange rate adjustments. After 1957, however, the degree of depreciation seems to have been more a matter of counteracting fluctuations in foreign cotton prices. The exchange rates were used as a direct means of stabilizing domestic prices and incomes. This feature of the exchange rate policies is highly interesting and in line with a certain school of monetary policy which maintains that the exchange rates should be used in just this way. According to this school of thought a country has to choose between stable exchange rates with the domestic price level fluctuating in accordance with foreign trade prices, or to let the exchange rates fluctuate in order to counteract changes in foreign trade prices and keep the domestic price level stable; domestic stabilization thus requires fluctuating exchange rates[17]). A policy of the latter kind clearly contradicts the ideals of the IMF, and through a variable system of export and import taxes and subsidies similar results can in principle be obtained. From a practical point of view, however, it is a great advantage to have the possibility of allowing the exchange rates to fluctuate in order to dampen foreign price fluctuations. The new cotton trade system (see chapter 4.4.7) has to be seen against this background; in this system a buffer has been created which can keep domestic producers' prices constant (or let them vary in any desired way) in spite of fluctuating export prices, and without formally imposing export taxes or subsidies, or partial adjustments of the exchange rate.

7.4.3 The foreign trade regulations

Foreign trade regulations and government intervention are not peculiar to Egypt. Quite apart from the Eastern Bloc countries, where such intervention is an integral part of the prevailing economic philosophy, foreign trade regulations are familiar in most underdeveloped countries. There are obvious reasons for the use of direct Government intervention in foreign trade in such countries. One is deficits in the balance of current payments, which it has not been politically feasible to correct by other means. A second reason is the need to nurse infant industries[18]). A third, the need to manipulate the balance of payments to secure a greater import of capital goods, once again, other means being out of question for one reason or another. All this is commonplace and needs no discussion. The inconveniences arising

---

[17]) J. M. Keynes, *A Tract on Monetary Reform*, London, 1923.

[18]) Welfare considerations have led many economists to recommend direct subsidies to infant industries rather than support through tariffs or import regulations. Direct subsidization, however, requires corresponding taxes, and so the limited capacity for collecting taxes other than customs duties may prevent such policies in underdeveloped countries, but see below chapter 9.7.

from bureaucratic rigidities and misallocations are certainly not fewer in Egypt than elsewhere and need no detailed discussion either.

What we wish to point out here is that in spite of such inconveniences, and for completely different reasons, underdeveloped countries embarked on serious development policies will often have to control the balance of payments rigorously. To pave the way for progress it is often politically necessary to break the power and position of established ruling classes, e.g. feudal landlords. With private capital concentrated in the hands of these very classes, a tendency to capital flight can easily follow. In pursuing a policy of development it may be almost impossible to guarantee security and profits, and in general create the atmosphere necessary to keep domestic private capital in the country. This will be particularly so if the development policy has a strong social bias, as is in fact the case in Egypt. Even for a developing country which in principle encourages private activity and savings, some control over capital movements may be necessary. Now, it is well known from the experience of many countries, developed as well as underdeveloped, that if capital flight is to be effectively hindered, the Government must also control foreign trade and invisibles. By double invoicing and other tricks export and import deals can easily be used to move private capital out of the country, and if this abuse of foreign trade is sufficiently pronounced, even a full-scale nationalization of the trade may be necessary to stop the flight of capital. It is not our intention to present this as the sole or even major reason for the nationalization of foreign trade in Egypt in 1961, but we do wish to stress that it is a phenomenon that can make unregulated trade difficult in many developing countries.

Finally, we wish to stress also the special problems arising from trade with Eastern Bloc countries. During the last ten years, underdeveloped countries have expanded their trade with the Eastern Bloc considerably. Quite apart from the political circumstances which in many cases are to be found behind this development, such trade may have great advantages for these countries. Without doubt, the whole world is loosing from the suffocation of trade between East and West, and there are big opportunities here for both sides. Trade with Eastern Bloc countries, however, is something very different from trade with Western Europe and America. The governments concerned may have to step in one way or another to secure deliveries or purchases, and even to counteract monopolistic exploitation on the part of the Eastern Bloc trade authorities. And although Eastern Bloc countries have on the whole tended to trade more and more on the basis of so-called world-market prices, there is still such a big gap between official exchange rates and relative cost and price levels that special exchange rates or other special measures may be called for in commercial intercourse with the Eastern Bloc. The ideals of the IMF, with free, unregulated multi-lateral trade and capital movements, and convertible currencies with unified rates, are not always easy to reconcile with Eastern Bloc trade, and it may pay economically for a country to develop Eastern Bloc trade rather than live up to the IMF ideals.

CHAPTER 8

Savings, investments, and the foreign deficit

8.1 The institutional background

Before discussing the monetary aspect of savings, investments and the foreign deficit, we begin with a brief description of the credit institutions and their functions, the central bank and its policies, and the growing role of the Government in the field of finance. Government intervention culminated in the nationalization of banks and insurance companies in 1961, but it had begun five years earlier, and what has probably been more important for the flow of credit than the actual take-over of the credit institutions is the "nationalization" of investments and savings that has taken place, through the rapidly growing public share in them during the last 10 years. With 90 per cent of all investments in the hands of the Government, and public savings in a wide sense amounting to 50–60 per cent of total domestic savings, only a limited role would in any case have been left for private activity in the credit markets.

8.1.1 Early developments

The origin and early development of credit market institutions in Egypt are closely connected with the needs of agriculture and trade. Agriculture needed both long-term credits for land reclamation schemes and irrigation purposes, etc., and short-term credits to finance crops, in particular the cultivation and marketing of the cotton crop. The long-term credits were supplied mainly by foreign-owned mortgage companies, the first being established as early as 1880. Since these companies for various practical reasons concentrated on relatively large loans for agriculture and residential building, the Government established in 1932 a credit organization for small real-estate loans to individuals and co-operative societies for residential building. The cotton crop was financed in part, from the beginning of the century, by the commercial banks, whose main activities were to extend short-term credits to big cultivators, merchants and exporters, in particular during the cotton season. Most of the commercial banks were branches of foreign banks, British, French, Italian, etc., and they refrained from granting loans to small cultivators, mainly owing to lack of acceptable collateral and the heavy administrative expenses. The peasants were therefore forced to turn to private money-lenders and borrow on very unfavourable terms. During the last decade of the nineteenth century, however, the Government began to give loans to peasants at relatively low interest rates, and after the *National Bank of Egypt* was established in 1898, an agricultural bank was created in 1902 by the collaboration of the Government and the *National Bank*. The activity of this agricultural bank grew steadily, but after some difficult years for agriculture in 1907 and 1911, the Government stepped in to protect small cultivators by enacting the "Five Feddan Law", which forbade foreclosures in respect of owners of five feddans and less. This eventually led to the liquidation of the agricultural bank in 1931, and the *Credit Agricole* was created to fill the gap. The *Credit Agricole* was an Egyptian joint-stock company in which the Government held 50 per cent of the shares. Its object was to grant both short- and long-term credits to cultivators as well as co-operative societies.

8.1.2 The stock market and the joint-stock companies

The stock market was organized as early as the beginning of this century, but owing to heavy speculative activity and the small number of investors, it has never worked well, and by 1909 increasing Government supervision was already considered necessary. The capital raised directly through the stock market was always modest and most of the long-term capital of the joint-stock companies before World War I consisted of long debentures, to a large extent foreign. These early developments are interesting, nevertheless, because they already reveal at an early date an increasing degree of self-financing in agriculture and an increasing flow of credits for industrialization.

The long-term capital of joint-stock companies active in the field of agriculture and building shows a heavy fall, which took place mainly between 1914 and 1938, and was concentrated in the debentures, which were subsequently paid off. Ploughed-back profits were thus sufficient not only to satisfy credit demands, albeit declining, but also to pay off foreign debts. During the great wars, with their inflationary profits in agriculture, the

TABLE 8.1

Joint-stock companies, long-term capital (paid-up capital plus debentures, £E million)

Type of activity, end of	1914	1938	1945	1953/54	1962*
Agricultural and mortgage banks	54.6	22.6	11.7	29.8	—
Agriculture, building, canal, water and irrigation	36.5	24.6	24.6	28.4	—
Commercial banks and other financial institutions	5.8	6.3	7.5	10.5	—
Industry, commerce and transport	17.9	30.3	46.3	97.1	—
Other	1.7	3.2	1.2	1.7	—
Total	116.5	87.1	91.4	159.5	233.0

* Only a break-down on commercial (£E 113) and industrial (£E 120) is available.

SOURCE   *Economic Bulletin*, National Bank of Egypt, vol. 1, no. 4, Dec. 1948, p. 117, for the figures 1914–1945. For 1953/54 see *Annuaire Statistique* 1960–61, p. 360 ff. For 1962 see *Economic Bulletin,* NBE 1963. The classification for 1953/54 is not fully comparable with that of the earlier years.

demand for credits from agriculture seems to have fallen sharply. At the same time long-term capital invested in industrial companies grew considerably, although until 1938 the rise was less than the fall in "agricultural" long-term capital, and from 1938 to 1945 only slightly greater. Taking into account the threefold price increase between 1938 and 1945, the "real" value of outside long-term capital fell in industrial companies too. This indicates an increased degree of self-financing in industry during World War II, or at least a decrease in the importance of the open long-term market. In that respect development in Egypt would appear to resemble what has taken place in most industrialized countries. The bulk of the increase in the capital of industrial companies until the beginning of World War II was subscribed by the *Bank Misr*. The increase since 1945 in Agricultural and Mortgage Banks reflects mainly residential building activity, and the rest of the increase is in industry and commerce.

8.1.3 The commercial banks

As we have said, most of the commercial banks were – until the Egyptianization of 1956 – branches of foreign banks, and engaged almost exclusively in the short-term financing of agricultural crops and trade in general; apart from this, they looked mainly for investment opportunities abroad. Behind this pattern of behaviour there was on the one hand the fact that until the 'thirties there was very little demand for other credit, but also, on the other, the well-known conservative British banking theory to the effect that so-called self-liquidating commodity loans provide the only sound basis for commercial banking. This conservatism proved particularly unfortunate during the 'thirties, when a demand for industrial long-term credits grew up. During and after World War I, however, a need for industrial credits had already been felt, and this led in 1920 to the establishment of the purely Egyptian *Bank Misr*, which served during the following decades as a Gründer-bank, and was very active in promoting the early industrialization of Egypt. Bank Misr created a number of industrial affiliates and granted them advances. The Government placed funds at the disposal of the bank to grant loans to small and medium-sized industrial establishments, but the main activity of Bank Misr, in addition to its business as a commercial bank, was in the creation of large-scale industrial establishments.

To solve the problem of the dearth of credit to small enterprises, the *Industrial Bank* was established after World War II, with the Government holding 50 per cent of the capital; this bank was authorized to participate in financing industrial enterprises and granting both short-term, medium and long-term loans. Again the major obstacle to credit expansion in small and medium sized firms lay on the demand side, i.e. in the status and qualifications of the applicants.

Little is known about the balance sheets of the commercial banks before 1946, but it seems that their activities changed during World War II when Egypt accumulated big foreign exchange reserves and cotton stocks, as described in chapter 7. By that time investment in Government securities had already increased in importance. This development was strongly ac-centuated during the 'fifties, when the activities of the commercial banks changed completely, not so much because the banks were taken over by the Government between 1956 and 1961, but rather because of the change in the composition of production, real investments, and domestic savings. As public investment increases commercial banks of necessity change character, and tend to become passive savings banks investing an increasing part of the private savings deposited with them in Government undertakings. Also, as the pace of industrial development quickened in Egypt more loans and advances were granted to industrial establishments, which by 1963 absorbed about 40 per cent of bank credits. On the other hand, the increased share of domestic savings handled by the Government, the greater role of the Pension and Insurance Fund institutions, the active part played by the

Treasury in financing economic development, and the setting up of public organizations to control and create production units, all mean that banking activities will tend to stagnate.

8.1.4 The Central Bank and its policies

The *National Bank of Egypt*, founded in 1898 as a private note-issuing bank and an agent for the Government, was from the beginning modelled completely on the *Bank of England*, with Issue Department and all. It was a private joint-stock company also handling commercial banking business. The shares were mainly in foreign hands. Its position remained unchanged until 1951, when it was given legal status as a central bank empowered to regulate the volume of credit in the country. Passive policies were abandoned in favour of active management of the credit system. The reserve ratio of the commercial banks, and the right of the Bank to undertake direct commercial banking business, were the main devices for the regulation of the credit market, although in principle the Bank could, of course, work on the rate of discount and operate in the open market. As the bank continued to be a private joint-stock company whose shares were mostly held by foreigners, a Supreme Committee with a majority of Government representatives was set up to settle all questions of monetary, credit, and exchange policy.

Until 1947 Egypt was almost a country without monetary policies of its own. Movements of funds between London and Cairo were free, and this enabled the commercial banks, since most of them were branches of foreign banks, to rely on their head offices abroad for funds to finance the cotton crop, etc. In these movements the *National Bank* served mainly as a passive transfer agent, and the Egyptian credit market thus became closely connected with foreign credit markets, mainly London, and the state of domestic liquidity was passively determined by developments in the balance of payments. The abandonment of the Gold Standard consolidated this system. Commercial banks gradually adopted the habit of keeping a reserve balance with the *National Bank*, but this was mainly for clearing purposes. The first attempt to pursue a more active domestic credit policy did not come until World War II when, as a special war-time measure, the commercial banks agreed in 1943 to keep a reserve of 15 per cent in cash or in deposits with the *National Bank*.

When Egypt left the Sterling Area in 1947 the situation changed radically, and transactions with the Sterling Area became subject to the same controls as those applied to other monetary areas. The need for a fully-fledged central bank with all its measures closely co-ordinated with other public policies became obvious, and this led in 1951 to the central bank legislation mentioned above. From that year the *National Bank* pursued more and more active policies, and although for several years they were still mainly governed by foreign exchange considerations, the stabilization of domestic production, together with prices and income, and development financing, gradually became important concerns of the Bank. Its main weapon after 1951 was the stipulation concerning reserve ratios, but following on the Egyptianization of the foreign commercial banks and the issue of the Bank and Credit Law of 1957, which considerably increased the *National Bank's* control over other banking institutions, and finally the complete nationalization of the banking system in 1961, there was also direct consultation between the Government and the commercial banks, and between the central bank and the commercial banks, concerning the investment policies of both commercial and specialized banks. The old attitude of the banks, with their strong preference for "self-liquidating" commodity loans, has in this way gradually been replaced by a more positive approach to long-term investment.[1]) Finally, to complete the co-ordination between monetary policies and other policies, in 1960 the old *National Bank* was made a state-owned bank and split into two, the *Central Bank of Egypt*, which was invested with all the authority of a modern central bank, and a new *National Bank of Egypt*, which took over the commercial banking activities of the old *National Bank*. From the point of view of monetary policy this was probably a step backwards, because it deprived the central banking authority of the possibility of interfering in the short-term market through direct commercial activities, but after the rest of the banking system was nationalized in 1961 this became of no importance.

8.1.5 The pension and insurance funds

The Government can interfere with the credit market directly by changing the institutional structure of the credit system. If the credit institutions are privately owned, controls and regulations can be applied to their current activities. And ownership itself may be assumed by the Government. In all these respects there has been a far-reaching intervention in the credit market

---

[1]) Girgis A. Marzouk, *Recent developments in monetary policies*, Institute of Banking Studies, Cairo 1962 (in Arabic).

during the period since the Suez War. Of equal interest from the point of view of the national economy is the change in the credit flows which has followed from the Government's investment and savings policies. The credit flows and the general state of the credit market are closely related to investments and savings, and their composition. Government policies have in an indirect way caused a rapid change in the nature of the credit market. The Government's investment policies and general budget policy will be dealt with below. Here we will only discuss certain special, non-budgetary measures taken by the Government to increase domestic savings, the most important being the compulsory pension and social insurance schemes, which have led to large accumulations of funds that have been utilized to finance development projects.

In 1956 a pension and insurance fund for Government civil servants was established. To this fund Government employees contributed 10 per cent of their salaries, while the Government contributed a further 10 per cent, and after 1961, 12½ per cent. The scheme was later extended to include all Government employees, and also to cover years of service prior to 1956 against additional payments from both the employee concerned and the Government. In 1960 and 1961 the scheme was reorganized and certain benefits granted to pensioners. The direct object of this fund is, of course, to give Government employees pension rights and certain other post-service benefits. In 1961/62 the scheme covered about 625 000 Government employ-

TABLE 8.2

Public organization for insurance and pensions for government staff; accumulation of funds

Year	Number of beneficiaries (thousands)	Excess of receipts over payments (£E million)	General reserve (£E million)	Return from investments (£E million)
1956/57	204	7.3	24.4	0.7
1957/58	221	12.5	36.9	1.1
1958/59	228	12.3	49.2	1.3
1959/60	582	15.7	64.9	2.0
1960/61	600	20.8	85.8	2.5
1961/62	625	24.9	142.2*)	4.7
1962/63		27.9**)		

*) In 1961/62 certain other Government funds were included in the general reserve.
**) Budget forecast.

SOURCE　　*1961–1962 Annual Report of the General Organization for Insurance and Pensions* (in Arabic), p. 4.

ees, whose families numbered over 3 million persons. In addition to the social security enjoyed by the employees considerable funds are accumulated annually; as in all other pension schemes ingoing payments during the first decades will greatly exceed outgoing payments and a rapid fund accumulation will take place.

The figures in the second column of table 8.2, excess of receipts over payments, do not represent a net addition to domestic savings. About half the annual receipts consist of payments by the Government; these payments will automatically decrease public savings, in the budget, by the same amount, and do not represent any net addition to domestic savings. The other half is deducted from the salaries of the Government employees, who, by the way, got no compensatory wage increase when the scheme was introduced, and to this extent represents additional savings. To the extent, however, that Government employees have cut down other kinds of savings to compensate for the enforced saving through the pension scheme, the additional savings will be lower. Since next to nothing is known about the savings patterns of Egyptian families, all we can say is that the net savings created through the pension scheme probably amount to something between nothing and half the figures of column two [2]).

The balance sheet of the Organization shows that while more than 60 per cent of the funds were invested in Government securities and undertakings, the Organization also acquired some shares and securities in the private sector, and granted long-term advances to a number of industries in both the public and the private sector for fixed investment; the rate of interest paid on long-term advances varies between 4.5 and 5 per cent.

Similarly, an insurance and provident fund for non-Government employees was also established in 1956. Originally workers in the private sector paid 5 per cent of their wages, while the employers contributed a further 5 per cent, but in 1959 the employer's contribution was raised to 10 per cent to cover the additional cost of insurance against employment injury. In 1961 the provident fund system was changed into a regular pension scheme and the total contributions raised to 24 per cent, of which 7 per cent is paid by the employee and the rest by the employer. Initially, the amounts accumulated under this scheme were considerably smaller than those ac-

---

[2]) In principle even a negative net effect on savings cannot be excluded. The "life-time income" of Government employees must have increased during the scheme, and this could theoretically lead to an increase in current consumption. Experience from other countries, however, shows that pension arrangements usually lead to a net increase in savings.

cumulated under the Government employees' pension scheme, but as it is gradually extended to cover all production units the funds to be accumulated here are expected to exceed those under the civil service scheme. Here again most of the surplus is invested in Government undertakings and long-term loans for investment purposes.

TABLE 8.3

Social insurance surplus, 1956–1963 (£E millions)

	Total receipts	Total expenditure	Surplus
1956	1.1	0.2	0.9
1957	2.3	0.7	1.5
1958	3.1	0.7	2.4
1959	4.1	1.0	3.1
1960	7.5	1.8	5.7
1961	12.7	3.6	9.2
1962			20.9*)

*) Budget forecast.

SOURCE   *Annual Report of the Egyptian Organization for Social Insurance, several years.*

8.2 Monetary survey 1951–1962

8.2.1 Credit transactions through the banking system

A substantial part of the flow of credit is canalized through the banking system. To give a picture, therefore, of net borrowing and lending, as between sectors, we have summarized in table 8.4 the net credit movements passing through the system, which is here taken to include the Central (National) Bank of Egypt and all commercial banks. The sectors considered are the Government (not including public companies), the private sector (including public companies and excluding central and commercial banks), and finally, the rest of the world. Net foreign assets in table 8.4 include US counterpart funds. Net claims on the private sector includes all circulating currency (money,) which is considered a claim by the private sector on the banking system[3]). Outside the scope of the table are, in particular,

---

[3]) This claim is, of course, a fictitious one, but the fiction is useful in this connection because an increase in currency outstanding implies borrowing by the banking sys-

direct credit transactions between the Government and the private sector, mainly in connection with the land reforms and the nationalizations; credits between firms; and direct Government credits to and from foreign countries not passing through the banking system.

Table 8.4 shows first of all a permanent net foreign borrowing, mainly through a fall in foreign assets, which has already been dealt with in chapter 7. At the same time there has been an almost continuous, though very uneven, increase in the net claims of the banking system on the Government. The net lending to the Government of £E 94 million in 1951 and 1952 was partly connected with the cotton policies, the Government's purchases being financed by bank credits. In 1953 and 1954 the Government lent or borrowed only small amounts, while during 1955 and 1956 its net borrowing reached £E 48 and 70 million respectively. Behind this lay an expansion in Government investment in agriculture and industry on the one hand, and on the other the effects of the Suez War. In 1957 and 1958 the Government again almost disappeared from the scene, but after 1959 Government borrowing expanded rapidly, to reach the record figure of £E 94 million in 1962; this development is connected with the Government's need to finance the investment programmes, and with the big increase in public consumption after 1961/62. The net position of the private sector with the banking system has also developed in quite an irregular way; to some extent it is correlated inversely with Government borrowing. Since 1959/60 there has been a permanent increase in the net claim of the private sector on the banking system. From the point of view of the banking system the period as a whole has thus been characterized by increasing net lending to the Government and net borrowing from abroad, owing to a fall in foreign assets, with a tendency towards increasing net borrowing from the private sector. These tendencies gained momentum towards the end of the period. We shall comment further in section 8.3.

8.2.2 Liquidity in the private sector

The liquidity of the private sector has some bearing upon the development of private demand for commodities and services. Liquidity, however, is not a very clear concept and many definitions are possible. Here we have at our

---

tem. And since only a negligible part of the currency in circulation will be in the hands of the Government or outside the country, changes in circulating currency will by and large imply credit transactions between the banking system and the private sector.

TABLE 8.4

Lending and borrowing through the banking system, 1950–1963 (*£E millions*)

Change 1 Jan.–31 Dec.	1951	1952	1953	9154	1955	1956	1957	1958	1959	1960	1961	1962
Net foreign assets	− 11	− 60	− 8	− 15	− 37	− 42	− 25	− 22	− 42	− 46	− 27	− 70
Net claims on government	31	63	− 6	− 8	48	70	18	− 2	23	60	61	94
Net claims on private sectors	− 12	− 1	0	22	2	− 28	− 7	30	17	− 1	− 51	− 12
Unclassified items	− 9	− 2	14	1	− 13	0	14	− 8	2	− 13	17	− 12
Total	0	0	0	0	0	0	0	0	0	0	0	0

SOURCE   *International Financial Statistics*, Supplement to 1963/64 Issues, IMF, p. 234, and *Credit and Banking Development*, Central Bank of Egypt, several issues. Government includes semi-government institutions, such as the Authorities (Railways, Suez Canal, etc.) and the General Organizations, but not public companies affiliated to the organizations; such companies are included in the private sector. Net claims on Government and private sector are all loans and advances less deposits and currency. Agricultural Bank and Industrial Bank Bonds sold to the banking system, though guaranteed by the Government, have been considered claims on the private sector, the Agricultural Bank and the Industrial Bank being included in the private sector. Net Foreign Assets include counterpart funds.

disposal two different statistical measures of private liquidity, the quantity of money (currency plus private demand deposits) and the net claims (other than on capital account) of the private sector on the banking system. We shall relate these two liquidity measures to gross private disposable income in order to get a measure of the real cash balances, and real net bank position per unit of real income of the private sector. A fall in real cash balances in this sense may be supposed to exert a downward pressure on private spending, and vice versa; the same importance may be attached to the real net bank position. Both real cash balances and real net bank position show a heavy fall from 1952/53 to around 1960 and 1961. In 1962/63 both of them rose again somewhat. Private liquidity may accordingly have exerted a dampening effect on private spending until 1961/62, but after 1962/63 there may have been a slightly expansive effect. Compared with the early 'fifties, private liquidity was still quite low in 1962/63[4]).

What is called the "private sector" here includes the nationalized enterprises, and all other public companies. This procedure has been adopted in order to obtain comparable series. It would have been better to keep the nationalized companies separate, but this has not been possible. To the extent that the public companies are able to dispose of their deposits and take on bank loans, it may be justified to include them in the private sector for the purpose at hand. High liquidity in public companies may, after all, lead to increased spending, e.g. for stock building, just as much as in private companies. But public companies are not entirely autonomous with respect to the use of their financial assets.

---

[4] The development means an increase in the income velocity of money from 1952 to 1961, and later a small fall. This increase in velocity is sometimes interpreted as a sign of inflation: a flight from money should have led to a rise in prices and accordingly to a fall in *real* cash balances. *A priori* this interpretation cannot be excluded as impossible, but it does not seem very relevant for the period in question. First of all this is a mechanism which works mainly under conditions of hyperinflation, or, at least, rapidly rising prices, but in Egypt prices have actually been very stable and most of the fall in real cash balances and the rise in income velocity is related to the increase in real national income. Secondly, the income velocity has been stagnant, and has even fallen since 1959, and it is exactly during the last few years that some signs of domestic inflation have appeared. Finally if anything, there has been a flight from land, shares and other kinds of property considered to be in the danger zone of nationalization, to small businesses, residential buildings, and also various kinds of cash. For all these reasons we find the interpretation *(à la* Patinkin) in the text the soundest.

TABLE 8.5

Private liquidity, 1952–1963

Year	Private disposable gross income (£E million)	Quantity of money, beginning of year (£E million)	Net claims by private sector on banking system £E million		Money per £E of private disposable gross income (£E)	Net claims on banking system per £E of private disposable gross income, £E	
			Mid-year	Beginning of year		Mid-year	Beginning of year
1952/53	754	342.5	280.2		0.45	0.37	
1953/54	801	349.1	281.6		0.44	0.35	
1954/55	846	346.1	248.8	297.1	0.41	0.29	0.35
1955/56	860	324.1	256.4	260.2	0.38	0.30	0.30
1956/57	924	342.9		281.8	0.37		0.30
1957/58	943	391.4		295.6	0.42		0.31
1958/59	1 003	375.1		244.4	0.37		0.24
1959/60	1 107	358.8		223.8	0.32		0.20
1960/61	1 194	393.1		224.1	0.33		0.19
1961/62	1 280	409.8		273.6	0.32		0.21
1962/63	1 359	467.7		311.2	0.34		0.23

SOURCE   Private disposable gross income, see Bent Hansen, "Savings in the UAR (Egypt), 1938/39 and 1945/46 to 1962/63", *Memo. no. 551*, INP, 1965, Table 1. Quantity of money (= notes in circulation plus private demand deposits) and net claims by private sector on banking system, see *International Financial Statistics*, IMF, and *Credit and Banking Development*, Central Bank of Egypt, several issues. Both private disposable gross income and quantity of money include public companies.

8.3 *Savings and investments*

As in many other countries, private savings can only be estimated statistically as a residual and errors in the statistics have an unpleasant tendency to cumulate in the residual. For Egypt the situation is even worse. Usually private savings can be obtained as a residual in several ways, as private disposable income less private consumption, or as gross investments less foreign borrowing less public saving, and some check on accuracy can be obtained. In Egypt available national accounts permit only one residual estimate, and unfortunately the basic series contain systematic errors which distort the private savings figures. Full tables for the years 1945/46 to 1952/53 and 1952/53 to 1962/63, the two periods being based on different estimates, do exist[5]). Here we will show only the last few years, together with some average figures for two earlier periods for which we believe the statistical errors to be relatively small, and which are sufficient to show the main trends.

8.3.1 *Domestic, public, and private savings*

Domestic savings, measured as a percentage of GNP, seem to have been very stable at a level of 12 per cent during the post-war period; the years excluded from table 8.6 show some variations year by year, but apart from two exceptional years, the percentage has stayed within the limits of 10–13 for all the post-war years. This means that the whole increase in the ratio of gross investments to GNP has been financed through foreign borrowing, which has grown from almost nothing (0.8 per cent) in 1948–50 to 6.4 per cent of GNP in 1962/63.

Public savings remained relatively constant in absolute amount until the end of the 'fifties, when they reached a peak of £E 65 million, at about 6 per cent of GNP. Since then they have been falling, both absolutely and relatively, to the present 2 per cent level. This development is closely related to budget policies, i.e. to the expansion of public consumption and public current net income, respectively. In chapter 1 we looked briefly at the development of public consumption, and in chapter 9 we shall consider the revenue policies of the Government budget. Here we would only point out that while tax increases, together with the increase in revenue connected

---

[5]) Bent Hansen, "Savings in the UAR (Egypt), 1938/39 and 1945/46 to 1962/63", *Memo. no. 551*, INP, 1965. See also Statistical Appendix.

TABLE 8.6

225

Savings and investments

£E million (at current market prices)	Average 1948–49	Average 1954–56	Average 1960/63	Average 1962/63*
1. GNP	773	1043	1565	1679
2. − Public current net income (including pension and social insurance fund accumulations and income of authorities like the Suez Canal)	117	190	288	320
3. = Private disposable gross income (including gross profits in public companies)	656	853	1278	1359
4. − Private consumption − $(x + y)$	596	764	1118	1189
5. = Private gross savings − $x − y$ (including gross profits in public companies)	60	89	160	170
6. + public savings (including pension and social insurance fund accumulation etc.)	40	38	34	30
7. = Domestic gross savings − $x − y$	100	127	194	200
8. + Foreign borrowing + y	6	32	67	107
9. = Gross investments − x	106	159	261	307

Percentages

10. Gross investments/GNP	13.5	15.2	16.7	18.3
11. Domestic gross savings/GNP	12.8	12.1	12.4	11.9
12. Public savings/GNP	5.2	3.6	2.2	1.8
13. Private disp. gross income/GNP	84.9	81.9	81.5	80.5
14. Private gross savings/private disp. gross income	9.2	10.5	12.5	12.6

* Preliminary figures.

SOURCE   Bent Hansen, "Savings in the UAR (Egypt), 1938/39 and 1945/46 to 1962/63" *Memo. no. 551,* INP, Cairo 1965, table 1. The level of investments for 1945/46 to 1952/53 in that table has been adjusted £E 20 million upwards to tally with the estimate for 1952/53 to 1962/63; other figures are adjusted accordingly. Owing to roundings, figures do not always add up to totals. Two important sources of error have been indicated, x being unrecorded stock-changes, y being unrecorded capital imports (leads and lags in commercial payments). For the years 1948–50 and 1954–56 we believe these two sources of error are of minor importance. Foreign borrowing corresponding to Russian High Dam deliveries are not included in full. If included they affect the figures for foreign borrowing and private consumption upwards, and the figures for domestic savings and private savings downwards, by about £E 5–10 million for the years 1960/62, corresponding to 1/2 per cent of GNP. Observe that in the table as well as in the text the "Authorities" (railways, Suez Canal etc.) are not included in public companies but in public current net income in the budget.

with the nationalization of the Suez Canal, succeeded in raising net budget revenues more than public consumption until 1958–59, the following years witnessed a very modest development in the current net budget income, though we must add to it the accumulations of the pensions and insurance funds mentioned earlier in this chapter; even taken together, budget net income and fund accumulations were only just able to keep the share of public current net income in GNP more or less unchanged, and with a big increase in the share of public consumption after 1961/62, public savings had by 1962/63 fallen to less than half their absolute level in 1957/58. It should be stressed, however, that we have not included the profits from Government-owned companies in public current net revenue. After the nationalizations of 1961 these profits add greatly to total public savings, but since this increase is of an essentially different nature from changes in public savings connected with tax policies, etc., we have left them in the private sector here; but we shall return to these profits in the next section.

Private savings are more closely related to private disposable income than to GNP. During the post-war period there has been a fall in the share of private disposable income in GNP from about 85 per cent to about 81. Most of this fall took place before 1954, and since 1955 the share has remained relatively constant at a level of 81 per cent. From private disposable income we have excluded the pensions and social insurance fund accumulations, and so the development of private disposable income simply reflects the development of public current net income discussed above. Private gross savings measured as a percentage of private gross disposable income show a rising trend during the post-war years as a whole, from about 9 per cent in 1948/50 to 12–13 per cent in 1962/63. To understand this trend it should be realized that private gross savings include not only the retained gross profits (after taxation) of private companies, but also, for the period 1960/63 and 1962/63, the gross profits (after taxation) of public companies. This distorts the picture from a savings propensity point of view. Company profits have most probably risen proportionately during the period, and at the end of it a large number of the private companies were made public by nationalization decrees. To judge the effect of these factors is difficult owing to lack of information about company profits, private as well as public. But we will make an attempt.

According to the budget estimates for 1962/63 the profits of the public companies (excl. Authorities) should be in the region of £E 90 million. The realized profits will most probably have been a little lower, say £E 80 million. This reduces private gross savings to £E 170 million less 80 million, or £E 90

million, which makes 7 per cent of private disposable income (net of public
company profits). Most of this must be household and personal business
savings, since the bulk of companies are now public. Let us then go back to
1948–50 when public companies were negligible. No estimate of company
profits exists, but we know that the value of dividend coupons amounted to
£E 10–13 million for these years [6]), and we know that during the 'fifties
around 40 per cent of company gross profits were distributed [7]). Applying
the latter percentage to the dividends in 1948–50 we find that gross profits
at that time may have been £E 25–30 million, and retained profits £E 15–20
million. Deducting these retained profits, we find a personal gross savings
ratio of 7 per cent in 1948–50. This figure should be roughly comparable to
the 7 per cent obtained for 1962/63. If anything, these figures point to an
unchanged gross propensity to save for households and personal business.
This might seem surprising, taking into account the equalization that has
taken place in income distribution, and the introduction of pensions and
social insurance schemes with compulsory payments. The main part of the
income redistribution has been between big landowners and small peasants,
and perhaps the small peasants in spite of their poverty are better marginal
savers than the big landowners; in developed countries peasants are known
to be big marginal savers, and the big landowners were known as big spenders.
Also of interest is the level of private personal savings. If our calculations
are correct, the level of net personal savings cannot be lower than five per
cent of disposable net income, which compares well with the 6–8 per cent
personal savings ratio of, for instance, the United States.

8.3.2 *Financial savings in the public and private sectors*

In table 8.7 we have tried to construct the distribution of savings and
investments in the public and private sectors in order to arrive at an impression of financial savings, i.e. the net lending or borrowing of each sector.
This will also give us an impression of the net income generation from each
sector; for the public sector table 9.1 should be consulted. A snag here is
again the public companies. Since the financing of investments in the public
companies is now a Government budget problem (see chapter 10 below), we
have tried in this table to include both the savings and investments of public

---

[6]) *Bulletin Mensuel des Valeurs Taleur Traites aux Bourses du Caire et d'Alexandrie*,
Cairo, several issues.

[7]) *Economic Bulletin*, NBE, 1958 and 1960.

TABLE 8.7

Savings and investments in the public and the private sector

£ E million	Average 1948–50	Average 1954–56	Average 1960–63	1962–63*
1. Public savings in budget	40	38	− 6	− 21
2. + Pension and insurance fund accumulations	0	0	40	51
3. = Public savings	40	38	34	30
4. + Profits of public companies	—	—	(40–50)	(80)
5. = Total public savings	40	38	(74–84)	110
6. − Public gross investment	30	69	230	277
7. = Public financial savings	10	− 31	(− 146– − 156)	− 167
8. Private gross savings	60	89	160	170
4. − Profits of public companies	—	—	(40–50)	80
9. Private gross savings proper	60	89	(110–120)	90
10. − Private gross investments	76	90	31	30
11. = Private financial savings	− 16	− 1	(79–89)	60
12. Total domestic financial savings	− 6	− 32	− 67	− 107
13. Foreign borrowing	6	32	67	107

* Preliminary figures.

SOURCE   Bent Hansen, "Savings in the UAR (Egypt)", op. cit., and "The National Outlay of the UAR (Egypt)", op. cit. The figures for Profits in Public Companies for 1960/63 are our "guestimates". For earlier years such profits, being very small, are included in public savings. Profits in public companies do not include revenue from Authorities like the railways, the Suez Canal, etc., and Organizations which are included in Public savings in budget. Concerning the level of investments, see table 8.6.

companies in the public sector. Public company profits were negligible in 1948–50 and 1954–56 and about £E 80 million in 1962/63. For the years 1960–63 we assumed the average level of public company profits to be £E 40–50 million, which is a very rough guess. We find then that while in 1948–50 each sector more or less financed its own investments, which is what one would expect in an economy in which a balanced budget and an even balance of payments were considered the two great aims of policy, development since then has been for the Government to run a big and growing financial deficit, covered partly by a financial surplus in the private sector, and partly by foreign borrowing. The private sector's financial surplus has been channelled into the public sector mainly through the banking system, while the foreign borrowing has been partly through direct Government borrowing abroad, and partly through a fall in the banking system's net foreign assets.

This change in the financial structure of the country is a consequence of the nationalizations and the general expansion in public investment activities that has taken place, at the same time as investment activities in the remaining private sector have been restrained by licensing measures, credit restrictions, etc.

8.4 The balance of payments deficit and the problem of inflation

Confronted with a large, persistent and growing balance of payments deficit, and with rapidly growing public expenditure, increasingly deficit-financed by borrowings through the banking system and from abroad, it is tempting to diagnose the situation as a simple demand-inflation emanating from the public sector's excessive spending and net income generation, coupled possibly with an overvaluation of the domestic currency. In the chapter on foreign trade we postponed discussion of these matters when we found that shifts in the composition of domestic demand and production could only partially explain the current deficits. Attention had to be turned to the level of total demand. Having now analysed the development of total demand in terms of savings and investments, we are ready to take up again the general balance of payments problem in its relation to the domestic economic situation.

8.4.1 Is there inflation in Egypt?

Concerning this question there is a good deal of confusion. On the one hand it is pointed out that prices and costs have been remarkably stable throughout the whole post-war period. In spite of a depreciation by 25 per cent and rising prices in most of the outside world, domestic prices seem in general to have increased by only 30–37 per cent from 1945 to 1962/63; and during the last 5–6 years, when the main increase in Government spending has taken place, prices have risen by only about ten per cent for the period. Behind the relatively stable prices we find a very modest development in money wages, and wage costs, only interrupted in 1961/62 by the various Government measures described earlier (chapter 5, section 5.6.3). Apart from that single year there is no basis for speaking of a general cost inflation. The rapid increase in the supply of labour has helped throughout to keep down wages in general, although there has been some increase in wages for skilled labour in construction activities. But in spite of the ample supply of labour there may be an excess demand for commodities, which would have led to price increases in the absence of price controls and price subsidies. In other words the inflation may be a suppressed inflation, limited mainly to the commodity markets.

To measure the existence and extent of a suppressed inflation is always a difficult matter. It shows itself in depletion of stocks, a backlog of orders and straightforward shortages of goods, coupled with tendencies to black-market prices. Stock and order statistics are too incomplete to allow any conclusions, and shortages of goods and black-market prices are as always not subject to official statistics. It is obvious to everybody, however, that there are some shortages of commodities and some tendencies to black-market prices. Earlier these were limited mainly to certain imported manu-factured consumer goods, and this was felt only by the upper-income brackets; for the population in general there was no shortage of the relatively few, domestically-produced goods entering its budget. In addition there are long-standing complaints from industry about a serious shortage of spare parts. During the last year or two there have also been periodic shortages of some elementary goods such as rice, meat and fat. The authorities have explained this as the result of bad co-ordination in the system of distri-bution, and maintained that there has always been a sufficient stock of goods somewhere. But it has also been officially explained as the outcome of incorrect public forecasts of production and consumption for these goods, plus an increase in demand, and this points of course to definite shortage[8]. However, the shortages may still be the sign of a partial disequilibria rather than the result of an overall internal excess of demand. The existence of an overall excess demand could be disclosed by an inflationary gap calculus of the traditional *ex ante* type, based on forecasts of investment, consumption, exports, etc., but unfortunately the official published figures for the budgets of the public enterprises are out of touch with realities and cannot be used for this purpose.

We pointed out earlier that disregarding capital goods the import controls

---

[8] See *The Egyptian Gazette*, Febr. 12, 1964.

keep back a substantial demand for import goods; we mentioned a figure in the region of £E 30 million. It is likely, however, that a relaxation of the controls and the switch in demand towards foreign goods that would follow would also be a switch in demand away from domestic goods, and this would result in an internal deflation. The import controls make people to buy domestic commodities which they may not otherwise buy, but this does not in itself mean that there is a general internal excess demand. So far, therefore, we can only say that there are obvious partial internal imbalances between demand and supply of commodities; it is less clear whether there is a general internal excess demand, too, although it seems likely. Finally, it should be pointed out that the increased demand for imported capital goods, which explains, say, one quarter of the current deficit, has not been and could not be directed towards domestic products to any large extent.

What we have discussed so far is only part of the problem, namely whether there is a general internal imbalance between demand and supply of commodities given the level of total demand and the level of imports and exports, that is within the fence of import and export controls. Irrespective of the existence or non-existence of such an internal inflationary demand pressure, it is clear that total demand for commodities and services must exceed total domestic supply by the deficit in the balance of current payments. Apart from capital goods this may be considered as a spill-over of domestic purchasing power keeping imports at a high level and exports at a low level. Whether this spill-over, which does not exert pressure on domestic prices, should be called inflation is a matter of terminology, in itself rather uninteresting; but since the notion of inflation is usually apprehended in a teleological sense, implying a recommendation of certain policies, it is better to be careful here in the choice of terminology. It is elementary economics that if a country wants to borrow (net) from abroad it has to have a deficit in its foreign balance of goods and services; and if it wants to have a deficit in its foreign balance it has to have an excess of demand over domestic supply of commodities and services (but not factors, of course[9]). If then a country actually has sufficient foreign finance available to cover the deficit, and it succeeds in expanding its demand for commodities accordingly without creating internal excess demands for commodities and factors, there is little point in speaking of inflation, since there is no need

---

[9]) The distinction between excess demand for commodities on the one hand and factors on the other is indispensable in discussions of foreign deficits and inflation, see Bent Hansen, *The inflation problem in small countries,* CBE, Cairo 1960.

for corrective policy measures. Until 1959 the deficits in the Egyptian balance of payments were in fact covered by a drain on the very large exchange reserves, and it was clearly sound policy for a poor country to try to transform such big reserves into fixed capital. From 1960 onwards it has been the deliberate policy of the Government to finance development partly through loans from abroad. So far it is only logical also that a total excess of demand over domestic supply of commodities has been allowed to develop, and so far there is no reason to discuss the deficit in the balance of payments under the heading of inflation. The Government may not have been successful in avoiding internal inflationary demand pressures, but this is quite another matter and it should be discussed as a separate problem from the balance of payments deficit; the latter should be judged on its own merits or demerits, which means that it should be judged from the point of view of repayment. This brings us to the problem of the possible overvaluation of the Egyptian pound. But before entering upon this topic, a few words on the so-called monetary inflation-indicators are necessary.

In the spirit of primitive quantity theory of money the IMF has tried to make money supply a main indicator of the financial soundness of a country. In particular, the growth of money supply in proportion to real GNP is assumed to be a condition for inflation-free development. Under special circumstances this may of course be true, but by this yardstick there has been little sign of inflation in Egypt during recent years, as we saw earlier. From 1952 to 1962 the supply of money rose 37 per cent, compared with a 56 per cent increase in real national income, and although most of the increase in the supply of money took place during the period after 1959/60 (30 per cent, compared with 19 per cent in real GNI), how the supply of money develops is not much help in understanding the domestic demand situation and the balance of payments deficit. As a matter of fact, it is the balance of payments deficit and the fall in the exchange reserves that have helped to keep down the increase in money supply. Furthermore, the "permissible" increase in the supply of money depends very much upon institutional arrangements and on the distribution of investment and savings by sector. This primitive approach is therefore not very useful in discussing economic policies.

8.4.2 Is the Egyptian Pound overvalued?

In simple terms of purchasing power the Egyptian pound became grossly overvalued during World War II; domestic prices trebled, while the Sterling

rate was kept unchanged. During the 'fifties this overvaluation was diminished, partly through the favourable development of unit labour costs,
and partly through the depreciation of the Egyptian pound. Whether these
developments were sufficient to eliminate overvaluation in this particular
sense is an open question. To this it must be added that the problem of
overvaluation cannot be solved by simple comparisons of price levels or
unit costs. Shifts in the terms of trade and in the composition of demand
are also important factors. Compared with pre-war and immediate post-war
conditions the terms of trade may have improved somewhat; the shift in
demand towards capital goods had an opposite effect. On balance these two
factors have probably improved the situation.

To settle the problem of overvaluation we must decide exactly what we
mean by an "overvalued" currency. We need in other words to define the
"equilibrium rate of exchange", and this cannot be done without knowing
the particular aims of economic policy and the economic policy instruments
to be used, the rate of exchange being regarded as one such possible instrument. Traditionally the problem of the equilibrium rate of exchange has
been discussed on the assumption that the balance of current payments
should be kept even continuously, or at least on an annual basis[10]), without
foreign exchange controls. In addition we can add, as minimum requirements, that full employment, of labour, and/or capital, and/or land, should
be maintained and that the level of investment should be sufficient to secure
a certain target rate of growth[11]). There is hardly any reason, however,
why the notion of an equilibrium rate of exchange should be confined to
the target of maintaining a zero surplus on current payments. Indeed, in
the development of poor countries it is much more appropriate to consider
a long-run balance of payments target which includes an initial period of
Government borrowing and a subsequent period of repayment. Now the
UAR has in fact planned for an expansion of the country's foreign borrowing
to implement the 5-year plan during the period 1960–65 to even larger

---

[10]) Net flow of free capital movements can be included in this definition of the equilibrium rate of exchange.

[11]) The fulfilment of these three targets requires the use of at least three policy instruments, which may or may not include the rate of exchange. If there is a solution with
three instruments not including the exchange rate, then there is no reason for speaking
of overvaluation. If there is no solution without including the rate of exchange among the
instruments, and the solution shows that an increase in the exchange rate is necessary,
then and only then can the currency be considered overvalued. This argument holds,
of course, for any number of targets.

amounts of foreign borrowing than already taken on; the 5-year plan also envisaged a substantial surplus and a beginning of foreign debt repayment in 1964/65. It would be natural then to relate the question of the equilibrium exchange rate to this plan for foreign borrowing and repayment, and already now it seems pretty clear that in this respect the 5-year plan will not be automatically fulfilled. To some extent this may perhaps be connected with the fact that the investment programme of the 5-year plan will not be completely fulfilled either, but the main reason is simply inadequate and over-optimistic planning for foreign trade during the period. We shall return to all this in chapter 11; what matters here is that within this officially adopted 5-year policy frame it can be argued that the currency is overvalued.

But even this does not settle the matter. Once it has been apprehended that the original programme of foreign borrowing and repayment is not going to fulfil itself, something has to be done about it. Two possibilities may then be open. One is to try to take adequate policy measures, without changing the foreign exchange rates, to secure that *inter alia* a balance, or, in the present case, a surplus, in current foreign payments is accomplished at the time originally planned. The other possibility is that the Government changes the targets of its plan and prolongs the period of borrowing. What the Egyptian Government's actual choice will be remains to be seen, but it would be quite natural if it preferred the second solution. Policy always works with a certain lag, and it may not be feasible at all – given the other targets – to create a surplus as early as from 1964/65 with or without changes in the exchange rates; and if feasible, the burden imposed on the population may be considered too heavy. In what follows we will show that the Government may have good reasons for thinking so. If then the Government finds it well-advised to prolong the period of borrowing at unaltered exchange rates, and is able to design a new feasible and realistic policy programme which includes debt repayment within a specified time at unaltered exchange rates, there is still no basis for talking about an overvaluation of the currency[12]. The feasibility of this new programme will depend, of course, on whether the Government can find lenders abroad who are willing to finance the programme and its prolongation, and whether the terms, interest, etc., are such that the Government itself really wants to stick to its own new programme. Here we meet a new difficulty, namely that no perfect inter-

---

[12] Feasibility is one thing; it is another matter whether the programme is also optimal. Here we come up against the whole problem of the optimum savings pattern, the solution of which is in the last analysis a matter of policy decisions.

national credit market exists where Governments can borrow what they want on terms determined "by the market". The majority of credits nowadays are given by Governments and international bodies to Governments, and so on the supply side too the question of international loans boils down to a question of political decisions. When therefore a lender argues against a borrower-country that the latter's currency is overvalued and that a depreciation is necessary, this may simply be a concealed way of saying: we don't like your targets and we don't want to finance your programme. (By this we have no wish to deny, of course, what in practice often happens, that a lender may find the borrower-country's programme a piece of bad economic thinking, and unrealistic in the sense that a surplus will again not be realized in the way the new programme envisages; but this is an entirely different matter.) In this environment the notion of overvaluation loses much of its meaning. Since the lender is usually in the stronger position, he can also determine the amount available to the borrower, and hence also to what extent the borrower-country's currency is overvalued. But this is something very different from the classical notion of overvaluation; we can no longer on objective criteria alone determine whether a currency is overvalued.

This may be an unsatisfactory answer to our question, but the answer lies in the nature of the problem. Summing up, we can only say that the question of overvaluation depends on the country's long-term plan for its balance of payments and other targets and the attitude of foreign lenders to it – and no such long-term plan (extending beyond 1964/65) exists at present for the UAR. It will be one of the most important issues of the next 5-year plan (for 1965/70) to work out a feasible solution to the balance of payments problem, and this solution will have to include definite assumptions with respect to foreign exchange rates.

8.4.3 How can the internal and external imbalances be rectified?

The need to curtail demand and increase domestic savings may arise then either because there is an internal inflationary excess demand, given the controlled levels of imports and exports, or because the balance of payments deficit for some reason is considered inappropriate. Concerning the internal inflationary excess demand, we have already pointed out that if it exists it is confined to certain particular commodities, and the natural remedy would be to increase the price of these goods through increased indirect taxation. Under the present organization of trade this means that the Government would have to increase the profit margins on these commodities or diminish the price subsidies. Public savings would then increase and private "forced savings" disappear, but the standard of private consumption in the country would not diminish; the available quantities of consumer goods might even increase. This problem is a relatively simple one, but it should obviously be handled by selective measures directed against the particular markets where the excess demands appear, rather than by general demand-curtailing measures; a change in relative prices is necessary.

Let us then consider this internal balance problem as solved and turn to the problem of rectifying the balance of payments deficit. Whether the deficit should be rectified in the short run or not is essentially a political question to be decided by the country's Government and its creditors; among the circumstances which will have to be taken into account when the decision is taken are, of course, the implications of policies for improving the balance of payments in the short run.

A balance of payments deficit is always accompanied by a discrepancy between investments and domestic savings, and a policy which is to restore balance in the foreign payments of the country must, by definition, be a policy which equalizes domestic savings and investments. But it does not follow from this that *any* increase in domestic savings or fall in investments will solve the economic problems of the country. The balance of payments is not the only concern of the country's economic policy. If the balance of payments is to be adjusted, and investment and domestic saving brought to equality, it has to be done in a way which does not jeopardize other policy targets. Among these other targets the most important are to keep current production as high as possible, and to increase current production at a certain rate, mainly through capital investments. There are numerous other Government policy targets to be taken into account – connected with income distribution and price stability, for instance – but we will ignore them for the moment and concentrate on those connected with total production; even so the problem is difficult enough.

We must first recall the development of the balance of payments during the last ten years, during which an increasing real national income and national product has been accompanied by a stagnating level of exports, an increasing level of imports other than capital goods, and increasing capital goods imports. We must also recall the discussion in chapter 7, section 7.4, where it was shown that simply halting net investment activity would not be sufficient to close the gap in the balance of payments, quite apart from the fact that it would put a serious brake on growth and so jeopardize one of the central policy targets mentioned above. For this reason, we disregard such "solutions" to the balance of payments problem. It could be asked, however, whether a less import-intensive investment policy could be followed. Since the domestic production of machinery and equipment is still negligible, this would mean a greater emphasis on construction and building, and this again would probably mean a shift in investments towards residential building and agriculture, for irrigation. Construction and building mean, however, an increased demand for cement, which would reduce exports of cement, and perhaps also increase steel imports. Thus, marginally, construction and building may be quite foreign exchange consuming and the improvement obtained small. To this must be added the possible reduction in the rate of growth caused by such a shift in investment activity. We therefore disregard the possibility of cutting down capital goods imports to any appreciable extent; the pronounced shortage of spare parts and the fact that Government investment plans have never been fully executed point in fact to the need to expand capital goods imports if Government policy targets are to be fully realized. We shall also disregard the possibility of reducing imports of raw materials and manufactured goods; as shown in chapter 7, import restrictions are already so severe that there is little further scope here without hitting current production. It is true that there are still some imports which seem luxuries, e.g. parts for television sets, cars, passenger aeroplanes, etc., but these things after all add up to comparatively small amounts. We shall also disregard the possibility of improving the net of invisibles; the Suez Canal dues are by and large determined by external factors, and the heavy Government expenditure abroad we shall consider as a politically given factor in the problem.

The solution must therefore be sought either in diminished imports of food, and this means in practice American surplus wheat, or on the export side. The problem is then whether an increase in domestic savings through decreased domestic consumption, private or public, will also bring about imports or increased exports *to the same extent* as consumption is reduced. The italicized words are added because with the given policy targets the reduction in consumption must not be allowed to lead to a fall in domestic production. This means again that a reduction in consumption will be a solution only if the consumption in question consists of import goods, or is competing directly with foreign demand for exportable goods, or the resources set free are absorbed in the production of exportable goods, which will also be in fact sold abroad. In an ideal competitive society, in which rapid movements of factors are called forth by relative commodity and factor price adjustments, this will take place automatically and instantaneously if consumption in general is cut down. And when increased domestic savings in general are recommended the "model" behind such advice is usually just this kind of ideal society with full mobility of resources. But economic realities in Egypt do not conform at all closely to this theoretical picture. The Egyptian agriculture and textile industry cannot suddenly pour out machinery and equipment for domestic investments, nor will the shoe-shiners start exporting just because there are no shoes to be polished. Consumption must be cut, but it matters a great deal just how this is done.

As an illustration of how *not* to solve the balance of payments problem, given the targets of maximum current production and a certain growth rate, we will discuss the effects of a simple cut in public consumption through the dismissal of redundant employees in public administration, and a corresponding immediate increase in public savings and decrease in public net borrowing through the banking system. This is a natural problem to discuss because it is quite clear that the aggravation of the balance of payments deficit during the last three years is closely connected with the vigorous expansion in public consumption. The direct decrease in the production of the public services can be disregarded as being negligible; for it is in the Government sector that disguised unemployment in Egypt is to be found. But the fall in private disposable income following the dismissals will be accompanied by a certain fall in private spending, which will have multiplier effects of the usual kind, and the demand for all types of consumer goods will fall[13]). With one important exception imports can be assumed not to be directly affected – with the given import controls incomes would have to

---

[13]) It has been maintained (V.K.R.V. Rao, "Investment, Income and the Multiplier in an Underdeveloped Economy", *The Indian Economic Review,* Feb. 1952, repr. A. N. Agarwala and S. P. Singh, Ed., *The Economics of Underdevelopment,* London 1958) that owing to low and even negative supply-elasticities in underdeveloped countries multiplier effects on *real* national income should be negligible. If all supply-elasticities really are low, or even negative, this is obviously true, but this assumption does not hold for Egypt, and probably not for any other modern underdeveloped country either. Many domestic consumer goods industries have actually had idle capacity during the post-war period. This is particularly true of the textile industry. And in the service sector a real expansion is always possible in underdeveloped countries. If, furthermore, it is assumed that in agriculture the marginal propensity to save is negligible, it will be understood that whatever the supply-elasticity in agriculture, every penny of purchasing power which is directed towards agricultural products will return in full as demand for industrial products, or services. No purchasing power is therefore "lost" in agriculture and the "real" multiplier proecss will continue with full force within the industrial and service sectors as if agriculture and its reactions did not exist, although it is true, of course, that the reactions

decline sharply before imported consumer goods would remain unsold. The exception is wheat, which is bought only as American surplus commodities and paid for by the accumulation of counterpart funds, but a fall in demand for this particular type of import would be rather pointless as a means of improving the payments situation, while US Public Law 480 is in force. Besides, the income-elasticity of the demand for wheat is low, and unless further measures were taken the effects would be small. In addition to the import of wheat, foreign borrowing would automatically be curtailed. Nothing would be obtained from an immediate foreign *payments* point of view, but if the task is to balance current payments this contribution should, of course, be taken into account.

Let us turn next to the export side, and distinguish between food, textiles and footwear, and other domestic manufactures and services. Concerning domestic food, an automatic increase in exports could probably be expected only in the case of rice and certain vegetables, while a fall in domestic demand for textiles and footwear would not automatically lead to increased exports. Both of these industries are indeed export industries, but the limiting factor here is foreign demand and foreign import restrictions, and not the capacity of the two industries; both of them have idle capacity and would be able to increase exports only if they could lower their selling prices. However, even if the fall in domestic demand really had deflationary effects on wages and other costs sufficient to bring about a lower export price, we should run the risk that these two industries in their markets abroad would meet falling demand curves with an elasticity lower than one; the result then might simply be a fall in the country's export income[14]). The fall in domestic demand for textiles, on the other hand, would set free raw cotton for export; and a similar effect might follow from the fall in demand for food, which might lead to an increase in cotton cultivation. With an elastic demand abroad this would obviously improve the payments situation. Finally, it is quite clear that a reduced domestic demand for other home-manufactured consumer goods and services would not lead to increased exports, but only to a fall in production, with the possibility, of course, of reduced raw material

---

of agriculture will contribute to price increases. With uncontrolled foreign trade, the combination of a low standard of living with an inelastic domestic food supply may, on the other hand, greatly enlarge leakages through imports and exports, so that for this reason the real national income multiplier may be low. But in a country like post-war Egypt, one can safely apply multiplier theory, particularly downwards.

[14]) Nor should we forget the possibility that price cuts might be ¦considered dumping and lead to increased im port restrictions abroad.

imports; even at substantially lower costs and prices these new industries are far from competitive, in particular because the quality of their products is still too far below that of foreign products.

Thus a simple cut in public consumption will have certain positive effects on the balance of payments; but there will also be substantial – and most probably much larger – negative effects on domestic production. For this reason it is not a short-run solution to our problem, and there is relatively little to be obtained in the long run from factor movements; the capital cannot be moved and labour in most sectors is available in sufficient quantities, the agricultural seasonal peaks being one of the exceptions. We have dwelt at some length on this example because it shows all the major elements and the major difficulties to be taken into account in finding a method of improving the balance of foreign payments without jeopardizing current production and growth.

It is by now clear that the structure of our policy problem points to decreased wheat imports or increased exports of textile manufactures, raw cotton, and other agricultural products as the only alternatives if an immediate, substantial improvement in the balance of current foreign payments is to be obtained.

If the consumption of wheat is to be cut down in order to diminish the American deliveries, a price increase for wheat and flour would be necessary. The price elasticity is probably very low (existing estimates show an income elasticity for cereals and starches of 0.4) so the price increase would have to be very substantial. The necessary rise could be achieved by abolishing the present price subsidies and, if necessary, increasing the Government's trade margins on wheat. If a shift to other cereals or pulses is to be avoided such prices would have to be increased too. With present trade organizations this could easily be done, though it might create a great problem in direct black-market trade between farmers and consumers, if the present negative margin between producer and consumer prices is changed into a large positive margin. But, as we have said, with PL 480 in existence there is little point in cutting down wheat imports. Greater interest attaches therefore to possibilities on the export side.

Let us begin with cotton, Egypt's classic export commodity. During the last seven to eight years the cotton area has, mainly because of the area restriction policies of the Government, remained on average about 10 per cent below what can be considered the maximum cotton area (see chapter 4, section 4.4.3). An increase in the area to its maximum might, everything else being equal, increase the cotton crop by at most 6 per cent[15]). With a domestic raw cotton consumption equal to about one third of the present crop, the export volume could be increased by at most 9 per cent. At a foreign demand-elasticity of, say, 2–4, the increase in foreign exchange receipts from raw cotton sales should increase by 4 to 6 per cent, or by £E 5–8 million. The shift in agricultural production towards more cotton would thus cover only a minor part of the balance of payments deficit. There would be a simultaneous fall in the production of other agricultural products, mainly food grains, which might fall by as much as 5 per cent; and to this extent consumption would have to be curtailed. We are assuming that this re-allocation of agricultural land could be made without affecting the deliveries of wheat, etc., from American surplus commodities in a negative way, an assumption which is far from obvious; American aid under Public Law 480 is seldom given without strings. We are also taking for granted that the PL 480 wheat deliveries would not be increased.

If we look around for other exportable agricultural products that could easily be sold abroad, we can probably find only one "big" commodity of this type: rice. The production of rice would hardly be affected by an increase in the cotton area. The total domestic consumption of this commodity amounted at the end of the 'fifties to about 700 000 tons; and the export value of this quantity of rice might amount to almost £E 20 million, which together with the above £E 5–8 million from increased raw cotton exports, would by and large cover that portion of the structural deficit in the balance of payments which is not covered by counterpart fund accumulations. Before we proclaim this as a possible solution, however, there are two problems we must discuss.

The first is the burden to be carried by the population. The fall in the supply of domestic wheat and other cereals, coupled with the complete disappearance of rice from the Egyptian table, would amount to a fall of almost 20 per cent in cereal consumption, which in turn would mean a fall in the total caloric intake of the population by about 15 per cent, i.e. a fall from about 2500 to about 2150 calories per day per capita. This would bring the caloric intake down to a low level, and would obviously impose sufferings on the population, although the level of caloric intake would still be higher than in countries like India, Ceylon, Taiwan, etc. And we are assuming, it must be remembered, that the American wheat deliveries would continue at their

---

[15]) Of two estimates of the cotton production function, assumed to be of the Cobb-Douglas form, one shows a land coefficient of 0.3 and the other 0.6, see H. Kheir El Din, op. cit. and B. Hansen, "Cotton vs. Grain", op. cit.

present level. Such a policy of austerity would recall the hardships endured by the population during the regime of Mohammed Ali a century and a half ago, when capital accumulation was financed through an exorbitant taxation of agricultural products, combined with forced labour; the first five-year plan of the Soviet-Union is a more recent example. It can be done, but...

The second problem is implementation. To call forth the proposed increase in the cotton area, a simple abolition of the existing area restrictions would probably be sufficient (to some extent it might also be possible to change from a three-year to a two-year rotation). If this should prove inadequate, a relative increase in the producer price of cotton and a fall in the producer price of wheat, etc., would have to be contemplated. This part of the policy would be relatively easy to implement. Since the consumer demand for wheat, etc., must at the same time be reduced somewhat, a price increase in the consumer prices of bread and flour would be necessary; but since the wholesale distribution of grain is in the hands of the Government, this could be managed. The big problem would be with the rice. Part of the rice crop is consumed directly by the farmers; the rest is sold to Government agencies. What is sold to Government agencies could be exported directly, but the problem is to make the rice farmers stop consuming rice themselves, and prevent them from selling directly to the rest of the population. Compulsory deliveries and forceful methods would certainly lead nowhere, and it seems the only procedure would be to keep the producer price for rice very high while at the same time forcing the farmers, by keeping their total cash income down, to sell all their rice in order to cover their needs for cash; this would mean that the producer prices for cotton and the other cereals would have to be fixed at relatively low levels, or that taxes would have to be levied on cultivators' incomes. The latter seems now technically possible (see chapter 9, section 9.7). We should thus have to have a large increase in the consumer prices of not only rice but other cereals, and perhaps also other domestically consumed agricultural products, pulses, vegetables, fruits, etc., a large increase in the producer price of rice and probably a fall in the producer prices of cotton and the other cereals, larger for other cereals than for cotton. To accomplish these price changes would in itself be no problem with the present organization of the internal trade in cereals and cotton. The magnitude of the price changes would mainly depend on the elasticities of demand for rice and other cereals. These elasticities are most probably low, even in the long run, and this means that strong shifts in the price structure would be necessary. We would also get therefore strong shifts in income distribution, and the necessary gap between consumer and producer prices of cereals might, if too big, lead to direct black-market transactions between farmers and the rest of the population; to avoid this price gap an income tax for cultivators would be very helpful and probably even necessary.

In this way it might in principle be possible to cut down consumption of exportable goods without affecting the level of current production, or the rate of growth, disregarding the possible effect on production which the deterioration in nutrition might have. Exports and export revenues would increase, and public savings would increase correspondingly, through the margins between the buying and selling prices of the agricultural products handled by the Government agencies, the abolition of the present price subsidies, and the increased income tax revenues following from a tax on cultivators' incomes. However, quite apart from practical difficulties in making the scheme work, some of which are mentioned above, the hardships involved are great. A fall in the foreign deficit by £E 25 million corresponds to about 2 per cent only of private consumption, and although the average standard of living is low, this does not appear too bad; but the way it has to be brought about makes it hit much harder, the real burden being indicated by the 15 per cent fall in the caloric intake, together with the fact that the traditional diet of the population would be radically changed. In the event of a further improvement being necessary through a decrease in food imports, the remedies would be the same, but more severe; and so too would be the hardships.

There seems, therefore, to be every reason to seek solutions which do not hit the caloric intake of the population to such an extent. This means in practice that the domestic consumption of textiles should, if possible, do some of the job. This would ease the burden on the population; for in the Egyptian climate it is, after all, easier to be naked than hungry. By how much the export of textiles could be increased, and what the net improvement in foreign receipts would be, is doubtful. If textile production and exports are increased at the expense of raw cotton exports, the net foreign receipts will only increase if the marginal revenue from textile exports exceeds the marginal revenue from exporting the corresponding amount of raw cotton. This again is a question of the elasticities at the actual present volume of exports. About this we know very little, but since the foreign raw cotton elasticity may be at least 2–4, a substantial foreign demand elasticity for textile products would be needed to make a switch from raw cotton exports to textile exports socially profitable[16]). What makes it hard to judge foreign

---

[16]) The fact that at existing export prices one ton of raw cotton incorporated in textile

demand elasticities is not only that cotton textile exports consist of both yarn and fabrics, which probably have very different price-elasticities, but also that the markets in which the Egyptian cotton textile products are sold are very different. Fabrics are to a large extent sold in the Middle East, including the Sudan, while yarn is mainly sold to Eastern Bloc countries. Sales to Western Europe and the USA are a minor part of the textile export, and they are regulated through the GATT World Textiles Agreement, which in a most effective way prevents low-cost producers from expanding their exports to Western Europe and the USA; also, as far as this highly protected part of the world market is concerned, lower prices do not necessarily lead to increased sales; accusations of dumping may easily be the actual result. In the other markets the textile products are often sold within the framework of bilateral trade agreements, in which official negotiations about packages of export and import goods determine the patterns of trade in a complicated way. Even within such a framework there may be a definite price elasticity and marginal revenue from individual export items reflecting market demands, but most likely the methods of trading would make it impossible to trace the marginal revenue of any individual item. Finally, a challenging question: if trade negotiations have in fact succeeded in carrying the trade in all single commodities to a social optimum, would this not mean that all the marginal revenues are already equalized, so that further attempts to increase textile exports at the expense of raw cotton exports would result in lower total export revenues?

The problem is in principle the same if domestic textile consumption is to be reduced in order to increase exports. The problem is then whether the country should attempt to increase its textile exports or cut down textile production and increase its raw cotton exports. The answer has been given above. The implementation of this kind of policy would consist in raising domestic prices and lowering export prices for textiles. With the existing organization of trade and production, this in itself presents no problem; and it is interesting to note that this is the very course followed since 1960/61 by the Government's textile price policy, as it has shown itself in the raw cotton

------

manufactures brings home a larger amount of foreign money than the direct export of the raw cotton, and that the capital and labour could not be used for any other purpose, is no answer to our question. The marginal revenues may be very different from the export prices. If, for instance, the price per ton of textile manufactures is double that of raw cotton, and the foreign demand elasticity for raw cotton is 4, the foreign demand elasticity for textiles has to be larger than $1\frac{3}{5}$. At a raw cotton elasticity of 2 the textiles elasticity has to be larger than $1\frac{1}{3}$, etc.

selling price policies of the Egyptian Cotton Authority (see chapter 6, section 6.4). From the present size of textile exports and the total size of textile production and consumption it is clear, however, that at best only a minor part of the balance of payments deficit can be covered in this way.

Hitherto we have discussed balance of payments policies at given, fixed exchange rates. The reason for this is simply that the mechanism by which the balance of payments situation is improved is very much the same whether or not the exchange rates are altered. A change in the price structure is in any case necessary, with an increase in the relative prices of exportables, cotton, wheat and rice being the most important ones. The level of prices must also inevitably be raised compared with money wages. One difference between making the price adjustments at fixed exchange rates and making them with an increase in the exchange rates is that in the former case public savings would increase much more, through the abolition of price subsidies and the increase in certain Government trade margins, while in the latter profits would increase correspondingly; since a substantial part of the profits would accrue to public companies this may be of minor importance. A more important point, therefore, is that if the policy is pursued through a depreciation the whole burden would fall on workers and salaried people outside agriculture, unless it is combined with an income tax levied on cultivators; while the policy at fixed exchange rates, even without an income tax on cultivators, could be designed in such a way that consumption in agriculture too is forced down. This difference in the effects on income distribution may be decisive for the choice of policy. A point in favour of depreciation is the allocative improvements which may be obtained.

From a long-run point of view – long run taken to mean a decade or so – the problem changes character. New industries should grow up, and the cut in the share of consumption will not need to hit cereals to the same extent, and perhaps not at all. Shifts in the price relationships will probably still be necessary, and since there is little reason to expect the private propensity to save to increase to any considerable extent, public savings will have to increase its share in GNI. The natural way to do this without altering the exchange rates, is to make money wages, including fringe benefits, grow more slowly than productivity, or rather to let unit costs grow less rapidly than abroad. This would mean a return to the wage policies of the 'fifties, when unit costs fell and company profits rose; the only difference would be that while the increased company profits at that time were private, in future they will mean increased public savings.

Public finance and fiscal policy

9.1 Brief historical survey

Before 1930 fiscal and budget measures were very passive, and the country was tied to a policy of almost complete economic laisser-faire with a minimum of state intervention. The so-called Capitulations, under which foreign residents in the former Ottoman Empire had extra-territorial rights and intervention in foreign trade was restricted, prevented the Egyptian Government from raising tariffs to promote domestic industries, and limited its possibilities in the imposition of new taxes to increase the revenues of the state. The fiscal system at that time was primitive and degressive [1]). Besides the general customs duty of 8 per cent *ad valorem* and certain excise duties, only two taxes were imposed, the land tax and the buildings tax. To levy a general income tax would have been futile, because almost the entire foreign community would have had to be exempted. Both the land tax and the buildings tax were levied at flat rates on yearly rental value, as periodically estimated by committees that systematically underestimated the rental value of properties belonging to big owners. Consequently these taxes, like the commodity taxes, hit the small tax-payers hardest. Owing to wide fluctuations in the cotton prices, tax collections too fluctuated widely and irregularly. The Government therefore kept special reserves to draw upon when revenue failed, and this practice may have had some countercyclical effect. Only relatively small funds were appropriated for public investments, and such funds were invested wholly in irrigation, roads, and public utilities. Basic agricultural investments, in particular irrigation and drainage facilities, have always been considered the responsibility of the Government. In industry the Government made no direct investments, though certain

---

[1]) Dr. Hussein Khallaf, "The Taxation System During the Last 50 Years", *Research on the Fiftieth Anniversary*, Société Egyptienne d'Economie, Cairo 1959 (in Arabic).

industries, e.g., sugar, were sponsored in various ways. It also encouraged the establishment of Bank Misr, which, as mentioned earlier, played an important role in the early industrialization of the country.

When Egypt gained tariff autonomy in 1930 and duties were raised Government revenues began to increase. It became possible for the Government to spend larger amounts on the development of public utilities, and these, coupled with the protection secured through the tariff system, provided a basis for industrial growth. After the termination of the Capitulations in 1937 the tax-system was overhauled and reconstructed to the advantage of the landowners. Taxes were introduced on commercial and industrial profits, interest and dividends, wages and salaries, and professional incomes, all of which were taxed at source. At the same time the land tax was considerably reduced. In 1942 a temporary excess profits tax was imposed, and in 1945 an inheritance tax followed. In 1949, finally, a progressive general, personal income tax was superimposed to replace an earlier surtax; and with this tax the structure of the present system was established.

Since 1952 numerous changes have been made in exemptions and in tax rates, but they have on the whole left the system unchanged. Tariff rates have been altered to make the tariff system more protective, while income tax rates have in general been increased, with certain subsistence and family exemptions, in order to make the tax more progressive, and, finally, the taxation of industrial and commercial profits has been revised so as to encourage investment. Since the radical direct interventions in private ownership and the distribution of wealth – the Land Reforms, sequestrations, and nationalizations – the tax system has lost some of its importance with respect to income distribution and incentives. At the same time para-fiscal devices such as the pension and insurance funds have gained importance and should be considered part of the taxation system.

9.2 *The budget in the national economy*

In earlier chapters we have touched upon the development of public expenditure for consumption and investment on the one hand, and public net income on the other. The following table gives the details behind these findings.

These figures tell the same story as we presented in the last chapter in terms of investments and savings, and show in the last column the great expansion emanating from the public sector, in particular during the years

TABLE 9.1
Public expenditure and income

	1948/50 (average)		1954/56 (average)		1960/63 (average)		1962/63*	
	£E million	per cent of GNP	£E million	per cent of GNP	£E million	per cent of GNP	£E million	per cent of GNP
Public consumption	77	10.0	152	14.6	254	16.2	290	17.3
Public investments	30	3.4	69	6.6	230	14.7	277	16.5
Total public expenditure on final goods and services	107	13.8	221	21.2	484	30.9	567	33.8
Current net income in budget	117	15.1	190	18.1	248	15.8	269	16.0
Pension and insurance fund accumulations	—	—	—	—	40	2.6	51	3.0
Public company profits	—	—	—	—	40–50	2.6–3.2	80	4.8
Total public sector income	117	15.1	190	18.1	328–338	21.0–21.6	400	23.8
Net income generation from public sector (= net borrowing)	−10	−1.3	31	3.0	156–146	10.0–9.3	167	10.0

* Preliminary figures.

SOURCES   Bent Hansen, "The National Outlay of the UAR (Egypt)", op. cit., and Bent Hansen, "Savings in the UAR (Egypt)", op. cit. Current Net Income in Budget is the net of all income transfers to and from the budget, i.e. taxes, fees, and net income from Authorities and Organizations *less* interest payments and price subsidies (social direct transfers being negligible). Owing to rounding the figures for Net Borrowing do not coincide exactly with the figures in table 8.7.

1960–63. Total public expenditure on final goods and services has expanded since 1948–50 by more than twice the increase in total public sector income. From almost nothing the net income generation from the public sector has increased to 10 per cent of GNP.

In table 9.2 we give budget revenue and expenditure in some detail, and arranged in a rather traditional way. Since 1962/63 the state budget has been presented in a radically different way from before. The new budget presentation includes all gross transactions of public companies and other Government enterprises. It is divided into a service budget and a business budget. The service budget consists of the traditional Government activities, including authorities and organizations, and the business budget all public companies. Because of gross accounting and plenty of double accounting the budget has become enormous and its income and expenditure exceed the national income. In a sense it is more rational than the old budget presentation, because it is more like a piece of national accounting, though the double accounting makes it difficult to penetrate. In order to make comparisons possible with earlier years and with other countries, we have chosen to present 1962/63 in the same way as earlier years. The old budgets were divided into an ordinary budget, several annexed budgets, and, after 1956/57, a special development budget, consisting largely of investment expenditure, but also some current expenditure. The ordinary budget and the annexed budgets contained mainly current revenue and expenditure, though some capital transactions, in certain years very large, were in fact included on the revenue side and some investment outlays and capital transfers on the expenditure side. We have as far as possible removed all capital transactions from Total Budget Revenue, but Total Current Budget Expenditure, including annexed budgets, includes public investments until 1954/55. From 1959/60 investment expenditure is shown separately. Finally, we also had to remove the gross transactions of public enterprises from revenue and expenditure; instead we have entered their net result on the revenue side. Neither pension and insurance fund accumulations nor public company profits are included among the revenues after 1959/60, but they are to be found at the foot of the table. The resulting figures for borrowing differ slightly from those obtained earlier (table 8.7). We have tried in this way to obtain comparable figures from 1938/39 to 1962/63. The result is not perfect. During the whole period there have been continuous changes in the details of the budget classification and we cannot claim that we have succeeded completely in overcoming this obstacle, but the errors are probably relatively small and do not disturb the general picture.

TABLE 9.2

The state budget and national product (absolute amounts in £E million)

	average					
	1938/39	1948/50	1952/53	1954/55	1959/60	1962/63
1. GNP at current market prices	200	773	905	1014	1372	1679
2. Total budget revenue	35.6	129.2	166.6	176.7	259.5	323.3
per cent of GNP	17.8	16.7	18.4	17.4	18.9	19.3
a) Taxes on income and wealth	7.0	23.7	41.3	34.3	48.6	52.9
per cent of GNP	3.5	3.1	4.6	3.4	3.5	3.1
b) Commodity and other taxes	20.0	72.7	97.4	109.6	116.8	159.8
per cent of GNP	10.0	9.4	10.8	10.8	8.5	9.5
c) Other revenues*	8.6	32.8	27.9	32.5	94.1	110.6
per cent of GNP	4.3	4.2	3.1	3.2	6.9	6.6
3. Total current budget expenditure	39.0	135.8	177.9	185.1	252.1	349.8
per cent of GNP	19.5	17.6	19.6	18.3	18.4	20.8
a) Education	4.5	17.7	23.6	27.7	44.7	66.2
per cent of GNP	2.2	2.3	2.6	2.7	3.3	3.9
b) Defence	5.0	34.5	36.4	56.0	76.1	94.7
per cent of GNP	2.5	4.5	4.0	5.5	5.5	5.6
c) Interest and price subsidies	3.3	12.5	15.2	9.1	15.0	54.0
per cent of GNP	1.6	1.6	1.7	0.9	1.1	3.2
d) Other ordinary expenditure	26.2	71.1	102.7	92.3	116.3	134.9
per cent of GNP	13.1	9.2	11.3	9.1	8.5	8.1
4. Total public investment expenditure	—	—	—	—	155.0	277.0
per cent of GNP	—	—	—	—	11.3	16.5
5. Total public expenditure	39.0	135.8	177.9	185.1	407.1	626.8
per cent of GNP	19.5	17.6	19.6	18.3	29.7	37.3
6. Total public expenditure less budget revenues	3.4	6.6	11.3	8.4	147.6	303.5
7. Available public fund accumulations and company profits	—	—	—	—	(30)	(130)
8. Total public sector borrowing	3.4	6.6	11.3	8.4	(118)	(173)

* From 1956/57 incl. Suez Canal net income.

SOURCE   1938/39 to 1954/55, *Annuaire Statistique,* several issues and Bent Hansen, "Savings in the UAR (Egypt)" op cit.; for 1959/60 and 1962/63 also information from the Treasury. All figures are actual, closed-account figures, including those for 1962/63, which are provisional but not forecasts. Government enterprises enter in principle only with their gross profits but we may not have been entirely successful in this respect, in particular for the earlier years. A sign of this is the surplus of £E 10 million for 1948/50 according to table 9.1 and the deficit of £E 6 million according to this table. Profits from companies with public participation or fully owned by the Government are included in Other Revenues until 1954/55, but were negligible. For 1959/60 and 1962/63 they are kept under 7. Income from Authorities (Suez Canal, Railways, etc.) and Organizations are for all years kept under other Revenues. Until 1954/55 some Government investment expenditure is included in Other Ordinary Expenditure; the investment figure for 1954/55 includes only so-called Development Expenditure that year. Taxes on Income and Wealth include the land tax, the tax on buildings, all income taxes, the inheritance taxes and the Ghaffir-tax (a tax for police guards). Commodity and Other Taxes include customs duties and excise taxes, stamp duties, property sales tax, entertainment tax, port and lighthouse fees, and taxes on automobiles and water transport. Other Revenues may include some capital transactions, such as sales of land, etc., which are unimportant, at least after 1948/50. In the earlier years some capital transfers and credits may be included among Other Ordinary Expenditure.

We have already observed how the development of Government income caused a decline in private disposable income, including company profits, from about 85 per cent to 81 per cent of GNP during the post-war period. To judge from table 9.2 pre-war disposable income seems to have been about 85 per cent of GNP, but this figure may be too low, owing to the inclusion of certain capital transactions and gross revenues from public enterprises in spite of our efforts to keep them out. Concerning the post-war fall in the share of disposable private income in GNP, it is interesting to notice that this fall is not due to increased ordinary taxation. In 1948/50 the share of taxes in GNP was 12.5 per cent; in 1962/63 it was only 12.6 per cent, after having been as high as 15.4 per cent in 1952/53. This peculiar development is the outcome of changes in the tax legislation. Until the beginning of the 'fifties efforts were directed towards increasing tax revenues proper. From 1953 onwards, however, the Government introduced on the one hand, tax exemption for company investments, an increase in the subsistence and family exemptions, exemption for land reform areas, and finally, in 1961, a reduction in the building taxes; and on the other hand, a progressive increase in income tax scales and a special defence tax, which was merely an increase in the rates of taxes that already existed. The latter was introduced in 1957 and raised in 1961. Finally, we have the changes in the customs duties discussed earlier, and the abolition of the export taxes. The outcome of all these many changes is the above-mentioned fall in taxation measured as a percentage of GNP. By and large we can say that from the end of the 'forties to the beginning of the 'fifties increased taxation helped to bring down the share of private disposable income in GNP from 85 per cent to 82–83 per cent. After the beginning of the 'fifties the decreasing tax burden, and the increasing price subsidies and interest payments, would have restored the share of private disposable income to the level of the 'forties, had not pension and insurance fund arrangements and the nationalization of the Suez Canal slightly more than counteracted the relative fall in taxation[1]). Since 1961 the big nationalizations have, of course, led to a heavy fall in private disposable income, excluding profits of public companies, from about 81 per cent to about 76 per cent of GNP.

Public current expenditure on goods and services, i.e. public consumption, has increased by about £E 50 million more than current net income in budget (total budget revenue less price subsidies and interest payments), but this has been almost exactly counterbalanced by the rise in pension and insurance fund accumulations. Public savings have thereby remained more or less unchanged in absolute amount but fallen to about one half, measured as a share of GNP (see table 8.6). On the expenditure side the most vigorous expansion has been in defence and education. The former now takes almost 6 per cent of GNP, and the latter 4 per cent.

At the same time as the whole of the ordinary Government net income increase, including pension and insurance fund accumulations, has thus been absorbed by the expansion in public consumption, public investments have increased greatly. Part of this increase, of course, consists simply of the formerly private investments that are now undertaken by the Government; but beyond these there is a real expansion in public investments, which have created a need for outside borrowing. The general picture is thus one of a rapidly increasing Government share in the national economy, which is particularly evident when we look at the Government share in national outlay. It is clear that the sharp increase in total Government expenditure must have pushed real national income vigorously upwards not only directly through the increased Government activity, but also indirectly through multiplier effects on actual demand, and the increased employment and productivity which Government investments have made possible through increased capacity. And here we have also the key to an understanding of the balance of payments deficit. The problems thus created have already been discussed in chapter 8.

---

[1]) The nationalization of the Suez Canal and other foreign property led not only to an increase in GNI and in Government income, but also to a certain transfer of GNI to the Government.

9.3   Budget policies

The budget policies of Egypt until World War II were probably neither better nor worse than those of most other countries. Compensatory fiscal policy is a recent invention; the theory grew up in the 'thirties, and as practical policy it was not generally recognized as "sound" until the post-war period. That a systematic compensatory fiscal policy was not ventured upon in Egypt until 1953 should not therefore give rise to surprise, although some earlier budgetary practices might seem to imply certain counter cyclical effects. During World War II a substantial budget surplus developed and put a brake on wartime inflation. This surplus, however, reflected mainly the rise in incomes and prices, although income tax rates were increased somewhat during the war years. Apart from this, and from the excess profits tax introduced in 1943, policy was passive, and what might look like a compensatory fiscal policy was largely the automatic reactions of the budget revenues. After the war the budget surplus disappeared and was changed into a large deficit during the Korean boom. During the Korean boom and its aftermath, budget policy was probably as bad as it could possibly have been. The official surplus dropped from £E 13 million in 1948/49 to £E 2 million in 1950/51, and for 1951/52 a deficit of £E 39 million was recorded. This change in the budget position was mainly due to an increase in expenditure beyond the automatic increase in budget revenues which followed from the high export prices and the increased imports; it is characteristic of the Egyptian budget, as it is of many other underdeveloped countries, that automatic revenue changes are related, not to the national income but to imports, through the customs duties. The rise in expenditure arose partly from the Government's stock purchases of cotton to support the high prices ruling in 1950 and 1951, but also from increased expenditure on defence after the Palestine crisis in 1948, and increased price subsidies. When the Korean boom was over, and the Egyptian economy was influenced the other way by the general tendency to a world recession in 1952, the Government changed its policy and introduced deflationary measures, at a time when there were only deflationary tendencies to combat. The budget for 1952/53, which was planned and approved by the old Government, showed a deficit of only £E 8 million, achieved mainly by a cut in expenditure.

In connection with the first budget presented by the Revolutionary Government, for 1953/54, new principles of budget policy were formulated, namely, the encouragement and development of production, the provision of social services, in particular education, and the adoption of compensatory fiscal policies with deficit financing to combat the deflationary tendencies and to promote growth. The closed budget for 1953/54 in fact came out with a surplus of £E 9 million, mainly through a reduction in the price subsidies for cereals arising from a revision of domestic price policy; but during the following years deficit financing became the rule. In 1953/54 a special development budget was instituted in addition to the ordinary budget; expenditures in this budget were planned to be covered by borrowing. From then onwards the general trend was a simultaneous expansion of total expenditures and receipts, with total expenditures running far ahead of receipts, as shown in section 2. In the years immediately after the Suez War there was a certain slowing up of the expansion policy, but from 1959/60 both expenditures and receipts went ahead again.

Once this expansionist budget policy had been chosen, with its deliberate spending of the existing exchange reserves, there was little reason to alter its main lines as long as foreign exchange reserves or foreign credits were available in sufficient amounts. The policy continued therefore and reached its maximum during the three budget years 1959/60 to 1962/63, when the over-all deficit reached an annual amount of about £E 170 million. We have already discussed the consequences of this policy, see chapter 8, section 8.4.4. The final exhaustion of the foreign exchange reserves in 1962, accelerated by the cotton crop failure in 1961, and the difficulties in expanding short-term credits abroad called for changes in fiscal and monetary policies in 1962[2]). In connection with the IMF loans, income taxes and certain indirect taxes were increased, and a tightening of credit market policies was announced. To judge from the budget figures the effects of these policies were negligible. The increase in budget revenue was mainly due to the large increase in imports, and no effective brake seems to have been put on Government expenditure.

9.4 Public investments

As development in Egypt has become more and more a question of public investments, development planning is now almost identical with public investment planning. Public investments seem to have grown from something

---

[2]) Girgis A. Marzouk, *The U.A.R. monetary and credit policy under the 1962/63 stabilization programme*, Banking Studies Institute, Cairo, 1963, (in Arabic).

like £E 20–30 million in 1952/53 to about £E 200 million in 1961/62, and about £E 275 million in 1962/63. This growing activity has created a need for special organizations to co-ordinate and execute the public investment policies.

The first development plan was launched immediately after World War II, when the old Government drew up a programme for spending altogether £E 36 million during five years. Annually this amounted to only 1–2 per cent of GNP at that time. The bulk of the investments were in agriculture and public utilities. As a percentage of GNP it has been calculated that total public investments grew from 2 per cent to about 4 per cent during those five years. The capacity to make the plan materialize was low. Between 1945/46 and 1950/51 only 63 per cent of the amount appropriated in the budget for "new works"[3]), which, by the way, included expenditure on repair and maintenance, was actually spent. In the report of the financial committee of the Chamber of Deputies[4]) at that time the underspending was ascribed to difficulties in acquiring the necessary imported materials, the incapacity of the Government administration, and insufficient technical and financial preparations.

After the Revolution of 1952 the new Government formed a permanent Production Council early in 1953 to examine and recommend development projects and to present an integrated programme of national economic development. The appropriations earmarked specifically for development projects were still modest, however. A sum of £E 21.6 million was appropriated for projects extending over four years; to this should be added £E 35.5 million for electrification projects. However, increasing sums were in fact appropriated for Government investments during the following years.

The decisive change in investment policy came in 1957. For the fiscal year 1956/57 a special development budget already included expenditure to the extent of £E 46 million (4 per cent of GNP). To concentrate all public investments under one administration, the Economic Organization was established in January 1957, as mentioned earlier (chapter 6, section 6.7). Furthermore, a National Planning Commission was instituted with which the earlier Production Council was amalgamated. The Planning Commission was responsible for the preparation of a comprehensive plan of economic development. Since the preparation of this plan would take some time, the

---

[3]) *Economic Bulletin,* NBE, 1951, p. 48 and 1952, p. 53.
[4]) *Economic Bulletin,* NBE, 1949, p. 83.

Ministry of Industry – instituted the same year – at once prepared an interim five-year plan for industrial development. This foresaw an investment expenditure of £E 500 million during the following five years. To execute the plan, a special organization was created, and in 1958, to harmonize investments within the frame of the plan, the Ministry of Industry was given control over all industrial investment by subjecting every new establishment to licence. A permit had to be obtained before any industrial undertaking could be set up, expanded or changed with respect to its line of production or location, and the Ministry was in principle authorized to issue obligatory specifications concerning methods of production, raw materials to be used, etc. At the same time a number of former private industrial organizations were reorganized to ensure co-operation between private industry and the Government. In 1960 the comprehensive plan worked out by the Planning Commission was adopted by the Government, and after 1960/61 public investment expenditure rose steeply. Coupled with the nationalizations of 1961 this created a need for a new system or organization, which was set up during 1961, with some alterations in 1963. With these changes the present system was established; it will be reviewed in detail in chapters 10 and 11.

9.5 The present system of taxation

Underdeveloped and socialist countries rely more on commodity taxes including tariffs than on taxes on income and wealth. This is certainly true of Egypt. While the share of total taxation in total budget revenue, as defined in table 9.2, rose from about 75 per cent before World War II to about 85 per cent in 1952/53, by 1962/63 it had fallen again to about 65 per cent. The share of taxes on income and wealth in total tax revenue has remained almost unchanged at one quarter, and other, indirect taxes at three quarters. In the 'fifties there was a slight shift towards income and wealth taxes, but this trend has recently been reversed. However, if we include the Pension and Insurance Fund accumulations[5], among the taxes on income and wealth the picture changes somewhat. Of total public revenue (including these accumulations) taxation contributed about 70 per cent, and the share of taxes in income and wealth in total taxes becomes about 40 per cent for 1962/63.

---

[5] The payments enterprises make into the insurance funds might be considered as an employment tax, and therefore classified with the taxes on commodities.

The income tax system consists of a basic structure of relatively complicated specific income taxes levied at source and differentiated according to
the nature of the source, and on top of these a general income tax, i.e. a
surtax levied on each person's total income. Income is thus in principle
taxed twice. Differentiation in the basic structure of specific income taxes
utilizes both the distinction between income from "movable" and "immovable" property, and that between "earned" income, from labour, and
"unearned" income, from capital and land. The treatment of different kinds
of "unearned" income is far from uniform, however, and the same holds to
a lesser degree for "earned" income. Progressive tax scales are applied to
most "earned" incomes, while with one exception "unearned" incomes are
subject to flat rates. The surtax, finally, is progressive and increases very
steeply for the higher income brackets. As part of the income and wealth tax
system there are also certain local taxes, mainly levied on land and buildings,
and an inheritance tax. Indirect tax revenues come mainly from customs
duties and, to a minor extent, excise duties. In the system of indirect taxes one
should also reckon the indirect subsidies on certain elementary necessities.

9.5.1 Taxation of personal income

Although the distinction between personal income tax and corporate income
tax does not apply, strictly speaking, to the Egyptian tax system, we shall
nevertheless retain it for purely expositional reasons. This may help the
European or American reader to understand the system.

In table 9.3 we have tried to give a systematic description of all taxes to
which *personal* income is exposed. In the left half of the table we have the
specific income taxes levied at source. For each tax a short description is
given of the tax base, the exemptions and the tax rate(s). Concerning the tax
rates, the additions referred to as "defence tax" are the increases in the
various taxes which were made after the Suez War, and again in 1962.
In the right half of the table we have the general income tax levied on the
total income of each person. Here information is given about tax base,
exemptions and tax rates, while in principle the source of the income is
immaterial. The table may speak for itself, but for a better understanding
of the various taxes and their possible effects, we add a few comments on
each tax.

a) *The land tax* is in principle a tax on rents, or rental value, as fixed by
special commissions. As already described in chapter 4 section 4.2.1. rents

TABLE 9.3

Personal income taxation, 1963

	Specific Income Taxes (Taxes at source)			General Income Tax (Surtax levied on person)		
(1) Source	(2) Tax base	(3) Exemptions	(4) Tax rate(s)	(5) Tax base	(6) Exemptions	(7) Tax rates
Land (cultivable)	Rent or annual rental value as fixed by commissions *minus* £E 4 if total tax less than £E 20	Land distributed under Land Reform Acts	14 per cent + 7 per cent (defence tax) = 21 per cent (plus 11–15 per cent municipal tax)	Total income of an individual from all sources as assessed for the payment of the specific taxes at source *minus* interest on loans payable by taxpayer; premiums for pensions,	Incomes less than £E1000 plus the deductions allowed for dependents.	8–90 per cent (according to size of income).
Buildings (in specified cities)	Rent or annual rental value as fixed by commissions *minus* 20 per cent for expenses	Buildings with an annual rental value of less than £E 18 per tax payer	10–40 per cent (according to rent per room) + 5 per cent (defence tax) = 15–45 per cent			
Interest, dividends and other income from "movable" capital	Interest, dividends, owner shares, fees of board of directors and shareholders, etc.	Mainly to avoid double taxation	17 per cent + 7 per cent (defence tax) = 24 per cent			
Commercial and industrial profits	Net profits of all business transactions *minus* rent of premises, "normal" depreciations, other taxes paid, certain donations, appropriations to provident and pension funds, interest and	Income under £E 150–250 (depending on family). Incomes within twice this size free of half of the tax	17 per cent + 7 per cent (defence tax) = 24 per cent			

(1) Source	(2) Tax base	(3) Exemptions	(4) Tax rate(s)	(5) Tax base	(6) Exemptions	(7) Tax rates
Wages, salaries, pensions, and annuities	Total amount of income *minus*, for Government officials, pension contributions; for all others, 7.5 per cent	Incomes under £E 150 (single) £E 250 (with family). Incomes within twice this size free of half the tax	2–22% (according to size of income) + 1–4 % (defence tax) = *3–26%*	specific taxes; certain donations; £E 50 for wife and each child up to £E 200, if taxpayer's income is less than £E 2 000.		
Wages paid daily (workmen)	Total wage	Daily wages less than 30 piasters	30–60 pt: *1 per cent* over 60 pt: *2 per cent*			
Income from non-commercial professions	Total net income	As for wages, salaries and annuities	11–22 per cent (according to size of income) + 7 per cent (defence tax) = *18–29 per cent*			

were fixed in 1952 at seven times the land tax at that time, which was in fact based on assessments from 1949. For big owners in particular these assessments were even then much below actual rental value. The land tax, which is 14 per cent (plus 7 per cent defence tax), i.e. about 1/7 of the rent, has thus been frozen since 1949 at a level which must be considered very low, compared with what rents and land tax would be to-day without controls. This does not benefit absentee owners, who also get the prescribed low rents, but for the owner-cultivator it is, of course, an advantage. Also, it should be pointed out that the socially motivated £E 4 deduction is conducive to land fragmentation, as it is levied on single parcels of land and not on each owner's total area.

b) *The buildings tax* is based on rents fixed by the authorities. Rents have been controlled since World War II, with the result that the level is very different in old and new houses and for old and new occupants, and usually much higher in new houses and for new occupants. The effect of the progression in the buildings tax must be judged accordingly. The progression according to rent per room, introduced in 1962, was intended to put a brake on the building of new luxury houses, but it has obvious side-effects in discriminating in favour of those who live in old houses.

c) *The tax on interest, dividends* and other income from "movable" capital is closely co-ordinated with the tax on commercial and industrial profits, to prevent double taxation of profits. The tax includes all payments to boards of directors and shareholders, except salaries to not more than two managing directors, whose salaries up to a total of £E 3 000 per year are treated as "earned" income (see below, e)).

d) *The commercial and industrial profits tax* applies in principle to all profits from business except agriculture and real estate, whether incorporated or personal. Certain specific rules that apply to companies only will be dealt with below. The reason why rent of premises and interest and dividends paid are deductable is to prevent double taxation at source. The other deductions show that at this point the tax system is quite up-to-date, allowing deductions for certain donations, and appropriations to provident and pension funds. It is also noteworthy that losses one year may be carried over to the following year and deducted from the taxable net income of that year. A loss may be carried over in this way to not more than three consecutive years. The tax rate is 17 per cent (plus defence tax of 7 per cent), which is the same as, for instance, dividends, etc. On the whole the rules for taxation here have been formulated to secure equal taxation at source of all business profits.

e) *The tax on wages, salaries, pensions, and annuities,* i.e. the "earned" incomes, is a progressive tax, in contrast to those on "unearned" income, levied after deduction of the compulsory contributions to pension and social insurance schemes (10 per cent for Government officials and 7.5 per cent for all others). The progression begins at a taxable income of as little as £E 100, though the marginal rates are very low. At an income of £E 1 000 the marginal rate is still only 7 per cent, while the average rate is about 5 per cent. At an income of £E 4 950 the maximum marginal rate of 22 per cent is reached, though the average rate here is still only 13.5 per cent. To this must be added, of course, the defence tax, which also has a certain progression.

f) To understand the tax on *workmen paid daily wages,* we will merely recall that the legal minimum wage in industry is 25 piasters per day, and in agriculture 18 piasters. But workmen's wages are often lower than this.

g) *The tax on income from non-commercial professions* is peculiar for its high initial tax rate (11 per cent), applied to even the lowest taxable income. The top marginal rate, however, is reached at the same income as in the case of wages, etc.; but the defence tax is higher, namely 7 per cent.

h) Concerning finally the *general income tax,* which is levied on top of the specific taxes and is based on personal declarations to the tax-authorities, it is to be noticed above all that income (before deductions) is assessed in almost exactly the same way as for the specific income taxes. This is particularly important in the taxation of income derived from land. Under the present rules, cultivators' incomes are grossly underestimated. The average net income per feddan in agriculture may at present be in the region of £E 60–70, while the average rent per feddan is about £E 21. The income of an owner-cultivator, if he pays general income tax at all, is assessed at the official rental value, and will therefore on average be assessed at less than half his actual net income, while a lessee (disregarding local taxes) will go completely free of tax; it will be recalled that the limits imposed on the size of holdings, whether owner-holdings or lessee-holdings, do not prevent a substantial number of cultivators having net incomes from the cultivation of land above the exemption level for the general income tax.

The progression in the general income tax is steep in so far as a marginal rate of 90 per cent is reached already at incomes of £E 10 000 and over. For medium-sized incomes, on the other hand, the marginal rates are modest; at £E 5 000 the marginal rate is still only 25 per cent. There is thus a steep rise between £E 5 000 and 10 000. However, the progression in the general income tax cannot be judged finally without taking the specific taxes into account; an appraisal is made below.

9.5.2 Taxation of companies

Companies, partnerships and so on, are in principle taxed according to the rules of the specific tax for commercial and industrial profits (see above, d, and table 9.3), which in theory applies to all joint-stock companies and business undertakings, no matter what their activities may be. Dividend payments, and all other payments to directors and share-holders, from which the company itself deducts the specific tax on interest, dividends, etc., before payment is made, are deductable, and so only the retained profits of a company are taxed, with deductions for dividends and interest received from other companies, banks, etc. This means that in principle all profit income arising from business (other than agriculture and buildings) is taxed at a uniform rate of 17 per cent (plus 7 per cent defence tax). This system differs from that of most European and North American countries, where incorporated business income is usually taxed according to completely different rules from personal business income. However, various rules that apply only to companies make the uniform treatment of income from "movable" capital rather fictitious.

First of all, companies are not subject to the general income tax or any other surtax; retained company profits are thus treated more mildly than personal business profits or interest and dividends, etc., which may be subject to the general income tax, depending upon the recipient's total net income. Secondly, there are special exemptions for companies whose activities are considered to be of particular importance from a national development point of view. The rules here are that companies founded after 1953, the year the rules were introduced, are exempted from tax on commercial and industrial profits and from tax on interest, dividends, etc., if the money which should have been paid as tax is used in new investment projects. A similar rule applies to companies that increase their capital. Also, companies whose principle activities are in the field of industry, motive power, etc., may be exempted from half the tax on commercial and industrial profits; in 1962 about 80 companies benefited from this rule. Finally, special exemptions may be extended to companies that are considered important from a national economic point of view.

With all these exemptions the taxation of retained company profits is obviously much milder than that of distributed profits; this was intended both to encourage corporate savings and also to stimulate company investments. Compared to that in industrialized countries Egyptian company taxation is very mild. After the nationalizations of 1961, moreover, the rules for company taxation have become rather unimportant, Government-owned companies being exempt from the tax on commercial and industrial profits.

9.5.3 Inheritance taxation

With certain exemptions a progressive tax is imposed on the distribution of the estates of deceased persons, to be calculated on the net share of each heir. On the shares of the descendants, spouses, and parents, the tax ranges from 5 per cent on the first £E 5 000 to 22 per cent on amounts in excess of £E 65 000. For heirs more remotely related to the deceased, the tax rates are doubled, trebled and quadrupled.

9.5.4 Stamp duties

These duties are levied on a wide range of contracts, documents, printed papers, etc. They are mentioned here separately because the amounts collected from them are actually larger than the receipts from some of the income taxes. Also important is the tax on transfers of fixed property. This tax is a registration fee which seems to cause much confusion in the registration of land due to evasion.

9.5.5 Commodity taxes and subsidies

The bulk of commodity taxes derive from customs duties, including tobacco duties which amount to about half the total. The customs duties are mainly duties on imported goods. Export taxes played a substantial role during the 'fifties, when cotton export taxes were very high, but since the lowering and abolition of these taxes and the concentration of the cotton trade under the Cotton Authority, this item has almost disappeared (see chapter 4, section 4.4.4). However, profits accruing to the Cotton Authority and other

Government agencies for buying and selling agricultural commodities could be considered as commodity taxes. It is often difficult to say what constitutes taxes and what profits in public enterprises and other public activities. The system of import duties has already been described in detail in chapter 6, to which the reader is referred.

The excise duties are levied on various consumer goods and should be judged in connection with the price subsidies on elementary commodities such as wheat, maize, sugar and kerosene. Some of these subsidies are given to commodities that are also taxed by excise duties. This is the case with sugar and kerosene, the intention being to give the population a rationed minimum amount of these commodities at low, subsidized prices. Price subsidies now add up to more than half the total receipts from commodity taxes other than customs duties.

9.5.6 The structure of tax revenue

For a comparison of the quantitative importance of the various taxes the budget estimates in table 9.4 for 1962/63 will be helpful. Of the receipts from land and buildings the greater part is from the land tax. The modest role played by the various income taxes can be clearly seen; exemptions are very important and free the majority of the population from paying income taxes. Of total private income perhaps as little as 3 per cent is paid in income taxes, while net commodity taxes may take some 10 per cent.

9.5.7 An appraisal of the tax system

An appraisal of the present tax system in Egypt has to take into account the trite observation that the current tax system of any country at any point of time is the outcome of a historical process – tax-systems are not changed every day – in which economic ideals of taxation have had to compromise with political considerations and limitations in the administrative capacity of the country in question. This applies to Egypt as much as to any other country, but in Egypt, as in most other underdeveloped countries, the practical administrative possibilities have been a serious hindrance to the introduction of tax systems which from the point of view of the Government's policy targets could be considered rational.

From a glance at the tax system described above the tendency to raise taxes where it has been practically possible is apparent. The tendency to tax at source is a clear indication of this, and the predominance of customs

TABLE 9.4

Budget estimates of tax receipts 1962/63 (£E million)

Income taxes		Commodity taxes and subsidies	
Land and buildings	9.0	Customs duties	113.6
Interest, dividends etc.	8.2	Excise and commodity duties	45.3
Commercial and industrial profits	15.7	Other commodity duties	17.2
Wages and salaries, etc.	9.1		176.1
Non-commercial professions	0.7	*minus* price subsidies	36.5
General income tax	5.0	Total net commodity taxes	139.6
Estate (inheritance) duties	1.9	Property transfer fees	1.1
Total income and wealth taxes	49.7	Stamp duties	8.0

SOURCE *Economic Review,* CBE 1962, no. 3, p. 288.
The actual outcomes were for total income and wealth taxes £E 53 million, total commodity taxes including stamp duties etc. £E 160 million, and price subsidies around 50 million.

and excise duties can also partly be understood in this way, though here "infant industry" nursing has played an important role. Within the field of income taxes the distinction between income from "immovable" property (land and buildings) and "movable" property (interest, dividends, etc., and commercial and industrial profits) originates in administrative considerations, bearing traces of old French influence, and with probably very little of economic or tax justice thinking behind it. The distinction, on the other hand, between "earned" and "unearned" income, which is also an integral part of the present system, is clearly derived from special ideas, partly under British influence, about just and unjust types of income, but seems also to be based on ideas of equity. The tax progression that runs through parts of the income tax system is a tribute to the ability-to-pay principle of taxation; and, finally, some recent changes in the system have been dominated by development considerations. With this hotch-potch administrative and ideological legacy behind it, the present tax system can hardly be expected to be very satisfactory from any point of view; a final judgement, however, should be made only after a careful empirical study of the factual impact of the tax system on the economy, taking into account existing general economic policy targets. A study of this kind, which would include problems of shifting and incidence, would require detailed statistics and information far beyond what is available even in the most developed countries. All we can do here therefore is to give some very crude indications of possible virtues and shortcomings in the system.

From an *equity* point of view the system does not live up to very high standards. Even if we agree that "equity" does not require an equal treatment of "earned" and "unearned" income, the unequal treatment of incomes within each group is hard to justify. The fact that high "earned" incomes are taxed more heavily than corresponding "unearned" incomes is quite inexplicable. But perhaps more important for equity than the difference in the tax rates applied to different kinds of income are the tax bases and the possibilities for evasion. Concerning the tax bases, we have already pointed to the very mild taxation of cultivators in agriculture. To judge the extent to which evasion is taking place is difficult. Only a rough estimate of total private income and its breakdown into types of income is available, and next to nothing is known about the distribution of income according to size. It is the opinion of informed observers, however, that although efficiency in the assessment and collection of taxes is increasing, there is still substantial evasion, profitable in particular to incomes from personal business and non-commercial professions.

From the point of view of *ability to pay,* and *income distribution equalization,* the tax progression is of special interest. Table 9.5 gives the total result of income taxation, disregarding deductions other than taxes to be deducted from the general income tax, and taking into account exemptions.

The income tax system alone would, if assessments and collections were effective, accomplish a substantial equalization of income distribution by size. Apart from incomes from rents of land and buildings small incomes are completely exempt from income tax, and already at an income of £E 5 000

TABLE 9.5

Average and marginal rates of total taxation for various types of personal income (per cent)

Size of income £E	Source of income							
	Rent of land		Profit from personal business		Wages and salaries		Non-commercial professional activities	
	average rate	marginal rate	average rate	marginal rate	average rate	marginal rate	average rate	marginal rate
100	21	21	0	0	0	0	0	0
500	21	21	24	24	5	7	18	18
1 000	21	21	24	24	8	13	18	18
3 000	26	29	28	32	16	30	24	32
5 000	28	33	30	35	25	44	28	40
10 000	39	64	41	66	40	67	42	68

before taxation, 25–30 per cent is removed; at £E 10 000 the total tax is over 40 per cent. The equalization accomplished, however, is larger for "earned" than for "unearned" incomes. The higher average tax rates in the small and medium brackets of "unearned" income could, of course, be justified by the fact that the recipients of these incomes will also be property owners with a higher ability to pay, but from this point of view it is hard to understand why the highest "unearned" incomes are taxed less than corresponding "earned" incomes. Here, however, the direct effects of the Land Reform Acts and the nationalizations must be taken into account. Since ownership of land was limited to 100 feddans in 1961, the average income from rents for absentee owners must be about £E 2 000 and will rarely exceed £E 3 000; the tax rates on the higher incomes are therefore of no interest here. Concerning rents from buildings, commercial and industrial profits, and interest and dividends, there is no doubt that nationalizations and sequestrations have greatly affected the top incomes, though many such incomes still exist. Wages and salaries, too, have been affected by direct intervention. In connection with the nationalizations in 1961 certain upper income limits were fixed for salaried people in Government service and in nationalized enterprises, the general upper limit being £E 5 000 per year. For the general manager of a big bank, for instance, this might mean a cut in income by about one third. And although these rules have since been relaxed to some extent, it is very rare to find salaries to-day above £E 5 000 per year. In equalizing incomes these direct interventions have probably done more than any system of taxes could have achieved.

When we turn to the *incentive effects* of the tax rules the marginal tax rates, which are also shown in table 9.5, have to be taken into account. High marginal tax rates are usually supposed to have a negative effect on both willingness to work and on the willingness of business to invest and take risks. From this point of view it is very difficult to understand why the marginal rates of taxation (disregarding the smallest incomes) are higher for profits than for incomes from rents of land and buildings. For incomes from labour we find lower marginal rates for smaller and medium-sized incomes than for incomes from land; but in the higher income brackets the opposite holds true. In an overpopulated country like Egypt there is every reason to create incentives to work for trained labour, skilled workers, engineers, and every other kind of specialist, which is in very short supply; but these are the very people who tend to be found in the higher income brackets, where the tax laws actually discriminate against income from labour.

As incentives to invest the special rules for incorporated business enterprise described above, are probably more important than the general tax rules for business income. The tax exemption allowed to companies making investments are in principle so important that one would have expected them to provide a substantial impetus for increased private investment. At least, that is what one would have expected from the success similar tax rules have had in certain highly industrialized countries. But in point of fact, total industrial net investment hardly increased at all from 1953, when the rules were introduced, until the effects of the Five Year Industrial Plan of 1957 made themselves felt in 1958/59; and since Government industrial investment increased, there must actually have been a fall in private industrial investment. Whatever the cause – after the Land Reforms and the many sequestrations the climate was not very auspicious for private investment in industry, in spite of the tax laws – the failure of these incentive tax rules was one of the reasons why the Government "lost patience" with private business after 1957 and stepped in with big investment programmes of its own.

The large share of indirect taxes in total taxes might be expected to make total taxation less progressive and even degressive. The indirect taxes are to a large extent levied on so-called "non-essential" goods, which, apart from tobacco, are not consumed by the lower income brackets; and for these income brackets the indirect subsidies, on wheat, maize, kerosene, and sugar, will probably more than counterbalance the indirect taxes paid. The net effect of total taxation, for the given income distribution before taxation, is most probably an increase in disposable income for the lowest income brackets, with the possible exception of small incomes from land rents, and a fall in disposable income for the higher income brackets. In saying this we have assumed that all indirect taxes are shifted on to the final consumer in full, and that income taxes are not shifted. However, if in addition we take into account the effects on income distribution *before* taxation, the picture may become a completely different one. We have already described, in chapter 6, sections 6.2 and 6.6, how the increased protectionism of the 'fifties, in which customs duties played an essential role, led to a strong shift in income distribution before taxation in favour of profits. Taking into account these primary effects of the tax system on incomes before taxation, the total effect of taxation itself may after all be a shift in income distribution in favour of the higher income brackets.

Finally, a few words about the *flexibility* of the tax system, i.e. its ability to make Government tax revenues rise with increasing economic activity. Both from a short-term stabilization point of view, and from a long-term development point of view, it is an advantage if tax revenues *automatically* tend to increase more than in proportion to the national income. The idea of the budget as a built-in stabilizer is well known, and an automatic growth in public savings will, of course, be conducive to development. As mentioned earlier, total tax revenues actually fell in relation to national income during the decade 1952/53 to 1962/63, but this can hardly be taken as proof that the tax system is badly designed from this point of view. It is true that the frozen land and buildings taxes have tended to put a brake on the growth of tax revenues, but apart from that the progression in the income taxes ought in principle to make the income elasticity of tax revenues greater than one. What has kept tax revenues down has been, until 1961, partly the stagnation of foreign trade, which together with the shift in the composition of imports has called forth a stagnation in revenue from customs duties, and partly the many exemptions to the income taxes, in connection with the Land Reforms, nationalizations, etc. After 1962 tax revenues would have fallen further compared with GNP, had it not been for the increased revenues from customs duties. These are probably the main factor making for flexibility, for they relate budget revenue closely to fluctuations in imports. This is probably rational in countries with an unstable foreign trade.

9.6 *The public debt*

Published figures on the public debt in Egypt are incomplete; they do not show the net debt, and in particular they do not give full information concerning the foreign public debt for post-war years. To obtain such figures, we have assumed in the table below that the public foreign debt at the end of 1952 was negligible; in 1943 all regular public debts in foreign currency were either converted into obligations in Egyptian pounds or redeemed, and probably only very little remained on foreign hands in 1952. The 1963 figures have then been calculated as the difference between the cumulated value of the yearly total net borrowing[6]) from 1952/53 to 1962/63,

---

[6]) From 1952/53 to 1958/59 net borrowing is equal to total budget expenditure less total budget revenues, as given by the UN Statistical Yearbook. From 1959/60 to 1962/63 net borrowing is equal to Public investment expenditure less Public savings in the budget (see Hansen, "Savings in the UAR (Egypt)" op. cit., table 2) less profits in public companies, which have been assumed to be £E 80 million in 1962/63 and 1961/62 and 40 million in 1960/61. Since investment in public companies is included in expenditure, it is natural in this connection to try to deduct company profits.

TABLE 9.6

The public debt, 1939–1961

£E million	31 March 1939	30 June 1952	30 June 1963
Domestic debt[a]	3[c]	156	586[d]
with domestic banks (gross)	...	106	547
Foreign debt[b]	92[e]	(0)	(224–274)
Total public debt	95	156	810–860

[a]) With deduction for Government deposits with the banking system.
[b]) Russian High Dam deliveries in principle included.
[c]) Short-term debts not included.
[d]) Agrarian Reform Bonds and Government guaranteed bonds not included.
[e]) Debt in foreign currency; only £E 39 million were actually held abroad.

SOURCES   United Nations, *Statistical Yearbook* 1960, *Economic Review*, CBE 1962, no. 3, IMF, *Financial Statistics,* and *Economic Bulletin,* NBE 1952.

and the increase in domestic public debts from the end of 1952 to the end of June 1963. We obtain then as a residual the figures £E 224–274 for Government total foreign borrowing from 1952 to 1963, and for Government foreign debt in the middle of 1963. There are various sources of error in this calculation. Certain domestic Government credit transactions are not included in the published domestic public debt figures; advances and capital transfers from public enterprises and the public pension and insurance funds are one possibility, and short-term "trade credits" between the Government and the private sector or foreign countries are never recorded in state budgets.

Measured as a percentage of GNP, the total public debt fell from 47 per cent in 1939 to 16 per cent in 1952, and rose again to 50–55 per cent in 1963. Of the total debt the domestic part is in itself less interesting. Most of the domestic debt is kept with the nationalized banks, and almost all the rest, disregarding the Agrarian Reform Bonds, which constitute claims on the new owners of redistributed land, is kept with the pension and social insurance funds, the nationalized insurance companies and other public companies. The "real" domestic public debt consists therefore mainly of the net claims of the private sector on the banking system, pension and insurance funds and insurance companies; and as we have already seen, the claims of the private sector on the banking system have been falling compared with the national income, while the pension and insurance funds represent highly consolidated loans from the private sector, if they can be considered loans at all. The domestic public debt therefore gives rise to no problems of importance, and its formal composition of short and long term loans is of little interest from a national economic point of view.

The foreign debt fell from 46 per cent[7]) of GNP in 1939 to probably nothing in 1952, and rose again to 15–20 per cent of GNP in 1963. The latter figure may be too high, owing to possible domestic loans obtained without collateral and not included in the domestic debt. Perhaps some £E 20–30 million should be moved from foreign to domestic debts on this account. On the other hand, it should also be remembered that the foreign debt figure does not include loans arranged through the banking system. The public foreign debt should actually be identified with the total net foreign debt of the banking system and the Government together with the public companies. This net debt may have amounted in 1963 to something like £E 350 million, to judge from the position of the Government and the banking system. Of this foreign debt about one half is US counterpart funds, and a good deal of the rest consists of long-term debts to foreign Governments and international organizations. Among the short-term debts, there are in particular the drawings on the IMF, which at the end of 1962 amounted to £E 40 million; however, there must also be substantial short-term credits from foreign commercial banks. It is, of course, this part of the public foreign debt that constitutes the acute foreign debt problem; the US counterpart funds are only amortized slowly, although their future liquidation is highly uncertain and unpredictable, while the Russian High Dam loans began to be paid off in 1964. Amortization obligations are, however, rapidly increasing and will after a few years constitute a heavy burden on the balance of payments.

9.7 The tax raising capacity of the administration

The limited capacity of the public administration to raise taxes in an appropriate way is usually supposed to be one of the greatest obstacles to the domestic financing of investments in underdeveloped countries. If public savings could be increased in an appropriate way, development programmes could always be financed domestically. Whatever the actual situation in other underdeveloped countries may be, however, there is no doubt that

---

[7]) 19 per cent if we include only debts on foreign hands.

in Egypt the taxing capacity of the administration is far from fully utilized. If we define taxing capacity as the ability of the administration to reduce the share of private disposable income in gross national income at market price, there is first the possibility of removing the price subsidies (negative indirect taxes), which in 1962/63 amounted to almost 3 per cent of GNI. Concerning the possibility of increasing the revenue from taxes on commodities, it is clear that wherever the trade in a commodity is at some stage completely in the hands of Government agencies or companies, taxation can offer no administrative problems. With the nationalization of foreign trade, big industry and wholesale trade, and with the marketing of all major agricultural crops in the hands of the co-operatives, which are in fact semi-official bodies, the technical opportunities for raising commodity taxes and profits of public companies at the wholesale trade stage must have increased enormously.

Turning to the taxes on income and wealth, we would first point out that the nationalizations can be considered as a 100 per cent income tax on the nationalized enterprises. Concerning the other income and wealth taxes, it is clear from the fact that they have fallen relatively during the last decade that more could be collected in this way. Revenue from the land and building taxes has even fallen absolutely from 1952/53 to 1962/63, although money income from agriculture and housing has almost doubled. There is particular scope in the taxation of agricultural income; for it is interesting to note that with the sale of all the major cash crops, and the purchase of all fertilizers, seeds, pesticides and weedicides and fuel concentrated in the hands of the co-operatives and Government agencies, it should be possible from 1963 to check most of the cash receipts and costs (except for hired labour) of each individual farmer. Since income in kind can easily be estimated on the basis of the area of each farmer, it now seems possible both to assess and collect income taxes from farmers with a low degree of evasion, and to choose the tax basis, gross or net income, actual or standard income, according to what is found appropriate from an income distribution and incentive point of view. Rents are already taxed, and could be taxed more heavily, but cultivators' incomes above the level of the regulated rents are almost free from taxation[8]). There seems to be a wide field for increased income taxation here, and also in the case of the buildings tax, which was greatly reduced

---

[8]) "Pharaoh by the advice of Joseph contented himself with a fifth, but the Pasha (i.e. Muhammed Ali) is scarcely content with two thirds". The present Government has been satisfied with about 2–3 per cent of agricultural income and is really modest compared

in 1961; again, increased taxation offers no technical difficulties. And so too with salaried people in the public sector.

In general, therefore, we can conclude that technically the opportunities are available for increasing Government revenues substantially. It is not the limited taxation capacity of the Government administration that explains the present modest degree of domestic financing of investments in Egypt. It would almost certainly be technically possible to increase public savings by an amount equal to the deficit in the balance of payments (£E 107 million in 1962/63) through increased tax revenues and the abolition of the price subsidies, without cutting Government expenditure on goods and services by one penny. Whether this should be done, and if so exactly how it should be done, is another question, which we have already dealt with at length in the previous chapter.

---

with both Pharaoh and the Pasha! The quotation is from a British consular report in 1826 see Helen Anne B. Rivlin, *The Agricultural Policy of Muhammed Ali in Egypt,* Harvard Middle Eastern Studies 4, Cambridge, Mass., 1961, p. 102.

CHAPTER 10

The new economic system

10.1 The new ownership structure

It is evident from our description of development in the individual sectors that far-reaching structural changes have taken place in the Egyptian economy during the last decade. A capitalist private enterprise economy has been transformed into "Arab Socialism". What then is the actual content of this kind of socialism? Or, to put it another way: how exactly does the Egyptian economy work to-day? This is not an easy question to answer. The present system is new and still undergoing transformation and consolidation. Furthermore, with a growing and dominant Government influence, the working of the system depends to a large extent on administrative mechanisms that may be difficult to observe, and are in any case extremely difficult to map out. A final description and appraisal of the new economic system will therefore be possible only when it has become fully consolidated, when permanent forms of organization have crystallized and temporary arrangements vanished, when statistical records of the performance of the economy under the new system for a series of years are available, and when careful studies of internal Governmental administrative principles and practices have been made. Until all these conditions are fulfilled – and this may take years – any description and appraisal, including the following one, must of necessity be tentative and even to some extent speculative.

According to a modern way of looking at things, an economic system is characterized by the way in which economically relevant decisions are taken and carried out; this then is what we need to know something about. Ideologies, however, socialist ideologies in particular, are usually more concerned with problems of ownership of the means of production and have little to say specifically about decision making and implementation. Apart from the old Utopian variety, socialist ideology does not tell us "how to run a nationalized bassoon factory". To be sure, one of the reasons why socialists do in fact want to change the patterns of ownership is that they want decisions to be taken in a way different from that obtaining under private capitalism. It is also obvious that ownership in itself does have some impact on decision making. But in themselves neither socialism nor public ownership implies any particular system of decision making. The contrast between Soviet centralization and Yugoslavian decentralization illustrates this point. A simple survey of the changes in ownership that have taken place in Egypt during the last decade can therefore provide only a limited understanding of the changes in its economic system, but as a background to such an understanding it is, of course, indispensable.

Before 1952 Egypt was a private enterprise economy with foreign influence in many fields and with some direct, though limited, Government interference. Through the Land Reforms, the Egyptianizations and sequestrations, the nationalizations, and also through direct Government investments, foreign influence was wiped out and the Egyptian economy became a mixed economy from both an ownership and a production point of view. The Government owns or dominates practically all big and medium-sized industry, all big transport and finance, the main part of domestic wholesale and foreign trade, together with construction. Private activity on the other hand predominates in agriculture and retail trade (although in both of these fields Government controlled co-operation makes itself increasingly felt) small-scale industry and handicrafts, housing (through the private ownership of residential and office buildings), and personal services. About 40 per cent of the gross national product seems now (that is, in 1962/63) to be created in Government-owned enterprises and public administration, 23 per cent of gross national income accrues (net) to the Government. Government spending on goods and services for final use corresponds to almost 35 per cent of the gross national product while 90 per cent of all gross investment, and 45 per cent of gross domestic savings take place in the public sector.

In itself the distinction between public sector and private sector does not tell us very much about the influence of the Government. Through its more general economic policies and regulations, the Government exerts a strong influence on parts of the private sector, while at the same time it seems to interfere less with the current activities of the publicly owned enterprises than it could in fact do. Being a mixed economy from an ownership point of view, it is highly regulated, with a good deal of Government intervention in the private half, and decentralization in the public half.

In the previous chapters we have already mentioned, and to some extent discussed, the most important ways in which the Government regulates and intervenes in private economic activity: area restrictions, price controls and policies, import licensing, wage policies, credit market policies, etc. We now need in addition a description of the present organization of the public business sector, and the content and method of planning.

10.2 The organization of the public business sector

The main principles behind the present organization of the public business sector are laid down in Law no. 60 of 1963 concerning General Organizations; besides this law certain Presidential Decrees are also important for an understanding of the organizational structure[1]). Altogether there are over 40 public so-called General Organizations, each one concerned with a particular branch of economic activity. Outside the system of General Organizations fifteen older, so-called Authorities, such as the Railway Authority, the Suez Canal Authority, etc., continue their previous activities, attached directly to the central administration in a traditional way. Each General Organization controls a certain number of the five hundred or so Government enterprises. The Organizations are attached to the particular Ministry most naturally concerned with their activity. The majority of organizations thus come under the Ministry of Industry; companies active in finance (banking, etc.) and trade come under the Ministry of Economy. Each Organization has a Board of Directors presided over by the Minister to whose Ministry the Organization in question is attached. The Minister has at his side an advisory committee to assist him in studying the technical, economic, financial and organizational problems of all the Organizations under his Ministry. As an over-all governing body a Supreme Council for Public Organizations, presided over by the President of the Republic and consisting of Vice-Presidents and Ministers, was instituted in 1961. The Supreme Council has so far never met.

The individual Government-owned establishments, apart from the Authorities, are usually organized as joint-stock companies. In the direction, supervision, and control of them, we thus find the following three levels: the Board of Directors of the company, the Board of Directors of the General Organization to which the company is affiliated, and the Minister to whose Ministry the General Organization is attached. The company's General

---

[1]) Concerning earlier organization, see chapter 6, section 6.7.1 and chapter 9, section 9.4.

Assembly of Shareholders is left out of the picture, since "the Board of Directors of the General Organization presided over by the Supervising Minister exercises the duties of the General Assembly of Shareholders" (art. 25 of Law 60, 1963). Secondly, the Chairman of the Board of the affiliated company has to report decisions of the Board to the chairman of the Board of Directors of the Organization, and seek their approval on matters concerning rules and regulations, the budget forecast, the general balance sheet and final accounts, the production plan, the marketing and exporting plan, and the investment and finance programme of the company (art. 14); in addition to this, the Board of the Organization "has the authority to rectify the decisions of the Board of Directors of affiliated companies and establishments concerning the utilization of reserves and provisions in terms not specified in the budget of the company or establishment" (art. 25).

Thirdly, "the Chairman of the Board of the Organization submits the decision of the Board to the Minister concerned for approval" (art. 11). The Minister's general authority is defined in art. 32, which gives him "the supervising, directing and controlling authority over the organization". With these regulations in force there seems to be no doubt that the Board of the Organization can interfere with any decision of the affiliated companies, and that the Minister can interfere with any decision of the Organizations. It is worth noticing that if the Minister wants to interfere in an affiliated company, he has to do so through the Board of the Organization, where, however, he has only one vote; in principle therefore he may be outvoted and unable to carry out his intentions. Also, there is nothing in the general regulations which forces the Minister to interfere actively and continuously; the approvals which are necessary in some cases, mentioned above, may boil down to mere routine without any real content. Under an earlier law (no. 265 of 1960), it was provided (art. 8) that an affiliated company had to seek approval for any decision taken by the Board of Directors of the company; this regulation was abolished by Law no. 60 of 1963, which can thus be regarded as a step towards increased decentralization. The legal frame now seems to permit varying degrees of centralization or decentralization. To what extent Ministers and Organizations do in fact interfere in the current management of the companies is a question that could only be answered by means of a series of case studies; and we know of none. However, in a presidential decree (no. 1900 of 1961) concerning the authority and duties of the Ministers in relation to the Organizations under their control, there is an interesting passage which may be read as some kind of programme. In connection with the above-mentioned advisory committee, the decree speaks about "the achievement of both centralization of planning and supervision and decentralization of management and execution" (art. 5). What this may mean is best understood in connection with a discussion of the system of planning applied.

In addition to the supervision and control of affiliated companies, the General Organizations are entitled to form new joint-stock companies or co-operative societies, give or guarantee loans to companies or bodies under its supervision, and acquire shares and securities in other companies. Each organization has its own budget, but is limited in its transactions by the total appropriations in the State Budget. An appropriation is made for each Organization as a whole, and the Organization is entitled to exceed the appropriations for any particular company by drawing on the appropriations of the others. In this way too a certain degree of decentralization is created.

10.3 *The content and method of planning*

It was not until 1957 that planning on a broad scale was introduced in Egypt. In that year two 5-year plans, for industry and for agriculture, were adopted and started. The present comprehensive 5-year plan for the period 1960/61–1964/65 can be considered in some ways as an extension of the two earlier ones. The industrialization plan and the corresponding plan for agriculture were in fact two investment programmes, each consisting of a priority list of concrete investment projects. In the present 5-year plan the investment plans cover the whole economy, and a set of national accounts was constructed to show how the economy is supposed to develop during the five years as a consequence of the investments made during the plan-period [2]).

The backbone of the 5-year plan is the investment programme. It was intended to make the majority of investments (about 90 per cent) through public authorities, on the assumption that the rest of the plan would then be realized automatically, without detailed specification, through the re-actions of private enterprises and households, as influenced by general policies, fiscal, monetary, etc. While the investment programme is thus a clear, detailed and specific working scheme for the Government, the rest of the 5-year plan is more a mixture of targets and forecasts of a rather

---

[2]) See *General Frame of the 5-Year Plan*, op. cit.

vague nature, conditioned as it is by policies to be specified in the annual budgets. Looking back at the first three years of the plan, it is quite clear that what has actually happened is that the Government has pushed a big investment programme as far as technical resources and foreign finance have permitted, and that the rest of the economic policy has been determined from year to year according to the circumstances. We shall return to this question; but we would say at once that in our opinion this may be quite a rational way of designing a development policy. We will also take up in a later section the question of the methods used in drawing up the investment programme. What matters here is that given the investment programme the rest of the plan was supposed to be realized through the automatic response of the economy, as influenced by policies left open for later specification. Concerning these policies, nothing was said in the plan itself, but from the context and from the fact that at the time the plan was drawn up, the great majority of enterprises in industry and trade were still private, it seems clear that the policies that were to complement the investment programme in the realization of the whole plan were to be of a general nature, and that it was not the Government's intention to run a centralized economy with detailed production targets and allocation plans for the individual enterprises and commodities. The individual enterprise was supposed to react to the demand of the market, given all the other circumstances. In this sense the economy was supposed to continue as a planned market economy with a rapidly expanding Government sector owing to the predominance of public investments. The nationalizations of 1961 and 1963, which were not foreseen by the plan, do not seem to have been undertaken in order to abolish the market economy. There is no doubt that the Government, including the Organizations, is by now able, should it so wish, to give direct orders concerning any detail of production in the Government enterprises. It is also obvious that such orders are in fact sometimes given – the big employment drive in 1961, with its detrimental effect on labour productivity (see chapter 5, section 5.5.3) is a case in point. But on the whole, the complete, direct control of savings and investments rather than of current production was one of the main economic motives for the nationalizations.

The machinery of planning follows a traditional administrative pattern. The individual Ministries and the Organizations attached to them suggest and prepare schemes and investment projects within their own field. These suggestions are collected by the Ministry of Planning, whose technical secretariat is the special National Planning Commission. The National Planning Commission is supposed to harmonize the proposals and schemes submitted by the various Ministries. To guide them in this work, the Commission has general economic and social targets fixed in advance by a Supreme Council for National Planning, headed by the President of the Republic. The Planning Commission submits its proposal for the comprehensive plan to the Supreme Council for approval; under it the Supreme Council has a huge number of advisory committees, headed by a ministerial committee for planning affairs. That the Supreme Council is more than just a nominal body was seen in 1960, when just before the first 5-year plan was launched the Council asked for a radical change in the plan, changing the target of doubling the national income per capita in 20 years as suggested by the Planning Commission to doubling total national income in 10 years.

Alongside the machinery of planning, there is a follow-up system which studies the performance of the economy and compares it with the plans.

The 5-year plan is subdivided into annual plans. To what extent these annual plans and their investment priorities have been revised during the plan period in the light of actual achievements and experiences, is not quite clear. That the annual plans must have modified the investment plans somewhat follows from the simple fact that actual investments are lagging behind the original plan for the first years. It would seem, also, that certain important changes in the investment plans have in fact taken place, in the plans for the High Dam, for instance.

The annual state budget is the main instrument for realizing the investment plan; the budget therefore contains the necessary provisions for the investments to be carried out in accordance with the plan. As already mentioned, the appropriations for each General Organization are considered as a whole, which implies some decentralization in the investment decisions. In recent years the gross budgets of the whole of the Government business sector, that is, not only the investment budgets, but also the current business budgets of Government enterprises, have been published along with the traditional state budget. The figures published for current sales revenues and production costs are not appropriations, however, in the sense of a traditional state budget, but simple, non-committal forecasts. It is significant, finally, that until early 1964 Planning and the Treasury were one Ministry under the same person.

10.4 How the system works

After this survey of the structure of public organizations and planning, can return to the question of the working of the present economic system. we

Beginning with price formation, the mixed nature of the system comes out very clearly. Prices are to a large extent administered, but the method of administering them is very different for different kinds of commodities. Agricultural prices are in a sense market prices: the Government buys and/or sells the "big" agricultural commodities from stocks at the desired prices, and gaps between domestic demand and supply are in some cases balanced through import (wheat and meat), or export (cotton, rice and onions). For some basic raw materials and consumer goods the Government fixes the prices directly, but the most common method of price control is to fix profits margins by law at levels which are considered to be "fair". These legal profit margins vary between commodities, and between importers, producers, wholesalers and retailers. This system of price-fixing for import goods and domestic industrial products is quite old and dates back to pre-war days when the protection of domestic industries began, and it was felt by the authorities that domestic producers and traders should not be allowed to take full advantage of the monopoly positions thus created. It gained in importance, however, on the outbreak of World War II, and even more after 1952/53, when import licensing became the rule, and it became necessary to prevent monopoly profits. This point is important in understanding the working of the system, as we shall see below. The products of small-scale industry and handicrafts sold directly to consumers are outside the price controls. In this field traditional oriental bargaining prevails; prices here are really competitive in the theoretical sense of the word. Rents of both buildings, i.e. flats, and land are regulated by law and have been kept unchanged for more than a decade, with a certain reduction in rents of buildings in 1962[3]), while the prices of the buildings and the land themselves are free.

Wage formation takes place mainly through the forces of supply and demand. This is particularly true for agricultural wages, where the legal minimum of 18 piasters per day until recently was a remote dream only, and actual wages stayed at a level of 10–12 piasters per day until the last few years. For industrial enterprises a legal minimum wage of 25 piasters per day is laid down, and this minimum wage is to-day probably by and large respected by the nationalized industries; but even in big enterprises, collective wage agreements are rare and individual wages seem mainly to be governed by

---

[3]) Average rents in houses must of course have increased with an increasing share of houses built at higher post-war costs and with rents in such houses fixed correspondingly higher.

supply and demand, with the enterprises in a favourable, monopsonistic position. An attempt is now being made to develop a system of graduated wages in the nationalized industries, but to what extent this will really change the method of wage formation, is still an open question. If successful it will make all wages in the public sector Government-administered.

Leaving prices and turning our attention to quantities produced, bought and sold, we can begin with the *household*. Disregarding normal conscriptions for the military forces, etc., choice of occupation is "free" in the usual Western sense, limited only by the individual's natural capacity and his opportunities for getting an adequate education; that for the majority of the poor, illiterate population these limitations reduce the choice of occupation in practice to almost no choice at all, is obvious. In the same sense the choice of consumption is "free", limited only by the pecuniary resources of the person in question. Only a few consumer goods are rationed, e.g. sugar and kerosene, and those who want to buy rationed goods in excess of their ration, can do so at higher official prices. Certain consumer goods are in short supply or not available at all, mainly manufactured import goods, but also certain foodstuffs such as meat and fat; or available only in qualities below what the consumer would prefer to buy; this is true of both many domestically produced consumer articles and some of the commodities imported from Eastern-Bloc countries. Concerning housing there is, at least in Cairo, a certain shortage of flats. These limitations in the choice of consumption make themselves felt mainly for families in the higher income brackets, though the great majority of families with small means have also experienced shortages of certain consumer goods.

Turning to *enterprises* and production, we must make a sharp distinction between fixed investments and current production. Since the time of the first development plans the aim of the Government has been to bring *fixed investments* more and more under the direct decisions of the Government. All major new investment projects are now decided upon and executed directly by the Public Sector, and investments within existing enterprises or by small private entrepreneurs will in any case need investment and import licences, and, in the case of Government-owned enterprises, approval by the Organization and the Ministry. For *current production,* and investment in stocks, the situation is different. In agriculture, where the majority of the land is in the hands of small private cultivators, production, given the external conditions of climate, water supply, etc. is determined by the cultivator's response to the Government-administered market prices for outputs and inputs. The Government exerts some direct influence on production through the area restrictions and deliveries of seeds, etc., through the production co-operatives in the land reform areas, and through the administration of the irrigation system. But in the main, the Government has to rely on the price mechanism if it wants to influence production decisions in agriculture. In private small-scale industry and handicrafts the Government has very little influence except perhaps through making raw materials and spare parts available, and the traffic works of course as everywhere else in the world; those who pay will be served. In medium-sized and big industry things may be different. Most of these industries are now nationalized, the Government is able to give them any order that it finds appropriate, and, finally, it is a fact that in connection with the plans, the planning authorities work out special commodity balances for a large number of basic articles. In spite of this, industrial production decisions seem by and large to be decentralized. The commodity balances are national forecasts rather than detailed production instructions, and the Ministries do not seem in general to force through particular production targets. Enterprises seem on the whole to produce for the satisfaction of the current market demand, including demand from the public authorities, which in most cases seem to secure a position of indisputable preference in the production programme of the Government enterprises. Stock-piling may of course be continued for some time if approved by the Organization and finance is made available, but should the enterprise have to turn to the nationalized banks for assistance, it will usually meet with very much the same response as in a private bank: finance will be supplied if the stock-piling is considered "sound". Direct intervention by a Minister may, of course, also take place here, but this seems to occur only in special cases. It would seem therefore that current production, even in the nationalized enterprises, is on the whole determined by current market demand, and that enterprises function very much as profit maximizing enterprises would do within the given frame of price fixing, import licensing, etc. This is particularly true for consumer goods industries, where the greater part of the demand is private. For enterprises which mainly sell direct to the Government it is more difficult, of course, to speak of production as being determined by a market demand. A Government decision to buy will in practice easily become an order to the enterprise to produce. However, it is important to note that competition for orders does actually take place between Government enterprises, in connection, for instance, with big construction works such as the High Dam; in fact a usual procedure is that public purchases and sales are subject to tenders and adjudications, whereby the most favourable offer has to be chosen. The aim of profit maximization has been stressed in several Government declarations, and the system of profit-sharing makes it almost a logical necessity.

With such a system the country might be expected to experience frequent shortages of domestically produced commodities; gluts would be counter-acted by the profit maximization of the individual enterprises and the behaviour of the banking system. When prices are kept down through price controls, profit margin regulations, etc., the expectation is that supply will fall short of demand, and that shortages and bottlenecks will appear in the system. Such shortages have appeared, and they have undoubtedly become more frequent and include even certain primary foodstuffs. An economic system having automatic built-in mechanisms to prevent gluts, but with no automatic built-in mechanisms to prevent shortages, will tend to become a shortage economy. However, such shortages cannot be said to dominate the economy in all fields. The explanation lies in the origin of the price controls, which arose from a situation in which monopoly positions had been artificially created through foreign trade regulations; from the outset therefore their task has been to keep down monopoly prices and profits rather than to prevent a general excess demand from pushing up prices. It is in the latter case that we can expect a supply shortage as an immediate consequence of Government price-fixing. In the case of a mono-poly price controls will have the immediate effect of leading to an expansion in the amount produced, and supply will tend to be equal to market demand; here production will only fall short of demand if the price is fixed so low that at the demand called forth by this low price, the marginal costs of the monopoly enterprise are higher than the price. Even if the price is fixed at the outset so as to equate demand and supply, a shortage will, of course, eventually occur if the demand later expands beyond what the monopoly enterprise can profitably produce at the given price[4]. It is partly along these lines that explanations for the frequent shortage situations of recent years must be sought.

It goes without saying that what we have discussed here will at most be true for the "representative" firm and commodity, from which there are certainly many exceptions. Direct interference with current production de-

---

[4] Two simple diagrams will clarify the arguments in the text. Assume that, as in figure (a), we have a situation with a demand curve D, a supply curve S, and a fixed maximum price $\bar{p}$. There is an excess demand equal to $q_D q_S$, and supply is lower than it would be without price controls; a shortage will appear here unless the Government steps in and fills the gap from stocks or imports.

cisions does take place, and in at least one important situation, namely in the case of import licences for necessary raw materials and spare parts, the Government has had to take sides directly and systematically in the production plans of the individual producer.

10.5 Price and foreign trade controls, and efficiency in current production

A main point in the appraisal of any economic system must be whether it is conducive to efficiency in current production. This again is a question of the allocation of existing resources amongst various lines of production and the use actually made of the resources alllocated for a specific purpose. Comparisons between the productivity of various factors of production in Egypt and abroad show a low productivity of labour, a high productivity of land, and a relatively rapid increase in labour productivity in industry; but none of these circumstances in itself provides any answer to the question of whether the system as such is conducive to efficiency in production. Land and labour in Egypt are factors of production very different from land and labour in Europe and USA. And the relatively rapid increase in

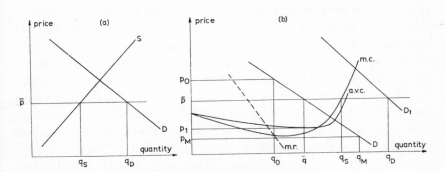

In the other case, we have a given import price, p_M, which is too low to permit domestic production, which would obey the cost curves m.c., and a.v.c. Domestic demand is D and the quantity imported is q_M. Let imports now be forbidden and domestic production started. Without price controls the price would be p_0, and the quantity produced (= quantity in demand) would be q_0, With price controls and profit maximization we may then have the lower price $\bar{p}$ and the higher production $\bar{q}$ – still equal to demand, unless the price is fixed lower than p_1. If then later the demand curve shifts to the right to D_1 and the price $\bar{p}$ is kept unchanged, while wage stability ensures unchanged cost curves, then a situation with shortages will appear; demand becomes q_D, while the supply is only q_S.

labour productivity, which by the way suffered a temporary setback owing to the employment drive in 1961, the year of the big nationalizations, may have been obtained at the cost of too-large capital inputs. Unfortunately, there is no simple method for measuring efficiency in current production in the sense we shall be discussing here, i.e. as "nearness" to the optimum. All that we can do is to discuss the question in a general way.

Public discussion in Egypt concerning the efficiency of the present economic system centres mainly on the capability of the Government administration and the possible strangling effects of "red tape" and excessive bureaucracy, in brief the dangers that the nationalizations may have brought to otherwise efficient production establishments through a destructive dependence on officialdom. The loose and rather elastic legal basis of the present system, together with the notorious general over-organization, slowness, and incompetence of the Government administration, make such fears understandable. We would not wish to belittle them; it is known, for instance, that in building and construction costs have risen substantially owing to the setting up of Governmental supervisory and controlling bodies. If far-reaching reforms, nay, revolutions, and improvements are needed anywhere in Egypt, it is precisely in the Government administration. And yet the efficiency of the present system is not only, and perhaps not even principally a question of the capability of the Government administration proper. If our interpretation of the working of the system is correct in its main lines, it would seem that its efficiency must be judged in particular from three points of view: first, the principles behind the investment decisions; this is a question of the allocation of capital, i.e. the allocation of existing physical resources and foreign exchange for capital formation; secondly, the effects of the present price system on efficiency in current production; and thirdly, the day-to-day administration of foreign trade in commodities other than capital goods, the long-term development of foreign trade and the day-to-day administration of capital goods imports being to a large extent questions of investment and general wage policies. The last two points are both concerned with the allocation of existing physical resources and foreign exchange for the production of intermediary and final products. For the moment, we will confine ourselves to this problem; investment policies will be discussed in chapter 11.

Publicly administered prices and nationalized foreign trade do not necessarily mean inefficiency in resource allocation, nor do uncontrolled private pricing and foreign trade automatically imply maximum efficiency. Everything depends on how it works. In the case of Egypt, monopolies and other limitations on competition in the major commodity markets would in any case justify some kind of Government intervention precisely from an efficiency point of view. And in foreign trade we have mentioned earlier how the tendency to capital flight makes public control of foreign trade almost a necessity in the present circumstances. In discussing price policies and efficiency we shall take it for granted that prices should in any case be fixed so that demand and supply tally. Shortages and bottlenecks are clearly detrimental to efficiency and give rise to various kinds of inconvenience. This aspect of the price policies has already been discussed, and found to be one in which the price policies have been far from perfect.

The aim of present Government price policies is mainly to accomplish a certain income distribution. In industrial and import price fixing the idea of "fair" or "reasonable" profits plays a dominant rôle; prices high enough to cover costs and allow for a "fair" profit margin, even in infant and otherwise incompetitive industries, are permitted while the monopolistic exploitation of consumers is frowned upon. In agricultural pricing too the same idea is at work, though agricultural price relationships have been moved more and more into line with world-market prices; around 1954 a major adjustment in agricultural prices was undertaken with the idea of influencing production. We do not need to explain here how and why cost-plus pricing based on ideas of "fair" profits may lead to inefficiency in resource allocation and production, and why marginal cost pricing is theoretically superior from this point of view. And although marginal cost pricing needs some modification if it is to imply full efficiency in production, such modifications would certainly not lead to the present Egyptian principles of pricing. So far it is easy enough to recommend a change from present price policies to marginal pricing. Such recommendations, however, may miss the point.

It very often happens in practical politics that governments try to influence income distribution by interfering with price formation without realizing that this may violate the conditions for efficiency in production, and that other policy means are available for the same purpose, such as direct taxes and subsidies. But the situation may be more complicated than this. First of all the interference may in fact improve resource allocation at the same time as it improves income distribution; this is the case when the Government controls monopolies. Here if the Government really succeeds in fixing all prices at the "competitive" level, it may obtain full efficiency in resource allocation at the same time as it shifts income distribution in favour of the lower income brackets. Secondly, a government may interfere with price formation for the sake of income distribution simply because no other ways are open to it. It is a very common situation in underdeveloped countries with limited administrative capacities that the number of policy instruments available is small compared with the large number of policy ends or targets which the Government wants to see fulfilled. The degree to which the individual targets are fulfilled will then turn out to be correspondingly low, and a lot of compromising between the various policy targets becomes necessary. Maximum achievement in economic policy usually requires that the number of policy instruments are at least equal to the number of ends to be taken into account[5]). In this sense, economic policy in underdeveloped countries will always tend to show a lower degree of achievement than economic policy in developed countries. This is also what makes nationalizations and direct interference with prices, etc., so tempting and attractive to policy-makers in underdeveloped countries; if you are not master of a sufficient number of methods of indirect interference, fiscal, monetary, and so on, and if this is the reason for the low degree of achievement in policy, why not widen the range of available instruments through direct interference?

It is against this background that the price policies pursued in Egypt during the last decade should be judged. To adjust income distribution in favour of the majority of the population and accomplish greater equity in a satisfactory way through direct taxes and subsidies has until very recently been an administrative impossibility. It must have been possible, however, to increase the taxation of incorporated business; yet a policy of reducing such taxes through various exemptions and investment-stimulating deductions was in fact adopted, in conformity with the policy of promoting private investments which the Government followed until around 1957. Excessive profits tended to arise, as we have seen, in connection with the increased import controls. The way out of this dilemma chosen by the Government was to prevent them through direct price-fixing, regulating profit margins, etc., with whatever consequences, positive or negative, which this might have had on resource allocation through its effect on price relationships. A better way out of this dilemma could certainly have been found; and with more appropriate methods for controlling the balance of payments, the income distribution problem might have become easier to solve without direct price controls; we shall return to this question below. What we wish to point out here is that with the nationalizations in industry

---

[5]) The reader will understand that here we are talking about "targets" or "ends" and "instruments" in the sense of the Tinbergen theory of economic policy.

and wholesale trade, together with the fact that it is now possible to force private retail profits down through the activities of the network of co-operative retail shops, most of this dilemma has simply disappeared. The idea of "fair" profits loses its meaning when enterprises are nationalized and the profits accrue in any case to the Government. From an income distribution point of view, the profits of the nationalized enterprises will be of importance mainly for the distribution of total national income between households and Government. In spite of the broad nationalizations under-taken, particular groups of the population may of course be affected in particular ways by the general level of profits and the individual profits of the Government enterprises; but the whole issue then becomes more a question of the distribution of the tax burden, whether direct or indirect taxation is preferable, and in this kind of problem there is no room for "fair profit" thinking. It is true that in agriculture there is still an income distribution problem (between sugar farmers, rice farmers, etc.), which may be difficult to handle except by acting on the price relationships for agri-cultural outputs; although the system of co-operative marketing adopted since 1963 seems to give the Authorities ample opportunities to tax or subsidize individual farmers. But in any case it is obvious that the need to use the price relationships to influence income distribution has diminished enormously with the change in ownership that has taken place, and the way should be open for a radical reform of the Government's price policies with respect to the *principles* of pricing. Thanks to the nationalizations, an inter-esting circumstance resource, allocation can now be given a much higher priority without jeopardizing other economic policy targets.

Various methods of pricing are possible. One solution would simply be to leave price fixing to the individual Government enterprises. From an administrative point of view this would be very attractive, but it would result in monopoly-pricing for most manufactured goods, and in the ex-tractive industries. Total Government income might perhaps increase as a consequence, and this might be considered good from a savings point of view, but the detrimental effects of monopoly-pricing on resource allo-cation are well known: monopoly-pricing implies restrictions on the quantity produced and unemployment or transference of resources to employments with lower productivity. Another possibility would be to continue with cost-plus pricing based on "normal" rather than "fair" profits[6]). With certain long-run equilibrium conditions ruling everywhere in the economy, this

---

[6]) Under the circumstances discussed "normal" does not refer to the "supply price" of

might indeed imply full efficiency in production and lead to the same result as "marginal pricing". In dynamic real life, however, the short-run deviations from this state of affairs might be large, and even in the long run cost-plus pricing with "normal "profits might lead us astray from an allocation point of view. We are left then with the ideal of marginal pricing, where prices are fixed so as to make demand and supply meet, and with enterprises ordered to extend their production up to the point where marginal costs equal the price. We would then have a society of competitive socialism along the lines advocated by Oscar Lange and A. P. Lerner, with centralized price-fixing and public ownership, as envisaged by Lange, in industry, finance, traffic and wholesale trade, and with the "counterspeculation" of Lerner, i.e. Government purchases and sales from stocks, coupled with private ownership, prevailing in agriculture and retail trade. To what extent marginal pricing would change the present price relationships is difficult to say; the largest changes in the price structure would probably appear if the principles of marginal pricing were applied also in the field of foreign trade. Before we turn to the problem of foreign trade administration, we would just point out that although there is much to be said in favour of central price-fixing and "counterspeculations" *à la* Lange-Lerner, the difficulties in administering such a system should not be overlooked – in particular in an underdeveloped country with a weak administration. The performance of the present price administration has certainly not been too brilliant. The great advantage of competitive socialism is that it decentralizes decisions concerning current production and in this sense frees it from "red tape", but it requires on the other hand, and so much the more, a good administration for price fixing and "counterspeculation"; obviously, the price side of the problem will work only if practical, *simple* rules of behaviour for the price authorities can be constructed; but economists interested in the idea of competitive socialism, have in fact done very little to create such practical rules [7]).

The reader may wonder why we have not included the management problem among the important aspects of efficiency. As a matter of fact, we have omitted it deliberately. This is not because we are unaware of the

---

capital; "normal" profits in the public companies should be fixed at a level sufficiently high to balance total demand and supply, given the structure of taxation.

[7]) One of the authors has discussed the problem of price fixing under competitive socialism in a structure like the present Egyptian one, see Bent Hansen, "Prices in a Socialist Economy", *Memo. no. 294,* Institute of National Planning, Cairo 1963, and "A Note on the Rules of Behaviour for Competitive Socialism", published in *Festschrift* to Oscar Lange. Warszawa 1964.

importance of efficient management and the well-known risks of inefficiency in Government enterprises. Nor are we unaware of the fact that management improvement is a crucial matter in Egypt, but this was also the case when the enterprises were privately owned [8]). Our problem is whether the present system as such is conducive or not to efficiency, and in our opinion it should not, at least in principle, prevent efficiency in management. With the adoption of profit-maximization as a general norm for the public enterprises, the "success-indicator" is theoretically the same as under private ownership [9]). The two new problems are that the identity of interest as between owner and manager has become smaller, and that with public price-fixing, etc., it becomes uncertain which standard of reference should be adopted in judging the success of an individual enterprise in making profits. The first of these problems could easily be solved by linking the manager's income directly to the profits of his enterprise. This idea has already been adopted in the profit-sharing system, which sets a maximum limit of £E 50, however, as the most a single person may receive annually; the only change needed in the present system therefore is to increase this maximum limit or at least relax it for the top management. The need for such a change in the system is of course different for different kinds of activities; the reform is particularly needed in industrial and commercial enterprises. Concerning the standard of reference it could perhaps be decided upon in connection with the selection of each single investment project. In principle there is thus no reason why there should be any great problem, but it means of course that the Government must be as alert and ruthless as any capitalist in removing inefficient managers. If the inefficiency of Government administration proper should spread to the enterprises, and the managers become just like traditional civil servants, production would suffer greatly.

Foreign trade is the main field where productive enterprises in the UAR, whether public or private, have to be in current contact with the central authorities, and where the Government's administrative decisions have a direct impact on the details of current production. If an enterprise does not get the raw materials or spare parts it needs, it will not be able to meet the market demand; in such cases the Government's actions are decisive for the volume and direction of production. And in exports similar problems arise in connection with the fulfilment of trade agreements.

---

[8]) F. Harbison and I. A. Ibrahim, op. cit.

[9]) That profit maximization is not under all circumstances a good success-indicator from an efficiency point of view is another matter.

Since the beginning of the 'forties, imports, and also to some extent exports, have been subject to licenses from a Government authority. In connection with the nationalizations of 1961, all import trade was concentrated in the hands of 12 public companies, and the main part of the export trade came under publicly-owned companies. This system has since been relaxed somewhat in that individual enterprises themselves can now get import licences for their raw materials or spare parts. However, the essential thing is that no import or export takes place without a licence being issued by the central authorities. At the beginning of the 'fifties tariffs were raised considerably for manufactured goods and "luxuries" and lowered for "necessities" such as raw materials and capital goods. At that time the high domestic prices of imported goods in many cases effectively limited imports, but to-day there is no doubt that in probably every case it is the *licence* that limits imports: at present import prices, including tariffs, etc., imports would in general, if they were adapted to current demands, tend to be higher than they actually are.

A full discussion of the problem of pricing in foreign trade would include the general balance of payments problem and its possible solutions. This question has been discussed at some length in chapters 7 and 8, and the conclusions were that any solution – with or without a depreciation of the Egyptian pound – which reduced import controls to a minimum would require strong shifts in the price relationships and in the structure of production. There is little doubt moreover that a general increase in both export and import prices, compared with domestic prices and wages, would be required. We also touched there upon certain optimum problems connected with the fact that in the foreign raw-cotton markets, and probably also in the foreign markets for Egyptian textile manufactures, Egypt meets sloping demand curves which may make it profitable for her to limit the quantities sold abroad in order to get the highest export proceeds. This means that for these commodities the optimum domestic price structure will deviate from the world-market price structure. Added to this is the necessity for an infant industry policy, which may also lead to strong, albeit temporary, deviations between the domestic and foreign price structures. All these deviations, however, could be handled by appropriate import and export taxes, or taxes on licences, which was in fact the kind of policy pursued during the 'fifties, and for which the present system opens up ample opportunities; though Egypt's recent joining of GATT does limit the freedom of the country considerably in this respect. What happens at present, however, is that direct controls in the form of licences are used instead of prices. The problem is, then, to what extent this affects efficiency in production.

To judge the effects of the present foreign trade controls, we have on the import side to distinguish between capital goods for fixed investments, raw materials and intermediary products for further processing in the country, elementary foodstuffs, and other mainly manufactured consumer goods. The import of capital goods is a question of fulfilling the Government's investment plans and must be judged in that connection (see chapter 11). The import of elementary foodstuffs takes place mainly under United States P.L. 480, title I, concerning sales against local currency of American surplus commodities; it consists mainly of wheat and wheat products. It is a kind of aid, and its volume is determined by direct negotiations between the US and the UAR Governments. During recent years the size of these imports has in fact satisfied domestic demand for wheat at given unchanged domestic prices. Domestic consumer prices for wheat are heavily subsidized, and it could be questioned whether it is rational under the circumstances to keep up domestic producer prices and domestic production; most probably, however, domestic production has been taken for granted in the negotiations about the size of the aid. American aid pays little attention to optimality in production. Other manufactured consumer goods are the goods which the import controls cut down most severely compared with what could be sold at current import prices plus import duties. The aim is partly to protect certain domestic "infant" industries, and partly to eliminate certain imports which are considered "luxuries" but for which no domestic substitutes exist. To the extent that the domestic price structure deviates here from the international, it may be justified by the infant industry argument [10]), but the gaps which do exist between demand and supply for certain commodities of this kind indicate that the system is inefficient at this point. We have already remarked that this is the main field where the principle of consumer sovereignty is clearly violated by the present system. This kind of problem could be handled by means of appropriate taxes and/or subsidies. We are left then with the imports of raw materials and intermediary products, including spare parts, which are important for efficiency in production in a very direct sense. The policy of the Government here has been to keep up imports of raw materials, etc., in all cases where domestic equivalents do not exist. Shortages of some raw materials have been noticed,

---

[10]) Theoretical welfare considerations lead to a recommendation of supporting infant industries by direct subsidies rather than through protection, and thus condemn such price deviations. Such a policy, however, requires that the country is able to handle the administrative problems connected with distributing the subsidies and collecting the taxes necessary to cover the subsidies.

there are continual complaints about delays in deliveries and difficulties in getting spare parts, and qualities (from some Eastern Bloc countries) are often bad; but on the whole such shortages seem to be due to "red tape" rather than to conscious Government policies. The policy throughout is to cut down other imports to allow production to go on and expand undisturbed by raw material shortages. But in spite of this, by and large it can safely be said that it is in foreign trade, exports as well as imports, that the influence of bureaucracy and "red tape" is most seriously felt, and it is probably here also that prices are most out of line with marginal optimum requirements.

10.6 Final remarks

The present chapter contains very little factual material apart from an account of some of the legal regulations and provisions. We have discussed the institutional structure of the system and commented upon it from one main point of view, in which the question of efficiency in particular has been considered basic. This led above all to a criticism of the methods of Government price-fixing, which does not seem to be conducive to efficiency; the present pricing system tends to make the economy a shortage economy. But all this does not fully and definitely answer the question: how does the system work? We have tried to describe how the system is designed rather than how it works; blueprints and actual performances are entirely different things. For the latter we need not only statistics concerning the relevant success indicators, such as productivity, per capita income, etc. We need also standards of reference. Concerning the statistics too short a time has passed to make it possible to produce any significant conclusions concerning the performance of the new economic system. As for the standards of reference, where shall we take them from? Certainly not from theoretical ideals, for although they may be used to suggest improvements, no country lives up to them. Nobody will ever know what would have happened had the new economic system not been introduced, and if we want to make comparisons with earlier performances we can choose between the old state of stagnation and the short period of rapid expansion at the end of the 'fifties before the big nationalizations took place, both of which periods have been discussed in detail earlier. In the future, when sufficient statistical material is available, students of Egyptian growth will perhaps find it appropriate to compare Egypt with other poor countries with different economic and political systems. The present authors, at least, would do so.

CHAPTER 11

The five-year plan

We will end this analysis of the Egyptian economy with a description and appraisal of the 5-year plan for the years 1960–65. for three years of the plan period we have already statistics and it is possible to form an opinion of the degree to which the planotto will be fulfilled. Since the Government is at present preparing the second 5-year plan for the period 1965–70, a discussion of principles is also appropriate. Nobody expects a country's first plan to be a masterpiece, but unless the faults of the first plan are recognized, the second will be no better than the first. We will try therefore to draw some lessons from the first 5-year plan.

11.1 The main objectives of the 5-year plan

The principal objectives of the present plan, which contains a broad 10-year plan superimposed on a more specific 5-year plan, are:

(1) to double the national income over 10 years. This means an average annual rate of growth of 7.2 per cent. For the first five years a 40 per cent increase was planned, corresponding to a growth rate of 7 per cent per year. This implies a per capita growth rate of 4.0–4.5 per cent;

(2) to achieve larger equality of opportunity, as well as a more even distribution of income and property;

(3) to expand employment opportunities.

Let us begin with the national income target. Compared with the actual annual rate of growth of about 6 per cent obtained during the so-called base period 1957/58–1959/60, the 7.2 per cent required for the ten-year period and the 7 per cent planned for the 5-year plan period do not seem very ambitious. However, special factors such as the nationalization of the Suez Canal and the general revival after the dislocations connected with the Suez War, together with a good deal of idle capacity, made the rate of

growth particularly high during the three years preceding the plan, and
the annual rate of growth achieved during the three first years of the plan
period did not exceed the previous growth rate, see table 11.1; in fact it
was perhaps slightly lower. Nevertheless, at almost 6 per cent it approached
the target growth and would amount to doubling the national income over
12 years. For the individual sectors growth rates during the first three plan
years show wide deviations from those planned. Against a planned growth
rate of 5 per cent in agriculture the actual rate was only about $1\frac{1}{2}$, in spite
of good crops in 1962/63; obviously the 5-year target for agriculture is
out of touch with realities. For industry the achieved rate approaches the
planned rate, and the same is true for Commerce and finance and Others.
In Building and construction development has been radically different
from the plan. The plan foresaw a slight decrease in this sector, which was
very strange, while in fact the sector has grown by 11 per cent per year
during the first three years. Part of the explanation seems to be the changes
in the construction schedule for the High Dam that were decided upon after
the 5-year plan was drawn up. In Transportation too the actual rate of
growth has exceeded that of the plan considerably, owing to a complete
underestimation of the increase in Suez Canal traffic. At the present rate
of growth – and it seems unlikely that the next two years will change the
picture radically – it would seem that at the end of the first 5-year period
GNP (in real terms) will have increased by about 30–35 per cent, against
40 planned, while the share of agriculture in GNP will have fallen further
than planned and Building and construction, and Transportation and
communication, will have increased their shares compared with the plan.

Over the 10-year period a more vigorous growth in both GNP and the
agricultural sector is likely, since a sizable part of present investment
activity, in particular the High Dam, land reclamation and irrigation works,
will begin to bring in some returns in the second half of the 'sixties. That
the growth in GNP for the 5-year plan period will most probably fall somewhat short of what was intended does not therefore necessarily imply that
the great target, doubling in ten years, is out of reach; but everything will
depend, of course, on investment policies and other policies pursued during
the second five-year period.

Turning then to the second major objective, we notice that the 5-year
plan has certain broad socio-economic objectives which would ultimately
imply a socialist pattern of society. Apart from the income redistribution
which the plan indicates, without discussing the means by which it is to be
achieved, this socialist pattern is to be realised mainly through the pre-

TABLE 11.1

The development of gross value added 1959/60–1964/65; planned and actual at fixed 1959/60 prices

Sectors	Actual 1959/60		Planned 1964/65		Annual rate of increase *planned* 1959/60–1964/65 per cent	Actual annual rate of increase *achieved* 1959/60–1962/63 per cent
	£E million	per cent	£E million	per cent		
Agriculture	400	31	512	28	5.1	1.7
Industry and electricity	273	21	540	30	11.5	9.3
Building and construction	52	4	51	3	− 0.4	11.3
Transportation and communic.	97	8	117	7	3.9	11.0
Commerce and and finance	127	10	163	9	5.2	6.2
Others	333	26	413	23	4.2	5.9
Total	1282	100	1795	100	7.0	5.7

SOURCE   *General Frame of the 5-year Plan for Economic and Social Development, July 1960–June 1965,* Cairo 1960, together with information from the Ministry of Planning.

NOTE   Total value added in this table does not coincide with GNP at market prices for 1959/60 for two reasons. Some revisions of the GNP estimates for 1959/60 have been made since the plan was published, and secondly, for some peculiar reason it does not include customs duties and is therefore only partly at market prices. The total growth rate of 5.7 per cent is for this reason slightly lower than the actual growth rate measured at market prices. This also explains why the sector distribution is somewhat different from that of table 1.1. The actual increases are calculated on a basis and sector distribution which is almost identical with that of the *General Frame.*

dominance of public investments, which would eventually place the greater part of the productive apparatus in the hands of the Government. In this respect the plan was similar to Indian socialist policies; no nationalization of private enterprises was involved. Since then the nationalizations of 1961 and 1963 have rapidly accomplished what current Government investments would have achieved only slowly, and in the National Charter of 1962 the socialist character of the future society has been stressed.

The third objective of the plan is to employ almost all the projected increase in manpower. Since some unemployment already existed at the beginning of the plan period, no full employment policy is therefore involved. During the 5-year period employment is intended to expand by one-sixth, i.e. one million persons, while the projected increase in manpower is slightly larger. Agriculture is to absorb one half of the expansion, services about one quarter, and industry less than one fifth. It is interesting to compare this feature of the employment plan with, on the one hand, the actual stagnation of the agricultural labour force during the last 25 years and on the other, certain fashionable views on development policy, according to which surplus labour should be drawn away from agriculture to be employed through industrialization. The employment policy of the 5-year plan has been criticized on just these grounds, that it does not conform to this way of thinking; but most probably it is the plan that is sound in this respect. As pointed out earlier, it is doubtful whether a surplus of labour exists in Egyptian agriculture in the sense that a number of persons could be moved permanently from agriculture, *ceteris paribus,* without decreasing production. The marginal productivity of labour in Egyptian agriculture seems definitely positive, and may even be larger than going wages in agriculture. If zero-productivity of actually employed labour is to be found anywhere in Egypt, it is most probably in Government administration. This points definitely towards an increase in employment in agriculture, even without additional investments. We shall return to this problem in connection with the discussion of the investment policies. During the plan years the attitude of the Government to the employment problem seems to have changed somewhat. Employment for social reasons now seems to be accorded a larger value than at the time when the 5-year plan was drawn up. In 1961 a great employment drive took place, including an increase in employment in Government administration and in the newly nationalized industries; in the latter it was connected with a reduction in the working week from 48 to 42 hours. This employment drive led to a large increase in industrial and governmental employment – with adverse effects on pro- ductivity in both spheres. While the total increase in the number of industrial employees was intended to be 204 000 over the five plan years, the actual increase from 1959/60 to 1961/62 amounted to 131 000. Employment in industry, measured in number of persons, has thus been running ahead of the plan, while production is lagging a little behind. However, this tendency will most probably be reversed in the last years of the plan, and the "over-employment" in industry may turn out to be a temporary phe- nomenon only. In Government administration "over-employment" will almost certainly continue to be a serious problem, because the Government has committed itself to employ *all* university graduates.

11.2 The investment programme

As we have explained, the investment programme is the only policy programme laid down in the plan frame, the rest being forecasts and targets based on unspecified policies. The plan envisages an increase in the share of investments in GNP (at market prices) to 20 per cent on average for the five-year period as a whole, with total investments amounting to £E 1636 million. The plan itself did not specify how investments should develop during the plan period[1]), but annual investment plans have since been published for the first four plan years. Until 1962/63 they can be compared with actual achievements.

The annual plans envisaged a big jump in investment activity from 1959/60 to 1960/61 and after that a certain further increase year by year. A glance at the annually planned figures, however, shows that they are going to add up to considerably more than the total £E 1636 million of the 5-year plan.

TABLE 11.2

Gross investments 1959/60–1964/65; planned and realized

	Planned gross investments £E million	Actual gross investments £E million	Unfulfilled investment plans £E million	Percentage implementation
1959/60		171		
1960/61	305	229	76	75
1961/62	355	248	107	70
1962/63	399	307	92	77
1963/64	406			
1964/65				
Total 1960/61–1964/65	1636			

SOURCES   For annually planned investments, see *Detailed Plans* published by Ministry of Planning; for actual investment, Ministry of Planning. Actual investments in 1959/60 were estimated in the plan at £E 204 million, but this figure has since been revised down to 171 million. We expressed some doubts about this low figure earlier on.

---

[1]) Only for the last year did the *General Frame* specify the amount of investments, and strangely enough it seems to assume a higher share of investments during the first years than during the last.

This may be due to changes in the plan, the High Dam investments, for instance, exceed the planned figures by far, but it may also be because the annual plan figures are most probably at current prices, while the total planned is a fixed-price figure, and there have in fact been some price increases in the investment sector. In spite of all this, there is little doubt that investments are lagging behind the 5-year programme. If we assume that actual investments for 1963/64 and 1964/65 will reach the average of about £E 350, which does not seem over-optimistic, the total for the 5-year period will be about £E 1480 million. Even taking into account the fact that this figure contains some price increase, this would mean about an 80 per cent fulfilment of the original investment plans for the 5-year period as a whole. With an incremental capital-output ratio of about 3 – which is the over-all incremental ratio assumed by the 5-year plan (see below table 11.3), and the actually observed ratio for 1946–1962/63 (see chapter 1, section 1.3) – the one per cent, roughly, by which actual growth is lagging behind the plan, would have required additional investments totalling about £E 250 during the 5-year period, which is about what the unfulfilled portion of the investment programme may amount to. This shows that the over-all assumptions of the plan concerning total investment requirements must have been fairly realistic. For the individual sectors table 11.3 gives the main figures.

In the interpretation of this table, it should be noticed that the sector Agriculture, etc., includes the High Dam, which contributes to the investments, by almost £E 50 million according to the plan [2]), without contributing to the value added of this sector until the second half of the 'sixties. Disregarding the High Dam lowers the capital-output ratio for Agriculture to around 3, which is still rather a high figure. Behind it lies the nature of the irrigation system, which requires investments with a very slow turn-over. The capital-output ratios shown by Transportation, etc., and Dwellings are rather high; the ratio for Transportation, etc., is pulled up somewhat by the low income forecast for the Suez Canal.

Concerning actual investments it will be readily understood, on comparing the above with the distribution of investments for 1962/63, see table 1.2, that the sectorial investments target will be fulfilled to varying degrees. For the period as a whole Agriculture and irrigation (including the High Dam) was supposed to absorb some 24–25 per cent of total investments; the actual

---

[2]) Actual spending is much higher, owing to changes in the plan and price increases. Up to the end of 1963 £E 110 million had been spent.

TABLE 11.3

Capital formation, value added and employment by sectors (at fixed 1959/60 prices)

	Planned total capital formation during 5-year period £E millions (1)	Projected increase in annual gross value added £E millions (2)	Projected increase in employed persons 000's (3)	Projected incremental capital output ratio = (1)/(2) (4)	Planned capital invested per person employed = (1)/(3) £E (5)	Projected gross value added per person employed = (2)/(3) £E (6)
Agriculture and irrigation (including High Dam)	383	112	555	3.4	609	202
Industry, electricity and construction	575	266	204	2.2	2 328	1 304
Transportation, communication and storages (including Suez Canal)	269	20	7	13.5	38 429	2 857
Dwellings	140	11	4	12.7	35 000	2 750
Services (including public utilities)	149	104	256	1.4	581	406
Stock changes	121	—	—	—	—	—
Total	1 637	513	1 026	3.2	1 595	500

SOURCE   *General Frame of the 5-Year Plan for Economic and Social Development*; the sector breakdown used in this table is not a happy one, but the breakdown used in the source varies from table to table, and we had no other choice.

share in 1962/63 was 22–23 per cent, in spite of a large increase in the planned
and actual High Dam investments. Industry and electricity was supposed
to absorb some 35 per cent; the share in 1962/63 was 31 per cent only.
Transport, communications and storages in 1962/63 seem to have had exactly
the share envisaged by the plan. For both Dwellings and Services the actual
share in 1962/63 was somewhat higher than in the plan, 12.5 against 9 per
cent, and 14.7 against 9 per cent, respectively[3]). The actual over-all incremental capital-output ratio is somewhat lower than that assumed in the
plan, namely 2.6 against 3.2, and also lower than the measured capital-
output ratio for 1946–1962/63 which was 3.1. But as mentioned earlier,
capacity utilization has increased. To check the sectorial capital-output
ratios assumed by the plan is not possible. The sectorial breakdown of
investments is available only at current prices, while the sectorial breakdown of value added is available only at fixed 1959/60 prices. Also, it has little
meaning to calculate incremental capital-output ratios for so short a period.

To appraise the investment programme, it is necessary to know the
underlying value judgements, the targets. Since doubling the national income
in ten years was taken as a primary policy postulate, and since, furthermore,
raising the standard of living of the population is the ultimate concern of
the plan, it is clear that the investments necessary to achieve this objective
should be minimized. However, some regard has also been paid to employment. If we look at table 11.3 we find very large sectorial divergences
between the values in columns (4), (5) and (6), which are related to these
criteria. Now it is well known that no matter which criterion is chosen as a
basis for decisions about the pattern of investments, an optimum pattern
of investment always requires that the quantitative measures of the criterion
in question should be the same for *marginal* investment projects in all the
individual sectors. About this table 11.3 says nothing, of course. A full
appraisal of the investment programme would involve getting down to the
individual investment projects.

To scrutinize each project would be an enormous undertaking, which
would, of course, be impossible for us to take up[4]). All we can do here is

---

[3]) The stock changes cannot be checked owing to lack of statistics. It is worth mentioning
that the planned figure is sensible. If total stocks amount to, say, one quarter of GNP,
a growth rate of 7 per cent would require stock investments to the extent of about
£E 140 million for the five years in order to keep the relation between stocks and GNP
unchanged.

[4]) One of the authors was a member of an investment appraisal Committee, and has
therefore seen the work done "from the inside".

to describe the actual process of reaching investment decisions and the principles involved. The process seems to have started from above, in the sense that the National Planning Commission, on the basis of the over-all targets laid down by the Government, fixed the sectorial, or rather ministerial, investment allocations. To do this, the NPC proceeded in a way which perhaps can best be described as an application of the Tinbergenian step-by-step method[5]. From the given over-all growth-rate target and a series of income-elasticities for consumer goods, obtained by informed guesses, there followed the distribution of consumer demand by sectors; to this was then added Government current demand. The over-all capital-output ratio gave the total amount of investments, which were roughly divided into construction and imports of capital goods. To find the necessary total production by sectors the NPC then tried to utilize a small Leontief input-output model, but without much success. The sectorial production targets were therefore determined in a rather intuitive way, and the total investments needed for each sector were estimated by the application of sectorial capital-output coefficients, obtained from historical studies of domestic development, from engineers, and from experience abroad. After each Ministry had received its broad investment frame, it was asked to fill it in with concrete investment projects according to the best judgement of the Ministry. Since the selection of projects within each sector was thus left to the Ministry in question, there was nobody to compare the individual projects as between Ministries. The work done by the individual Ministries was probably of quite different quality, and in some Ministries ambitious attempts were made to estimate future returns in terms of value added, employment and import-saving effects. Regard was paid to these various aspects of the individual projects, but certainly not in any systematic way. All we can say, therefore, is that there may have been a tendency within each Ministry to choose projects with high value added returns, high employment, and high import-saving capacity, but how these factors have been weighted against each other is impossible to know. The method of selection may also have varied from Ministry to Ministry. Furthermore, special considerations for individual projects may have come into the picture. About 1400 investment projects were selected, and a substantially larger number must have been scrutinized[6]. It is worth stressing that all the public in-

---

[5] Jan Tinbergen, *The Design of Development*, Baltimore 1958, and "The Appraisal of Investment Projects", *Memo. no. 383*, INP, Cairo 1963.

[6] I. H. Abdel Rahman, "Comprehensive economic planning in the UAR", *L'Egypte Contemporaine*, July 1963.

vestments envisaged by the 5-year plan are expressed in terms of concrete investment projects. Proposals for the investment programme were then submitted from the Ministries to the National Planning Commission, which in turn worked out its final proposals. These proposals met with strong criticism in the Supreme Council, which at the eleventh hour revised the whole plan substantially: in particular, the capital-output coefficients with which the NPC had worked were revised downwards considerably, a revision which actual developments seem to have justified.

It is clear from this brief account of the procreation and birth of the 5-year plan, that the investment programme contained in it cannot claim any high degree of co-ordination and optimality. There is no reason to condemn the plan on this account; the time available for the Authorities was desperately short, the persons and offices involved had little experience in drawing up an over-all economic long-term plan, and the lack of statistics and background studies must have been frustrating. The NPC in fact did an impressive amount of data-collecting and economic analysis as a preparation for the plan – the memoranda of the NPC are still one of the best sources of information about post-war developments – but there is no doubt that there are many "informed guesses" behind the plan figures. In any fair appraisal all these difficulties must be taken into account. What should be criticized, however, are some matters of principle, where it is doubtful whether the principles actually applied could ever have led to an optimum plan, even if sufficient time and information had been available.

The first point to be raised is the "open" nature of the plan. We have stressed several times that the plan consists of an investment programme plus a forecast for the rest of the economy based on the automatic responses of enterprises and households, as influenced by future policies. There is much to be said in favour of this kind of procedure, the main argument being that the future contains so many unknown elements impossible to forecast 5 years ahead that it seems better to decide general policies subsequently, when external conditions concerning technical knowledge, foreign trade, climate conditions, etc., are better known, or at least easier to forecast. The unspecified policies should then be determined in connection with the annual budgets, etc. It can be questioned, of course, whether it is at all possible to work out an optimal long-term investment programme under such circumstances, and most probably the investment programme itself must undergo changes during the course of time. But apart from that, it would seem that the least that should be done is to study whether the conditioned forecasts can be accomplished at all with the available policy instruments. A fundamental study of the possibilities of implementing the plan does not seem to have been undertaken.

Secondly, the principles for selecting investment projects can be questioned – quite apart from the lack of co-ordination described above, which could, of course, only be completely avoided by the application of a comprehensive planning model. We have already said that the rate of return on capital in terms of value added has played a role in selecting investment projects. This seems natural when the task is to minimize the amount of investments necessary to accomplish a given national income increase. This procedure presumes, however, that other factors of production are free, in particular that labour is a free factor (disregarding the agricultural investments, which should increase the cultivable area to some extent, land is a minor factor of production in most of the investment decisions). Here the planners have obviously been working on the standard assumption that in underdeveloped countries labour is an abundant factor of production. As mentioned in chapter 3.4.2, this is doubtful, and some evidence against the existence of an absolute surplus of labour in Egyptian agriculture is available. The marginal productivity of labour in agriculture in Egypt seems to be in line with, or even above, agricultural wages, which means that in appraising investment projects labour costs evaluated at about current wages should have been deducted before the rate of return on capital was calculated. One would then have been left with a profitability calculus for each investment project. Such a change in evaluating the rate of return would have implied a tendency towards the selection of more capital-intensive projects than the principle actually applied. Egyptian Ministries, packed with engineers, have often been accused of being biased in favour of capital-intensive projects. This may be true, as it also seems to have been with private industrialists in Egypt[7]), but taking into account the bias in the opposite direction suggested by the assumption of labour as a free factor, it seems doubtful whether on balance too high or too low a capital intensity has been chosen. The problem we are discussing here is the general one of market prices *versus* "shadow" prices in investment calculations. Our argument is that the shadow price principle may be wrong for the labour factor in Egypt. It may be asked whether similar problems were met with on the capital side. As posed here, the fundamental policy problem was to minimize the amount of capital necessary to obtain a given increase in national income. Under these circumstances no shadow price for capital comes into

---

[7]) El Gritly, op. cit.

the picture; projects should simply be selected from above according to their rates of return until a sufficient total increase in GNP is obtained. This gives rise to no questions of principle, except in cases where capital is available for a certain special purpose only. Such cases of course would have to be treated separately, the investment being decided upon if the rate of return on capital exceeds the cost of obtaining the specified amount of capital. This problem very often crops up in connection with foreign loans, the main example in Egypt being the Soviet loans for the High Dam.

Thirdly, it can be asked whether the procedure for selecting investment projects has led to an optimal structure of foreign trade. The leit-motif for the plan in this respect has been import substitution and self-sufficiency. The Suez War may have left its mark here, but more generally the planners have acted on the view that an underdeveloped single-commodity exporter should diversify her production in order to depend less on foreign trade. For a single-commodity exporter, this may perhaps be a sound rule of thumb at the beginning of its development. Any import substitution will then make the country less dependent on the traditional export commodity; foreign trade will decline compared with national income and this in itself will make the country's economy less sensitive to fluctuations in foreign trade and crop conditions. But even in the first stage of development, it matters greatly just which commodities the country chooses to produce itself instead of importing them; there may be natural advantages to be taken care of. This point of view has obviously been considered by the Egyptian planners, as can be seen from the big expansion in the production of fertilizers, cement and oil, which are all based on existing natural resources. Since these commodities also happen to be in strong domestic demand, the exploitation of natural advantages and self-sufficiency are compatible policies. To this extent self-sufficiency has probably also been an optimal policy. But one-sided investments for import substitution and self-sufficiency will not make the country less of a single-commodity exporter. After 30 years of industrialization Egypt is in its foreign trade still highly dependent upon raw cotton. In this sense very little "diversification" has been obtained up to now, and this is at least partly due to the principles applied in the 5-year plan. Furthermore, the lucky coincidence between natural advantages and self-sufficiency does not continue to apply. Sooner or later the country has to ask itself whether a commodity should be produced at home, or whether it should produce another one, sell it abroad, and import the commodity it needs. The answer depends, broadly speaking, on which method will require the largest amounts of domestic productive resources. This question has not been answered by the 5-year plan; it has not even been posed. It may have been relatively unimportant up till now, as we have said, but as development progresses the simple idea of self-sufficiency will make the composition of both domestic production and foreign trade more and more inoptimal. Poor countries in particular should take as much advantage as possible of foreign trade.

Fourthly, and closely connected with the second and third points, it seems that even apart from the shadow-price problem for labour mentioned above, the method of project selection may have led to inoptimalities owing to another "shadow-price" problem related to foreign trade. To some extent project selection has been based on the return on capital in terms of value added. It seems, however, that the prices used for calculating future sales revenue and costs, other than wages costs, in order to arrive at value added, have been *domestic* prices rather than *foreign* prices, i.e. prices at the frontier. Some authors, such as Tinbergen, consider this to be part of the general shadow-price problem, although it is a question of choosing between two sets of actual existing market prices rather than choosing between market prices and invisible social opportunity costs. In any case, it is obvious that to arrive at the social profitability of a capital investment, both sales and costs should be calculated at the future prices[8]) at which the commodities involved can be bought or sold abroad: these represent the true opportunity costs or revenues of the activity in question[9]). Instead, it seems that domestic

---

[8]) Strictly speaking, the marginal revenues or costs in selling and buying abroad. For Egypt this is important in all problems connected with cotton.

[9]) This point has been stressed by Tinbergen in his advisory activities, also in Egypt, see Tinbergen, "The Appraisal of Investment Projects", op. cit., but it does not seem to be taken into account by Ragnar Frisch in his present work for the Institute of National Planning, Cairo. Says Frisch: "The strength of Egypt as a competitor in the World's export markets in any given year in the planning period depends, of course, on the quality of its export goods, on the price it is able to offer and on whatever export drives it has carried out. In the reasoning in the sequel I shall assume that these basic conditions for export are given. "See Ragnar Frisch, "How to Plan", *Memo. no. 380* (being Memo. no. 102 in the new series of Professor Frisch), INP, Cairo 1963, p. 40. This means, of course, that what is generally recognized as the central problem in Egyptian foreign trade planning is ignored. The way to take it into account in Frisch's model seems to be to recalculate the commodity flows, on which the model is based, in *international* prices, i.e. at the prices at which the qualities produced could be bought or sold abroad during the plan period, while in Frisch's model past domestic prices seem to be used. Let it just be added that Frisch's earlier work in Egypt did not have any practical influence on the shaping of the first 5-year plan. The work referred to here is being carried out during the preparation of the second 5-year plan, for 1965–70, but does not seem to get any practical influence on this plan either.

prices have been used, including tariffs and/or monopoly profits conditioned by protection from foreign competition; unless the infant industry argument is involved, this must imply that comparative advantages have not been fully taken care of. A further foreign trade shadow-price problem, also stressed by Tinbergen (op. cit.) is that of the exchange rate applied. Tinbergen's position here is not very clear, but it seems that he relates the judgement of the overvaluation of the domestic currency to the *current* deficit of the balance of current payments. As we have argued earlier (see chapter 8, sections 8.4.2 and 8.4.3), the question of overvaluation should be judged as a long-run problem, taking into account the other public instruments used to realize all the targets. The rate of exchange may or may not be one of the instruments. Even if the current deficit is large, therefore, the actual exchange rate may be the correct one to use in the problem of optimizing foreign trade.

Fifthly, it is worth mentioning that with respect to foreign payments, the plan expects a substantial export surplus to arise as early as 1964/65. This surplus is expected to arise not only through import substitution, which should help to keep imports slightly below the level of 1959/60, in spite of a planned 40 per cent increase in production and income, but also through increased exports of both agricultural products and manufactured commodities. In many fields the investments planned will lead to excess capacity as compared with domestic demand; it is then taken for granted that the excess production will automatically turn into exports. Whether there will really be a foreign demand at the prices at which the Egyptian industries can produce does not seem to have been the subject of any more deepgoing studies, which is, of course, just another example of the general deficiencies in the principles of planning with respect to foreign trade.

11.3 The financing of investments

Total investment expenditure in the 5-year plan amounts to £E 1636 million. Of this £E 1096 million were supposed to be financed from domestic savings and the remaining £E 540 million from foreign sources. This means that about one third of the investments were planned to be financed from abroad. Annual distribution over the 5-year period is not given in the plan, but since it specifies that in the last plan year, i.e. in 1964/65, a surplus of £E 40 million should be obtained in the balance of current payments, the implication is that for the four years 1960/61–1963/64 foreign borrowing should on average amount to about £E 145 million per year, which for these four years would correspond to 40 per cent of the investments.

Actual development has been somewhat different from what was planned in so far as both investments and foreign borrowing have been running at a lower level than planned. Total investments have actually been £E 783 million from 1960/61 to 1962/63, while net foreign borrowing during the same period amounted to about £E 220 million. Borrowing for these three years is therefore only about half the amount envisaged by the plan, although the share of investments financed from abroad comes near to thirty per cent. Foreign financing has increased rapidly during these three years. The share of foreign-financed investments was only about 14 per cent in 1960/61, but in 1962/63 it was almost 35 per cent. It is clear, however, that for the four years 1960/61 to 1963/64 as a whole, the planned share of 40 per cent foreign financing cannot be reached. This means, on the other hand, that for these years domestic savings are running at a relatively higher level than envisaged by the plan. For the years 1960/61 to 1963/64 the plan implies total domestic savings of £E 706 million. For the three years 1960/61 to 1962/63 actual domestic savings were £E 562 million, and with domestic savings of perhaps £E 250 million for 1963/64 the plan figures for the years 1960/61–1963/64 will clearly be surpassed.

For the last plan year, 1964/65, however, it is difficult to see how the plan figures can be fulfilled, or even be approached. The plan envisages a surplus of £E 40 million in the balance of payments, which in its turn implies domestic savings of about £E 390 million. In 1963/64 the deficit in the balance of current payments may be in the region of £E 100 million, and domestic savings £E 250 million. What is needed then is an improvement in the balance of payments and an increase in domestic savings by £E 140 million, corresponding to 8 per cent of GNP. What policies can accomplish such a dramatic improvement?

The sharp increase in domestic savings envisaged by the plan, from about 13 per cent of GNP in 1959/60 – the actual figure for 1959/60 seems to have been below even 10 per cent – to about 20 per cent in 1964/65, was expected to be realized mainly through ploughed-back business profits, and, since Government business profits would to a large extent be paid into the budget, through increased public savings. Household savings were expected to increase only rather modestly. Household disposable income was to increase by about 30 per cent and private consumption by 26 per cent, which implies a marginal rate of savings of about 17 per cent. Whether this is a reasonable figure for Egypt we are unable to say. The relatively slow rise in household disposable income did not assume any substantial increase in taxation, but was based on the assumption that there would be a rapid increase in retained business profits, though nothing was said in the plan about how this should be accomplished. The nationalizations of 1961 may partly be seen as an implementation of this aspect of the plan, though it is uncertain what effect they have actually had on retained business profits and household disposable income. Estimates of disposable income and private consumption indicate that the share of disposable income in GNI was about the same in 1962/63 as in 1959/60, and the share of savings in private disposable income has increased only slightly, if at all. With an actual domestic savings ratio of only 12 per cent in 1962/63 the savings ratio in 1964/65 cannot be expected even to approach the plan target; the necessary policy measures will have to be very vigorous indeed, as follows clearly from our discussion of the balance of payments problem in chapter 8.

11.4 Availability and use of resources during the plan period

Any understanding or appraisal of the plan with respect to the availability and use of resources is complicated by the fact that the plan is not fully expressed in terms of market prices, and that the conceptions and classifications of the plan do not conform to the customary international standards. In table 11.4 we have tried to compare plan and achievements in terms of current market prices with the plans for the last year of the 5-year period translated into 1962/63 prices; a true fixed-price estimate for all years is not available. Furthermore, the breakdown of both availabilities and use in table 11.4 follows international standards. Concerning the availabilities, we have already discussed both the probable short-fall in the GNP development, and the assumptions of the plan concerning net imports. For the sake of comparison, we give the average percentage distribution for the use of resources during the years 1956/57–1959/60; the year 1959/60 had an unusually low investment share and an unusually high private consumption share.

First of all, we find that already in 1962/63 a share of investments was obtained which is equal to the share planned for 1964/65[10]). Since the 10-year target is to obtain a doubling of GNI, corresponding to 7.2 per cent

---

[10]) As pointed out earlier the share for 1962/63 may be exaggerated owing to price increases in the investment sector.

TABLE 11.4

Availability and use of resources for the 5-year plan period

£E millions at current market prices	Base year 1959/60	Actually achieved			Planned for 1964/65 (converted into 1962/63 market prices)
		1960/61	1961/62	1962/63*	
GNP	1375	1467	1550	1679	2021
Net imports	39	35	80	107	− 42
Total available	1414	1502	1630	1786	1979
Gross investment	171	229	248	307	369
Public con-sumption	193	211	260	290	253
Private con-sumption	1050	1062	1122	1189	1357
Total use	1414	1502	1630	1786	1979

Per cent of GNP	Average 1956/57 1959/60				
Net imports	2.4	2.8	2.4	5.2	6.4	− 2.1
Gross investments	13.5	12.4	15.6	16.0	18.3	18.3
Public con-sumption	14.3	14.0	14.4	16.8	17.3	12.5
Private con-sumption	74.5	76.4	72.4	72.4	70.8	67.1

* Preliminary figures.

SOURCES   *General Frame of the 5-Year Plan,* and information from Ministry of Planning.
NOTE   The recalculated plan figures for 1964/65 converted into 1962/63 market prices were obtained as follows. The implicit GNP deflator is known to have increased by about 5 per cent from 1959/60 to 1962/63. Since the plan is expressed in terms of 1959/60 prices, this price increase has been applied to all items of the 1964/65 plan (sectorial price indices are not available, unfortunately). Some difficulties of principle arise, however, owing to the system of concepts used by the *General Frame of the 5-Year Plan;* it does not use the categories of table 11.4, it is only partly expressed in market prices, and its assumptions for the base year are different from what is now statistically known about that year. This leads to the difficulty that in "translating" the plan figures we have either to stick to the plan in absolute terms or as percentage changes. The following way of "translating" the plan figures seems to us the most reasonable.

The GNP figure for 1964/65 was obtained by applying to the 1959/60 figure the 40 per cent increase in national income, which is the basis of the plan, with an addition for the 5 per cent price increase. The Net imports of − 42 millions were obtained by adding a 5 per cent price increase to the − 40 millions assumed by the *General Frame* for 1964/65.

On the use side 'gross investments' were set at the 351 million given in the *General Frame* plus a 5 per cent price increase. The concept of Public consumption does not appear in the *General Frame*, but those items in the Public Administration Sector Appropriation Account (p. 237) which come nearest to Public Consumption together show an increase of 25 per cent. This percentage, plus 5 per cent price increase, has been applied to the 1959/60 figure of table 11.4 to obtain the figure of 253 million. 'Private consumption', calculated as a residual, then shows a 23 per cent increase from 1959/60 (subtracting the price increase), while the plan assumed an increase of 26 per cent. The reason why we come out with a lower increase in planned consumption is that we have kept the absolute investment target, and this implies a larger relative increase in investments than assumed by the plan, because the plan assumed that actual investments were 204 millions in 1959/60. Concerning the method of inflation applied it can be said in general that since investment prices have probably increased more than public consumption and private consumption prices from 1959/60 to 1962/63, the inflated 1964/65 plan figures probably underestimate the investment target and overestimate the public and private consumption targets for 1964/65.

increase per year, the investment share planned for 1964/65 seems too low, at least with a capital-output ratio of about 3. For long-term purposes an investment share of about 23 per cent will perhaps be necessary in 1964/65, corresponding to an investment level of about £E 430 million, assuming that a GNP level of about £E 1850–1900 million will in fact be reached in 1964/65. To obtain such a level a strong upward investment push is still needed. Given the Net imports, this means that the share of public and/or private consumption for 1964/65 will have to be even lower than shown in the table.

Secondly, we observe that the share of public consumption in GNP has increased a good deal, while the plan foresaw a certain fall. Even if the absolute level of public consumption were to be kept constant during the last two years of the plan period, its share will still show a certain increase.

Private consumption, thirdly, has diminished its measured share from 74.5 per cent during 1956/57–1959/60 to 71 per cent in 1962/63. Whether this represents a real fall or merely statistical fallacy is uncertain (the heavy fall after 1959/60 is certainly so), it being recalled that private consumption is estimated as a statistical residual and contains some unrecorded stock changes and capital imports, together with the sum of all errors made in the estimates of the other items. We must also remember that table 11.4 is at current prices for the years 1959/60 to 1962/63; a fixed-price estimate might show an unchanged or even rising share of consumption, because investment prices have probably risen more than consumer prices. However, even if there has been some fall in the share of consumption, a further sharp drop is needed to reach the planned share for 1964/65.

Taken together private and public consumption seem to have maintained an unchanged share of GNP of 87–88 per cent during the years from 1960/61 to 1962/63; this is about the same level as the average for the years 1956/57–1959/60; the share of 90 for 1959/60 is again most probably a statistical fallacy. According to the plan, this share is to fall to below 80 per cent in 1964/65. To depress it by 8 percentage units in the course of two years is what is needed to fulfil the plan from the use of resources side. This is, of course, just another way of expressing the fact emphasized in the last section: that domestic savings need to be raised from 12 to 20 per cent of GNP in order to fulfil the plan. But now we have the additional information that public consumption has been the culprit rather than private consumption.

11.5 Future planning and policies

Summing up, we can say that the over-all rate of growth for the 5-year plan will most probably fall only a little short of the planned 7 per cent, while the share of investments may slightly exceed the too-low target set for 1964/65. In these respects the 5-year plan seems likely to be fairly successful. The sectorial production development shows quite important deviations from the plan, but here actual developments may have been sounder than the plan. The significant divergences from the plan are in the use of resources, where it is by now pretty clear that the plan targets cannot even be approached. The Second Five-Year Plan, which is now under preparation, will therefore meet other and greater problems than those assumed by the first Five-Year Plan. During the second plan period, 1965/66–1969/70, the problems left unsolved by the Government in the first plan period will have to be cleared up in addition to the problem of creating an annual growth of almost 8 per cent.

The rate of growth in itself will perhaps not be the worst problem of the Second Plan. The share of investments has already been brought half-way towards the necessary level, compared with the pre-plan level of 13–14 per cent of GNP, and administrative and technical machinery now exists for pushing investments up further. Also, during the first plan period certain important investments were carried out, or begun, which will begin to bear fruit only in the Second Plan period, the High Dam and the related irrigation and land-reclamation works being the most conspicuous example; for agriculture the blessings of the High Dam will already be forthcoming during the second 5-year plan period, although electricity, which constitutes 40 per cent of the estimated value added contribution, will not appear until 1970. From our discussion of the principles of planning that were applied in drawing up the First 5-Year Plan, it followed that a good many improvements were needed in the planning of investments, but some of the conditions for making such improvements seem to have been fulfilled. First of all the planners have some experience, which they did not have at the time the first plan was prepared. Secondly, methods of planning have improved considerably, too. Some work is at present going on at the Institute of National Planning, Cairo, in the application of Ragnar Frisch's colossal decision models on Egyptian planning problems. This work, however, is still in a preliminary stage and badly in need of improvements, as pointed out earlier, and it may be decennia before it reaches the point of practical application. One great obstacle is the lack of statistical information. Another more fundamental difficulty is the problem of determining the "objective function", which is a common problem in all attempts to apply maximization methods to policy-making. Thus even if, as is most probable, the second 5-year plan too is put together by some crude stage-by-stage method, which is theoretically inferior, of course, to the ideal simultaneous approach, great improvements are possible. First of all, Tinbergen himself has pointed to improvements in the stage-by-stage method concerning that very point which represents the major weakness of the first 5-year plan: foreign trade[11]). Comparative advantages can now be better taken care of. Secondly, the statistical information available is much greater to-day than it was five years ago, although still clearly insufficient for projects like Frisch's models. Income-elasticities can now be estimated from household surveys; a more detailed and reliable input-output table can be set up; more information on capital-output ratios exists – just to mention some crucial points. If then, in addition, returns on projects are calculated on the basis of foreign prices instead of domestic prices, and furthermore, an inter-Ministry comparison of investment projects is undertaken, great progress would already

---

[11]) Tinbergen, "The appraisal of investment projects", op. cit., where Tinbergen has explained his modified stage method based on the "semi-input-output" method. This method is probably the only planning method at present available which in a satisfactory way can take care of comparative advantages at the same time as it does not require more statistical information than may be at hand in underdeveloped countries. For an appraisal of Frisch's and Tinbergen's planning methods see Bent Hansen, *Lectures in Economic Theory*, 2nd rev. Ed., Part II, "The Theory of Economic Policy and Planning", INP, Cairo 1964, Lectures 15 and 16.

have been made. By applying simulation methods, the planners may be able to present the Government with a series of feasible solutions to choose from; in this way the problem of the objective-function is sidestepped.

The primary problem of the second 5-year plan should therefore not be the drawing up of a good investment plan, although this may be difficult enough. The real problems will come with the implementation, with the policies necessary to carry it out. Here, unfortunately, neither Tinbergen's nor Frisch's methods have very much to contribute; none of these models includes prices as determinants for enterprise or household coefficients, and there is no doubt that changes in the price structure will be an important part of the policies for the second plan period (see our discussion in chapters 8 and 9). It should be added also that models which consider agriculture as one sector can never be very useful for planning in underdeveloped countries; it is *within* this sector that some of the biggest policy problems are to be found. During the second 5-year plan period the country will in all probability have to improve its balance of current foreign payments, and perhaps even begin to pay back foreign loans, at the same time as investments are pushed further upwards. A solution to the problem of making private and public consumption grow more slowly than gross national production will then become imperative, and this may mean increased taxation, while wages and salaries will have to be prevented from increasing in step with productivity. For a successful wage policy the population pressure is in itself, sad to say, a great help; but increased employment, and better education and birth control, together with "rising expectations" and increased Government ownership, may make it difficult to repeat the development between 1939 and 1960, when money wages always rose less than productivity and helped to improve the low competitiveness of Egyptian industry. However, it is an advantage that profits are mainly under the direct control of the Government. If wages are prevented from rising in step with productivity, there is no risk of private spending from the rising profits; if the Government then restricts its own consumption spending sufficiently, domestic savings can increase simultaneously with the improvement in the international competitiveness of industry. Nevertheless, this may still be insufficient to keep an internal balance as well as improve the balance of payments. Taxes may then have to be increased to help prevent private consumption from increasing too rapidly. But increasing taxes will mean that the whole tax system will have to be reconsidered. As we pointed out in our discussion of the balance of payments problem, it matters greatly just how consumption is prevented from increasing too rapidly. Having been created at a time when private enterprise dominated the economy and needed strong protection against competition from abroad, when the inequality of income distribution was much larger than to-day, and when there was no serious balance of payments problem to solve, the tax system is badly in need of an overhaul. With rising incomes and increasing equality of income distribution, taxing the lower income brackets and agricultural incomes become indispensable, even if much may be gained through curbing existing tax evasion. Large shifts in relative prices may also become necessary, and to prevent undesirable effects on income distribution, the system of indirect taxes and subsidies may have to be revised. Clearly, also, a general change in attitude to the problem of creating export industries rather than import substitutions only, is necessary.

During the first 5-year plan period the Government was confronted with the problem of establishing machinery for pushing investments and creating income. During the second 5-year plan it will meet a new problem, namely that of establishing machinery for directing the use of income effectively. Without efforts from the country itself, the balance of payments problem of the UAR will not be solved. It needs to be stressed, however, that the UAR is not the only developing country in this position; and for the development countries as a whole, the balance of payments problem cannot be solved, of course, unless they are supported by adequate balance of payments policies in the developed countries. An improvement in the balance of payments of the developing countries requires a deterioration in the balance of payments of the developed countries; and some industries in the developed countries will have to suffer and perhaps even die. If the developed countries do not permit this, all efforts from the side of the underdeveloped countries will be in vain. The measures taken to increase domestic savings and check consumption will then in general have only deflationary effects on the domestic economies, with no effect on the balance of payments as a whole. Even under such unfavourable general circumstances an individual developing country such as the UAR could solve its balance of payments problem without harming its own development, but the hardships imposed on the population would be inhuman. The success of the Second Five-Year Plan of the UAR is not therefore the sole responsibility of its own Government; it is also a responsibility of the developed countries. Fortunately, the joint responsibility of developed and developing countries seems to-day to have become a generally accepted principle in international policies and it was endorsed unanimously by the U.N. Conference on Trade and Development. What is left then is only to act accordingly.

National income, national outlay, and savings in the UAR (Egypt) 1939-1962/63

The following tables, with some minor extensions and corrections, are reproduced from Bent Hansen and Donald Mead, "The National Income of the UAR (Egypt), 1939–1962", *Memo. no. 355*, Institute of National Planning, Cairo 1963; Bent Hansen, "The National Outlay of the UAR (Egypt), 1937–1939 and 1945–1962/63", *Memo. no. 377*, INP, Cairo 1963; and Bent Hansen, "Savings in the UAR (Egypt), 1938/39 and 1945/46–1962/63", *Memo. no. 551*, INP Cairo, 1965. For sources and methods of calculation, and critical appraisal, see these papers, which are available on request; here it need only be mentioned that the national income estimate for 1939–45 is based on Dr. M. A. Anis, "A study of the national income of Egypt", *L'Egypte Contemporaine,* Cairo 1950, while for the post-war period the estimates are based on certain estimates made by the National Planning Commission, all of them adjusted in various ways and brought on to a definitionally consistent basis. Although consistent as to definition methods of estimation vary as between periods. The reader should be careful, therefore, in comparing figures from various periods; in certain cases adjustments for differences in level have to be made on the basis of overlapping years. It must be appreciated also that some of the estimates are at fixed prices, others at current prices. Only within each table are the figures fully comparable. Two systematic sources of error, of unknown size, have been indicated by x, unrecorded stock changes, and y, unrecorded capital exports, in all tables for years after 1945. Since private consumption and private savings are estimated as residuals these two errors appear in both of these items.

TABLE A.1

Net national income at current and constant market prices, 1939-45

Year	Net national income at factor costs, current prices £E million	Indirect taxes minus subsidies*) £E million	Net national income at current market prices £E million	Wholesale price index 1939 = 100	Net national income at constant market prices £E million	Value added at constant 1939 prices £E million	
						Agriculture	Industry
1939	168	15	183	100	183	54	13
1940	191	15	206	113	182	49	15
1941	233	17	250	141	177	47	18
1942	326	19	345	189	182	40	20
1943	390	16	406	238	171	39	20
1944	464	24	488	271	180	43	20
1945	502	26	528	288	183	44	18

*) For the budget years 1 March to 28 February.

TABLE A.2

Gross national product and income, 1945–54 (£E million at constant 1954 prices, unless otherwise stated)

Year	Agriculture	Industry and electricity	Construction	Transportation and Communications (incl. Suez Canal)	Housing (ownership) of real estate	Commerce and finance	Other services incl. Government	Total: Gross Dom. Product at 1954 market prices	+ Net factor income from abroad	Gross national product at 1954 market prices	Net gains or losses (−) from terms of trade changes	Real gross nat. income at 1954 prices (incl. terms of trade effects)	Rate of increase over previous year per cent	Gross national product at current market prices [1]
1945	303	91	19	38	50	122	96	719	− 8	711	− 38	673	—	552
1946	302	92	22	43	51	142	101	753	− 9	744	− 40	704	4.6	535
1947	299	101	25	46	53	147	110	781	− 5	776	− 45	731	3.8	578
1948	328	113	31	61	56	169	122	880	− 3	877	31	908	24.2	718
1949	325	126	25	72	59	190	139	936	− 9	927	10	937	3.2	829
1950	303	133	22	78	62	210	148	956	− 11	945	68	1013	8.1	916
1951	304	132	36	81	65	209	157	984	− 13	971	113	1084	7.0	1016
1952	334	132	30	81	68	193	166	1004	− 12	992	9	1001	− 7.7	920
1953	315	134	37	86	73	181	166	992	− 11	981	− 25	956	− 4.5	888
1954	312	146	33	88	77	188	179	1023	− 13	1010	0	1010	5.6	936

Average annual rate of change compound per cent

	Agriculture	Industry and electricity	Construction	Transportation and Communications	Housing	Commerce and finance	Other services incl. Government	Total: Gross Dom. Product	Gross national product at 1954 market prices	Real gross nat. income at 1954 prices
1945–51	0.0	6.4	11.3	13.5	4.5	9.4	8.5	5.4	5.3	8.3
1951–54	0.9	3.4	− 2.9	2.8	5.8	− 3.5	4.5	0.7	1.4	− 2.3
1945–54	0.3	5.4	6.3	9.8	4.9	4.9	7.2	3.8	4.0	4.6

[1] This estimate of GNP at current market prices is the only one available for this period; it was made by Dr. El Sayed Hafez Abdel Rahman, *A Survey f the Foreign Trade of Egypt in the Post War Period*, University of Cairo, Faculty of Commerce Library (unpublished doctoral thesis). Definitionally, it should be comparable to the fixed-price estimate, but the 1954 figures show that the level of GNP is quite different in the two series.

TABLE A.3

Gross national product and national income 1952/53–1962/63 (£E million)

	Gross nat. prod. at current market prices [1]	Agricul-ture	Ind. and elec.	Con-struction	Transp. and commun.	Housing	Commerce and finance [2] I	Commerce and finance [2] II	Other ser-vices	Total I	Total II	Gains from terms of trade changes [3]	Real gross nat. income at constant 1953/54 I	Real gross nat. income at constant 1953/54 II	Rate of increase over previous year per cent I	Rate of increase over previous year per cent II
		Gross national product at constant 1953/54 market prices														
1952/53	905	305	137	25	54	59	167	142	217	964	939	+ 8	972	947	—	—
1953/54	963	295	140	27	55	56	158	158	232	963	963	0	963	963	− 0.9	1.7
1954/55	1014	298	149	26	58	62	161	163	235	989	991	+ 8	997	999	3.5	3.7
1955/56	1072	308	160	25	62	65	171	165	237	1028	1022	+ 10	1038	1032	4.1	3.3
1956/57	1125	318	170	28	58	67	172	151	236	1049	1028	+ 17	1066	1045	2.7	1.3
1957/58	1195	333	186	33	62	68	189	167	240	1111	1089	+ 14	1125	1103	5.5	5.5
1958/59	1256	352	198	38	69	70	205	172	245	1177	1144	+´17	1194	1161	6.1	5.3
1959/60	1372	367	209	42	88	73	213	184	259	1251	1222	+ 26	1277	1248	6.9	7.5
1960/61	1467	365	234	39	97	74	223	197	289	1321	1295	(+ 20)	1341	1315	5.0	5.4
1961/62	1550	338	257	55	111	76	228	204	280	1354	1329	(+ 20)	1374	1349	2.5	2.2
1962/63[4]	1679	386	274	62	121	78	275	211	302	1498	1434	(+ 20)	1518	1454	10.5	8.2

Annual rate of change comp. per cent

		Agricul-ture	Ind. and elec.	Con-struction	Transp. and commun.	Housing	Commerce I	Commerce II	Other	Total I	Total II		Real I	Real II		
53/54–56/57		2.5	6.7	1.3	1.8	6.2	2.9	− 1.5	0.6	2.9	2.2		3.5	2.8		
56/57–62/63		3.3	8.3	14.1	13.0	2.6	8.2	5.7	4.2	6.1	5.7		6.0	5.6		
1953–1962/63		3.0	7.8	9.7	9.2	3.8	6.4	3.3	3.0	5.1	4.5		5.2	4.7		

[1] Comparable with alt. II at fixed prices.

[2] In alt. I the contribution of 'commerce and finance' to GNP has been assumed to be proportional to the flow of commodities, defined as production in 'agriculture' and 'industry and electricity' plus imports. In alt. II the GNP contribution has been assumed to be proportional to employment in the sector itself. In our opinion alt. I is preferable.

[3] No estimate of terms of trade is available for the years 1960/61 onwards.

[4] Preliminary figures.

TABLE A.4

Availability and use of resources 1945–1956 (£E million at fixed 1954 market prices)

	1945	1946	1947	1948	1949	1950	1951	1952	1953	1954	1955	1956
GNI	673	704	731	908	937	1013	1084	1001	956	1010	1061	1093
Net import of commodities and services + y	− 47	14	24	8	4	11	14	50	8	4	34	29
Total available + y	626	718	755	916	941	1024	1098	1051	964	1014	1095	1192
Gross investment — x, of which		64	88	121	130	137	149	115	111	128	160	130
private fixed		55	77	99	117	122	115	87	70	72	94	72
public fixed		11	12	15	18	19	26	28	35	44	57	49
stock changes — x		− 2	− 1	7	− 5	− 4	8	—	6	12	9	9
Public consumption	46	50	55	75	99	108	118	128	124	138	152	170
Private consumption + x + y		604	612	720	712	779	831	808	729	748	783	892
Total uses + y	626	718	755	916	941	1024	1098	1051	964	1014	1095	1192
Shares in GNI (per cent)												
Net import + y	− 7.0	2.0	3.3	0.9	0.4	1.1	1.3	5.0	0.8	0.4	3.2	2.7
Gross investments — x		9.1	12.0	13.3	13.9	13.5	13.7	11.5	11.6	12.7	15.1	11.9
of which												
private fixed		7.8	10.5	11.0	12.5	12.0	10.6	8.7	7.3	7.1	8.9	6.6
public fixed		1.6	1.6	1.7	2.0	1.9	2.4	2.8	3.7	4.4	5.4	4.5
total fixed		9.4	12.1	12.7	14.5	13.9	13.0	11.5	11.0	11.5	14.3	11.1
Public consumption	6.8	7.1	7.5	8.3	10.6	10.7	10.9	12.8	13.0	13.7	14.3	15.6
Private consumption + x + y		85.7	83.7	79.2	75.9	76.9	76.6	80.7	76.2	74.0	73.7	75.2

y indicates capital exports due to changes in the leads and lags in foreign payments.
x indicates unrecorded stock changes.

TABLE A.5

Availability and use of resources[1], 1952/53–1962/63 (£E million at current market prices)

	52/53	53/54	54/55	55/56	56/57	57/58	58/59	59/60	60/61	61/62	62/63[2]
GNP	905	963	1014	1072	1125	1195	1256	1372	1467	1550	1679
Net import of commodities and services + y[3]	31	−10	25	39	20	46	17	36	36	69	107
Total available + y	936	953	1039	1111	1145	1241	1273	1408	1503	1619	1786
Gross investments − x	119	132	146	172	151	165	181	171[4]	229	248	307
of which Stock changes − x	3	9	12	12	1	15	1	− 13	4	− 10	18
Public consumption	133	135	140	164	175	172	173	187	211	260	290
Private consumption + x + y	684	686	753	775	819	904	919	1050	1063	1111	1189
Total use + y	936	953	1039	1111	1145	1241	1273	1408	1503	1619	1786
Shares in GNP (per cent)											
Net import + y	3.4	− 1.0	2.5	3.6	1.8	3.8	1.3	2.6	2.5	4.5	6.4
Gross investments − x	13.1	13.7	14.4	16.0	13.4	13.8	14.4	12.5	15.6	16.0	18.3
Fixed gross investments	12.8	12.8	13.0	14.9	13.3	12.6	14.5	13.4	15.3	16.6	17.2
Public consumption	14.7	14.0	13.8	15.3	15.6	14.4	13.8	13.6	14.4	16.8	17.3
Private consumption + x + y	75.6	71.3	74.3	72.2	72.8	75.6	73.1	76.5	72.6	71.7	70.8

x indicates unrecorded capital exports due to changes in the leads and lags in foreign payments.

x indicates unrecorded stock changes.

[1] Methods of estimation differ slightly for 1952/53–59/60 and 1960/61–62/63; but the figures may be considered comparable for all practical purposes.

[2] All figures preliminary.

[3] For each of the years 1959/60 and 1960/61 £E 10 million have been added to account for Russian deliveries for the High Dam. These deliveries are not included in the CBE estimates of the balance of payments for these two years. An earlier official estimate was £E 204 million, which seems to fit better with available capital goods flow statistics.

[4] The gross investment figure for 1959/60 is surprisingly low. With this investment figure private consumption would be only £E 1016 million and its share in GNI 74.1 per cent. This adjustment would also have important consequences for the savings estimate in table 8.

Public consumption and savings (£E million at current market prices)

Actual budget outcome¹)

Year²)	Current budget net revenue⁴) (1)	Interest payments and price subsidies (2)	Current budget net income (3) = (1) − (2)	Public consumption (4)	Public saving in the budget (5) = (3) − (4)	Pension and insurance funds accum. outside budget (6)	Total public saving (7) = (5) + (6)	Total public current net income (8)
1938/39	35.6	3.3	32.3	n.a.	n.a.	—	n.a.	32.2
1945/46	90.3	8.7	81.6	49	32.6	—	32.6	81.6
1946/47	94.1	9.0	85.1	50	35.1	—	35.1	85.1
1947/48³)	84.5	6.0	78.5	52	26.5	—	26.5	78.5
1948/49	120.8	16.0	104.8	70	34.8	—	34.8	104.8
1949/50	137.6	9.0	128.6	84	44.6	—	44.6	128.6
1950/51	160.3	14.0	146.3	117	29.3	—	29.3	146.3
1951/52	171.5	20.0	151.5	130	21.5	—	21.5	151.5
1952/53	166.6	15.2	151.4	133	18.4	—	18.4	151.4
1953/54	174.4	12.1	162.3	135	27.3	—	27.3	162.3
1954/55	176.7	9.1	167.6	140	27.6	—	27.6	167.6
1955/56	222.2	10.5	211.7	164	47.7	—	47.7	211.7
1956/57	205.7	13.1	192.6	175	17.6	8.5	26.1	201.1
1957/58	244.8	7.6	237.2	172	65.2	14.5	79.7	251.7
1958/59	249.3	11.6	237.7	173	64.7	15.0	79.7	252.7
1959/60	259.5	15.0	244.5	187	57.5	20.1	77.6	264.6
1960/61	263.6	18.8	244.8	211	33.8	28.1	61.9	272.9
1961/62	260.3	30.3	230.0	260	− 30.0	39.9	9.9	269.9
1962/63	323.3	54.0	269.3	290	− 20.7	51.0	30.3	320.3

¹) For 1962/63 the figures are provisional (but not forecasts).

²) The budget year until 1947 ran from May 1st to April 30th. From 1947 to 1951 the budget year was from March 1st to February 28th. Since 1951 it has been from July 1st to June 30th.

³) Ten months only.

⁴) Definition of this item differs slightly as between the periods 1938/39–1956/57 and 1957/58–1962/63. This should not, however, affect the comparability in any serious way.

TABLE A.7

Disposable income, savings and investments 1945–1952/53¹) (£E million at current market prices)

	1945	1946	1947	1948	1949	1950	1951/52	1952/53
1. Gross national product	552	535	578	718	829	916	968	904
2. *minus* total public current net income	82	85	79	105	129	146	152	151
3. Private sector disposable gross income (incl. retained profits in private and public companies)	470	450	499	613	700	770	816	753
4. *minus* private consumption $+ x + y^2$	433	459	495	573	661	721	761	704
5. = Private gross savings $- x - y^2$) (incl. retained profits in private and public companies)	37	− 9	4	40	39	49	55	49
6. *Plus* total public savings	33	35	27	35	45	29	22	18
7. = Total domestic gross savings $- x - y$	70	26	31	75	84	78	77	67
8. *plus* foreign borrowing $+ y$	− 45	13	21	7	4	11	34	31
9. = Gross investments $- x^2$)	25	39	52	83	88	89	111	98
Percentages								
10. Domestic gross savings/GNP	12.9	4.9	5.4	10.4	10.1	8.5	8.0	7.4
11. Gross investments/GNP	4.5	7.3	9.0	11.6	10.6	9.7	11.5	10.8
12. Total public savings/GNP	6.0	6.5	4.7	4.9	5.4	3.2	2.3	2.0
13. Private gross savings/private disp. gross income	7.9	− 2.0	0.8	6.5	5.6	6.4	6.7	6.5
14. Private disp. gross income/GNP	85.1	84.1	86.3	85.4	84.4	84.1	84.3	83.3

¹) Concerning the years, see note 2) to table 6.

²) The level of this investments series may be about £E 20 millions too low. The series for 'private consumption', obtained as a residual, is correspondingly £E 20 million too high. This reflects on the series for Private Gross Savings, obtained as a residual, which is £E 20 million too low.

TABLE A.8

Disposable income, savings and investments, 1952/53–1962/63 (£E million at current market prices)

	52/53	53/54	54/55	55/56	56/57	57/58	58/59	59/60	60/61	61/62	62/63[2]
1. Gross national product	905	963	1014	1072	1125	1195	1256	1372	1467	1550	1679
2. *minus* Total public current net income (incl. pens. and ins. funds accum.)	151	162	168	212	201	252	253	265	273	270	320
3. = Private sector disposable gross income (incl. ret. profits in priv. and publ. comp.)	754	801	846	860	924	943	1003	1107	1194	1280	1359
4. *minus* Private consumption $+ x + y$	684	686	753	775	819	904	919	1050[1])	1063	1111	1189
5. = Private gross savings $- x - y$	70	115	93	85	105	39	84	57[1])	131	169	170
6. *plus* Total public savings (incl. pens. and ins. funds accum.)	18	27	28	48	26	80	80	78	62	10	30
7. = Total domestic gross savings $- x - y$	88	142	121	133	131	119	164	135	193	179	200
8. *plus* Foreign borrowing $+ y$	31	–10	25	39	20	46	17	36	36	69	107
9. = Gross investments $- x$	119	132	146	172	151	165	181	171[1])	229	248	307
Percentages											
10. Domestic gross savings/GNP	9.7	14.7	11.8	12.4	11.6	10.0	13.1	9.8	12.5	11.5	11.9
11. Gross investments/GNP	13.1	13.7	14.4	16.0	13.4	13.8	14.4	12.5	15.7	16.0	18.3
12. Total public savings/GNP	2.0	2.8	2.7	4.5	2.3	6.7	6.4	5.7	4.2	0.6	1.8
13. Private gross sav./Priv. disp. Gr. Inc.	9.3	14.4	11.1	9.9	11.4	4.1	8.4	4.9	10.9	13.2	12.6
14. Priv. disp. gross income/GNP	83.3	83.2	83.5	80.2	82.1	78.9	80.0	80.7	81.4	82.6	80.5

1) See footnote 4) to table A.5.
2) Preliminary figures.

Subject Index

Name Index